THE CRISIS
of
EVANGELICAL CHRISTIANITY

THE CRISIS
of
EVANGELICAL CHRISTIANITY

*Roots, Consequences,
and Resolutions*

Keith C. Sewell

WIPF & STOCK · Eugene, Oregon

THE CRISIS OF EVANGELICAL CHRISTIANITY
Roots, Consequences, and Resolutions

Copyright © 2016 Keith C. Sewell. All rights reserved. Except for brief quotations in critical publications or reviews, no part of this book may be reproduced in any manner without prior written permission from the publisher. Write: Permissions, Wipf and Stock Publishers, 199 W. 8th Ave., Suite 3, Eugene, OR 97401.

Wipf & Stock
An Imprint of Wipf and Stock Publishers
199 W. 8th Ave., Suite 3
Eugene, OR 97401

www.wipfandstock.com

PAPERBACK ISBN 13: 978-1-4982-3875-5
HARDCOVER ISBN 13: 978-1-4982-3877-9

Manufactured in the U.S.A.   04/19/2016

New Revised Standard Version Bible: Anglicized Edition, copyright 1989, 1995, Division of Christian Education of the National Council of the Churches of Christ in the United States of America. Used by permission. All rights reserved.

Scripture quotations marked (NIV) are taken from the Holy Bible, New International Version®, NIV®. Copyright © 1973, 1978, 1984, 2011 by Biblica, Inc.™ Used by permission of Zondervan. All rights reserved worldwide. www.zondervan.com The "NIV" and "New International Version" are trademarks registered in the United States Patent and Trademark Office by Biblica, Inc.™

for Edwin

And he said to them:
'Therefore every scribe who has been trained for the kingdom of heaven is like the master of a household who brings out of his treasure what is new and what is old.'

—*Matthew 13:52*

CONTENTS

Preface | ix
Acknowledgments | xiii
Introduction | xv

PART ONE: CONTEXT
1 The Meaning of Evangelicalism | 3
2 Whatever Happened to Christianity? | 9
3 Whatever Happened to the Reformation? | 26
4 Theology, Science and the Reformation | 39
5 The English and Scottish Reformations | 55

PART TWO: FOCUS
6 The Roots and Character of Evangelicalism | 77
7 Multiple Confusions and Challenges | 95
8 Evangelicalism Wrestles with Liberalism | 112
9 Neo-Evangelicalism and the Great Crusade | 136
10 After the Great Crusade | 151
11 Evangelical Distress and an Integral Alternative | 178
12 Is Authentic Renewal Possible? | 198

Glossary | 227
Bibliography | 233
Index of Persons | 285

PREFACE

Protestant Christianity in western countries is in deep trouble. I have become increasingly aware of this situation since I professed the faith in 1961. This discussion is addressed to evangelical Christians particularly, and includes in that category those who might also define themselves as fundamentalist or Pentecostal or charismatic. My principal focus is evangelicals resident in the so-called Anglo-Sphere—North America, the British Isles, and Australasia. It is written for them and about them. American readers will find that they will be drawn to consider their spiritual roots in Europe and especially the British Isles. British, Australian and other readers will find themselves confronted by the immense influence of American Evangelicalism worldwide.

The marks of spiritual atrophy are evident on all sides. This is generally true even after we allow for exceptions. Among evangelicals some might yet remain in denial, perhaps with the thought that if only everyone was like them, then there would be no problem. While some still talk of growth, the reality is too often shallow. Youth clubs present an extraordinarily mixed picture. Youth ministries may wither as readily as they flower. The median age of many congregations is increasing perceptibly. Where the young are present they rarely stay. Where families are present they are usually those with very young children only. Of course, not all agree. The promoters of megachurches may think that they are bucking the trend that, in reality, they are not reversing but actually facilitating: by drawing on a wider demographic catchment area they help drain local congregations of vitality and commitment.

Over the last seventy or so years the numbers attending public worship have declined massively, especially when the figures are considered in the context of the overall demographic increase. Of course, the issue is not simply a matter of numbers. Membership rolls are not the ultimate issue, whatever church growth consultants might have us believe. The numbers are merely a symptom of a much deeper malaise that has been generations in the making. There are diverse symptoms. In many churches the Bible is given only scant attention. It is as good as silent, or only very inadequately explained in settings where those with discernment are left hungry for more. Other than where liturgical traditions have been retained, public prayer has become attenuated so as to make room for an almost compulsive and frequently repetitive singing of songs and choruses. Such tendencies accord well with a culture in which the iconic and sensate predominate. Christians who are caught up in these trends have little taste for serious Christian literature. Evangelicals who read discerningly and reflect seriously are not nonexistent, but they are not representative of the whole.

Yet the non-reading laity is not without its nagging questions and partly expressed misgivings. Why is it that institutional Christianity is so frequently inept and fumbling? Why is the ministry of word and sacrament so frequently unsatisfying—with all the resultant "Church hopping"? Why is it that now in so many churches the faithful are denied the possibility of singing psalms and hymns? Many congregation members "settle" for what their circumstances offer, and "make the best of it," but with reservations. They know that in some way things are out of focus, but lack the means to adequately pinpoint the problem.

For their part many of the clergy are deeply perplexed. More than is generally appreciated many endure persistent stress and anxiety. In countless situations, doing all that needs to be done is a practical impossibility. The demands and pressures can be overwhelming, but many ministers dare not express themselves candidly for fear of being accused of letting the side down. There is a great deal of apprehension, and looking over one's shoulder. Unable to preach effectively, some clergy take up counseling, only to realize that they might be in need of counseling themselves. Alas, frustration can come to expression in bullying conduct and other kinds of abusive behavior. And, as if we could forget, all churches should now hang their heads in shame at the sexual abuse that has taken place in their midst and for which they are responsible. A massive further decline in public respect and trust has ensued.

In the midst of all this there are nagging questions that simply will not go away. Why is it that present-day Christianity is so inadequate when it comes to addressing contemporary culture? Why is it that what is preached does not seem to grip the rails any more? Why does secularization seem inexorable? Is Christianity in the West in inevitable terminal decline? Why does so much of what was taught at training college or theological seminary not seem to help in the "real world"? Why is it so hard, in spite of all that training and study, to effectively grasp and communicate the meaning of Scripture in and beyond a church setting?

A perplexed clergy might instinctively turn for answers to the theological traditions within which they were trained, only to find the results less than adequate. Many have neither the time nor inclination to invest in reading the great number of volumes of relevant literature on offer. An apprehensive laity might seek illumination through online searching, only to be confronted with myriad competing voices, all claiming to be right and (at least implying) that others are wrong.

Such is the predicament in which the Christian religion, and not least evangelical Christianity, now finds itself in western countries. The discussion that follows offers an elucidation of the nexus of problems in which Evangelicalism is presently entangled. It does not purport to resolve all difficulties, and still less to provide a quick fix. It does address the "how" and "why" of our contemporary predicament. It considers the historical trajectories that have brought us to where we are now, and what a coherent response would require. It is offered in the hope that it will encourage Christian men and women to reflect with wisdom as they watch and pray, and to stimulate them to think carefully, soberly, and coherently on our contemporary situation, and to open up a way for constructive conversations to take place.

The challenges before English-speaking Evangelicalism are immense, and it must be prepared for many cherished assumptions to buckle under pressure. It has been said: "The scandal of the evangelical mind is that there is not much of an evangelical mind."[1] This discussion puts the rudder hard over, and takes a different tack. It asserts that there is at least a tacit evangelical mind and that along with many typically evangelical attitudes and practices it is a long way from being as authentically scriptural as many evangelicals have themselves assumed.

At the same time it will be argued that evangelicals generally exhibit a marked "intellectual deficit." The evangelical mind, it will be argued, is seriously deficient in biblically directed thought, and that therefore Evangelicalism is also seriously deficient in biblically directed action. Of course, this deficit will require consideration of the differing ways of understanding how the Bible is authoritative, ways that Evangelicalism inherited from the Protestant Reformation. This is an important issue, and evangelical Christians are here invited to contemplate a more biblically consistent standpoint that arguably preserves much of what they rightly value while also taking it to both a deeper level and broader application.

---

1. Noll, *The Scandal of the Evangelical Mind*, 3.

In a discussion of this sort it is impossible not to use terms such as Lutheran, Anglican, Calvinist, Puritan, reformed, evangelical, dispensationalist, fundamentalist, Pentecostal, charismatic and so forth. I have tried to use these terms clearly and to explain their meaning. In truth, millions of Christians worldwide have employed these terms as they have sought to define themselves, understand each other, and give expression to their faith. All such terminology has limitations and is capable of misuse, but here we use these terms in order to explain and answer the issues raised by our title. Of course, these terms can always be used pejoratively, but any ungracious misuse of them does not mean that we should shy away from using them clearly and respectfully.

This discussion therefore acknowledges the reality that there has been a process of self-definition at work in the use of these terms and we will consider the issues relating to them in a *historical* manner. This approach yields considerable insight. It recognizes that the Christian religion as we know it is not and never has been freshly fallen from heaven, but is a human and therefore creaturely *response* to the gospel message itself. At the same time, it should be emphasised that this is not a formal history of Christianity or of even just English-speaking evangelical Christianity. Footnotes have been kept to a minimum. A short glossary of terms has been provided. This is an overview intended to stimulate thought and encourage constructive debate and endeavour.

Readers may wish to know "where I am coming from." I was born in London and live in Melbourne. I have lived and worshipped in England, southern Ontario in Canada, the upper Mid-West of the USA, New South Wales and Victoria in Australia, and New Zealand. I am therefore well acquainted with the diversity within the Anglo-Sphere. I was baptised and confirmed in the Church of England as a teenager, was a member of reformed churches in my middle years, and currently attend my Anglican Parish Church in Australia. I did my doctoral research on the English historian Herbert Butterfield (1900–79) whose roots lay in Yorkshire Methodism.

ACKNOWLEDGMENTS

This book arises from many authors read, observations made, and conversations had for over fifty years. While I confess to being a Christian, the perspective offered here is that of a long-term observer rather than an evangelical insider. Earlier drafts of this work have benefitted from the scrutiny of readers across three continents and both hemispheres. They have saved me from some factual blunders and many more compositional infelicities. In both regards I would like to especially thank my wife Alida for her valuable comments on both style and content. Needless to say, I alone am responsible for the standpoint adopted, the arguments presented, and the conclusions drawn.

INTRODUCTION

Disciples of Jesus Christ in the twenty-first century have inherited a situation of bewildering complexity. Only in some places are they numerous. In many settings they are seriously secularized. They are frequently divided. They are profoundly confused on a wide range of issues. They can be stunningly inept at making clear what they believe, and deeply unsure about expressing the faith and putting it into practice. This discussion confronts this complex predicament. It is addressed to those who are "Bible-believing." In using this term I have no one particular theory of biblical inspiration in view. I simply mean receiving the Scriptures as inspired and authoritative. Of course, this raises questions concerning *how* the Scriptures of the Old and New Testaments can be said to be authoritative. Here we straightaway encounter matters that have separated Protestants from Christians of the Coptic, Eastern Orthodox and Roman Catholic persuasions.

As will become clear in the following pages, my standpoint is oriented towards the Protestant Reformation, without being bound to it anachronistically. Coptic, Orthodox and Roman Catholic believers are most welcome to "listen in" on this piece of protestant discussion. When all is said and done, by the grace of God, all Christians can say the ancient creeds with fervour and conviction.

As evangelical Christians contemplate the complications and confusions in which they are immersed, some are prone to call for rapid and radical surgery. They want the inherited baggage of the centuries to be jettisoned. They long for the everlasting gospel alone. They cry out for a sweeping aside of the great mass of accumulated impediments and a return to the pure and pristine faith and life of the New Testament church. "Forget the history," they declare, "just argue your case from the Bible."

At just such points an extra measure of circumspection is required. Although the questions before us cannot be settled without reference to the Bible, they cannot be settled by a quick flip through its pages either. We need to recognize that the Bible is never just "read," but always read in a specific way in relation to a specific context. No one is exempt. Furthermore, when we think we are engaging in *exegesis*, we may be producing *eisegesis*—reading *into* scripture our prior, uncritical assumptions. So we come back to the historical side of things by another route: because there is such a thing as the *history* of the reading and interpretation of the Bible. That history itself needs to be scrupulously and self-critically addressed. The historical side of things cannot be evaded. If we think that we can evade it, we are fooling ourselves. It is an unavoidable feature of the ordered creation of which we are a part. Moreover, those who say, "Forget the history! What does the Bible say?" are prone to forget that this attitude itself has a history, and is open to historical analysis.

It is therefore wise to study and ponder the history of the Christian religion, because that history can give us decisive insights into *why* Christians currently understand and live out their faith *in the way that they do*. Although some might write off the past as either dusty and drab, or formidably complicated, the present situation cannot be understood without making reference to historical lineages and trajectories.

Without being a work of formal theology, this study takes both the Bible and historical experience seriously, but never in order to set up some past era as a permanent template for Christian conduct. The standpoint adopted is critical, but not that of unbelief. We will regard the Scriptures as authoritative and we will proceed on the basis that they call us to respond obediently in the era and circumstances in which we find ourselves, rather than anachronistically attempt to re-enact anyone's version of what first century Christianity may have been like. Such a project should not be feared. A truly historical approach has ways of delivering us from the fetters of a blind or unexamined traditionalism. The aim is to sharpen understanding of what it means to be disciples of Jesus Christ in the twenty-first century.

Part One

CONTEXT

1

THE MEANING OF EVANGELICALISM

A Quadrilateral of Priorities

It is important to establish as clearly as possible what is meant here by the term "evangelical." It is also needful to remember that many who might not habitually define themselves as evangelicals also affirm with conviction the ancient creeds of the Christian religion—the Apostles', Nicene, and Athanasian Creeds. In addition, while the present divisions among the Christian churches are scandalous, the extent to which they and evangelical Christians are *doctrinally* divided should not be over-stated. The truth is that the vast majority of Christians concur in respect of those doctrines that are bedrock, that is, foundational to their faith, even though they may not always agree on how these beliefs should be expressed.

Nevertheless, although the term evangelical is derived from the Greek *evangelion*, meaning gospel or "good news," (from the Old English "godspell"), in the English-speaking world, it is almost universally applied to a certain kind of Protestant. So what is the meaning of the term in our present context? The question is challenging, because evangelicals come in a great variety of shapes and sizes. The sheer diversity can be very confusing, sometimes to evangelicals themselves, and certainly to those who contemplate Evangelicalism from beyond its bounds. The diversity arises, in the main, from multiple disagreements, which have resulted in divisions and fracturing.

Some evangelicals are willing to be present in denominational structures that include a variety of non-evangelicals. Others insist that separation from such "mixed" structures is necessary if doctrinal integrity is to be maintained. Some are in churches administered by bishops (Episcopal); others are subject to a hierarchy of assemblies (Presbyterian or Reformed), while others abide by the independence of the local congregation (Congregational, Baptist, Pentecostal or Free Evangelical). Some are willing to be called fundamentalists, others are not. The former are more likely to insist on what they term the "infallibility" and even the "inerrancy" of the Bible, than those who are content to simply affirm the inspiration and authority of the canonical scriptures. Some believe that under certain circumstances it is right to baptize infants—others are Baptists, believing that only those able to profess their faith should be baptized.

Moreover, among Evangelicals there are many different views on the return of Christ—the Second Coming. Some are a-millennial, believing that the single Bible passage that speaks of a thousand-year reign of Christ (Rev 20:1–6) is figurative rather than literal. Others are post- or premillennial, depending on their view of whether or not a more or less literal millennial reign of Christ on earth will take place after ("post-") or before ("pre-") the definitive second advent of Christ. Moreover, from the nineteenth century onwards, many premillennial fundamentalists have accepted a version of this viewpoint known as "premillennial dispensationalist," along with belief in a so-called rapture in which Christ collects believers from the earth prior to his full and final return.

As if these differences were not enough, evangelicals are also divided on the question of Pentecostalism. The Pentecostal movements and the churches they produced are part of the wider evangelical fold, but they teach that the charismatic gifts referred to in the New Testament are still present in the church, and emphasize a "baptism with the Holy Spirit." Pentecostalism has entered both mainline and separatist evangelical denominations in the form of the charismatic movement. While all evangelicals affirm the presence of the Holy Spirit in the life of the Christian, and the necessity of his work, not all concur that the charismatic gifts of the New Testament are imparted to contemporary believers, nor do all understand the baptism of the Holy Spirit to be an event subsequent to Christian conversion.

This wide diversity renders all the more necessary a definition of the meaning of the term Evangelicalism for the purposes of the present discussion. Certainly, many evangelicals will declare themselves to be against liberal theology, by which they mean theologies arising from the rationalist-critical approach to the Bible expressed in the thought of the Enlightenment, and modernism generally. However, such statements are inadequate for definitional purposes because they do not enunciate positive characteristics and emphases. Great movements should not be understood only in terms of what they are against. Often they are best understood in terms of what they declare themselves to stand *for*. In other words, we need to ask the question: What have evangelicals historically said that they actually stand for *above all else*? In 1980 the evangelical historian David W. Bebbington persuasively answered this question. He formulated four leading characteristics of evangelical religion in terms of a "quadrilateral of priorities":

> *conversionism*, the belief that lives need to be changed; *activism*, the expression of the gospel in effort; *biblicism*, a particular regard for the Bible; and what may be called *crucicentrism*, a stress on the sacrifice of Christ on the cross.[1]

This formulation has been widely accepted. It captures the heart of the evangelical commitment, and it signifies what is meant by the terms "evangelical" and "Evangelicalism" as used in this discussion. This formulation will be referred to as Bebbington's quadrilateral of priorities in this discussion. How these relate to fundamentalism and Pentecostalism will be discussed later.

Somewhat later the evangelical author Alister McGrath expanded on Bebbington's quadrilateral of priorities. McGrath spoke of "six fundamental [or "controlling"] convictions," as follows:

> 1. The supreme authority of Scripture as a source of knowledge of God and a guide to Christian living. 2. The majesty of Jesus Christ, both as incarnate God and Lord and as the Saviour of sinful humanity. 3. The lordship of the Holy Spirit. 4. The need for personal conversion. 5. The priority of evangelism for both individual Christians and the church as a whole. 6. The importance of the Christian community for spiritual nourishment, fellowship and growth.[2]

McGrath's six points are more doctrinal, while Bebbington's quadrilateral of priorities is more descriptive. Nevertheless, there is a substantial overlap between the two. Both emphasize the saving work of Christ and the need for conversion. In addition, Oliver Barclay (1919–2013) later added his gloss to Bebbington's formulation in order to distinguish between his preferred classical Evangelicalism, and liberal Evangelicals, and possibly also charismatic Evangelicals.[3] More recently, Timothy Larsen has offered another slight

---

1. Bebbington, *Evangelicalism in Modern Britain*, 3, 5–17.
2. McGrath, *Evangelicalism and the Future of Christianity*, 55–56.
3. Barclay, *Evangelicalism in Britain*, 10–14, 100, 116–117, 137–141.

expansion of the formula.[4] Nevertheless, it is Bebbington's formulation that has been widely received and has stood the test of time. It will be used here because it is commendably succinct and one that many evangelicals themselves would regard as a valid characterization.

Creation and Culture

It is highly significant that none of the points in Bebbington's quadrilateral of priorities, or of McGrath's controlling convictions, makes specific reference to the *order of creation*. By this term, and its synonyms, we refer not only to the divine act "at the beginning" (Gen 1:1), but also to God's sovereign ordering, upholding and directing of the entire cosmos in all of its diversity, both natural and cultural. The creational setting provides the context in which all human culture (and not just art and literature) is expressed. Moreover, as all human thought and endeavor is in the service of the living God, or of a presumed substitute for the Creator (idols, ideologies, making "absolute" what is only creaturely and relative), it follows that in this sense all human culture is ultimately religious in character, a response to our Creator, whether or not this is actually acknowledged.

This neglect of the order of creation is inextricably bound up with what Evangelicalism is prone to do with the gospel it proclaims. It tends to *reduce* the gospel to a message focused on the salvation of individual souls. This is a great deal less than (and arguably a distortion of) the proclamation of the *good news concerning the coming of the kingdom of God* that we encounter in the New Testament. Bebbington's quadrilateral of priorities, or McGrath's six points make no explicit reference to these biblical teachings. In this respect their characterizations are a true reflection of the evangelical outlook. In Evangelicalism, the dominant tendency has been to emphasize the repentant individual before the cross in a way that neglects what the Scriptures have to say about the order of creation and the kingdom of God. Evangelicalism is persistently prone to reduce all to an individual-road-to-personal-salvation narrative—and the result is a serious distortion of the biblical message.

Although the Reformation of the sixteenth century, at its best, exhibited an awareness of the order of creation, in the Evangelicalism that emerged later in the English-speaking lands the creation order is generally assumed to be at best a *natural* or *secular* prelude to an other-worldly *supernatural* salvation. Gordon J. Spykman (1926–93) was right when writing of "the

---

4. See Larsen, "Defining and Locating," 1.

eclipse of the creation . . . in many wings of evangelical Christianity."[5] This "creational deficit" across Evangelicalism has meant that even Evangelicalism's evangelism has characteristically fallen short of the biblical norm—the gospel has not been brought to every creature and to every part of life as the Bible teaches, but for the most part only to individual souls. This deficit has had a deep impact on the evangelical understanding of the Christian life and calling, characterised by a strong tendency to seriously under-recognize and under-proclaim the cosmic scope of Christ's redemptive work and kingship.

Moreover, among evangelicals, multiple unexamined assumptions, taken to imply that at least some aspects of human culture are religiously neutral, have resulted in unbiblical viewpoints being absorbed and tacitly attached to the gospel itself. We may therefore also speak of an evangelical cultural deficit arising from its creational deficit. This being so, what we are about to discuss is not a set of philosophical or cultural questions of concern only to a remote, intellectual elite. On the contrary, before us are issues that address our understanding of scriptural religion, the fullness of its character, and the consequences that all of this entails. At best, Evangelicalism has exhibited only a sporadic and fluctuating awareness of the religious significance of human culture, and of the truth that *all of life is religion*—in the sense of lived *coram Deo*; before the face of God. Yet this truth is central. It does not mean that everything is churchly, or that everything is to be understood in terms of theology. It means that the totality of our lives—our thoughts, words and deeds—is in the service of the one true living God or of an idol.

There arises from this insight an outlook that seeks to be *integral*. It is not interested in gaining leverage or acceptance (even for the purpose of preaching the gospel) by allowing the prevailing culture, as in the translation of J. B. Phillips (1906–82), to "squeeze" us "into its own mould" (Rom 12:2). It is not interested in any attempt to conjoin the supposedly sacred with the presumably secular. On the contrary, it seeks an *integrally* Christian standpoint that is free from such false dichotomies. At the same time it delights in the rich diversity displayed within the ordering of creation, even as it sees in every lawful expression of human culture an opportunity to honour the living God and be of service to humankind. This is neither idealism nor perfectionism, although it does foster an outlook that inevitably anticipates the full realization of the kingdom of God. This *integral* standpoint recognizes that there are no limits to Christ's call to "Follow me" (Matt 4:19; Mark 1:17). Accordingly, Christians are not at liberty to set limits on their discipleship.

---

5. Spykman, *Reformational Theology*, 176.

Of course, even this preliminary discussion raises many questions. What were the origins of Evangelicalism? How are we to explain its character, with its typical traits and persistent tendencies? How are we to explain the prevalence of what we have called the creational and cultural deficits in much Evangelicalism—even after we make allowance for some important exceptions? It is hard for many evangelicals to address these questions. They can always find other high-sounding priorities, not least their proclamation of their reduced and circumscribed version of the gospel message. And, it must be said, many evangelicals who have not lacked educational opportunities are nevertheless intellectually lazy. In such cases the creational and cultural deficits are reinforced by a further intellectual deficit arising from the prioritizing of feelings over thinking. It can be especially adverse to the kind of thinking that aspires to a scrupulous and coherent articulation across the encyclopaedia of the sciences.

To many evangelicals, even to those who are graduates of colleges and universities, this kind of thinking can sound very strange—maybe even weird. The questions abound. Is this approach really biblical? Why does some of this kind of probing sound so strange? Indeed, is it sound, or is it some sort of new heresy? What does this characteristic way of listening to Scripture have to do with the predicament of contemporary Bible-believing Christianity in the English-speaking world? How does the authority of the Bible function in our multicultural setting? How does all this relate to the contemporary church? Why have I not heard this kind of questioning at my local church? Why are there so many more seminaries and theological colleges than multi-faculty institutions of Christian higher education? Why have so many Christians claimed the benefits of the gospel as a private privilege having no public consequences? Is there a distinctively Christian approach to public life? Why is it so hard for Christians to agree on political questions? Why do so many Christian graduates have so little in the way of *distinctively Christian* intellectual clout? What about the Bible and science? Is it possible to be a Christian without being in intellectual denial, at some level, somewhere along the line? Why is it that so many contemporary church leaders are ignorant or suspicious of the issues discussed in this book? Is it really possible that we have got some important things so seriously wrong? And if so, what is to be done?

2

WHATEVER HAPPENED TO CHRISTIANITY?

An Evangelical Conversion

On May 21, 1738 there took place what John Wesley (1703–91) always understood to be the decisive turning point in his life. In his account of his "Aldersgate Street experience" he wrote

> In the evening I went very unwillingly to a society in Aldersgate Street [London], where one was reading Luther's *Preface to the Epistle to the Romans*. About a quarter before nine, while he was describing the change which God works in the heart through faith in Christ, I *felt my heart strangely warmed*. I felt I did trust in Christ, Christ alone for my salvation, and an assurance was given me that He had taken away *my* sins, even *mine*, and saved *me* from the law of sin and death.... I then testified to all there what I first felt in my heart.[1]

Much ink has been expended on exactly what was taking place at this stage in Wesley's life. Few would argue that this is one of the great moments in the history of Evangelicalism. Was this John Wesley's actual conversion, or was it a renewal of an authentic but distressingly unsatisfying pre-existing commitment? How can one tell the difference, given the incompleteness of our self-understanding, and our propensity for self-deception? And, were not

---

1. Ward and Heitzenrater (editors), *Works of John Wesley* 18, 249–50.

all sincere Protestants genuine Christians anyway? If not sincere, as much in the writings of John Wesley and his associates certainly implied, it has to be asked: "Was there a deficiency in the development of the Protestantism arising from the Reformation that required the emergence of something further, something along the lines of the Evangelicalism that arose some two hundred years later?" Clearly, the Protestant Reformation, which first began in parts of Germany and Switzerland between 1517 and 1530, and the Great Evangelical Awakening, which came upon Great Britain and its American colonies, especially in the 1730s and 1740s, are in no way unconnected even though they exhibit markedly distinct features. Wesley's experience came at a reading from Luther's writings. The Evangelicalism that emerged from the Awakening in the eighteenth century had a long lead-in period—it had been fermenting in the depths of post-Reformation Protestantism for an extended period.

As soon as we start to explore the origins of Evangelicalism in earlier Protestantism we discover the deep continuities of human history. Evangelicalism did not descend with a thunderclap from heaven, and neither did Protestantism itself. Scholarship of a high order has shown that the roots of early Protestantism lie deep in late-medieval Catholic philosophy and theology. In truth, Protestantism was hewn from the Catholic block. We need to remember that for the most part the habits of mind of the protestant reformers remained, by our standards, cast in the late-medieval mold. Martin Luther (1483–1546) never aspired to found a distinct entity called Protestantism. His priority as a reformer was to see Catholic Christendom reconstituted on the basis of biblical rather than papal authority. The circumstances of his time and place still shaped much of his teaching and outlook. These both had their limitations.

At first glance, when we look at the history of Christianity, it resembles much of the history of human culture in general. We are repeatedly faced with important developments and vast projects that are ground down, undermined, or deflected. In addition, remarkable transpositions are also possible, in which original beliefs, structures, and practices acquire new meanings and significance. Sometimes this transposition takes centuries, but it can happen within a lifetime. Accordingly, when reflecting on the passage and interaction of events, one should never infer original intentions from actual outcomes. The New Testament makes reference to the granting of the Holy Spirit to the disciples, but also to a coming apostasy (Acts 20:29–30; 1 Tim 4:1–3). In the future envisaged by the New Testament, neither cancels out the other. This may serve to prompt this question: what happened to Christianity after the earthly ministry of Jesus and the apostles?

Christianity and the Allurements of Pagan Thought

In responding to this question, we should not forget that the New Testament uses the term Christian only three times (Acts 11:26; 26:28; 1 Pet 4:16). The *Acts of the Apostles* just as frequently refers to "the way" (Acts 9:2, 22:4; 24:14). As we read the gospels and Acts, we ought to be struck by the fact that the gospel—the good news—concerns *the coming of the kingdom of God*. Over the centuries this truth was lost from view. Our language is now of "church" and "Christianity." In the New Testament, Christianity (named as such) is unknown, while the "church" (*ecclesia*) consists of all those who confess the kingship of Christ the risen Lord (Rom 10:9). In the New Testament, church is contextualized by kingdom, not the other way round. At the conclusion of the *Acts of the Apostles* we are given a magnificent vignette of Paul's manner of life in the environs of Rome towards the end of his days. The words are eloquent. He "welcomed all who came to him, proclaiming the kingdom of God and teaching about the Lord Jesus Christ with all boldness" (Acts 28:30–31 NRSV).

In Paul's teaching, Christ and his kingdom were inseparable. When, in subsequent centuries, either Christ or kingdom has been taught or sought in ways that obscures or eclipses the other, serious distortions in Christian teaching and living have taken place. The challenging truth is that over centuries we have transitioned from Christ and his kingdom to multiple versions of Christianity and the institutional church. It is important to remember that what we have come to call Christianity is a creaturely thing. It has arisen from our believing, always creaturely, responses to the gospel message, even though these have sometimes been seriously defective. Christians therefore need to pray for wisdom as they humbly, self-critically, and in the communion of the saints, check their understanding of the gospel continually against the teaching of the canonical texts.

In that process we discover the challenging historical truth that what we have come to call the Christian religion has undergone successive waves of deep historical change. Already functioning in a *milieu* predominantly shaped by Greek thought and attitudes, the first great historical change came with the absorption by early Christianity of characteristically Hellenic understandings of man and nature. These inevitably came to function in an unstable mix with authentic, biblical teachings—even as the church became decreasingly Jewish and increasingly gentile. The Old Testament view of creation—not so much creation as an initial event, but belief in the creation as the entire God-given and divinely-sustained created order—"the heavens and the earth and all that therein is"—was never explicitly repudiated by Christians, but became confused with, and overlaid by, Greek (and essentially pagan) ideas of nature. For example, a view of nature that sees things as possessing a certain inner essence, which somehow guarantees that they are what they are, is not compatible with a biblically-directed understanding which sees things as being what they are because *God says* (by his creating word) *that that is what they are to be*. In other words, a creature is not an independent self-directing entity or quality, but a response to the Word by which God has called that creature into being in order to be whatever he calls them to be. The latter view sees the Creator as unquestionably sovereign (and non-dependent), while everything else is creation and therefore dependent on the Creator.

The cosmos is not therefore a self-contained "closed system" but always and at every point dependent upon its Creator. In short, the order of creation is wholly contingent. This view undermines any Platonic notion of a "great chain of being," with the meanest thing at the base and God as the greatest being at the top. Such notions imply that God is God because he is the biggest or greatest of all beings, as if he were, so to speak, the greatest being on the creaturely block. Such an outlook blurs the distinction—ever present in Scripture—between the Creator and the creation.

Another example is the acceptance within Christianity, as it developed, of notions of "the eternal soul" that owe much more to pagan Hellenic philosophy than to the more integral view of humankind presented in the Scriptures. The resulting problems have been far-reaching. An accommodation to characteristically Hellenic modes of thought has dictated the way in which various biblical passages and turns of phrase are habitually understood and therefore translated into English and other languages. One consequence has been that many Christians are alienated from their own bodily physicality and experience a guilt-laden loathing towards their own and others' legitimate expressions of their sexuality. This has sometimes led to very serious crimes being committed in some Christian-institutional settings. The result is that all things Christian have been discredited in the world at large, even as some clergy continue to live in denial.

Tertullian's Question and the Issue it Represents

In the era that followed the time of the Apostles, and as Hellenic influences were becoming more pervasive in the church, Tertullian (c. 155–230) posed his famous questions:

> What indeed has Athens to do with Jerusalem? What concord is there between the Academy and the church? What has the heretic to do with the Christian? . . . Away with all attempts to

produce an intermixed Christianity of Stoic, Platonic and dialectical composition! We want no curious disputation after possessing Christ, no inquiry after enjoying the gospel. We believe we need nothing above our faith.[2]

Tertullian deserves respect for his desire to uphold the distinctive integrity of the Christian religion. He was arguing against the corruptions of the faith peddled by heretics. However, Tertullian's discussion of the question is open to more than one interpretation. It has provoked repeated discussion across the centuries, discussion that has reflected the uncertainty of many Christians about the answer. Tertullian prompts questions in return, such as: is it possible to oppose philosophy without having a philosophical standpoint? What about an authentically Christian philosophical response to the philosophies of Athens? What does a biblically oriented Christianity have to say about all those issues already raised by Greek philosophy, *including* the ways in which it raises those questions and seeks to answer them?

Arguably, Tertullian unintentionally confirms that philosophy cannot be discussed without a philosophical standpoint. An authentically Christian philosophical response appears to be precluded by his rhetoric. However, the articulation of an integrally Christian philosophy would be required if Athens was ever to be answered philosophically.

Of course, Paul warns Christians about "vain philosophy"—but in doing so he was *not* repudiating philosophical thought as such, but warning against what was vain, empty, or void *because it was not first founded in Christ* (Col 2:8). It is a long historical trek from Tertullian to Wesley, so why bring Tertullian into the discussion? The answer is that Tertullian can be read in a way that legitimizes a tendency that has become highly characteristic of Evangelicalism—towards a "just believe" outlook that depreciates Christian thinking, even as it sets a premium on *feeling*. The anti-intellectual temper of such Christianity defends itself against any analysis of how it is itself shaped by notions that might prove to be biblically questionable. That is a conversation it does not want to have.

Those who once sought to insulate the gospel from all intellectual activity, with the possible exception of *their* kind of theology, bequeathed to succeeding generations a problematic legacy with which many struggle. By contrast, we shall argue that a valid approach should reflect a distinction between thinking from a genuinely biblical starting-point on one hand, and thinking that has some other starting-point. A genuinely biblical starting-point certainly requires that we make distinctions, for example, between God and his creatures. Not all distinctions are invalid. The distinctions we

---

2. Tertullian, *De Praescriptionibus*, VII, 8; Osborn, *Tertullian*, 27–47.

make should be consistent with the way of viewing things to which the Scriptures *direct* us.

To some this may sound like "Bible-based Fundamentalism," but it is not. This *biblically directed* standpoint is not consonant with Fundamentalism because it does not confuse a biblically *directed* understanding of cosmos and culture with the scientifically questionable world-picture of the biblical characters and authors themselves. That world-picture is reflective of how reality was perceived and experienced in biblical times. We now need to be wisely self-critical about the way in which we make distinctions, constantly asking why we draw distinctions in the way that we do. To give a prime example, some things are visible and others invisible—but that does not make some things *secular* and others *sacred*, some *temporal* and others *eternal* as is often suggested. If we intrude unbiblical sacred and secular distinctions into our views of everything, it will greatly confuse our understanding of all things visible and invisible and / or temporal and eternal.

For this reason many Christians have come to regard the human body as visible and therefore natural and secular, while the soul is invisible, supernatural, and sacred—something for all eternity. In the midst of these problems, we should not forget that the Apostles' Creed does not speak of the eternal salvation of immortal souls but—to the scandal of the classical mind—of *the resurrection of the body* (see also Acts 17:32). When the Apostles' Creed was formulated, Christianity was not yet so far down the path of compromise with Hellenic philosophy as to inhibit its witness to the biblical standpoint.

The Misleading Notion of a Christian "Golden Age"

A further word of caution is appropriate. It would be wrong to suggest that the church of the apostles and prophets, and immediately thereafter, had all of its doctrine clearly, if still only basically, formulated. The truth is more complex. Pre-Christian Judaism was *already* variously influenced by Hellenic ways of thinking—as the writings of Philo of Alexandria (20 BC–AD 50) and some apocryphal books make clear. It was into this context that the apostolic message was first preached. The notion of a wholly uniform apostolic or post-apostolic church in a Christian "Golden Age" (another Hellenic idea!) that can function as a perpetual template for all later generations needs to be set aside once and for all. All hankerings to return to such a presumed "Golden Age" are doomed to repeated disappointment. The complexity and direction of the historical process precludes such a possibility.

Attempts to fly in the face of this norm of history always carry the marks of their own day and circumstance.

Such longings for a restoration of the supposed simplicity of the primitive church tend to display their own varieties of rigid traditionalism, coupled with romanticized distortions of the past that can be seriously misleading. We are better off envisaging the apostles and their associates preaching the good news of the kingdom of God, and at the same time discovering and wrestling with its challenging implications for humankind—starting with the new and perplexing reality of uncircumcised gentile believers entering the covenant community—rather than assuming the existence of, and setting out to find, a primordial, supposedly perfect church that had its teaching, thinking, procedures and practices perfectly in order.

It is therefore better for contemporary Christians to think in terms of having a calling, as disciples of Jesus, to think through and live out of a growing understanding of the gospel, and to view this as a God-given, trans-generational task. Such an understanding parallels the creational calling to populate and "have dominion" over the earth, a command incapable of being fulfilled in a single generation. Clearly, the witness and teaching of the apostles—the apostolic declaration or *kerygma*—is of unique and central significance to all Christians; but we are not now called to live in apostolic times. It is better to take the view that our calling is to hear and do the gospel of the kingdom of God in the time and circumstances in which we are placed. So, while the apostolic witness in the New Testament is indispensable, there was no "Golden Age" of the early Church. It was only after the time of the apostles that the church came to clarify its understanding of the person of Christ. Furthermore, the New Testament itself never mentions "the Holy Trinity" as such. Rather, it presents us with the truth of God; Father, Son, and Holy Spirit—the rest was the church's believing response thereto. These matters need to be understood with historical insight.

In other words, a *biblically directed* approach, as will be made clear, is not anachronistic. It recognizes that what we call Christianity is not directly God-given, but our creaturely response to the gospel message. It is what those who believe, rightly or wrongly—and arguably often wrongly—have made of that message. So tradition is neither sacrosanct nor irrelevant, but like us it is constantly in need of scrutiny and testing. And such processes are no spiritual picnic, because in testing the history of Christianity by the norm of the gospel there is much that will bring forth sorrow and tears as well as joy and gratitude. Such an exercise brings us face to face with ways in which the gospel has been distorted, misrepresented, even betrayed by those who have professed the faith.

The Transformation of Christianity: Constantine, Eusebius and Theodosius

All this must be kept in view as we consider a further great historical transformation that engulfed Christianity, one associated with Constantine the Great (c. 272–337), his fulsome and assiduous advocate Eusebius of Caesarea (263–341), and the Byzantine Emperor Theodosius I (347–395). At the outset, Christianity was *not* a *religio licita* within the Roman Empire. The Romans required that only specifically approved (licit) religions were to be practiced. As far as Rome was concerned, the early church was an *illicit* organization. Its members proclaimed that Jesus, and not Caesar, is Lord. This was not a piece of private devotional rhetoric but a public cultural assertion that challenged the existing imperial order to its core. It is hardly surprising that those expressing this conviction concerning the risen Christ were subjected to successive waves of sometimes fierce and hideous persecution. Rome was a great civilization. If, in retrospect, her culture and many cruel practices (such as crucifixion and gladiatorial combat) appear to us *barbaric* in the extreme, that is strong testimony as to how our concept of civilization has itself undergone historical change through the humanizing influences of Christianity.

The last great persecution of Christians (until modern times) was during the reign of Emperor Diocletian (245–311, ruled 284–305). Thereafter, a remarkable transformation took place, one that has inspired, perplexed, and appalled informed Christians ever since. Writing years later, so as to confirm the legitimacy of what had already transpired, Eusebius tells us that Constantine, then co-emperor, was engaged in a military campaign within the empire against a rival for imperial office. On the eve of battle, Constantine claimed to see a vision of a sign above the sun with the inscription: *in hoc signo vinces* (conquer by this sign). That night, according to Eusebius, Christ appeared to Constantine and gave him the sign of a Greek "chi" combined with a "rho," the first two letters of the Greek word for Christ (*Christos*). Constantine adopted this sign as his military standard and proceeded to triumph over his enemy at the battle of Milvian Bridge on October 27, 312.

This development raised the distinct prospect of what had been an unthinkable contradiction in terms—a Christian Caesar. In retrospect, one might think that something of this sort was becoming increasingly likely, given the growth of the church and the inner spiritual decay of late-classical paganism. Nevertheless, this was a development of immense significance. The following year, by the Edict of Milan, an already widely anticipated measure of toleration, which included Christianity, was confirmed. Only twelve years later, on July 3, 324, at the Battle of Adrianople, did Constantine finally achieve the military elimination of his great rival Lucinius (263–325). As might be expected, there remains considerable uncertainty as to the sincerity with which Constantine professed the Christian faith. Orthodox and Roman Catholic scholarship is much inclined to view his affirmation of the faith as sincere, in spite of lapses and the stunning irregularities of his family life. Among protestant authors his reputation is more mixed. Amongst Free Church Evangelicals, and especially Anabaptist writers, he is viewed with deep suspicion, as one whose ambition further undermined and incorporated whatever was left of the integrity of post-Apostolic Christianity.

There remains considerable room for debate. The documentary evidence that has survived is far from complete. This is not an unusual circumstance for the historian, but in this case the deficiencies are particularly tantalizing. Exactly how are we to assess accounts of his vision before battle? Constantine's actual convictions are not always clear. For many his status as a truly Christian emperor was confirmed by his championship of the Athanasius-led orthodox faction against the followers of Arius (256–336) at the Council of Nicaea in 325. He was present at the council's doctrinal debates, and the hundreds of bishops who attended all traveled and were accommodated at imperial expense. Who is to say what Constantine's true motivations were? They might well have been mixed, conflicted, and imperfectly understood even by Constantine himself.

Paganism at the time of Nicaea was not explicitly proscribed, although Christianity of the officially acceptable variety was now clearly privileged. Whether they liked it or not, Christians now found themselves becoming a favored group. If Christians found this pleasant, it is not surprising, after so many waves of cruel persecution. Certainly, the notion that Constantine "took over the church" is far too crude and lacking in nuance. The bishops were sufficiently free and powerful to take a strong line against Arius, notwithstanding Constantine's inclination towards the inclusion of his followers.

In all of this we need to be cautious when appraising the part played by Constantine's great Christian champion, Eusebius. His fulsome praises of Constantine should be read with all the circumspection we are able to muster. Eusebius was certainly a man with a mission. He was out (as our society would say) to "sell" Constantine the Christian Emperor to Christian opinion across the empire, especially to those who were ill at ease with such a prospect. Beyond this, Eusebius was setting a standard, "writing the book," so to speak, on such a Christian Emperor. Eusebius got to say what such an emperor was, what he would look like, and how he would conduct himself. Also in this respect his impact was seminal. He is best known for his *Ecclesiastical History* (*Historia Ecclesiastica*). His *Universal History* (*Chronicon*) is less well known. Taken in conjunction, they imply a certain sacred / secular duality. Most significantly, the point of integration comes in his panegyric work on Constantine himself, his *Life of Constantine* (*Vita Constantini*), as confirmed by the *Oration in Praise of Constantine* (*Laudes Constantini*).

The significance of what Constantine initiated, or the interpretation that Eusebius formulated and promoted for it, was not fully demonstrated during the lifetime of this first Christian Emperor. It is only *after* Constantine that certain of the questionable features of the new Christian-imperial culture became more fully manifested. There was nothing inevitable or permanent about any of this. As if to remind us of the play of contingency, the period after Constantine included the interlude of Julian the Apostate (332–363), the last of the Constantinian dynasty.

Julian's successors reversed his policy and restored the "Catholic" Christianity of which they approved. This trend was even more fully exhibited in the policies of the first emperor of the Theodosian line, Theodosius I (347–395), who came to the throne in 379. It was at this stage that the persecution of pagans set in with a vengeance. Moreover, under the prevailing order, if the emperor was a Christian, a persistent affirmation of paganism could be viewed as a challenge to the imperial office and title. In public life it became increasingly advantageous to be a Catholic Christian irrespective of your actual convictions.

Even though the full expression of the Christian-imperial system did not yet appear under Constantine himself, what took place under Constantine and Theodosius was transformational. Was the empire Christianized, or was Christianity *imperialized*? The answer has to be, "a bit of each." The suppression of pagan cults could mute or even terminate the evils they sustained. The positive public-cultural consequences of Christian belief and living could more readily flourish with imperial support. In such ways we may say that the general culture within the empire became somewhat Christianized, if not wholly Christian. Yet it is also true that the Church became more conspicuously imperial. Its bishops became more tied in with the imperial administration. Certainly, from Theodosius onwards, official Christianity emerges as a persecuting power that is repeatedly aligned on the side of the political, social and economic elites. Under the imperial authority of Theodosius, the *Edict of Thessalonica* (February 27, 380) defined true and approved Christianity, declaring all others (clearly including Arians) as madmen and heretics. Thereafter, Christian-imperial power was used to suppress both paganism and any version of heterodox Christianity. From that time, an imperially sanctioned version of Christianity could function oppressively towards the masses and the marginalized in a manner not contemplated by Christ and his apostles. Christianity was *reduced* to the church as an institution, with its approved practices and agencies. Of course, once Christianity was effectively constituted as the official religion, those with status and ambition—however unscrupulous they might be—were liable to associate themselves with it as the imperially approved religion.

How many so-called ordinary Christians, we might wonder, perceived a loss in the transformation that Constantine's actions initiated and in which Theodosius and many others persisted? Doubtless, there were those who sensed that an imperial co-option of the church robbed it of vital possibilities, even though the church remained the custodian of gospel truth. In impassioned passages Eusebius sought to allay their fears; his influence was considerable. Theodosius made the definitive division of the Roman Empire, effective upon his death in 395, between its Latin-speaking western portion, still centered on Rome, and its Greek-speaking eastern portion, based on Constantinople. The latter gave rise to the civilization of Byzantium, the context in which Eastern Orthodoxy came to its fullest expression. Byzantium became the great historical example of caesaro-papism, in which under God, the ruler was viewed as supreme in both church and state. And it was not so long before this same Byzantine Empire was being viewed as *the kingdom of God on earth*—a far cry from the coming of the kingdom as preached by Jesus around Galilee and beyond.

Augustine and the Legacy of Platonism

Further re-shaping developments lay on the horizon. In the century after Constantine, the Roman Empire in the West succumbed to the pressures long exerted by the Germanic tribes to the north. In the circumstances of collapse, the cry went up that Rome was now enduring the consequences of abandoning the old pagan ways of its founders by adopting Christianity. Augustine of Hippo (354–430) replied to the charge in his rambling yet seminal work *The City of God* (*De Civitas Dei*). Augustine set this "heavenly city" over against the "earthly city" (*civitas terrenae*). The ambiguities of this formula were to complicate the western understanding of what we call "church and state" for centuries to come.

Does Augustine primarily compare the "heavenly New Jerusalem," of a *future* age with the wickedness of the present age? Or does he address the *present* contrast between the Church as the communion of the saints, over against the "world"— the disbelieving city of the present age? Both sets of distinctions are in some sense applicable simultaneously. How then do they relate to each other? These difficulties planted a dualistic uncertainty into Christian answers to questions such as: How are Christians to live in the present age? The loss of a biblical sense of the order of creation, and of the religious character of human culture, has led to a confusing variety of Christian answers to these questions over the centuries. Some of the answers have helped foster a Christianity whose ethereal remoteness from earthly life could seem strangely at variance with the comprehensiveness of its claims over all of life.

Medieval and post-medieval appropriations of the Augustinian legacy have resulted in a plethora of "two kingdoms" theories about church and state, Christians and culture, and so forth. Today, many Christians wrestle with these questions, but become discouraged when they discover too many tangles and dilemmas that they cannot unravel, and so they become frustrated and give up. A great deal of this issue has to do with the importation of alien philosophical standpoints into the fabric of our thinking—as already noted—even into our habitual reading of the Bible. Such insoluble difficulties arise from the importation of dualistic assumptions alien to the full gospel teaching. These assumptions have affected all the main branches of Protestantism. The stark truth is that "two kingdoms" thinking is not *intrinsic* to the biblical texts. The gospel message is that the kingdoms of this present age (flagrantly disobedient as they may be) are *already* subject to the kingly rule of the risen Christ. In the New Testament there is only *one* kingdom of God.

The monastic movement had its origins in the East. Its introduction to the West is usually attributed to John Cassian (360–433). While the monastic orders performed important functions—including the preservation of biblical and classical texts and the advancement of learning—they also represented a defective response to the question: How are Christians to live in the present age? The sacred / secular, higher / lower dichotomy that had entered the thinking of Christians through the influence of Hellenic philosophy seemed to offer the alternatives of a "higher" life of celibate, monastic withdrawal and a lesser and "lower" life marked by varying degrees of "secular" defilement. The latter was not viewed as wholly "un-Christian," but it was not the best—not the "highest." Indeed, in the West, the clergy who served in parishes were eventually referred to as "secular clergy," as distinct from ordained priests in monastic orders. The latter were regarded as holier, being more withdrawn from the worldliness of ordinary life. Many centuries later, the notion of a "higher Christian life" was to have great appeal to many evangelical Christians and is strong evidence of how these early influences have served to distort our understanding of the gospel and the holiness to which we are called.

These tendencies arose from the pervasive influence of Platonic thinking, to which the prestige of Augustine's reputation for the next one thousand years gave a powerful boost. Notions of holiness consisting in a constant abstemiousness with respect to ordinary creaturely existence ran counter to the main thrust of biblical teaching with its strong creation-affirming orientation. The Reformation started an important turn around. Its reaffirmation of marriage and the wholesomeness of sexual activity within the marriage bond, also for the clergy, is a case in point.

Augustine's writings were immensely influential. His impact on western thought, not only in Roman Catholicism, is incalculable. He was highly regarded by both Martin Luther and John Calvin (1509-64). Luther became an Augustinian monk in 1505, and Calvin referred to Augustine more than any other post-New Testament author. Augustine's *Confessions* pioneered the literary *genre* of spiritual autobiography, laying down a path that Wesley followed when writing about his "Aldersgate experience." Augustine greatly influenced the way in which we think about religion: he shaped many of the categories that are habitually utilized when Christian doctrine is discussed and the Bible is translated and interpreted. He provided generations of translators and commentators with what we might call their conceptual furniture.

Augustine's writings exhibited a strong tendency to present Christian teaching by employing categories reflective of the philosophy of Plato (427-347 BC) and his later disciples, such as Plotinus (AD 205-270). In so doing, Augustine was strongly influenced by Ambrose, Bishop of Milan (c. 340-397), who had already mingled Platonism with Christianity. For example, in Augustine, Plato's notion of eternal, universal ideas became "ideas in the mind of God." The light beyond the cave in Plato's famous allegory of the prisoners in the cave becomes the light of the gospel. Eventually, God and all creatures came to be viewed within the continuum of a "great chain of being." We should not blame this exclusively on Augustine. Platonizing tendencies were already apparent in the writings of Justin Martyr (100-165), for whom the "word" (*logos*) of John's prologue (John 1:1-18) is to be understood platonically, rather than in the Old Testament context provided by the opening of the book of Genesis. Nevertheless, Augustine's immense reputation legitimized his persistent Platonizing in the eyes of many Christians over the centuries.

Augustine and his writings were to loom large in the thinking of the Latin Catholic West for more than a millennium, not only because of their quality but also because of the further great changes that took place across the Mediterranean basin following his death. The collapse of Roman rule brought an almost complete end to urban life across much of Western Europe for centuries, other than in Italy—and even there it declined seriously. The extensive municipal culture—"civilization," no less—in which

Christianity first spread had all but disappeared. It was under such conditions that the Latin-speaking church in the West eventually acquiesced to the claims of primacy asserted by successive bishops of Rome. For centuries something more akin to tribal society prevailed across much of Europe. These societies, founded by incoming Germanic tribes, eventually coalesced as feudal kingships under the watchful eyes of the Catholic Church.

Throughout this period the ideal of a "Christian Empire" still held great allure—witness the crowning of Charlemagne (742–814) as Holy Roman Emperor in 800, and the reconstitution of the Holy Roman Empire in 962 by Otto I (912–973). Furthermore, the degree to which post-Augustinian Latin Christianity in the Catholic West itself underwent a process of "Germanization" should not be discounted. Eventually there emerged an array of social structures, headed by pope and emperor, which in combination exemplified the medieval ideal of an ecclesiastically integrated culture: the *Corpus Christianum* of the medieval West.

The inheritance of Constantine, Eusebius, Theodosius, and Augustine found a place in the medieval ideal of *Christendom*. It can unquestionably be presented in romanticized terms, but its consequences should not be lost sight of amid any latter-day idealized depictions. Human history often presents us with a mixed picture, and medieval Christendom is no exception. Torture and death for heresy became a feature of this sort of society. Medieval Christendom bequeathed to us a dreadful legacy of Christian anti-Semitism. Even as the Papacy fought hard against any eastern-style caesaro-papism, it repeatedly asserted the supremacy of the Papacy over Emperor and Holy Roman Empire, and monarchs generally. As might be expected, the drawing of a boundary between holy church and holy empire became a vexed business, as the great "investiture crisis" for ultimate authority between popes and emperors during the eleventh and twelfth centuries made clear. Yet it was the actual existence of these two great centers of power and authority that generated in the West a level of sophisticated political and jurisprudential debate without parallel in the East. Also, the civilization of the medieval West fostered three great institutions without which our contemporary society would be unrecognizable: parliaments, universities and hospitals. The best that we might say of medieval Christendom is that it strove to be Christian, however defective its understanding.

Islam and Aristotle

Meanwhile, in the East, the rise of militant Islam threatened and eventually crushed the Byzantine Empire upon which Eastern Orthodox Christianity had been centered, a process completed by the Fall of Constantinople to the Ottoman Turks (1453). The West fought off the military challenge of Islamic *jihad* at Tours in France (732), although it was centuries before Islam was ejected from Spain (1492) and the western Mediterranean (1571). The last Turkish siege of Vienna was as late as 1683. Christianity was not unaffected by these trials. We can be shaped by what we oppose, and it has been argued that the Catholic West itself acquired a disposition to wage "holy war" (and mount Crusades) and a willingness to practice the enslavement of others from the contagious examples set by Islam. From Islamic scholars also came the medieval West's knowledge of the otherwise long-lost philosophy of Aristotle (384-322 BC). Thomas Aquinas (1225-1274) strove to synthesize this newly acquired Aristotelian philosophy with the received doctrine of the Catholic Church. The path was not easy—at one stage Aquinas found his teaching condemned—but eventually his massive accommodation of Aristotelian thought to Catholic doctrine prevailed. Thomism was born, and today it remains the official philosophical position of the Roman Catholic Church.

In certain respects, the synthesis of Thomas Aquinas represents the supreme intellectual achievement of western medieval Christianity. Its subtle dovetailing of the secular and the sacred, or nature and grace, or the physical and the metaphysical, reflected and legitimized the ecclesiastically integrated culture of the mediaeval era as pre-eminently expressed by the Holy Roman Empire and in Papal control of the Roman Catholic Church. Yet Thomism never reigned absolutely supreme. Indeed, it is possible to see in Thomism the beginning of the end of the medieval synthesis, even as it achieved its fullest expression. Aquinas saw himself as expanding and refining the position of Augustine, but the adjustments were considerable. For Augustine, theology was generally envisaged as *the* Christian philosophy. In Aquinas, philosophy and theology were distinguished in a manner that reflected the Aristotelian distinction between physics and metaphysics. Theology was now enthroned as the "queen of the sciences" (*theologia regina scientiarum*), with the other disciplines in a subordinate position. Often, and sometimes unwittingly, Christians have wrestled with the consequences of that view ever since.

Emerging Challenges: Nominalism and Reformation

The intellectual life of the medieval West was never as barren or futile as its latter-day critics have been prone to suggest. No sooner had Thomism become established, than it seems to have greatly stimulated the rise of nominalism. Hitherto *realism* had reigned supreme. According to realism, "universal ideas" (the abstract idea of "horse," for example) *really* (hence *realism*) did exist as objective, abstract entities—the spin derived from Platonism being that they existed "in the mind of God." Augustine and Aquinas were both realists. Now the "old way" (*via antiqua*) of realism was challenged by a "new way" (*via moderna*) of nominalism, frequently associated with one of its leading exponents, William of Ockham (d. 1347)—sometimes spelt Occam. Nominalism was to play a role in the coming of the Reformation. Its questions had the effect of undermining the realist assumptions upon which so much previous thinking had been based and had provided the outer framework for Aquinas's grand synthesis of Catholic doctrine and Aristotelian thought. Universals previously regarded as actual abstract entities were now viewed as mere requirements of linguistic expression—a necessary feature of the business of naming things and organizing knowledge. Accordingly, new issues emerged and old discussions could be formulated in new ways. Nominalists were deeply involved in reasserting the powers of the prince against the claims of the Papacy. Such polemics were prone to pull the mediaeval system apart.

Martin Luther could tell his students "My master was Occam." However, although Luther was definitely influenced by William of Ockham, we should not overinterpret his sweeping remark. He also said "I demand arguments [from Scripture] not authorities. That is why I contradict even my own school of Occamists, which I have absorbed completely."[3] We are on safe ground seeing Luther as backing nominalism against Aquinas and Aristotle. In seeking to break with the conventional realism, and to reflect the transcendence of God, nominalism could assert that God is "outside" or "above" his law (*Deus ex lex*). This dictum, however, though offered with the intention of asserting the sovereignty of God, nevertheless came with problems of its own. It appeared to open the way to a divine arbitrariness not encountered in the Bible. Moreover, it is important to keep in mind that the "new way" (*via moderna*) of thinking was never a monolithic school of thought, and that the version of nominalism which seems to have been most influential on the Reformers is the one arising from Gregory of Rimini (d. 1358), the *schola Augustiniana moderna*.

In this line of thinking, we may discern a blending of nominalism's rejection of realism with an Augustinian insistence on the sovereignty of God over all his creatures. It was in the protestant and reformed continuation of this line that the problem of the seeming arbitrariness of God was to receive its scriptural answer: God is sovereign, but not arbitrary; he keeps

---

3. Oberman, *Luther*, 120.

his word by being faithful to his *covenant* with his people and all creation. Even as the medieval synthesis waned, with the papacy discredited by exile, division, ambition, and corruption, much of Europe was traumatized by the horrors and aftermath of the Black Death. Arguably, the spread of various versions of nominalism both fed a growing sense of spiritual insecurity and stimulated the quest for a new certainty.

It was in this context that the mighty renaissance cry went up: *ad fontes*—"back to the sources." Of course, as might be expected, the sources proved not to be the same for everyone. For the ambitious Machiavelli (1469–1527), the authors of pagan Rome took center stage. For the troubled Luther the sources meant the text of the Old and New Testaments which he had been appointed to explain at the newly established, and definitely modest, University of Wittenberg. In this he was greatly assisted by the appearance in 1516 of the new edition of the New Testament in Greek by Desiderius Erasmus, often known as Erasmus of Rotterdam (1466–1536). Spurred on by agony over his eternal destiny and the scandal of the church's opportunistic and manipulative indulgence selling, Luther was the most conspicuous among those who took the first steps in distinguishing the teachings of Scripture from the doctrines and the traditional practices of the church. The New Testament provided by Erasmus was central in this process.

As we have seen, it was at a reading of Luther's *Preface to the Epistle to the Romans* that Wesley had felt his heart "strangely warmed" in 1738. His experience, and his understanding of his experience, arose from a Christianity that had undergone immense change over the centuries but referred directly to the Reformation of the sixteenth century, to which we will now turn. We must do this, because Wesley and the first evangelicals cannot be understood without considering the Reformation and its inner conflicts and their consequences.

So, what did happen to Christianity? A great deal—it became ensnared in Hellenic ways of thinking and Roman ways of organization. It lost sight of the robust appreciation of the order of creation so characteristic of the Hebrew Bible. It fell into dualistic attitudes. It misunderstood, as it misrepresented, the kingdom of God. The entire situation cried out for Reformation. In any serious discussion of Evangelicalism the Reformation cannot be ignored. The Bible translation work of Erasmus, Luther, William Tyndale (1494–1536), and others opened its books to the people, and without that increasingly available open Bible historic Evangelicalism is inconceivable.

3

WHATEVER HAPPENED TO THE REFORMATION?

Luther and the Reformation of Christendom

Between the assertions of his ninety-five theses (1517) and his legendary declaration before the Emperor Charles V at the Diet of Worms (1523), Luther was driven by force of circumstance to define his position. He repudiated papal authority and asserted that of Scripture. His actions were of world-historical significance, eventually changing the face of western civilization. Salvation could not be purchased or earned: it was granted by God's grace in and through Jesus Christ. The existing "cradle to the grave" sacramental system was rejected. Baptism and the Eucharist were retained, while the Roman Catholic doctrine of transubstantiation—best explained in terms of the Thomist utilization of Aristotelian categories—was repudiated, as was the notion of a celibate and sacerdotal priesthood. Monasticism was abandoned in favor of service in all legitimate walks of life. Human sexuality, within the context of married life, was positively affirmed. If we say that the Reformation did not go far enough, it was still an extraordinarily radical and constructive development in what remained by our standards a static society.

Luther was one of the truly exceptional men in the history of Christianity. His life and teaching were decisive. Long before being "born again" became a revivalist cliché, Luther could speak of himself being "straightway born afresh and to have entered through the open gates into paradise itself."[1] His message was one of deliverance and new life. We can stand in awe of his achievements: his bravery, his boldness, candor, lack of affectation, and his immense literary output, including the *Luther Bible*. We can also be appalled by his fearful harshness towards the peasants and his repulsive anti-Semitism. At every point it is imperative that we keep Luther in his context, and not anachronistically modernize him in our imaginations. Luther retained much that reflected the medieval outlook. This should not surprise us, especially if we have traced the origins of the Reformation deep into the life and thought of late-medieval Catholicism. If in Luther the Reformation made a stunning beginning, it should not surprise us that its full implications were not at every point immediately apparent. We should always remember that Luther never aspired to start another kind of Christianity called Protestantism. He sought the reformation of Christendom on the basis of biblical rather than papal authority. The term Protestant only emerged as his followers *protested* their treatment at the hands of the authorities. The "great schism" between Catholicism and Eastern Orthodoxy occurred long before the Reformation in the West. Further division *within* the western church became inevitable as the papacy actively opposed calls for doctrinal and institutional reformation. Catholic power in church and state failed to eliminate the emergent reformation movement by either force of argument or force of arms. The division of Christendom is not to be laid primarily at the doors of the protestant reformers. Due weight must be given to the intransigence of the Papacy.

As we proceed further, we need to keep in mind a number of points about the Reformers, and the movement they initiated. Above all, we need to recall that Protestantism never assumed the form of a single alternative movement. It was diverse from the outset, as Roman Catholic critics have not failed to observe. In truth, there was no generic Reformation as such, but a series of different, interrelated and interacting reformations across Europe. Nevertheless, as diverse as they were, the Reformers were foremost committed to the recovery and restatement of biblical doctrine, especially concerning the way of salvation (soteriology)—of how we are restored to a right relationship with our Creator in Jesus Christ. Any attempt to account for the Reformation in terms of its accompanying political, social or economic circumstances misses this key point. For the Reformation, the recovery of right doctrine was a prime consideration. Of course, any assumption that in the sixteenth century doctrine functioned in a compartment by itself is erroneous. On the contrary, doctrine had meaning for how life

---

1. Rupp and Drewery (editors), 5–6.

was to be lived. For this reason, all the Reformers saw that the reformation of doctrine and worship entailed the reformation of life and public culture. We also need to remember that the first Reformers inherited from the days of Constantine and Theodosius, via Augustine and the ecclesiastically integrated order of the medieval period, a view of society in which church and state were but two sides of the same collective Christian body—Christendom. As we have seen, this Christendom came to avow teachings that were an unstable amalgam of Christian and pagan features—many of the latter being derived from classical Greece, sometimes via the Islamic east. The reformations of the sixteenth century did not immediately address all of these problems; and it could be argued that it made some of them worse, at least in the short term.

A Diversity of Views on How the Scriptures Are Authoritative

At the heart of the Reformation was the question of authority. Where did final authority lie when it came to Christian belief and conduct? At first glance the Reformers all gave the same answer: the Bible is authoritative, not the pope, and while church councils might have their place, they can be in error. Only the Bible is a sure guide. So far, so good—but some serious problems emerged when it came to clarifying *how* the Bible was authoritative. Exactly *how* was the authoritative text to be interpreted, and *how* was it to function in the reformation of the teaching, worship, organization, and government of the church? And exactly *how* did reason and tradition function in this picture? While all the Reformers received the Scriptures as inspired and authoritative, they differed in their answers to these questions. They did *not* arrive at a single view of *how* the authority of the Scriptures was to function in the life of the Church and of God's people generally. From the very outset there were profound differences about how this authority played out in practice. These differences helped create a marked diversity within and across emergent Protestantism.

This key question of how the Scriptures are authoritative was answered in four distinct ways. These will be referred to as follows: (1) the *corrective* as adopted by Lutheranism and also in the Church of England; (2) the *regulative* as annunciated by Huldrych Zwingli (1484–1531) and later Heinrich Bullinger (1504–75) in Zurich, and by John Knox (1514–72) in Scotland; (3) the *exemplary*, as espoused by the Anabaptists in various parts of German-speaking Europe and beyond; and (4) the *directional* as exemplified by John Calvin and his circle in Geneva. These strands are all important because they exhibit different views of *how* the Bible, as God's word written, was considered authoritative.

These distinctions are generally applicable, provided that the limitations of too hard and fast a categorization are recognized. The point here is not to engage in a crude labeling but to gain historical insight into the structure and diversity of the Reformation situation. These differences had a significant impact on Protestantism in the British Isles and tell us much about the milieu in which English-speaking protestant Evangelicalism later emerged. These four different ways do not coincide precisely with the various denominational labels that subsequently became familiar, but they help to explain why denominationalism eventually emerged in the way it did.

The Corrective Way

The basic approach of Luther and his followers—the *Evangelische*—was the Lutheran-corrective way of understanding biblical authority. In German-speaking lands the term *evangelisch* meant "protestant" and pre-eminently protestant according to the Lutheran model. The *evangelische Kirchen* were the protestant churches. In Germany the term later became much broader than the English "evangelical." As Anglo-American Evangelicalism, much later, also impacted German-speaking Europe, the German language came to distinguish between *evangelische,* meaning Lutheran, and *evangelikal*, meaning contemporary, Anglo-American style evangelical.

The *corrective* model of biblical authority held that everything that was traditional in the doctrine and life of the church was to be retained, *unless it was expressly contrary to biblical teaching and example.* Matters not explicitly discussed by the Bible were liable to be considered as *adiaphora*—things indifferent. Such externalities, such as vestments, might be retained, or discarded if considered unseemly. In the Lutheran tradition there emerged a strong contrast between the inner spiritual and the outer temporal. It is consistent with the "two realm teaching" (*Zweireichslehre*) already expressed in Luther, inherited from Augustine, and articulated more systematically by later generations of Lutherans.

Undoubtedly, Luther stands as the first champion of the Reformation. William Wycliffe (d. 1384) and John Hus (d. 1415) appear to us as significant forerunners, but Luther was the man who effectively challenged the prevailing system. His immediate following was diverse. Philip Melanchthon (1497–1560) was more accommodating to the scholasticism of the late-medieval period than Luther, with his avowal of nominalism and aversion towards "the schoolmen." If there was no great breach between Luther and Melanchthon, this may in part be attributed to Luther's increasing conservatism from the mid-1520s onwards. If Luther flung open the door to Reformation, others entered more fully into its promise. Luther's corrective approach towards biblical authority disappointed some of his early followers. For example, Andreas von Karlstadt (1486–1541) eagerly sought more thoroughgoing changes in public worship than Luther's cautious corrective approach would sanction. It was not long before voices of reform more radical than those of Wittenberg were being raised in the Swiss Cantons—initially in Zurich. On the other hand, the reformed Church of England, from 1549 to 1552, and after 1558, adopted a version of the corrective approach, although it inclined strongly towards Zurich in its view of the Eucharist.

The Regulative Way

Early Protestantism was not exclusively German—a significant proportion of it was Swiss—and the Swiss reformation was both German and French speaking. In the Swiss cantons we encounter a non-Lutheran reformation that came to be labeled Reformed, in order to distinguish it from the *Evangelische* (Lutheran). These other Swiss reformations differed amongst themselves as to their view of the authority of Scripture, as well as the Lutheran standpoint expressed in the German lands and Scandinavia. The Reformation under Luther in Saxony may be contrasted with that of the Canton of Zurich under Zwingli (1522). In both localities the processes involved were deeply dependent on the acceptance, co-operation and protection of the civil magistrate. In Luther's case it was the protection of Frederick the Wise of Saxony, in Zwingli's that of the Zurich municipal authorities. The Reformation tended to take hold where it received, one way or another, support and protection from the Godly Prince or Magistracy. Zwingli died, with sad irony, on the field of battle, in 1531. Luther lived until 1546. If Luther had died earlier and Zwingli had lived to a ripe old age the Reformation may well have taken a significantly different historical trajectory. European Protestantism might have come to exhibit a more Swiss rather than a German character.

Heinrich Bullinger was Zwingli's successor in Zurich. The view of the authority of Scripture that came to expression in Zurich has come to be termed *regulative*. According to this view, *whatever had no explicit warrant in Scripture had no authorized place* in the doctrine and life of the church. Thus it was that Lutheran and non-Lutheran protestant churches—the latter often called Reformed—were liable to have a markedly different appearance from the outset. In the eyes of the Reformed, the Reformation in Zurich soon came to look much more Protestant than that of Wittenberg which seemed in some respects still rather Catholic. It was Zwingli and his followers who broke with all images, while the Lutherans retained the use of vestments and their version of the mass—substituting Luther's consubstantiation teaching for Catholicism's transubstantiation.

The Lutheran *corrective* view and the Zwingli-Bullinger *regulative* view were both influential. As has been noted, the Church of England adopted the *corrective* standpoint at the time of the Reformation. By contrast, the Reformation in Scotland ultimately followed the *regulative* approach—as did the "hotter sort of Protestants" in England, soon to be dubbed Puritans.[2] Bullinger outlived Calvin. His ministry in Zurich was appreciated and respected across Europe, outlasting—some might even say outflanking—Calvin's final and longest uninterrupted period at Geneva from 1541 to 1564. Bullinger composed the *Second Helvetic Confession* (1566), which was highly influential in Scotland, France, the Rhineland, Hungary, and Poland.

The *regulative* view exhibited a strong moral emphasis and commitment to public righteousness. At the same time the *regulative* view (sometimes referred to as "the regulative principle") has had the effect of limiting the application of biblical teaching only to those institutions explicitly referenced in Scripture—particularly to the church (as an institution), to the civil magistrate, to marriage, and to the family. What was not explicitly addressed in Scripture could too easily be viewed as *adiaphora*. How easy it is, then, to fall back into the old "two realm" teaching, and to say that the Bible only addresses what is sacred or supernatural and to leave the rest of human culture untouched by the gospel and the claims it makes on Christian discipleship. The regulative view saw questions of church order as falling within the sacred realm because certain Scripture texts explicitly addressed questions of ecclesiastical government and conduct. However, the exponents of this "Bible-based" regulative view—ever prone to search for explicit proof texts—have been at a loss to explain how the authority of Scripture applies specifically to culturally formed societal structures unknown to the biblical authors, such as the political party, the business corporation, and the labor association.

The proponents of the Zurich-based, Zwingli-Bullinger *regulative* view of the authority of Scripture were highly influential. They strongly influenced the kind of trans-national Reformed Protestantism that emerged towards the later sixteenth century. Some of this influence was immensely positive. Its leaders not only asserted the principle of *Sola Scriptura* (by Scripture

---

2. Collinson, *Elizabethan Puritan Movement*, 27.

alone), but also that of *Tota Scriptura* (by all of Scripture); they took the Old Testament seriously. They explored and articulated the biblical teaching of God as the LORD—the covenant-making and covenant-keeping God who always keeps his word to his people. Their view of the Old Testament, and not least the "moral law," was more positive than that of the Lutherans. Eventually the proponents of the *regulative* view added "godly discipline" as a third mark of the true church—along with the true preaching of the gospel and the right administration of the sacraments. Critics might argue that this presaged a narrowing of discipleship to little more than an adherence to the prohibitions enforced by church discipline.

The Exemplary Way

Among Zwingli's most fervent initial supporters were those who soon parted company from him completely. They often called themselves the brethren, but the term Anabaptist has stuck because they were conspicuous for their rejection of the practice of infant baptism. Recent historiography has used the term Radical Reformation to describe this group of movements. The Anabaptists were but one expression of various strands of popular commitment and piety that had for centuries persisted within, or on the fringes of, and sometimes beyond the confines of, and frequently in spite of, the officially constituted institutions of western Christendom. Anabaptist groups varied greatly from one locality to another. Offering generalizations about them is therefore especially hazardous. What was central was the persistence with which they sought to live out their vision of the Christian life with almost exclusive reference to the New Testament. The examples it provided were to be followed directly. When first viewed from the perspective of Wittenberg, the early reformation in Zurich could seem markedly Anabaptist in tone, especially as the *regulative* principle swept aside much of what the Lutheran *corrective* view retained. But there were crucial differences, and these became more conspicuous as Anabaptist leaders such as Conrad Grebel (1498–1526) and George Blaurock (1491–1529) broke with the "magisterial reformation" as represented by Zwingli and the Zurich magistrates.

Focusing on two key areas can highlight the grounds of Anabaptist separation from magisterial reformers such as Luther and Zwingli. Firstly, they dissented from the complicity of the magisterial reformation in the politico-ecclesiastical system of Christendom as inherited from Constantine and Theodosius. In their view, the system was a corrupt travesty. The true church was to consist only of those who made a credible profession of faith.

Living, as we do, in a post-Christendom era, many today who would not consider themselves Anabaptists would nevertheless agree with them at this point. However, the Anabaptists often reacted against the Constantinian-Theodosian system by withdrawing from both church and state—they repudiated and withdrew from state-controlled churches and refused to hold public office under such a system. The Anabaptists of Zurich were dismayed at Zwingli's apparent willingness to make the pace of reform contingent upon the approval of the magistrates. The Swiss Anabaptists refused to bear arms—as stated in the Schleitheim Articles of 1527. This refusal was viewed by non-Anabaptists as a duplicitous contracting out of society while still wishing to partake of its benefits.

Secondly, Anabaptists were conspicuous for their repudiation of infant baptism. Here the protestant exponents of paedo-baptism were dangerously exposed on two counts: (1) popular superstitions surrounding infant baptism, ascribing to it what amounted to a magical efficacy, and (2) the truth that any exponent of the regulative view of Scripture must acknowledge: that the New Testament nowhere contains a single verse that declares explicitly "You shall baptize the babies of believing parents." In meeting these challenges, Zwingli and Bullinger stressed the principle of *Tota Scriptura* and emphasized that the Bible envisages a single covenant people of God, a covenant that always included the children. The reformed churches followed Zwingli and Bullinger in understanding infant baptism in these terms. They took the view that it was not rendered illegitimate by the superstition of some, or the malpractice of others.

Zwingli used the continuity of covenantal teaching in both Old and New Testaments to uphold and maintain the practice of infant baptism. Bullinger helped to make the idea of the covenant much more foundational to reformed doctrinal understanding. Nevertheless, the Anabaptist ideal of "believer's baptism" was in the longer run to have immense appeal for many evangelicals. It was to resonate with their individualism and tendency towards pietistic withdrawal from the world. However, the historical path from the Anabaptists of the 1520s to a much later Evangelicalism is not direct but convoluted.

Anabaptist diversity must also be stressed. Sometimes they could seem to be revolutionaries; what they could not change they would condemn and seek to overthrow. Thomas Müntzer (1489–1525) led the Peasants' Revolt to its tragic end at the battle of Frankenhausen (1525). Very quickly the Anabaptists found themselves facing the persecuting and executing zeal of both Catholic and Protestant princes—the latter at this stage still profoundly embedded in the outlook and ways of medieval Christendom. Under the pressure of rejection and persecution it is hardly surprising that not a few

Anabaptists fell prey to wild apocalyptic delusions. Melchior Hoffman (d. 1543), who is often regarded as the founder of Dutch Anabaptism, proclaimed himself Elijah and informed the city of Strasbourg that it was to be the New Jerusalem—whereupon the magistrates imprisoned him for life. Even more troubling was the Anabaptist rule of the city of Münster by Jan Mathias of Haarlem (d. 1543) and then Jan of Leiden (d. 1535) in the years 1534-5. This "reign of the saints" was marked by an attempt to recover the commonality of property as in the early *Acts of the Apostles*. It resorted to polygamy in order to populate the New Jerusalem. Eventually the city was captured and put to the sword by the surrounding Catholic and Lutheran forces.

These tragedies largely purged the Anabaptist movements of violent millennialism. Jacob Hutter (c. 1500-36) in Moravia, and Menno Simons (1496-1561) in the Netherlands, forged a more pacific communalism, giving their names to the Hutterites and Mennonites respectively. Generally forsaking public life, the men and women of these spiritually introverted movements could be exclusivist and sectarian, but they have quietly done more good in the world than is generally realized. On occasions they suffered terribly at the hands of the authorities, but theirs was to be an honorable part in finding a way along the tortuous path to religious pluralism. They viewed biblical authority in literalist and exemplary terms—too often the actual words (*ipsissima verba*) of Scripture were to be literally understood and followed, as if there were no intervening historical development.

This was an attempt to live, so to speak, with a certain New Testament "freshness," but in a totally different cultural milieu from that of the first century—as if no biblically directed understanding of subsequent cultural change were needed. Contemporary Evangelicalism evinces something of the Anabaptist outlook when, among its myriad sub-divisions, we encounter examples of what might be termed the "chasm" view of the history of Christianity. Various groups envisage themselves as if they are in direct continuation of the *Acts of the Apostles*—with the intervening chasm between the Apostolic era and themselves being of little or no relevance until things got "back on track" at the beginnings of their kind of church or group. It is also noteworthy that in later times, when and where the exponents of the *regulative* view failed to gain or maintain control of national churches, they also could find themselves drifting into something like an Anabaptist posture. In seventeenth-century England and Wales, Puritanism long advocated the *regulative* view of biblical authority. Only after it lost all prospect of political power in 1660 did the congregational wing of what became "Protestant dissent" become increasingly susceptible to those arguments that repudiated infant baptism. For the most part, the Baptists of the

English-speaking world may trace their lineage to this source, rather than directly to the Anabaptists of sixteenth-century continental Europe.

The Directional Way

Yet the Reformation in Zurich was not the only Swiss reformation. We are right to ask, "Where does the great ministry of John Calvin in French-speaking Geneva fit in?" After all, it is to Calvin that we look for the most eloquent and cogent statement of reformation doctrine: his *Institutes of the Christian Religion* (first edition 1536, French edition 1541, definitive revised edition 1559). This sometimes inscrutable and always diligent man is never to be underrated. Calvin was not Swiss—in Geneva he was a homesick Frenchman in exile. He was certainly more in accord with the Zwinglian than the Lutheran reformation—as much as he appreciated Luther personally. At the same time, Calvin's view of the authority of Scripture was not exactly that of Zurich. It was *directional* rather than *regulative*. Calvin's view was contextualized by his biblically inspired awe of the order of creation. This was for him no romantically inspired reverence for "nature," but a constant declaration of the glory and majesty of the Creator. This awe before the order of creation is a repeated theme in much of his writing. While our fallen condition renders us spiritually blind and deaf, for Calvin both creation and Scripture bear eloquent testimony to the Creator.

This *directional* view does not downplay scrupulous attention to specific biblical passages—as any consideration of Calvin's immense standing as an exegete, demonstrated in his biblical commentaries, will confirm—but it seeks to understand each passage in terms of scriptural principle distilled from the whole span of the canonical writings. It was in such a manner that Calvin struggled to assert the distinctive calling and authority of the church in relation to that of the civil magistrate. Even in a "Christian commonwealth," he insisted that the office bearers and assemblies of the church, and not the civil magistrate, had the calling and responsibility to bar delinquents from the Lord's Supper. Contrary to the requirements of the regulative principle, Calvin recognized "doctors of the church" as a distinct ecclesiastical office. Particularly instructive was Calvin's approach when considering the question of the payment of interest. He did not consider only a few prohibitory texts, using them to dispose of the question in a cut and dried but anachronistic manner. He had regard for the wider implications of biblical principle and the state of the culture in which he was living. Calvin's approach to the text focused on the central question of meaning without being literalistic. His rejection of a false literalism is conspicuous in his handling of passages in Genesis and the Psalms in relation to the recent astronomical discoveries of his day. There lay implicit in Calvin's *directional* understanding of biblical authority the possibility of articulating a biblically-directed worldview that was not bound to the pre-scientific world picture (*Weltbild*) of those who wrote the biblical texts.

Mention of Calvin inevitably brings to our attention the problematic term Calvinism. The term itself would definitely not have met with Calvin's approval. It came into existence largely in recognition of Calvin's immensely authoritative standing amongst the Reformed—including in the perceptions of non-reformed (specifically Lutheran) writers. As the second and third generations of Lutheran traditionalists were threatened by Reformed inroads into the protestant German *Länder*, and the emergence of the so-called Crypto-Calvinists within their own ranks (who were sympathetic towards the reformed view of the Lord's Supper)—they became more critical of the Reformed, and as they focused on Calvin as their prime representative, they came to talk of Calvinism.

Some Inter-twining of Viewpoints

Perhaps inevitably the four different views of how Scripture is authoritative have sometimes become intertwined in practice. The *regulative* and *directional* views especially have sometimes co-functioned in a single ecclesiastical setting, sometimes uneasily, because they represent two distinct approaches. For example, within contemporary reformed Churches, the question of women in ecclesiastical office is liable to be decided in the negative where the regulative view prevails, and positively where the directional view has some influence. Reformed exponents of the regulative view may sometimes (and in all sincerity) describe themselves as Calvinists or as being Calvinistic. They often identify also with the Puritanism of the seventeenth century. They generally equate the two. For them, Puritanism is the very essence of Calvinism.

However, where the *directional* view has prevailed, the view more consistently expressed by Calvin and his circle, Puritanism, with the persistent proof texting that comes with the regulative approach, came to be viewed as a *negation* of a truly Calvinistic outlook. As will be seen, the great strength of the directional outlook is that it exemplifies an understanding of biblical authority *that makes possible the application of general biblical principles in circumstances unanticipated by the biblical writers*. They will seek to follow the general *direction* set by Scripture, recognizing that the *principles* that lie at the foundation of specific injunctions are important, and that the ways in which such principles are applied may certainly vary from circumstance to circumstance.

The *regulative* and *directional* approaches have often not only coexisted, but have sometimes found ways of collaboration. To their immense credit, Bullinger and Calvin came to an agreement on the Lord's Supper, as formulated in the *Consensus Tigurinus* (1549). Much was due to Calvin's desire for Christian unity. His stance differed markedly from that of Luther at the Colloquy of Marburg in October 1529, where Luther insisted against Zwingli that the words "this is my body" (*hoc est corpus meum*) be read literally. It is necessary to recognize that a false literalism can carry us *away* from what Scripture means to say by the words it uses. Arguably, among Reformed Christians, some are much more authentically Calvinistic, meaning *directional*, than others. Some whom we might assess to be less Calvinistic might be grievously offended thereby, so much has their view of Calvin been shaped by a literature that reads him in *regulative* terms or does not sufficiently discern the *directional* character of his biblical hermeneutics. On such grounds much literature on Calvin and the history of Calvinism is problematic. The best work on Calvin himself is that which places him in his context and gives to him what all should be granted anyway—the effort needed to place the men and women of the past in their historical context.

By carefully examining the problems left unanswered by Protestantism in the sixteenth and seventeenth centuries, concerning exactly *how* the Scriptures are authoritative, we can see the roots of the confusions that a later Evangelicalism was unable to resolve. Though Evangelicalism has sometimes sought to minimise the churchly consequences of these differences, it has never resolved and sometimes multiplied them. The Reformers faced immense challenges. The Scriptues enabled them to discern and expose the errors of Rome, which could be viewed as post-apostolic accretions. Yet there was no going back to the church of the apostles and prophets themselves. That, after all, was a church *without* the New Testament canon. The church that the Reformers sought to reform was a church *with* the New Testament canon.

The corrective and regulative ways exhibited a compatibility with prevalent (sacred / secular; church / world) dualistic tendencies, while the regulative and exemplary ways could get stuck with a static "Bible-based" biblicism that sought in different ways to recapture a supposed apostolic authenticity. The corrective, regulative and exemplary ways all admitted a place for areas of life that were supposedly neutral in relation to the gospel, and therefore declared them *adiaphoria*. These all came into play in the life of Evangelicalism as it developed from the eighteenth century onwards. By contrast, and without suggesting that everything in human life was of equal importance, the directional way offered a forward orientation that took the authority of the canonical Scriptures seriously and that in principle addressed the totality of human life before the face of God.

4

THEOLOGY, SCIENCE AND THE REFORMATION

Theology as a Problem, Including Reformation Theology

The more we reflect on the Reformation, the more we can conclude that it was a start that did not go far enough. Of course, such judgments must be tempered with historical understanding. The Reformation represented a very important change in direction, but it did not wholly undo the well-entrenched legacies arising from the penetration of Christian thought by pagan Hellenic concepts, and the Romanization of Christian institutions. For this reason the magisterial Reformers, as we have seen, still thought in broadly Constantinian-Theodosian terms. Certainly, our twenty-first-century notions of "freedom of religion" would have been repellant to them.

When it came to Christian doctrine, many still thought in terms of the old Greek (particularly Aristotelian) idea of theology, a viewpoint that the vast majority of Christians today—evangelicals included—take for granted without so much as a second thought. Many students of theology fail to reflect seriously on the basis, status, character and object of their discipline. Many assume that theology is something that one "just does." This assumption is not so surprising. Science and scholarship in the English-speaking world have for a long time failed to provide a philosophically rigorous and coherent account of the encyclopedia of the sciences. Important questions at the level of foundational *prolegomena* ("first words") are ignored as supposedly impractical. A given field of science is something that is done, as in "doing biology" or "doing theology." Accordingly, the status of theology as a discipline is rarely subjected to rigorous scrutiny, firstly in relation to the individual believer: should all Christians be in some sense theologians, because all should read the Bible? Secondly, in relation to the church: what is the relationship between churchly creeds and confessions, and extended theological articulation? And finally, in relation to the academy: what is the place of theology in relation to the encyclopedia of the sciences generally?

It is sometimes said that theology simply means the study of God. A moment's reflection shows that such an answer is seriously problematic. Almighty God is not open to scientific investigation. What we *can* investigate, to the extent that we have access to it, is the order of creation in its manifold aspects and structural diversity. All this we may subject to analysis as best we can, but we cannot subject God to analysis. We can count, survey, probe, analyze, and theorize about all aspects of creation and every creature to which we have access. This we may do, and in this sense these things are subject to us, but God is never subject to us—we are always subject to God. There can therefore be no science of God. Science can only investigate the order of creation, and there can only be sciences that look at different *kinds* of creatures (abstract, inanimate and animate)—such as botany, zoology and anthropology, and different *ways* in which creatures may function— such as physics, biology or history. In short, there can be no science of God because God is *not* a creature. By contrast, the sciences investigate the order of creation, in all its wonderful complexity and diversity. It is the task of philosophy to provide a theoretical account of the encyclopedic relationships between the various sciences.

As we have argued, the Bible teaches that all creatures—also in their mutual interrelationships—are dependent on their Creator, whereas the Creator is non-dependent. Of course, we may subject our religious beliefs (our Christian beliefs not excluded) to analysis because our beliefs are themselves creaturely. However, the long tradition of Christian thinking that contemplates a rational-theological science of God is testimony to the influence of pagan Greek philosophers on Christian thought for almost as long as Christian history. It should not surprise us that in the medieval period, theology came to be seen as "the queen of the sciences." This sort of thinking was reflective of the idea that God was the greatest being in a great chain of beings, and theology was the queen over all other sciences because it discussed the greatest being—God. And, because all was subservient to God, all disciplines should be subject to theology. Here lies the basis of the notion that Christian theologians should have some sort of veto over all Christian thinking—with the prerogative of pronouncing it sound or unsound. Here arises the presumption that the theology faculty ought always to be pre-eminent in the Christian academy—the guardians and gatekeepers necessary to keep everyone in line. Here also lies the root of the notion that theologians should have primacy in telling us all how to read the Bible, hear its stories, and live its good news.

The truth is that the term theology is itself highly problematic. It has pagan rather than biblical roots. It carries the connotation that God (*theos*) himself may be accessed by reason (*logos*) and thereby subjected to rational study. Such a view is, of course, profoundly at variance with the Bible. The Bible not only teaches that God is fully sovereign and therefore not subject to his creatures (including the laws of logic he created), but also that all of his creatures depend on him, and that he has revealed himself to us in Jesus Christ. If we want to know God—if we want to know what the God who wants us to know him is like—then the way is not endless metaphysical speculation. The way is Jesus Christ himself. In short, the classical and medieval view of theology is inconsistent with the biblical view of revelation.

So what then is the true focus of theology—if it cannot be God? For many Protestants the next candidate has been the Bible. After all, we do have the Bible, and access to the Bible has always been strongly emphasized by Protestants. The Bible, God's word written—and itself a whole library of books—is a gift from the Holy Spirit to humankind. It instructs us concerning God, humankind, and the created order of which we are a part. It also instructs us concerning our alienation from our Creator as the result of our presumed autonomy and consequential disobedience, and with respect to God's redemptive purposes in Jesus Christ, the giving of the Holy Spirit, and the ultimate renewal and consummation of all creation.

Would we therefore be right in giving theology another mandate—not the study or science of God but the study or science of the Bible? Certainly, such an alternative is less offensive. It does not presume to treat God as if he were a creature. Yet upon further investigation the "study of the Bible" alternative is also unsustainable. To grasp why this is so we need to clarify what the Bible is and how it functions.

The Bible certainly does *not* tell us all about all things. It does tell us what *all things are all about*. In other words, it addresses *the totality of things*. Using the language of the day, it employs its own style and idiom. Moreover, while the Bible is not a book *of* science—it is a book *for* science, and it is not just a book for one science; rather it is *a book for all sciences*. It is a book for all sciences, because it is a book for the totality of human life and endeavor, and science is itself one of the most magnificent of all human undertakings. Moreover, the Bible is a book *for* the sciences: *not* that it teaches or is a sourcebook for scientific theories or is in any way a substitute for scientific or historical or any other kind of research, but it teaches us about the relations between God and his creatures. It is a book for the whole of life. As all of life serves either the one true living God or an idol, this is inevitably reflected in everything we do, *and therefore also in the fabric of our theorizing.* There is no zone of neutral and therefore common reason or supposedly non-religious, objective thought. A great deal in the western intellectual tradition is stacked up against this truth and invested in the idea of *human autonomy*. By contrast, however, a consistently *biblically directed* theorizing will continually honor the *dependence* of all creatures on their Creator.

Furthermore, to assign to persons designated as theologians the pre-eminent authority in determining how we are to understand the biblical texts is to return by a more protestant-sounding route to the old medieval position of "theology as the queen of the sciences." Such a position would ultimately put the totality of Christian life under theological authority, of whatever variety, and grant to the theologian a presumed authority to sanction or prohibit each and every scientific theory. Having escaped the tyranny of a medieval priesthood, presuming with its sacramental system to stand between God and people, we can all too easily succumb to the tyranny of a theological professoriate presuming to stand between the written Word and our calling to follow Christ in all things.

The latter tendency can be particularly conspicuous where systematic theology is highly prized. Here—sometimes on the basis of an undisclosed or inadequately discussed starting- point—the texts of Scripture (often with insufficient regard for *genre* or context) are re-assembled into a logically organized architectonic structure, which is then presented as biblical truth and therefore right doctrine. This may be described as a "jigsaw puzzle" approach to the Bible. In the Bible, individual texts with their different teachings might seem to come to us very untidily, all jumbled up and in no logical order. Only by using reason can the theological expert sort out all the pieces of the puzzle for us and place them in their logical order so that we can make sense of the whole. The results of such doctrinal labor tend to have little or nothing to say, beyond ethical instruction, to the full lives of the Lord's people lived simultaneously as family members, marriage partners, parents, church members, citizens, voters, thinkers, producers, buyers, sellers and so forth. These static architectonic endeavors categorize and utilize the biblical texts in ways, typically devotional or spiritual in a restricted sense, that obscure and negate the actual *directional* character of the Scriptures themselves.

Many Christians sense something of the deficiencies of such theologizing. Their misgivings are sound. They prefer the Bible, even if at times it seems to be untidy and confusing. Yet many others are still in thrall to scholastic theology as here outlined—not least among evangelicals who have understandably reacted against the doctrinal superficiality that pervades Evangelicalism generally, and who might self-identify as Puritan and Reformed. Such latter-day champions of scholastic theology still tend to see the Bible as offering a "sacred" message with moral injunctions, but having at best only a minimal relevance for so-called "secular" life. Rather than *theology*, it would be better if we had a term that effectively captures the science that investigates belief (Latin *fides*, faith) in all its diversity. For the Christian such a science will of necessity take the Bible seriously, because the Bible does tell us what ought to be believed—clearly and richly, yet without using the terminology of scientific abstraction. Rather, the books of the Bible offer us *teaching* (that is, doctrine, *doctrina*), that is pre-scientific (*not* anti-scientific), utilizing ordinary discourse and reflecting the ordinary experiences and perceptions of the times and places in which they were written.

Our everyday experience of reality should never be viewed with contempt. It should be regarded as primary. Theorizing is second-order, requiring the abstractions that make theory-formulation possible. When we understand this distinction we realize that astronomers may still perfectly legitimately speak of "sunrise" and "sunset" without having lapsed into the errors of geo-centricity. They are simply using the language of our day-to-day experience of the cosmos—they are using language in exactly the same way as was employed by the biblical authors in their own day and that was reflective of the world picture of their times.

A science, by contrast, proceeds by abstraction. It is characterized by an abstracting process that theoretically distinguishes aspects of things, for the purpose of achieving analytical insight, leading to hypothesis construction and theory formulation. Science approaches the totality of creation with but one of its features or aspects specifically in view. The biologist focuses on the living aspect of things, the physicist on the material, the mathematician on the numerical, and so on. So we may also focus on the belief-side of human functioning—the acts of believing and disbelieving, and all of the beliefs (true or false) that humans espouse—but we need to remember that this side, and all other such sides remain aspects of a single creational order. So, if by theology we mean a science that addresses belief, then that science should not be seen as having a final or all-encompassing status and character. Such a science, one that examines the belief-side of human life, is one of a diversity of disciplines that may be pursued in order to glorify God and serve humankind with insight and understanding. It is not the "queen of the sciences"—even though this was the view that prevailed in much sixteenth and seventeenth-century Protestantism.

The Persistence of Scholasticism and Scholastic Theology

We have observed that although the Reformation challenged Roman error and repudiated Papal authority, it did not test with due diligence the philosophical and anthropological assumptions it had inherited. While the Reformers' view of the relationship between God and his creatures pointed *in principle* to an alternative that was free of the Platonism of Augustine and Anselm of Canterbury (1033–1109) and the Aristotelian formulations of Aquinas, *in practice* the Reformation movement never wholly broke free from such *scholastic* modes of doctrinal statement, even where the *via moderna* was favored over the *via antiqua*. Protestantism was still somewhat Catholic. The doctrines of grace, the sacraments, and the church were challenged, but those of the triune God, creation, providence and the fall were retained in ways that unduly deferred to the formulations offered by Augustine, Anselm, and Aquinas. This retention tended to reinforce and legitimize medieval notions of faith as a "higher" supernatural addition (*donum superadditum*) to what is natural and "lower," even though this view was at variance with the better insights of Luther and Calvin. The depth of the Reformation should therefore be neither over- nor understated. Rather than blame the Reformation for what it left undone, it would be better—and be in fuller accord with its true spirit—to see reformation as a continuing calling.

What precisely is meant by scholasticism in this context? The immediate meaning is "pertaining to the manner of the schools." In other words, it refers to the formal logical-technical mode of articulation used for instruction in medieval educational institutions. This may be contrasted with a more straightforward, conversational, and less abstract style of discussion offered by *humanism* in the Renaissance and early Reformation periods. In recent decades a great deal of ink has been expended discussing whether or not Calvin's standpoint is compatible with the conspicuously more scholastic style of theological statement that became standard in the universities and churches of the Reformation in the later sixteenth century onwards. Was Calvin a scholastic or a humanist as we have used these terms here? The practical reality is that many protestant figures in the sixteenth and seventeenth centuries (and this applies to both Lutheran and Reformed) were capable of both modes of discourse, depending on the circumstances. Those who might be labeled scholastic on the basis of their academic lectures and technical writing, might be deemed humanist for their accessible preaching style, or on the strength of literature written for general consumption. If much of the work of Calvin appears to us to be humanist rather than scholastic—particularly when compared to certain of his successors—it is not because the long shadow of Plato and the shorter shadow of Aristotle did not sometimes darken his thinking. Rather, it is because many of his publications, especially his published sermons, were written for the general educated reader of his day rather than theological specialists.

Mention of Plato and Aristotle brings us to the central problem of scholasticism. There can be no objection to the distinction between competent discussions prepared for the general educated reader and technically rigorous literature written specifically for the technically qualified. The problem with the technical sophistication exhibited by post-Reformation protestant scholasticism is its overriding orientation to the requirements of Aristotelian logic and to an anthropological ontology that clearly reflects pagan Greek concepts rather than an authentically biblical viewpoint. Indeed, it tended to construe the latter in terms of the former. Of course, such an Aristotelian-scholastic mode of statement was not religiously neutral. It was ultimately rooted in a pagan (and therefore unbiblical) view of reality. The results could be overly abstract and curiously unhistorical. Its characteristic tendency was towards a rational ordering of propositional statements according to the requirements of Aristotelian logic. Among the consequences was a greater license to engage in a metaphysics that could take the dogmatic theologian into realms of speculation way beyond what a prudent reading of Scripture allows. This speculative tendency was especially apparent in debates concerning the divine "decrees" of election to eternal life and reprobation to eternal perdition.

The influence of protestant scholasticism meant that logic came to override context in the interpretation of biblical texts. The point here is not that the Scriptures are of themselves illogical but that their coherence does not *depend* upon any system of logic. In other words, biblical teaching is not to be *reduced* to a system of interlocking syllogisms, and does not depend on Aristotelian categories for its arguments to be valid. Moreover, we need to remind ourselves that the Reformation was in part shaped by developments already underway at its inception. Foremost among these was the eventual arrival in Europe of movable-type printing.

The chapter numberings in the Bible with which we are familiar originated in the middle ages, while the verse numbers came after the introduction of printing. These numberings greatly facilitated the citation, divorced from context, of short fragments of the text and their utilization as proof texts in the reordering of the content of Scripture for logical-systematic purposes. This is the jigsaw puzzle approach to the Bible mentioned earlier. In the twenty-first century, we need to remember that the phenomenon of a chapter-and-verse-segmented, and privately owned, printed Bible is relatively recent in the history of Christianity. We should also remember that, the poetry and correspondence of the Bible notwithstanding, its preferred way of telling us the truth is in narratives. And for most of Christian history these narratives were imbibed liturgically, congregationally and communally. The triumph of scholasticism obscures such considerations. It is highly significant that in contemporary English-speaking Evangelicalism by far the greater part of the Bible reading that does take place is individual and private, not collective and public.

It was Calvin's successor, Theodore Beza (1519–1605), who insisted that the thought of Aristotle was to be the philosophical standpoint of the Academy at Geneva—one of the most important institutions of protestant higher education in its day. In a letter dated December 1, 1570 to Petrus Ramus (1515–74), Beza was emphatic concerning the "determination" of the Academy "to follow the position of Aristotle, without deviating a line, be it in logic or in the rest of our studies."[1] Here we encounter the spirit of *philosophia aristotelico-scholastica*—scholastic subservience to the thought of Aristotle—that was to rule much protestant theology for an extended period. Ramus was the assiduous advocate of an alternative "protestant logic" deemed unacceptable at the Academy. Beza had arrived in Geneva in 1558 and significantly influenced the context of Calvin's later ministry, as well as shaping his subsequent reputation, beginning with *La vie de Calvin* which appeared as early as the year of Calvin's death (1564). Two Italian Aristotelians significantly influenced Beza: Peter Martyr Vermigli (1499–1562) and Jerome Zanchius (1516–90). Both were of reformed doctrinal persuasion. However, it must be emphasized that Beza did not deliberately set out to subvert Calvin's teaching or distort his legacy.

At this time, immense forces were at work that served to propel late-Reformation and post-Reformation Protestantism towards an increasing emphasis on scholastic style articulation of the Aristotelian variety. First, it had failed to formulate an adequate alternative to the old medieval approach. Second, as Catholicism moved to define its position over and against Protestantism—not least in the work of Ignatius Loyola (1491–1556), the Society of Jesus, and at the Council of Trent (from 1563 onwards)—it utilized the resources of Aristotelian style scholasticism. All too often, their protestant (including the reformed) interlocutors responded in kind. So it was that the Thomist notion of sacred theology (including theology as queen of the sciences) was retained with little challenge, and the ways of scholasticism became the standard mode of technical theological expression amongst Protestants as well as Catholics.

The new scholastic reformed theology was exemplified in the extensive writings of men such as Zacharias Ursinus (1534–83), a pupil of

---

1. Aubert (general editor), *Correspondance de Théodore de Bèze*, XI, 295.

Melanchthon, the English Puritans William Perkins (1558–1602) and William Ames (1576–1633), the Huguenot Pierre du Moulin (1568–1658), and the Dutchmen Franciscus Gomarus (1563–1641) and Gisbertus Voetius (1589–1676). It was perhaps inevitable that the doctrinal-intellectual atmosphere that such writers generated and reflected led to a polarizing of opinion on a range of pseudo-questions concerning the presumed *logical* order of the divine "decrees." These are usually discussed as the *supralapsarian* and *infralapsarian* views of predestination. In the supralapsarian view, a decree to elect some and reprobate others logically preceded other decrees to create (and permit the fall of) man, while in the infralapsarian view, decrees to create and permit the fall of man logically preceded a decree to elect some and reprobate others. The consequences of scholasticism are well illustrated by the polarizing tendencies of such debates, which sought by logic to transcend the limitations to which we (also in our thinking) are subject as creatures. In such scholasticism we encounter a presumption that human rationality, if sufficiently rigorous, could somehow penetrate the secret council of the Almighty.

The great controversy surrounding the teachings of Jacob Arminius (1560–1609) and his followers in the Netherlands arose out of Arminius's attempts to address the theology of Dirck Volckertszoon Coornhert (1522–90) in a context already influenced by Beza's supralapsarianism. Arminius had studied under Beza and had not himself opened these discussions concerning the divine decrees. He clashed seriously with Gomarus in 1607. Arminius died before the deeper implications of his position became apparent. It seemed that reformed scholasticism, in attempting to logically encompass and explicate the secret council of God, had (fervent denials not withstanding) at least gone to the brink of making God the author of sin! In reaction, Arminius (who held Calvin in high regard as an exegete), and followers such as Simon Episcopius (1583–1643) and John Uytenbogaert (1557–1644), without ever denying humankind's need for a divinely provided deliverance, ceded to man a more participatory role in his own salvation. They drew up their Remonstrance in 1610, and the other side prepared their Counter-Remonstrance in 1611. The Remonstrants, who were soon called Arminians, were backed by the statesman Johan van Oldenbarnevelt (1547–1619), while the party representing reformed scholastic orthodoxy was supported by the Stadtholder of the United Provinces of the Netherlands, Maurits, Prince of Orange (1567–1625). The conflict had multiple dimensions. The Arminians looked to the civil magistrate for protection against the demands of rigorous doctrinal orthodoxy, while Gomarus and his followers upheld the distinctive integrity of the institutional church. In the Eighty Years War (1568–1648), the Dutch struggle for independence from Spain, Oldenbarnevelt and his party might be seen as moderates, while the orthodox Reformed and supporters of the House of Orange were hawks.

The Synod of Dort and the So-called Five Points of Calvinism

In the struggle that ensued, the party of reformed scholastic orthodoxy triumphed with the backing of the House of Orange. A National Synod of the Reformed Church of the Netherlands was called and met at Dordrecht in the Netherlands from November 1618 to June 1619. In addition to Geneva itself, reformed churches from various parts of Germany, the Swiss Cantons, and the established English and Scottish churches were also represented. Brandenburg was absent as a result of Lutheran opposition, and representatives of the Reformed Church of France were forbidden to attend by King Louis XIII.

It is hard not to come to the conclusion that the proceedings of the synod were seriously flawed. If the Remonstrants had expected a conference, what they got was an orchestrated trial and pre-determined (!) condemnation. Genuine debate was largely precluded. In five tightly worded canons the synod asserted the *Total* depravity of man (that humankind is subject to sin and unable to help itself); *Unconditional* election (that God saves his people unconditionally; without any regard to any presumed merit on their part); *Limited* atonement (that the actual intent of Christ's atoning death was to secure the redemption of his chosen people only); *Irresistible* grace (that we are so dead in sin that salvation requires a regenerative act on the part of the Holy Spirit for which we are unable to prepare ourselves), and the *Perseverance* of the saints (that those actually regenerate persevere in their faith and do not fall away). These five points, when so characterized in English, yield the mnemonic TULIP.

Eventually, people came to speak of "the five points of Calvinism"—but it is important to remember three things about these so-called five points. First, while certain of these teachings may be drawn from the writings of John Calvin, the actual formulation was unknown to Calvin himself. Calvin never heard of these five points as such. Second, these points are five responses offered to the issues raised by the Remonstrants, and do not in themselves represent the fullness of the reformed doctrinal standpoint, even if Calvinism subsequently became equated with the five points, especially in the English-speaking world. Third, the TULIP mnemonic works in English, not in Dutch or Latin. The mnemonic gained currency because the issues addressed at Dort re-emerged and were recontested in the early days of English-speaking Evangelicalism in the eighteenth century.

Moreover, it would be wrong to see the Remonstrants simply as humanists and their Counter-Remonstrant opponents as strident dogmatists. While neither side was deliberately setting out to subvert the gospel, both sides were the ensnared prisoners of scholastic assumptions and methodologies. Yet for all that, the Synod of Dort was endeavoring to state something of central importance that lay at the heart of the Reformation itself. We may legitimately dissent from its scholastic formulations, but that should not lead us to discard the doctrine they were seeking to enunciate and defend. What the synod was intent on defending was this: our human condition is such that humankind, in and of itself, is incapable and unwilling to seek and receive the deliverance that is offered to us by, in, and through Jesus Christ. To allude to a passage from the Gospel of John much cited by evangelicals, and to take the full force of its metaphor seriously, we can no more bring ourselves to Jesus Christ than we can will our own conception and birth (John 3:3). The point is this: that *we are wholly dependent on the grace of God for our deliverance.*

The issues here are not only soteriological—relating to the way of salvation—but also foundational and centrally relevant to this discussion. They are so because the reality of our complete dependence upon God as our Redeemer and Deliverer is contextualized by the reality of our complete dependence upon God as our Creator and Sustainer. In other words, the truth about redemption, that *we are wholly and continually dependent on the grace of God for our salvation*, is rightly contextualized by the *creational* truth that every creature—indeed the entire order of creation in all of its magnificent diversity and manifold interrelationships—*is wholly and continually dependent for its existence on its sovereign Creator.*

Of course, the Bible itself does not chop creaturely reality up into physical / secular and metaphysical / sacred segments. It invites us to make distinctions only within the framework set by its own integral starting-point. There can therefore be no truly scriptural view of things that does not recognize God's sovereignty over *all* of his creatures and their ongoing dependence on their Creator. This is a cosmos-wide, all-of-life standpoint. This was the deeper meaning of the Protestant Reformation and the context in which the underlying doctrine of the Synod of Dort falls into place. The dependence of all creatures upon their sovereign Creator is central to the biblically directed standpoint, and it at once transcends, undermines and ultimately sets aside the *philosophia aristotelico-scholastica* espoused by Remonstrant and Counter-Remonstrant theologians alike.

In addition, it should not be forgotten that the late sixteenth century and early seventeenth century not only witnessed the rise of theological scholasticism, but that this was paralleled by the concomitant emergence of what German historians have called protestant confessionalization (*Konfessionalisierung*). This process utilized the confessional statements of the churches to impose a disciplined conformity on clergy and laity alike. The tendency developed for biblical exegesis to be regarded as sound only if located within the parameters of the relevant confessional statement. The claim might still be made that the confessions were subordinate to the Scriptures, but confessionalization ensured that in practice the confessions now overrode the Bible.

The Dissenting Opinion of Moses Amyraut

Reformed scholasticism's tendency towards a logically tight systematics ran counter to the narrative, conversational, poetic, and sometimes visionary *genres* of Scripture itself. It theologized the Bible. A certain forcing of the text was required. In the case of the findings of the Synod of Dort, its teachings on the extent of the atonement (did Christ die for everyone or just for the elect?) and reprobation (is it right to envisage God as not only decreeing not to elect some but actively reprobating them?) both seemed—for the sake of the internal consistency of the system—to go beyond what the actual texts of Scripture plainly teach.

Eventually, Moses Amyraut (1596–1664) of the Reformed Church of France mounted a powerful challenge to the Canons of the Synod of Dort. He taught a universal view of the atonement and held that this view was consistent with both the language of Scripture *and* the teaching of Calvin. The point was clear: the more restrictive terminology of Dort, while it intended to be a clarification, was also in some measure a departure from primal reformed doctrine. Amyraut, a man whose significance ought not to be underrated and who merits greater attention than he has received, enjoyed the support of his colleagues Louis Cappel (1585–1658), and the Hebraist Josua Placeus (d. 1665).

It is not altogether surprising that this challenge came from the French quarter. Much of the French reformed community had stayed closer in temperament to the teaching of Calvin himself and were less fully committed to the techniques and systemizations of the prevailing scholasticism than their Swiss, English, Scottish, German, and Dutch brethren. To the discomfort of the latter, Amyraut asserted that his was the position most consistent with Calvin himself, not least in his *Defence de la doctrine de Calvin sur le suiet de l'election et de la reprobation* (1644). Nevertheless, Amyraut faced the criticisms of Pierre du Moulin (1558–1658), André Rivet (1572–1651), and also François Turretin (1623–87)—the leading theologian at Geneva in the post-Beza period and author of the *Institutio Theologiae Elencticae* (1679–85), arguably the literary high point of reformed scholasticism.

If we ask "What has all of this got to do with Evangelicalism?" the answer is that here again we see the roots of confusions that were inherited but unresolved by Evangelicalism itself. If Evangelicalism has sometimes sought to minimize these differences, it has never resolved and sometimes multiplied them. In the later seventeenth century—within the lifetime of John Wesley's father, Samuel Wesley (1662–1735)—the theological successors of the Counter-Remonstrants proceeded even further down the path of a logically rigid schematization. With Turretin and Johan Heinrich Heidegger (1633–98) of Zurich at the helm, they drew up the *Helvetic Consensus* of 1675. This statement was designed to halt the spread of what was now called Amyraldianism into the Swiss cantons. The Consensus' assertion that even the vowel-points of the Hebrew text of the Old Testament were divinely inspired ran counter to the implications of Louis Cappel's carefully formulated conclusion that the vowel points were relatively late in date, even post-dating the Vulgate, Jerome's (d. 420) Latin version of the Bible. The *Helvetic Consensus* therefore ran counter to the careful protestant study of Hebrew texts pioneered by figures such as the great Huguenot philologist Isaac Casaubon (1559–1614).

Turretin's *Institutio Theologiae Elencticae* was most influential in those pockets of Calvinism that survived the high tide of scepticism that came with the Enlightenment of the eighteenth century. In the USA, Turretin's *Institutes* and the *Helvetic Consensus* were held in high esteem at the (Presbyterian) Princeton Seminary in New Jersey (founded 1812). It was from this source that Evangelicalism—in reaction to what it termed liberalism or modernism—eventually was to acquire its characteristically fundamentalist definitions of plenary inspiration, along with infallibility and inerrancy. As we shall consider, this latter development helped to steer millions of well-intentioned evangelicals down the road of *biblicism*. They became committed to a static "Bible-based" view of how the authority of Scripture should operate in the thought and lives of Christians. In practical terms this too often precluded their thinking and acting in terms of a *directional* view of biblical authority. Dualistic outlooks were thereby sustained: the Bible provided a sacred revelation that could be rationally codified and organized into theology, while life and existence beyond church, missions and the "inner life of the soul," was secular and untouched by the gospel. This was a *reduction* of the full message of the coming of the kingdom that left vast areas of human life and culture untouched by its transforming impact.

Biblicism and the Rise of Science

The Reformation was not the only great movement to blossom in the sixteenth century. During the lifetimes of Luther and Calvin the development of modern science—especially in the fields of anatomy and astronomy—was of world-historical importance. The Lutheran reformer Andreas Osiander (1498–1552) actually saw the publication of *De revolutionibus orbium coelestium* (1543) by Nicolaus Copernicus (1473–1543) through the press. This work broke with the geocentricity that had been the hallmark of western astronomy since the days of Aristotle's first century disciple, Claudius Ptolemy. Copernicus advocated heliocentricity. This seemed to contradict the words of Scripture—as in the opening stanzas of Psalm 19. Consequently, Luther was less than cordial towards the new heliocentric thinking. On the other hand, the Wittenburg based astronomer Georg Joachim Rheticus (1514–74) supported the Copernican position. Already, new scientific ideas seemed to imply a calling into question of the authority of Scripture. The resulting unease helps to explain why Osiander, in his preface to the posthumously published work of Copernicus, led his readers to believe that the author was only advancing a hypothetical case and not advocating his thesis as actually true. Whatever his motivations, Osiander's action seems somehow to have anticipated the ambivalence that was later to afflict Christian views on science. This ambivalence was not inevitable and is not necessary in principle but became virtually inevitable as the theologians became ever more enamored of the *philosophia aristotelico-scholastica*.

And so it came to pass, that as the theologians embraced Aristotelianism, others whom we would now call scientists found that serious advances could be achieved by abandoning Aristototle and all his works. While the Reformation view of a law-ordered cosmos encouraged science, Aristotelian-minded theologians were to take Christian doctrinal understanding down a retrograde path that would eventually collide with advances in scientific understanding. At a later stage their view enabled secularist and materialist thinkers alike to utilize the achievements of science to *oppose and eclipse* Christian doctrine, as if Christian belief were nothing more than a disproved scientific theory.

Only by facing up to the shortcomings of the Reformation in failing to develop a *scripturally directed* understanding of the orderedness of creation—a shortfall inherited but unaddressed by Evangelicalism—can we begin to see why Protestantism (even including Evangelicalism) can be viewed as a secularizing force in history. It is here that we encounter the roots of one of the most pernicious notions of our time—the twin folly that somehow empirical science has supposedly disproved the Christian message, and that the Christian religion is intrinsically averse to scientific understanding. There have been, and are, outstanding evangelical scientists, but the more fundamentalist various segments of Evangelicalism have become, the less able they have been to address the discoveries and theories of physical and biological science without lapsing into denial and obscurantism. Only when we confront the philosophical inadequacies of the Reformation—not least the relapse of early Protestantism into Aristotelian scholasticism—can we understand how the pseudo-problems relating to the (presumed) logical order of divine decrees brought anxiety and confusion to subsequent generations. Even though many early evangelicals would have defined themselves as Calvinist, the great John Wesley, even after he felt himself "strangely warmed," along with his brother Charles, and their followers, retained their Arminian orientation. Evangelicalism inherited problems and divisions it was unable to resolve, given this legacy and its intellectual deficit.

Of course, it would be very wrong to assert that all of the research and writing done under the heading of theology should be discarded. What is argued here is that not only is the time-honored concept of theology more problematic than is generally appreciated, but its characteristic attempts of marrying authentically Christian doctrine (arising from the canonical Scriptures) with philosophical notions rooted in classical or modern paganism (often inadequately examined) is inevitably inconsistent with our calling to serve God with our whole heart, also in our thinking and understanding. Such repeated attempts to synthesize what is ultimately incompatible have been fraught with serious consequences.

In its continuing reaction to the deadening formalism of scholastic theology, much Evangelicalism has been deficient in achieving and maintaining its own doctrinal clarity. Today, for all the "battle for the Bible" rhetoric affirming the reliability and authority of the Scriptures, large portions of the evangelical rank and file are surprisingly ignorant of their actual contents. All too often inadequately grounded in the teaching of the Bible, they have been prone to be seriously misdirected. Among them, Bible texts, superficially understood, have been misappropriated to sustain cries of "Give us Jesus, not doctrine," or "the Holy Spirit, not Bible texts." And so it has been that significant sectors of Evangelicalism have been captivated by teachings and practices that are sub-Christian at best and in some cases carry folks across the line into the treacherous quagmires of Gnosticism. Accordingly, our call to recast our understanding of theology within the encyclopedia of the sciences in no way depreciates Christian doctrinal understanding as such. Neither is it intended to discourage Christians from becoming mature in the doctrine that they profess. On the contrary, it is fully in accord with what the Bible itself says about the importance of having understanding and getting wisdom.

Before turning directly to the character and development of Evangelicalism worldwide it is necessary to pay close attention to the Reformation in the British Isles. The great changes it brought about provided the context within which Evangelicalism first emerged in the English-speaking world. Moreover, what transpired in the British Isles was to have immense significance in the New World and beyond.

5

THE ENGLISH AND SCOTTISH REFORMATIONS

The Official (Magisterial) Reformation in England

Protestantism in the British Isles is central to this discussion because it provided the setting in which English-speaking Evangelicalism first came to expression. It was the context of John Wesley's archetypally evangelical "Aldersgate experience." No such experience takes place in a cultural vacuum. As continental Protestants look back to John Hus of Bohemia as a precursor to Luther; those of England look back to John Wycliffe, the leader of the Lollards. This popular movement of Bible preachers and readers preceded the Reformation and partly explains the early, latent minority support for the Reformation in England. The *official* provision of the Bible in English was pivotal, and the name of William Tyndale will be honored wherever the English Bible is read. In the case of England it is useful to think of two reformations: the official (magisterial) Reformation decreed from above, and the popular Reformation desired by some of the king's subjects, irrespective of royal policy. Initially, the Reformation only received minority support. The Reformation that England and Wales finally got was the Reformation that the English crown wanted them to have. Scotland and Ireland were different. In Scotland the Reformation triumphed in spite of the wishes of monarchs; in Ireland it failed notwithstanding the desires of the English crown.

The official Reformation was the creature of monarchs and their high appointees. Henry VIII (1491–1547) separated the English Church from Papal jurisdiction because Pope Clement VII (1478–1534) would not approve his proposed divorce from Catherine of Aragon (1485–1536). The solution proffered by Thomas Cromwell (d. 1540) was to separate the English Church from all Papal jurisdiction, and make the English monarch the head of the English church. This was done and the new Archbishop of Canterbury, Thomas Cranmer (1489–1556), obliged Henry in the matter of the divorce proceedings. The entire process was an exercise of the high Constantinian-Theodosian variety. Henry became his own kind of pope—"caesaro-papism" with a vengeance! By the later years of his reign, Cranmer had become a convinced "closet" Protestant. Henry kept his English church bound to Catholic doctrine, although he did allow the Bible in English to be set up in parish churches.

The official *Protestant* Reformation only commenced in the reign of the short-lived Edward VI (reigned 1547–53). The mass was abolished, protestant doctrine was adopted (42 Articles, 1553, formulated as 39 Articles in 1563), and worship in English according to a *Book of Common Prayer* was introduced. In addition to Archbishop Cranmer, the key figures included Hugh Latimer, Bishop of Worcester (1485–1555), and Nicholas Ridley, Bishop of London (1503–55). The Reformation under Edward was effected as royal policy, with genuine conviction, and with the assistance of continental Reformers residing in England. The old hierarchy of archbishops and bishops and other practices were retained as "not repugnant" to the Scriptures. This was the *corrective* view of the authority of Scripture in action.

However, the firmly protestant John Hooper (d. 1555) strongly objected to the use of certain vestments in connection with his being installed as Bishop of Gloucester. Hooper's arguments on this matter—which in 1550–51 brought him into sharp disagreement with Ridley and Cranmer—were strongly oriented towards the *regulative* standpoint. The fuller unfolding of these issues was cut short by the early death of Edward in July 1553. Nevertheless, in England, the differences between the official *corrective* view and the minority (eventually Puritan) *regulative* view of biblical authority were to last for centuries and give rise to repeated controversy. They were a principal cause of division between the Church of England as "by law established," and those who eventually came to be known as Protestant Dissenters, including English Presbyterians, Congregationalists, and Baptists. For more than three centuries these distinctions produced two different cultures and outlooks on public life in England: those of the Churchman and the Protestant Dissenter.

The Edwardian Reformation was thrown into sharp reverse when Mary came to the throne on the death of her half brother in 1553. The eldest daughter of Henry by Catherine of Aragon, she promptly returned England and Wales to Roman Catholicism. Thereafter, hundreds suffered martyrdom for their protestant convictions, including Cranmer, Hooper, Latimer and Ridley. Hundreds fled their homeland for the relative safety of the protestant cities of the Swiss cantons, the Rhineland, and beyond. On the continent these English Protestants were exposed to a variety of protestant polities arising not only from varying local circumstances but also from the diverse ways of understanding biblical authority previously outlined.

These circumstances provided a further instance of a clash between different views of how Scripture was authoritative in the sad set of episodes, usually referred to as "the troubles at Frankfurt." There, in 1554-55, a sharp disagreement developed between those inclined to follow the Swiss models, such as William Whittingham (1554-79) and John Knox, and those who followed Richard Cox (1499-1581) in insisting on "the true face of an English Church"—by which they meant worship according to the *Book of Common Prayer* (the second protestant version of 1552), framed according to the *corrective* view. Unable to get the better of an insistent Knox, Cox ousted him from Frankfurt by adroit political maneuvering. Knox received the support of Calvin in Geneva, where he and many other exiles settled for the time being.[1]

In retrospect, the Knox-Cox confrontation at Frankfurt not only presaged the future struggle between the leadership of the English Church and its more radical Puritan critics, but also foreshadowed the characteristic differences between the ethos of Anglicanism, with its strong emphasis on historic continuity in order and worship, and that of Presbyterianism with its greater orientation towards governance by ecclesiastical assemblies and open debate. The stand taken by Knox was arguably even more prescient than he realized: his defense of a more fully reformed church order entailed an opposition to monarchical absolutisms, an opposition that helped open the way to the idea of a civil society based on laws rather than executive power.

The Church of England under Elizabeth

Upon the death of Mary in 1558, Elizabeth (1533-1603) came to the English throne. The Reformation Settlement adopted at the commencement of her reign preserved many of the features introduced under Edward VI,

1. Ridley, *John Knox*, 189-214.

sometimes in slightly attenuated form. A basically protestant doctrinal standpoint was adopted. Yet throughout her reign it was persistently applied so as to inhibit any further reformation of the Church of England on Swiss reformed lines. Like Henry, Elizabeth was deeply conservative. John Jewell (1522–71), in his *Apologia for the Church of England* (1562), saw the new *status quo* in Constantinian-Theodosian terms. Church and state were two sides of the same body, with the monarch the divinely sanctioned head of both. Appropriating the Lutheran *corrective* approach, apologists for the new status quo argued that episcopacy and liturgical worship prescribed by the new *Act of Uniformity*, were to be retained because they were not contrary to Scripture, and acceptable to the "godly prince"—in this case Elizabeth.

It was during the 1560s, that the "hotter sort of Protestants,"—those who sought to further *purify* the Church of England on more *regulative* lines, acquired the epithet of Puritan. In the longer run this Puritanism—which itself underwent significant historical change—was to be of immense significance. Throughout her reign, Elizabeth thwarted all calls for the further reformation of the English Church. The critics were vocal and disappointed. In vain did Lawrence Humphrey (d. 1590) and Thomas Sampson (d. 1589) raise the issue of the Elizabethan requirements for clerical dress in the "vestiarian controversy." In vain did Thomas Cartwright (1535–1603) repeatedly challenge the episcopal structure of the Church of England. In vain did Walter Travers (d. 1635) call for a "godly discipline" on the Genevan model. In vain did men such as John Field (d. 1587) strive to introduce something like a classical reformed structure of parish governance, with a plurality of lay ruling elders. In vain did he and Thomas Wilcox (1549–1608) publish *An Admonition to Parliament*, pleading for the further reformation of the Church of England (1572). In vain did the sympathetic Archbishop Edmund Grindal (1519–83) seek further reform within the Church of England: Elizabeth put him under house arrest for insisting on the promotion of preaching.

Although unsuccessful, these projects remind us how early Puritanism still thought in terms of the Constantinian-Theodosian legacy. Men like Cartwright, Travers, and Wilcox still envisaged a single Christian nation committed to a single polity. Their objection was not against a national church as such—their objection was that the English church was a very long way from being sufficiently reformed in the continental European sense. Their turning towards Parliament as a way of attempting to put pressure on an unresponsive monarch was prescient. In the following century, the causes of Parliament and Puritanism were to coalesce in opposition to an emerging royal absolutism. Constitutional crisis and civil war ensued. For the duration of her reign, Elizabeth used the coercive force of royal authority to negate proposals for further reformation on the Swiss model. Eventually William Whitgift (1530–1604), one of Elizabeth's more conspicuously compliant archbishops, took a strong line against those Puritans who had become used to not conforming to various requirements they considered to be hangovers from the pre-Reformation era. By the end of the century his successor as Archbishop of Canterbury, Richard Bancroft (1544–1610), was asserting that episcopal governance was not only acceptable because sanctioned by the "godly prince" but also *divinely* sanctioned and ordained (*jure divino*). This was a new development, not anticipated by the initial advocates of the Elizabethan Settlement.

Resistance to further reformation on the part of Elizabeth and her bishops gave rise to two new phenomena. The first was *separatism*. Most Puritans remained within the Church of England down to 1662. Believing in a fully reformed national church, and willing to accept episcopal governance, they pressed for reform while valuing unity. Men such as Richard Sibbes (1577–1635) are in this category. However, by the 1590s, some Puritans had despaired of the situation, and followed the call of Robert Browne (d. 1633) for *Reformation without Tarrying for Anie* (1582). This separatist group, including John Greenwood and Henry Barrow (both executed in 1593), were only a small minority of English Puritans, but they came to be regarded as the founders of Congregationalism.

The second new phenomenon was *Anglicanism* itself. The initial set of compromises that had constituted the Elizabethan Settlement of 1559, with its combination of reformed doctrine, English-language liturgical worship that looked back to the early church, and episcopal government, became hallowed by familiarity and custom. Many came to see this set of compromises as a positive virtue. If it was unpatriotic to genuflect towards Rome, it was also disruptive to assent to Geneva. Richard Hooker (1553–1600) articulated the outlook and ethos of Anglicanism, in his *Laws of Ecclesiastical Polity*. This extensive work, only fully published posthumously, was written specifically in opposition to Cartwright and those who were calling for further reformation on Presbyterian lines.

Hooker stood for the due authority of Scripture, reason and tradition. Of course, these three are present in *all* Christian organizations. Even the most "Bible-based" Christian groups must give some *thought* to how to interpret the texts open before them, and inevitably find themselves doing so in an interpretative *tradition*. In Hooker's case, the charge may be made that his formulations allowed tradition and reason to curtail, restrain, check, and abridge the full and continuing application of biblical principle. On the other hand, Richard Hooker did not repudiate the Reformation, or neglect figures such as Calvin totally, although it seems that his occasional references to the Reformer were calculated to drive a wedge between Calvin's reputation and the advocates of further reform. Hooker thought in broad Augustinian terms, and his Platonism should be understood accordingly.

The writings of "the judicious Hooker" fostered the rise of *Anglicanism*, and validated the emergence of an *Anglican ethos*. That ethos has facilitated the long-term existence of parties within Anglican churches generally. Where high churchmen or Anglo-Catholics have emphasized tradition, latitudinarians and liberals have been more oriented to reason. In the sixteenth and seventeenth centuries the Puritan party (*within* the English church until 1662) emphasized the authority of Scripture in *regulative* terms. From the eighteenth century onwards, Anglican Evangelicalism emphasized the authority of Scripture mainly in terms of the *corrective* way. Arguably, the points of discussion between the various parties within worldwide Anglicanism pivot on the question of which of these three foci should have the overriding authority. At least to the extent that modern Anglican evangelicals credibly affirm the primacy of scriptural authority, they may legitimately claim to stand front and center in the life of their communion. Whether this is an adequate standpoint to adopt in relation to the multiple challenges confronting English-speaking Evangelicalism is a very different question.

The Scottish Reformation: a Distinctive Alternative

Scotland was profoundly different from England. The many differences may be recognized without subscribing to the mythologies of either Scottish or English nationalism. The history of Scottish Presbyterianism is highly instructive, especially when carefully cross-referenced to developments in England. In Scotland the Reformation came late, triumphing in 1560 with English aid. The contribution of John Knox was decisive. The regulative view of the authority of Scripture was eventually far more influential in Scotland than in England. In the manner of Zurich, all that was not expressly required by Scripture was to be set aside. Knox articulated this viewpoint forcefully, with a strong insistence on the authority of the Church in deciding admission to the Lord's Supper. Under Christ, the church was to be mistress in her allotted sphere. This principle implied a restraint on the authority of monarchs. That restraint became especially offensive to those monarchs attracted to notions of absolute monarchical authority as expressed in the idea of "the divine right of kings."

However, a Presbyterian polity was not introduced unambiguously and at all points in Scotland in 1560. The process took time. It was more systematically instituted under the leadership of Andrew Melville (1545–1622), who was strongly influenced by Beza. The historical origins of this system merit careful consideration. For a hierarchy of bishops and archbishops set over dioceses and provinces, it substituted a hierarchy of assemblies (local, regional, national). In the longer run of things it owed something to the late-medieval conciliar movement. More immediately, it drew upon arrangements made in places such as Geneva, where the Reformation was adopted, but where, unlike England, the former episcopate remained hostile. Nevertheless, something had to be done. The Word had to be preached, the sacraments administered, order maintained, and the *Genevan Ecclesiastical Ordinances* of 1541 were introduced accordingly.

The full Reformed-Presbyterian system of church government was a deliberate fabrication, providing the churches of the Reformation with a structural alternative to historic episcopacy, which in many places had proved to be an impediment to the furtherance of the Reformation. The principal architects of this system—which emerged from the 1570s onwards—were Theodore Beza, Thomas Cartwright, Walter Travers, and Andrew Melville. These men were key in the formalization of an impressive system that has lasted for centuries, and under which millions have lived and died. In Scotland, the episcopal office was formally abolished, and the Presbyterian system instituted, in 1592. However, while the advocates of the system might appeal to an array of New Testament proof texts, they were hard pressed to show it to have been the actual practice of the post-apostolic church. The system was actually the creation of exceptionally able men in the sixteenth century. The eventual triumph of Presbyterianism imparted to Scotland much of her distinctive national character. Many a dramatic episode has arisen from the struggles of its churches against the usurpations and presumptions of monarchs, noblemen and parliaments as they have sought to undermine the Presbyterian system—not least the principle that congregations have the responsibility to call qualified ministers of their own choosing. Where the English were subject to bishops who were in turn subject to royal authority, the Scots could look to "the courts of the church," as the Presbyterian assemblies were called.

For Knox, the Geneva of Calvin and Beza was "the maist perfyt schoole of Chryst since the dayis of the Apostills."[2] Knox tended to articulate and defend the Genevan example in terms of the *regulative* standpoint. Calvin and Knox were men of dissimilar temperament: where Calvin would work

2. *The Works of John Knox* (edited by Laing), VI, 240.

earnestly within the historical process while moving in a certain direction, Knox was disposed to be peremptorily prescriptive. This tendency in Knox is attributable to his *regulative* approach to the authority of Scripture, not least when compared to the more *directional* approach of Calvin. The regulative standpoint drove Knox to act as if there could only ever be one way of obedience. By contrast, Calvin, who, although he could never be rightly called a pragmatist, understood Scripture in a directive manner, and was therefore more open to take cultural circumstances into consideration. In this connection, the surviving correspondence between Knox and Calvin, from the crucial year of the Reformation in Scotland (1560) to Calvin's demise in 1564, merits careful attention.³

A definite discontinuity existed between Zurich and Geneva on the issue of admission to the Lord's Supper. Zurich would assign the power to prohibit access to the Lord's Supper to the civil magistrate—within the ambit of what was understood to be a Christian polity embracing church and state. By contrast, Geneva, without a hint of secularization, insisted that admission to the Lord's Supper was an *ecclesiastical* responsibility alone. This issue came to a head in the Palatinate, at the University of Heidelberg, in the 1568 controversy between George Withers (d. 1605) and Thomas Erastus (1524–83). Withers took the Genevan standpoint, Erastus that of Zurich.

The Reformed-Presbyterian system lay implicit in the work of Calvin; it was made explicit by Beza and his Anglo-Scottish associates. The first major airing of the new system was by Thomas Cartwright in lectures on the *Acts of the Apostles* given in the University of Cambridge in 1570. Students were animated, and the authorities were not amused. Cartwright lost his professorship, and eventually his fellowship at Trinity College. The new polity was advocated in terms of the *regulative* view of biblical authority. This was to be its undoing at the hands of Hooker. He could argue that it was a construct based on a way of interpreting and utilizing specific biblical texts that produced a system of ecclesiastical governance hitherto unprecedented in the history of Christianity.

Those who adopted the *corrective* standpoint could argue that if there was a specific polity explicitly taught by the New Testament, it was nevertheless far from conspicuous, if not remarkably well hidden. The rise of scholasticism (with its preference for static formulations) from Beza onwards, drove the *directional* viewpoint towards eclipse. The men of Geneva and Edinburgh could respond that Hooker's articulation of the *corrective* standpoint legitimized an Anglicanism in which too much of the old order was allowed to continue, and that the longer this lasted, the more likely would

---

3. *The Selected Works of John Calvin* (edited by Beveridge and Bonnet), VII, 184.

be an eventual regression towards an unreformed Catholicism. They had a point: those who followed the teaching of the "Caroline divines" of the early seventeenth century—men such as Lancelot Andrewes (1555-1626), William Laud (1573-1645), Jeremy Taylor (1613-67) and John Cosin (1594-1672), and especially members of the Oxford Movement of the nineteenth century, would draw Canterbury away from the Reformation and back in the direction of Roman Catholicism. At the same time, as we shall see, the advocates of the *regulative* approach failed to make good their actual claims.

The Troubled Era of Stuart Rule, 1603-1714

English Puritanism kept a low profile in the 1590s. It faced repressive measures and was discomfited by Hooker's critique. Elizabeth died in 1603, and King James VI of Scotland, of the House of Stuart, assumed the title of James I of England. Puritan expectation was high—was not the new monarch from Scotland, where the Presbyterian polity had triumphed? However, at the Hampton Court Conference convened in 1604, even the most moderate of Puritan hopes were dashed. Back in Scotland, James had chafed at the way in which a national Presbyterian Church was not constituted to be the compliant tool of "godly princes." He did not relish being addressed as "God's silly vassal" by the likes of Melville.[4] James professed the reformed version of Protestantism but advanced the notion of "the divine right of kings" and was resolved to be answerable to no man on earth. Melville and his associates upheld a principle of immense importance: that while the state—the civil magistrate—was also called to hear the word of God in following its calling, the church as an institution was not a department of state and is called to obey Christ directly, irrespective of prevailing political policies and conditions.

The declaration of James at the conference: "no bishop no king," suggests that he had discerned a deeper truth—that in the reformed version of Protestantism there lay something antithetical to royal authority unchecked by something like effective parliamentary government.[5] James had discerned that reformed Protestantism, if it were true to itself, was bound to come into conflict with his notions of royal absolutism. In threatening to "harrie" the Puritans "out of the land" unless they conformed, James showed himself unwilling to contemplate in England what he already disapproved of in Scotland.[6] At the same time, the out-maneuvered Puritans of later

---

4. M'Crie, *The Life of Andrew Melville*, I, 391-392.
5. Neal, *History of the Puritans*, I, 326.
6. Usher, *Reconstruction of the English Church*, I, 327.

Elizabethan times (not all of whom were anti-episcopal from the outset) had discerned that if episcopacy were allowed to run to a highly authoritarian prelacy, and otherwise unchecked, then in seventeenth century conditions it could open the way to a counter-reformation in England.

If it is remembered at all at the beginning of the twenty-first century, the Hampton Court Conference is associated with the decision to embark upon a new translation of the Bible into English. The result was the "Authorized Version"—known in the United States as the "King James Version." It was designed to supplant the *Geneva Bible*—a version of the English Bible completed in that city in 1560. William Whittingham was the organizer. He had taken the side of Knox at Frankfurt. The *Geneva Bible* was immensely successful. While favored by Puritans, it was disagreeable to monarchs because of the anti-monarchical and anti-hierarchical cast of its text and accompanying annotations. The new translation authorized by James appeared in completed form in 1611, and was not an immediate success. This Authorized Version was conservative, lacking the radical marginal comments that came with the later editions of the *Geneva Bible*. After 1604, James I and the Church of England continued to profess a protestant and reformed doctrinal position. During James's reign the English Church officially concurred with the outcome of the Synod of Dort. Nevertheless, the proceedings at Dort caused offense to English participants and observers, and this did not hinder Arminianism from sometimes being given a sympathetic hearing in the doctrinal life of the Church of England. The reaction against Dort was complemented by a tendency towards a more ornate and ritually complex mode of worship, as practiced by the "Caroline divines."

The Puritan pressure for further institutional reformation might have abated following the check administered by Hooker, and in the face of continuing royal displeasure, had it not been for the constitutional views of James I and the political and ecclesiastical policies recklessly pursued by his son, Charles I (1600–49). James's view of the rights of the crown brought him into repeated confrontations with the House of Commons, especially in 1614 and 1621. Viewed in retrospect these crises were prescient, although almost everyone at the time believed that the monarch could exercise great powers under God. The big question was just how much latitude the monarch actually possessed. In the House of Commons—and increasingly amongst common lawyers and antiquarians—the resistance that emerged was not to royal authority as such, but to its definition and prospective exercise in absolute terms and in an unrestrained manner. The trend was towards increasing assertions of royal authority, and the implications became clearer as both Parliament and Puritanism responded with their own counter-assertions. The constitutional crisis provided a pathway for the re-opening of those ecclesiastical concerns that were close to the Puritan heart and that had never actually gone away.

During the reign of James's successor, Charles I (1625–49) things fell apart. Parliamentary-constitutional and Puritan-ecclesiastical opposition to Charles's absolutist claims took England to the brink, and then into civil war. Eventually, all parts of the British Isles were caught up in an expanding range of conflicts, resulting in a *proportional* loss of British lives that was only exceeded by the slaughter on the western front during the First World War (1914-18). As Charles's appointment of Laud as Archbishop confirmed, he supported the rise of ornate ritual in the Church of England. Questions of high constitutional law inevitably arose as opponents of this policy were punished, as Charles sought to tax and rule without parliamentary sanction, and as the crown refused to heed parliamentary criticism of its ecclesiastical policies (1629-40). The constitutional issue prompted a resurfacing of the various Puritan objections to the Elizabethan settlement. As Oliver Cromwell (1599–1658) was later to put it "religion was not the thing at first contested for . . . but God brought it to that issue at last . . . and at last it proved to be that which was most dear to us."[7] A tense situation was rendered critical by Charles's stunningly foolish attempt to impose an English-style liturgy on the Church of Scotland. This policy was repudiated by those Presbyterians who subscribed to the *Scottish National Covenant* (1638). They saw the *corrective* view as far too open to the old ways of Catholicism: for them the rigor of the *regulative* view should apply, and ought to apply throughout the British Isles. They repudiated the bishops that had been re-imposed on the Scottish Church, as well as the *Book of Common Prayer* so hotly contested at Frankfurt.

It was these Covenanters who first took up arms against Charles I and invaded England in 1640. Charles, desperate for the revenue necessary for an effective military response, finally called a Parliament, only to find that, under the able leadership of John Pym (1584-1643) the House of Commons rejected his policies. Parliament refused the voting of subsidies until its grievances concerning civil and ecclesiastical policy were addressed. By the end of the year, Parliament had impeached Archbishop Laud and Thomas Wentworth, Earl of Strafford (1593-1641), the latter on charges relating to the use of Irish troops in Great Britain in support of the royal cause. The following year saw calls for the abolition of episcopacy in England and Wales, and an anti-protestant uprising in Ireland. The situation was further inflamed when, in early 1642, Charles attempted and failed to arrest five

---

7. *Letters and Speeches of Oliver Cromwell*, (edited by Lomas), III, 76.

members of the House of Commons. Thereafter, Charles raised his royal standard at Nottingham. England slid into civil war.

The *Solemn League and Covenant* was concluded between the Covenanters and the English Parliament in 1643. It provided for an exclusively Presbyterian church polity in Scotland, England, Wales, and Ireland. The long habit of Constantinian-Theodosian thinking was still in operation—the presumption was that it was lawful for the civil magistrate to settle the affairs of the Church of God, and that all within the realm were to conform to a uniform practice. It should be noted that it was *Parliament* that instituted the Westminster Assembly to address the problem of the further reformation of the Church of England. Parliament took the initiative, and the Assembly was answerable to the House of Commons. This was not a situation that Scottish Presbyterians such as George Gillespie (1613–48) found easy to live with.

The Assembly embarked upon its labors when the parliamentary cause was far from sure. By the time it concluded its deliberations the political and ecclesiastical terrain had changed significantly. For Parliament, the military tide only turned with the formation of the "New Model Army," under the command of men such as Oliver Cromwell, which imposed a decisive defeat on the king at Naseby in 1645. Meanwhile, the Scots had become increasingly critical of English proposals to make the envisaged (Presbyterian) English national church subject to Parliament. By late 1646 Parliament had moved to abolish episcopacy and the Westminster Assembly had produced its *Confession of Faith*. Charles surrendered himself to the Scots in May 1646 and came into the hands of Parliament the following year—but the end was not yet. There was growing discord between those in Parliament who still tended to favor some form of Presbyterian settlement, and its own New Model Army, in which Congregational and more radical views, such as those of the egalitarian Levelers, were becoming more conspicuous. Seeking to exploit the divisions of his enemies, Charles's machinations succeeded in igniting a second civil war (1648), with the New Model Army led by Cromwell eventually purging Parliament ("Pride's Purge," 1648), and Charles being tried and executed for high treason (January 1649).

By the time the Westminster Assembly had finished its work in 1648, producing its *Confession of Faith* (1647) and also the *Larger* and *Shorter Catechisms* (1647–8)—the Westminster Standards—as well as *The Directory for The Public Worship of God* and *The Form of Presbyterial Church-Government* (both 1645), the balance of power in England had moved away from Parliament and Presbyterianism. It now inclined towards the New Model Army and its more radical ideas: of congregationalism, and to a greater degree of diversity than had previously been acceptable, and of those far-reaching ideas pertaining to church and society expressed in the wide-ranging Putney debates (1647). Already, in the debates of the Westminster Assembly, five dissenting brethren had rejected Presbyterianism. They were Thomas Goodwin (1600–80), Philip Nye (1595–1672), Sidrach Simpson (1600–55), Jeremiah Burroughs (1599–1646), and William Bridge (1600–70). While they accepted the *regulative* view of biblical authority, they did not concur with the conclusion that the inevitable result was the Presbyterian view of church government. They could find no gradation of ecclesiastical assemblies in Scripture but only "the congregational way." Their standpoint was enunciated in the statement known as *An Apologetical Narration* (1644). The regulative view of biblical authority failed to resolve the differences between Presbyterian and Congregationalist. This is why we encounter Cromwell pleading with the General Assembly of the Church of Scotland: "I beseech you in the bowels [depths] of Christ [to] think it possible you may be mistaken."[8] As men such as Richard Baxter (1615–91) were to find out, the Presbyterian moment in English history was short indeed.

Oliver Cromwell dominated the Commonwealth and Protectorate eras (1649–58). He was made "Lord Protector of the Commonwealth." He fought in both Ireland and Scotland against Roman Catholic and Presbyterian exclusivism. Cromwell and the men around him, such as Henry Ireton (1611–51) and John Milton (1608–74), concurred with the view that the Reformation had not gone far enough. Milton asserted: "new presbyter is but old priest writ large." It was he who called for the "reforming of Reformation itself."[9]

The 1640s and 1650s were remarkable times in English history. Ideas and thoughts that had long been suppressed could now surface. Long overdue debates on governance, representation, law, and justice could now take place, and they have reverberated down the centuries. Pen and press were prodigiously productive. Milton had already called for the freedom of the press in his *Areopagitica* (1644), and in *The Tenure of Kings and Magistrates* (1650) he called for a law-state (*Rechtstaat*) over against the arbitrariness of royal absolutism. Yet, there were problems on all sides: if royal absolutism was constitutionally questionable, then a Parliament purged of opposing members, and the rule of major-generals were also constitutionally untenable—as long-time opponents of royalist absolutism such as William Prynne (1600–69) did not fail to declare. Following the execution of his father, Charles II (1630–85) renewed the struggle against Parliament, now with the Scottish Covenanters as allies—they being intent on imposing *The*

---

8. Ibid., II, 156.

9. Milton, *Complete Poetry and Selected Prose*, 1950, 84, 714.

Solemn League and Covenant on a recalcitrant England. Having triumphed in Ireland, Cromwell and the New Model Army defeated the Scots at Dunbar (1650), and Charles II at Worcester (1651). Charles II escaped to the continent.

After an extended period of repression under Charles I, and the repeated civil wars of 1642–51, England needed decades of repose if she were to be successful in developing an acceptable republican constitution. It was not to be. The Protectorate collapsed following the death of Oliver Cromwell in 1658. Although republican sentiments never completely disappeared from English life, it was across the Atlantic in New England that they were eventually reasserted with powerful effect.

Anglican Divisiveness and the Emergence of Protestant Nonconformity

Out of the confusion following Cromwell's demise came the restoration of the monarchy, marked by the return to England of Charles II in 1660. Charles, who had previously assented to the *Solemn League and Covenant*, now in his Declaration of Breda (1660) offered liberty of conscience to all Protestants. However, the restored Parliament, thick with Royalists and Laudian high churchmen, smarting from past indignities and defeats, and intent on a full restoration of the previous order in church and state, would have none of it. A new *Act of Uniformity* (1662) was passed containing much to please Laudian opinion, along with certain features expressly designed to be unacceptable even to more moderate Puritan opinion. As a result, and culminating on August 24, 1662—long known as Black Bartholomew's Day—almost two thousand clergy of the Puritan persuasion quit the Church of England rather than subscribe to terms that were deliberately framed to achieve their exclusion.

The Church of England was thereby party to one of the most schismatic actions that has ever disfigured the annals of a protestant church. The Puritans may not have had everything right, but they had persistently stood for further reformation in the English context—and now they were decisively repudiated. Thereafter they were exposed to the tyrannies and penalties of the Clarendon Code, which was designed immediately to marginalize and eventually to drive them out of existence as a distinctive group. For the triumphant Laudian "high church" party, it was not simply that the Church of England was to be *the* national church—it was to be *their* Church of England.

The years 1662-88 were dark times indeed for those who did not conform, now termed Protestant Nonconformists or simply Dissenters. They were people of principle, disparaged and yet feared by their sneering opponents. Suffering many disabilities and indignities, they endured and survived the extreme official prejudice with which they were now confronted. Their counterparts in Scotland—the Covenanters—could be treated with pitiless severity. If it is asked why it is necessary to spend so much time on these pre-evangelical matters, the answer is that when the Evangelical Revival came, its initial leadership was *not* drawn from amongst the Protestant Dissenters—but from men of the Church of England. In England, Evangelicalism found its first home, and its most prominent expression, in the dominant ecclesiastical tradition whose leadership once repudiated further reformation. This imparted both strengths and weaknesses. Tendencies towards further reformation were liable to be checked by the deep-seated conservatism characteristic of so much Anglicanism.

It was also during the reign of Charles II, and especially in relation to the "exclusion crisis" of 1678-81 (over whether the king's Roman Catholic brother James might ascend to the throne) that there emerged the Whigs and the Tories—the two great parliamentary parties that were to dominate British politics for almost two centuries. The Whigs and Tories were both largely controlled by great aristocratic English families, and they both supported the Church of England. The Whigs favored a limited measure of toleration for Protestant Dissenters, while the Tories were more astringent in their stance and more likely to favor an exclusively high church viewpoint.

Charles II was an Anglican, although somewhat sympathetic towards Catholics. His brother and successor, James II (1633-1701) was a convinced Roman Catholic. In his short reign (1685-8) James managed to unite both Tory and Whig against him—for both had strong grounds to fear his Roman Catholic absolutism. When Parliament offered the crown to William III of the Netherlands, it was with the support also of the marginalized Protestant Dissenters. The resulting Glorious Revolution of 1688 opened the way for the Toleration Act of 1689, which, although it did not provide Protestant Dissent with anything like parity alongside the Church of England, at least conceded the right to build and maintain places of non-Anglican protestant public worship. In 1690 James II was defeated at the battle of the Boyne in Ireland, which fastened the Protestant Ascendency on Ireland in the eighteenth century. It was to prove increasingly unsustainable thereafter.

In England and Wales, where the crown or the nobility might fund new Anglican churches, Protestant Dissenters built churches out of their own pockets. Their ministers were elected and not imposed on congregations by patrons. Excluded from England's universities, they built protestant dissenting academies. Excluded from Parliament, they might thrive in business. From 1689 to the early twentieth century, protestant dissent cultivated a distinct, principled and alternative Christian culture in England and Wales. Advocates of Christian unity should note that up to 1662, the vast majority of Puritans had sought to live and serve within the Church of England. They challenged the status quo but were not in practice as divisive as their opponents maintained. An exception was those Puritan separatists who had previously quit the English Church (such as those who sailed on the Mayflower in 1620) and who were at that stage only a small fraction of the Puritan whole. After 1662, and especially after 1689, such separatists were joined by large numbers of those forced from the Church of England by the 1662 Act of Uniformity.

However, as those who would not conform to the Act of Uniformity were forcibly cut loose from the pale of the English national church, the inadequacies of the regulative view—already exposed by the five dissenting brethren—came to fuller public expression. Even as the Act of Uniformity forced Puritans out of the English church, the failure of the *regulative* view of biblical authority to settle key questions entailed a forfeiture of public unity. The regulative view could not definitively resolve questions concerning the baptism of infants, or determine the full relationship of one congregation and its office bearers to another. Perhaps inevitably, distinctive alignments of Presbyterians, Congregationalists (swelling the ranks of their separatist precursors) and Baptists (not to be confused with continental European Anabaptists) emerged. The Laudian inflexibility of men such as William Juxon (1582–1663), and the inadequacy of the regulative view, combined to produce English protestant denominationalism.

Scholasticism and Pietism in Late Puritanism

The mid-to-late seventeenth century saw Puritan scholastic theology reach its apex in the extensive literature produced by writers such as Thomas Manton (1620–77) and John Flavel (1627–91), and Congregationalists Thomas Goodwin (1600–80), Thomas Brooks (1608–80), and John Owen (1616–83). Works such as *The Display of Arminianism* (1642) and *The Death of Death in the Death of Christ* (1647) by Owen confirm the close orientation of these writers towards the Counter-Remonstrant scholasticism as epitomized by the Canons of the Synod of Dort.

Scholastic theology has pastoral consequences. Any systematic theology featuring predestination that turns on the *absolutum decretum* is always open to the charge that it drives folk down an ever-darkening path of agonized inner speculation ("Am I or am I not elect?") rather than to Jesus Christ himself. Puritanism was not immune to such a charge, at least since William Perkins published his *A Golden Chain or, The Description of Theology* (1592) in which the divine decree apparently precedes the person and work of Jesus Christ—even though Jesus Christ himself declares that *he* is *alpha* and *omega* (Rev 21:6; 22:13). After 1662 something also happened to Puritanism itself. The movement had once been capable of wide visions and agendas of comprehensive reform. Now, however, excluded from the established church, from political life, and the universities, Protestant Dissent took on an increasingly introspective character. This tendency was driven partly by a loss of public standing but also by the dynamics of a scholastic theology that drove its adherents in the direction of ever more assiduous introspection. Puritanism became increasingly introverted, in a word, *pietistic*. This trend had its parallels also in Scotland, and in the *Nadere Reformatie* movement in the Netherlands. The pietistic cast of later Puritanism and early Protestant Dissent is particularly relevant for our discussion because it was the Puritan writers expressive of this pietistic tendency whom subsequent generations of evangelicals were most readily able to appropriate for their own devotional use. The prime examples are John Bunyan's (1628–88) *Pilgrim's Progress* (1678, completed 1684) and Matthew Henry's (1662–1714) much used *Commentary on the Holy Bible* (1708 onwards).

Over a century ago the German sociologist Max Weber (1864–1920) floated a thesis to the effect that the inner drive to verify one's elect status and thereby achieve assurance markedly changed the behavior of Protestants, especially of the puritan and reformed variety. He saw this drive as inducing in them, among other things, an exceptional willingness to forgo ease and pleasure—a kind of "protestant asceticism." This greatly facilitated productivity, the generation of profits, and the accumulation of capital. This work ethic did not create capitalist-style economic relations, but certainly advantaged in the market place those who were so motivated to be diligent and frugal, especially when invention and enterprise were added to the mix. Weber's thesis might have been better formulated and substantiated, and his interlocutors might at times have misunderstood and misrepresented him seriously, but the fecundity and persistence of the debate over the protestant work ethic indicates that he was pointing in the right direction.

These considerations help explain how the Protestant Dissenting type of Christian emerged. Belief, piety, and devotion were primarily inward, and these, combined with the scrupulous adherence to a high standard of moral rectitude in interpersonal relations, tended to confirm a self-perception of elect status. The use of the Ten Commandments as a "rule of thankfulness" could spur Protestants down this path. Pietism could produce a supposedly private Christianity seriously deficient on the public and corporate side: the church was but an *accumulation* of "saved" individuals meeting on Sundays. For the rest of the week an *individualistic opportunism* might prevail in workshop, market and counting house. Suffice it to say, this was a far cry from what Calvin originally had in mind. Now, however, efficiency could become an overriding consideration, and charity restricted to the "deserving poor." Certainly, these Protestant Dissenters, and Quakers also, were to be very important in the commercial development of Great Britain. If it is a mixed picture, we should not forget that many a hard-nosed, dissenting businessman was insensitive to those considerations expressed by the arts and literature because he had been deliberately excluded from the universities of England by the multiple forms of statutorily imposed discrimination that prevailed after 1662 and that survived well after 1689. From 1732 onwards the Protestant Dissenting Deputies struggled with noble persistence against the discrimination and stigmatization they endured, eventually taking up the question of Jewish civil liberties.

The pietism of late Puritanism and the Protestant Dissent of the late seventeenth and early eighteenth centuries was not yet Evangelicalism. Although it was eventually to greatly facilitate evangelical revivalism, it lacked the full expression of those features so well highlighted by Bebbington's quadrilateral of priorities. A forerunner was Joseph Alleine (1634–68). Impressive figures such as Thomas Boston (1676–1732) and Ebenezer Erskine (1680–1754) in Scotland, Griffith Jones (1683–1761) in Wales, and Isaac Watts (1674–1748) and Philip Doddridge (1702–51) in England were at once pivotal and transitional. In them we encounter the best of late Puritanism coupled with a partial inclination towards and merging with the rising tide of Evangelicalism.

Across the Atlantic, Jonathan Edwards (1703–58) belongs only partly in this transitional group, because he cannot be denied a place in the first rank of those who were the initiators of English-speaking Evangelicalism. He struggled with the issues presented by the revival without having previously resolved the problems presented by the contestable philosophical underpinnings of his theology and anthropology. The roots of this inner struggle were not always clear to his contemporaries, because many of his philosophical writings were only published posthumously. They were not included in the two-volume edition of *The Works of Jonathan Edwards* edited by Edward Hickman dating from 1834 and extensively reprinted thereafter. The Yale edition of *The Works of Jonathan Edwards* (1957 onwards) presently extends to twenty-six volumes, with much more material made available online. The additional material now available offers insight into the philosophical underpinnings of his theological writings, and not least his theological anthropology.

Part Two

FOCUS

6

THE ROOTS AND CHARACTER OF EVANGELICALISM

German Protestant Pietism and the Moravians

A great transition took place from the mid-1720s to the early 1740s. It affected the German-speaking lands, the British Isles and British North America. Its character cannot be adequately grasped unless we consider the developments in German Pietism as seminal to the birth of English-speaking Evangelicalism. We must remember that scholasticism was certainly not unique to Puritanism and the reformed wing of continental European Protestantism. After all, scholasticism arose out of the failure of early Protestantism to develop a philosophy inherently true to its own basis and starting-point. Lutheran scholasticism may be traced to the earliest days of the *evangelische Kirchen*—not least to Philip Melanchthon's *Loci communes* (1521, definitive version, 1555), through the formative writings of Martin Chemnitz (1522-86), and to the immense elaborations of Johann Gerhard (1582-1637) and Abraham Calovius (1612-86). Also among the Lutherans, rational system-building led to a certain spiritual aridity, and here also a pietistic reaction to scholastic rationalism emerged.

In the German *Länder*, this reaction was expressed by Johann Arndt (1555-1621), whose *Vier Bücher vom wahren Christenthum* (*Four Books on True Christianity*, 1605-9) already warned against formal assent without a commitment of the heart. For some, Philipp Jacob Spener (1635-1705) author of *Pia Desideria* (1675), meaning "pious longings," stands as the founder of Pietism. Spener did not champion an exclusively introverted piety. He also sought to revitalize *public* worship: protestant public worship could be stunningly funereal in those days. He was centrally involved in the founding of the University of Halle (1694), which in due course became renowned as a bastion of Pietism. However, the traits fully characteristic of Pietism were more amply exhibited in the life and work of August Hermann Francke (1663–1727), who was appointed Halle's first professor of Greek and Oriental Languages. It was Francke who laid strong emphasis on a decisive conversion experience rather than a gradual growth in grace.

These developments presaged what was to come. The group that was to shape the evangelical movement decisively were the Moravians, founded and re-constituted under the aegis of Count Nikolaus Ludwig von Zinzendorf (1700–60), an exceptional man who was for some a second Luther (*Lutherus vere redivivus*). The Moravians were a seminal influence on the character of Anglo-American Evangelicalism, much more decisively than the reformations of Switzerland or the doctrinal scholasticism of later Puritanism. This Moravian influence, imparted at the formative stage, gave to Evangelicalism many of those characteristic tendencies, practices, and traits familiar to many who have participated in evangelical life or who have made it a study. It is among the Moravians that we encounter the "prayer chain" and the "quiet time," and the strong emphasis on singing that remains characteristic of Evangelicalism and its derivatives.

As a group, the Moravians arose out of the *Unitas Fratrum* ("Unity of the Brethren") movement that had emerged in Bohemia and Moravia after the execution of Jan Hus (1415). Sometimes referred to as the Ancient Moravian Church, it traced its lineage as an episcopally organized entity from its institution at Kunwald in 1457. It was finally crushed by the Habsburgs, following the defeat of the protestant cause at the Battle of White Mountain in 1620—but not before it was influenced by Lutheranism, and later by reformed teaching as well. Driven underground and into exile, the prolific Jan Amos Comenius (1592–1670) strove to retain the cohesion and promote the recovery of the Moravians. In some measure influenced by the Lutheran mystic Jacob Böhme (1575–1624), Comenius sought to give Christian articulation to an educational vision that was intentionally post-medieval and impressively progressive for its time, also in its preferred teaching methodologies.

Zinzendorf's conversion experience was iconic rather than textual, though doubtless informed by strong pietistic influences. Where Luther wrestled with Scripture, and thereby found himself "born afresh," Zinzendorf's moment of crisis came; we are told, with his contemplation of a painting of Christ—*Ecce Homo*, attributed to Domenico Feti (1589–1624). In

1722 Zinzendorf purchased the estate of Berthelsdorf. There he fostered the Moravian settlement of *Herrnhut* (meaning "The Lord's Watch"), following representations from members of the Moravian Brethren who were fleeing Habsburg-instigated, anti-protestant persecutions. In 1727 Zinzendorf took up residence at *Herrnhut*, and in August of that year the community experienced a profound upsurge of spiritual intensity that was particularly evident at the celebration of the Eucharist. From this development dates the Renewed Moravian Church, or Renewed Church of the *Unitas Fratrum*. Some unusual practices arose among them, including praying to the Holy Spirit, and referring to the Spirit as "Mother" (as Christ is the Son). The Count was a Lutheran of the pietistic variety, and these events seem to have been closely related to his realization, derived from the writing of Comenius, that the Moravians were not a sect but the remnants of a protestant-type episcopal church that antedated even Luther.

In the beliefs and actions of the Renewed Moravians we first encounter all of Bebbington's evangelical quadrilateral of priorities with their characteristic balance and interrelation. There is the *conversionism* with its call for a changed life; there is a Bible-centered approach to truth, with a strong tendency to stress conscience (*conscientia*) over, even against science (*scientia*); there we encounter a gospel-*activism*, especially in the form of missionary endeavor at home and abroad; and there (especially so with the Moravians) an intensely devotional *crucicentrism*, with a sometimes highly emotional focus on the wounds, blood, agony and dereliction of Christ crucified. If there was much about these characteristics that evoked the spirit of Catholic Counter-Reformation devotion, there were also resonances evocative of the piety of the cantatas and oratorios of Johan Sebastian Bach (1685-1750). Such *crucicentrism* has always been a feature of Evangelicalism, and has been particularly prominent in movements such as the East African Revival, where the Moravian influence remains clearly discernable. An ardor for Christ that becomes fixated on "the blood and the wounds" can of course produce unwholesome consequences. In later years, during the "time of sifting" (1743-50) Zinzendorf struggled to address and redress the problems generated by the intensely crucifixional focus that he himself had fostered. Here we may discern one of the leading tendencies of Evangelicalism: a strong tendency to elevate the cross in such a way as to obscure, even dismiss as a mere prelude, the order of creation.

This dismissal was to play out across a wide arc. In his justifiable opposition to arid formalism, Zinzendorf repeatedly stressed heart (*Herz*) over head (*Kopf*). There is, of course, a sense in which this is entirely scriptural. The heart (in the religious and not merely anatomical sense) is central. However, the Moravian way of teaching a religion of the heart (*Herzensreligion*) came to be suspicious, even dismissive, of intellectual understanding (*Kopf-wissenschaft*). Science, scholarship and theory were at a discount. There was little awareness that *these legitimate endeavors also belonged to Christ*, and that he was to be served in these also. This deficiency has been decisive in forming the character of Evangelicalism. In this respect it represents a *further reduction* of the Christian message, with its virtually exclusive focus on individual salvation, inward, personal holiness, and a predilection for feelings over clarity of understanding.

There have been and are evangelical scholars, but overall the movement has exhibited a serious and systemic intellectual deficit—especially beyond the specific field of biblical studies. Those scholars and scientists who are present in Evangelicalism are not typical or expressive of the movement overall; most evangelical scholars and scientists are unknown to most evangelicals. At the more foundational level, when addressing general philosophical questions or issues in the special sciences, almost all writers in the pietistic-evangelical line see no need to start from an integrally biblical starting-point. They have little or no sense of how this is possible, and are inclined to assume that secular viewpoints are religiously neutral. They occasionally attempt to integrate these viewpoints with received Christian teaching. This deficiency may be traced to Evangelicalism's very inception. Arguably because of its neglect of the order of creation and the religious significance of human culture, Evangelicalism came to see any biblically-directed cultivation of science and scholarship as of marginal importance, or simply superfluous. Such work was not "preaching the gospel." The Bible is believed, but in the life of the evangelical believer it functions as little more than a *devotional resource* for challenging or comforting thoughts.

Zinzendorf spent 1726–36 consolidating the life and work of the "renewed brethren" at *Herrnhut*. Thereafter, he spent 1736–55 in extensive travel across northern Europe, to Great Britain, and across the Atlantic to the American Colonies. He was assiduous in preaching his message and in acting on behalf of the Moravian movement, weathering doctrinal and financial storms. His final years (1755–60) were spent at *Herrnhut*, but not before his efforts secured the statutory recognition of the brethren in Great Britain as "an ancient Protestant Episcopal Church." At a strategic time the Moravians enjoyed a standing that was denied to the Protestant Dissenters. The Moravians were viewed as much more compatible with the *ethos* and assertions of the Church of England. At the time of John Wesley's conversion, the Moravian message of active, individual dedication gained significant acceptance within the Church of England, characterized as it was by deep institutional conservatism. These traits have lasted. Even when advocating major changes, the Moravians emphasized retaining as much of existing structures as possible and working within them wherever feasible. Theirs was a moral earnestness that rarely saw structural reformation as a high priority.

A Transatlantic Movement—Britain and America in Interaction

By the time John Wesley felt his heart "strangely warmed" in 1738, English Protestantism had been through two centuries of troubled history. Great Britain was capable of envisaging itself as a protestant bastion. Rising from the ashes of the great fire of 1666, St. Paul's Cathedral, London, was designed as a protestant architectural response to St. Peter's Basilica in Rome. Nevertheless, the magnificence of St. Paul's belied the actual condition of eighteenth century English Protestantism. In the cities especially, many parish churches were poorly attended. At the same time, in spite of the challenges represented by the Stuart-inspired rebellions of 1715 and 1745, Great Britain seemed to have discovered the secret of political stability—a "mixed monarchy," an independent judiciary, and policies that blended tradition and innovation. These developments greatly facilitated the increasing volume and sophistication of market-based commerce after 1689.

The Evangelicalism that emerged in the 1730s both played to and arose from this increasing commercialization of culture. Many British Christians were preoccupied with the implications of increasing material prosperity. The *Fable of the Bees* (1714) by Bernard de Mandeville (1670–1733) disturbed many church leaders and moralists. The message of the *Fable* was that private vices might be public benefits, which seemed to legitimize sin. Nevertheless, with an abatement of the doctrinal-ecclesiastical conflicts of the seventeenth century, it was found that a measure of toleration was good for business, trade, and commerce. The Agricultural and Industrial Revolutions were gaining momentum. They would eventually transform many parts of Great Britain and, in due course, much of the world. Some Christian observations concerning the functioning of markets are therefore appropriate. An open market, rightly governed, justly and equitably conducted, in lawful goods, especially when operating in conjunction with a stable monetary system, has a legitimate and highly constructive place in human affairs. At the same time, from a Christian standpoint, the functioning of the markets as we experience them can never constitute a norm for right conduct and valid decision-making because the behavior of the market reflects not only legitimate needs grounded in the order of creation (not a problem) but also the ever-present sinful inclinations and erroneous understandings of its participants (definitely a problem).

Evangelicalism as it began to emerge in the 1730s and burgeoned thereafter, was powerfully shaped by its increasingly commercialized milieu. Simultaneously, it drew upon the greatly increased emphasis on the individual that was characteristic of the early Enlightenment, even as its emphasis upon feelings ("*I felt my* heart strangely warmed") anticipated the rise of Romanticism, with its aversions toward Enlightenment rationalism. Indeed, it might be argued that Evangelicalism—along with various forms of German Pietism and mysticism—profoundly contributed to the emergence of Romanticism in the late eighteenth and early nineteenth centuries. Moreover this milieu, characterized by an expanding market, was one in which individual market decisions could be worked on by techniques designed to sway sentiment. By the earlier eighteenth century, all the arts and techniques of mass advertising were about to come into their own. The first evangelicals may not themselves have fully appreciated this influence, but they concurrently benefited from and contributed to this tendency.

Jonathan Edwards

The three great exemplars of first generation English-speaking Evangelicalism were Jonathan Edwards, John Wesley, (already mentioned), and George Whitefield (1714–70). It would be impossible to discuss the beginnings of the movement in the English-speaking North Atlantic world without considering each of these three men.

Jonathan Edwards was a congregational minister in Northampton, Massachusetts. Much about him reminds us of later Puritanism and Pietism—its emphases were his primary concerns. He also exhibited the kind of awe for the order of creation that was a feature of the Calvinistic reformation. When the "awakening" came, he sided with its advocates, the pro-revival "new lights," against the "old lights" who could not discard their reservations, committed as they were to the conventions of an earlier Puritanism. Edwards was a man of undeniable intellectual stature and candor. He entertained serious reservations as to the authenticity of some of the behaviors he had witnessed under "revival" conditions. His seminal works on the awakening—*A Faithful Narrative of the Surprising Work of God* (1737), *The Distinguishing Marks of the Work of the Spirit of God* (1741), *Some Thoughts Concerning the Revival of Religion in New England* (1742), *A Treatise Concerning Religious Affections* (1746)—are pervaded with a prescient sense that the awakening, though authentic, might propel protestant Christianity towards a wild and deluded subjectivism. He exudes an awareness of being part of something that contained unresolved tensions of definite if unfathomable consequence. The caution of Jonathan Edwards deserves to be respected and merits the serious reflection of latter day evangelicals who so readily talk about promoting revival. He discerned that the "religious affections"—what we ultimately set our hearts upon—ought not to be confused with transient emotional states of affairs, even when these are described using fervently pious language.

It can be argued that features already present in Edwards's not so well known philosophical reflections were unintentionally instrumental in eventually giving leverage to the tendencies he decried. In *A Careful and Strict Enquiry into the modern prevailing notions of the Freedom of the Will* (1754) he left the door ajar to notions of human autonomy that became commonplace in later Evangelicalism. His writings exhibit the dangers inherent in a synthetic philosophical position in which biblical teaching and questionable Enlightenment assumptions are uncomfortably combined. He was philosophically eclectic. Where his reflections on the revival were empirical and measured we may detect the influence of Francis Bacon (1561–1626) and John Locke (1632–1704), even as he was capable of expressing his conclusions using an idealistic terminology reminiscent of Nicole Malebranche (1638–1715) and George Berkeley (1685–1753). He assumed that the doctrinal statements of Protestantism expressed a "revealed religion" that could be innocuously melded with contemporaneous versions of natural philosophy.

More specifically, the retention of a dualistic anthropology, already legitimized by the theological and confessional utilization of the *philosophia aristotelico-scholastica*, facilitated a distinction in Edwards's thinking on the will between humankind's *natural ability* and *moral inability* to respond positively to the gospel message. Much in the evangelical future lay implicit in this distinction. The door that was left ajar was flung open by later Evangelicalism. The older insights into the human condition emphasized by Augustine, Luther, and Calvin, teachings that Edwards never intended to abandon, were gradually set aside as Evangelicalism adjusted its preaching of the gospel to the purportedly autonomous individuals envisaged by eighteenth-century thought and society.

George Whitefield and the Wesley Brothers

In certain respects George Whitefield was the center figure of the movement. This has not always been clear to subsequent generations. In America the intellectual stature of Edwards can result in his dominating the discussion, while in Great Britain, the historical reputation of John Wesley, as the founder of Methodism, along with his brother Charles (1707–88), overshadowed that of Whitefield, who founded no movement or denomination that took his name. Nevertheless, Whitefield was *the* central man. It was he who, at the invitation of Edwards, brought his style to Massachusetts (after an earlier revival there in 1734), and it was he (rather than Edwards) who maintained a long-term relationship with John Wesley. Although Whitefield adhered to a soteriology inherited from Puritanism, his style was powerfully new. He brought to the *business* of preaching a singular oratory, capable of evoking great dramatic intensity. He worked with agents and representatives and boosters of the cause, and could exhibit considerable *entrepreneurial* flair—here is the key to his otherwise puzzling friendship with the indefatigably enterprising Benjamin Franklin (1706–90).

John Wesley was a leading light in the Holy Club, founded at Oxford by his brother Charles in 1729. His father, Samuel, brought up a Protestant Dissenter, committed to the Church of England in the 1680s—perhaps influenced by *The Unreasonableness of Separation* (1682) by Edward Stillingfleet (1635–99). After 1662 there remained within the Church of England a small number of Puritans who conformed—such as John Trapp (1601–69) and William Gurnall (1617–79), but its clerical leadership was either high church or, as the Whigs came to dominance in the eighteenth century, latitudinarian.

In the later seventeenth century, Anglican thinking began to be influenced by the latitudinarians, especially those known as the Cambridge Platonists—chief among whose leaders were Benjamin Whichcote (1609–83), Henry More (1614–87), and Ralph Cudworth (1717–88). They repudiated the kind of elaborate dogmatic constructions facilitated by the *philosophia aristotelico-scholastica* and advocated a simpler and more elevated Platonic approach. They called for an attitude of tolerance between high churchmen and latter day Puritans; they were men of latitude, hence the term latitudinarians. They were influenced by the intellectual posture adopted by the "ever-memorable" John Hales (1584–1656) and members of the Great Tew Circle such as William Chillingworth (1602–44), who in the 1630s had sought a way through the looming confrontations of mid-seventeenth-century England. If the high church party did not abandon its shibboleths—including non-resistance to the monarch as "the Lord's anointed"—they were not unaffected by a return to a more Platonic orientation, which, after all, was the general philosophical standpoint of Richard Hooker, whose final works were only published in this period.

John Wesley and his brother Charles were brought up on high church principles in the rectory at Epworth, the irascible irresponsibility of their father Samuel being overcome by the iron determination of their mother, Susannah Wesley (1669-1742). It was in such a context that John and Charles earnestly read rigorous works such as the *Serious Call to a Devout and Holy Life* (1728) by William Law (1686-1761), and it was from such a background that they went up to Oxford where they participated in the life of the Holy Club. But the holiness John Wesley sought was beyond his reach. He was a beaten man when he sought spiritual solace in the company of the Moravians in London, having first encountered the "renewed brethren" on his 1735-8 visit to Georgia. This was the immediate context of his Aldersgate experience. It took the Moravian presentation of Luther to bring Wesley a measure of conscious deliverance. Ever the man of action, within weeks Wesley departed on a pilgrimage to *Herrnhut*.

The Moravians as Formative Contributors to the Evangelical Ethos

The historical process is wonderfully complex, and formulas can be misleading. It is tempting to propose a formula such as: Late Puritan Pietism + Lutheran Pietism + Renewed Moravian Pietism = Evangelicalism. Certainly, the Moravian strand of activist-pietism exerted immense influence on early Evangelicalism during the formative decade of the 1740s. As has been argued, it was from the Moravians that evangelicals acquired their modes of thought and expression and their characteristic emphasis upon the crucifixion. It is from the Moravians that late Pietism acquired such an intense missionary zeal, without which the revivalist and crusading character of Evangelicalism cannot be adequately explained. The Moravian strand of Lutheran Pietism, at this decisive stage, influenced both Whitefield and Wesley. The essential roots of Evangelicalism therefore lie deep in the ethos of Lutheran Pietism—as mediated to the British Isles and North America by the Moravians. Only later did Whitefield and Wesley express serious reservations about certain Moravian viewpoints and practices. By the time the Moravians had gone through their "time of sifting," their formative impact on Evangelicalism was already on the wane, but by that stage the die had been cast.

Although the Evangelical Revival eventually boosted the ranks of protestant dissent in England and Wales, Evangelicalism in England found its first and true home within the Church of England. From the outset, the leading English evangelicals were committed members of that church. As we have seen, historically both Lutheranism and Anglicanism had adopted the *corrective* view of how Scripture was authoritative. This helps to explain why so many evangelicals have been ready to adopt versions of the Lutheran "two kingdoms teaching." This view has served to put effective limits on the discipleship of Christians, by restricting its scope to devotions, church, and missions. The characteristically evangelical, pietistic outlook, with its emphasis on inner personal holiness, accorded well with this *corrective* view of the authority of Scripture. Questions of external polity could still be seen as falling within the realm of *adiaphora*—as did much of supposedly secular life. Formal denominational structures became the context in which a "church within the church" of the truly converted might function, even as the same churchly structure might, as conditions permitted, be used as a platform from which to preach the gospel to the unconverted.

The princely rulers of the protestant German *Länder* appreciated pietism for its Lutheran tradition of subservience to monarchs. Across the North Sea this attitude chimed in well with Anglican habits of non-resistance to royal authority. John and Charles Wesley cannot be adequately understood apart from their high church background. They and Whitefield were Church of England men all their lives. They were central to the formation of the evangelical party in the Church of England. Moreover, they both accepted the ecclesiastical standpoint articulated by Richard Hooker and subsequently enforced by the Act of Uniformity of 1662. It was in this intellectual, doctrinal and churchly *milieu* that Evangelicalism strove to establish itself from the late 1730s onwards. In all the years following, Anglican evangelicals have repeatedly defined themselves as the champions of the Church of England "by law established." It was this Anglican-based Evangelicalism, conveying its own appropriation and adaptation of Lutheran-Moravian Pietism that was to have immense influence on Evangelicalism worldwide.

The Evangelical Impact

What took place in the later 1730s and early 1740s is known in America as the Great Awakening, and in the British Isles as the Evangelical Revival. Both terms imply a revivifying of what was already present but had decayed to a moribund state. The missionary zeal of the first evangelicals was characterized by a willingness to engage in outdoor preaching, on occasions to large numbers. When preaching, Whitefield could play the part of the dramatic showman. In such preaching, a pre-existing general knowledge of Christian doctrine, often acquired from church sources, could be worked on with great effect by the new dramatic techniques. Prime examples include

Edwards's sermon on "Sinners in the Hands of an Angry God" (1741), delivered at Northampton, Massachusetts, as well as Whitefield's sermons at Cambuslang, Scotland (1742). It was Whitefield's preaching to the miners at Kingswood Hill near Bristol, England (in 1738) that had already convinced a very "proper" John Wesley to take up open air preaching. The parish system was not sacrosanct. The gospel was more important. Whether the local parish minister liked it or not, there were "souls to be saved" and that is what mattered. To this end both Whitefield and Wesley traveled extensively. Both men crossed the Atlantic, Whitefield thirteen times. He died in Massachusetts in 1770.

There can be little doubt that these evangelicals caused a great stir in the land, especially as they developed their array of promotional and publicity techniques. An extensive biographical and autobiographical literature exists testifying to the manner in which the new preaching had a decisive influence on the lives of many. From the 1740s to the 1790s they contributed to changing the face of large parts of Great Britain. Of course, when confronted with the remarkable events of the awakening or revival, readers may adopt the view of the unbelieving cynic or skeptic. They may say that all this was only so much foolish emotionalism whipped up by opportunistic preachers. Some have dismissed a great deal of the revival as mere enthusiasm. On the other hand, it would be unwise to view the revival exclusively through the eyes of, and in the terms adopted by, those who were then or who are today its fervently committed advocates. The key point here is not to dispute that we have experiences, nor that coming to and living a life of discipleship is something that is inevitably *experienced*. We can misinterpret and therefore misrepresent our experiences. So neither extreme skepticism nor crass gullibility is required but the discernment that comes with the gaining of wisdom.

In what follows, it will be assumed that if there is authentic faith in Jesus Christ anywhere on the face of the earth, it is exclusively attributable to the work of the Holy Spirit. It will also be assumed that whenever the Holy Spirit uses persons and other means, their instrumentality does not sanction to the full the persons or means so used. Even the briefest reflection will show that this is necessarily so. To say that the Holy Spirit only uses that which is *wholly consistent* with the divine will is to limit his power and make it conditional where it is sovereign. This side of the restoration of all things (Acts 3:21), the Scriptures teach that the Holy Spirit always uses people and means that are incomplete and inadequate. A critical assessment of Evangelicalism, and not least the techniques of *contrived* revivalism, is not an *ipso facto* denial that the Holy Spirit might work in and through such circumstances, but it may assert that that such contrivances are not therefore to be regarded as normative.

It is clear that the first evangelicals developed an impressive dexterity in the arts and crafts of publicity and promotion. Written representations of revival both defined and advocated the phenomena and its leading features. In addition, it is hard not to see something along the lines of a personality cult status coming to be attached to some leading evangelical preachers. Organizers, authors, publicists, and facilitators often buttressed their efforts. In assessing the Evangelical Revival or the Great Awakening, the Christian historian must therefore proceed with exceptional care. The historian should not rush to ascribe to the Holy Spirit what may be of intentional or unintentional human contrivance. At the same time, heeding the Bible, neither should he or she exclude from our understanding of any situation the silent but effectual workings of the Holy Spirit. The historian never sees all, but should aspire to understand with wisdom and circumspection.

Moreover, the historian of Evangelicalism is not dealing with a single protestant denomination, but with a complex of interrelated movements and initiatives, within and across denominations, spanning the English-speaking world. Some evangelicals were assiduous trans-Atlantic communicators. The attitude of evangelicals towards existing ecclesiastical structures was simultaneously a strength and a weakness. It was a virtue in Evangelicalism in that it tempered the harshness of some of the barriers set up by the exclusivity of the Act of Uniformity in 1662. Remaining a Church of England man, Whitefield did not scruple to preach at locations such as the Tottenham Court Road Chapel in London and once declared the (Presbyterian) Church of Scotland "to be the best constituted National Church in the world."[1]

Yet past conflicts left abiding legacies. Such was the gulf between church and dissent in England, that it took courage and magnanimity for Protestant Dissenters such as Isaac Watts and Philip Doddridge to extend the hand of fellowship to men such as Whitefield. Wesley appropriated the extensive literary legacy of western Christendom, including Puritanism, *on his own terms*. As much as figures such as Doddridge longed for renewal, Protestant Dissent was not immediately disposed to adjust to the pragmatism of the new-style Evangelicalism. At the same time, across the British Isles, the revival was given momentum and depth by support arising from innumerable pockets of Protestant Dissent scattered across the land.

---

1. Whitefield, *Letters*, 515.

Hanoverian expectations of ecclesiastical subservience produced predictable results in Scotland. Early in the eighteenth century, the Church of Scotland was stirred by the Marrow Controversy, which arose when the General Assembly adopted an adverse stance towards the 1718 republication of *The Marrow of Modern Divinity* (1645-49), attributed to Edward Fisher (d. 1655). This work discussed the free offer of the gospel in a manner that was profoundly influenced by the ministry of Thomas Boston, but that the ecclesiastical leadership had rejected on the grounds of its supposed antinomianism. The minority who supported *The Marrow* in this affair was soon caught up in a secessionist movement led by the brothers Ralph (1685-1752), and especially Ebenezer Erskine. They formed the Associate Presbytery in 1733. The central issue was the imposition of unelected ministers upon reluctant congregations. Whitefield met with the Erskine brothers on his first visit to Scotland in 1741. Although they were in many ways kindred spirits, Whitefield could not accede to their request that in Scotland he align himself expressly with the Associate Presbytery. For their part, the Erskine brothers, having endured much for high principle, were unwilling to accede to his ecclesiastical pragmatism. It was a turning point; henceforth Whitefield was to be represented in Scotland by the Church of Scotland minister John Gillies (1712-96), author of *Historical Collections Relating to the Success of the Gospel* (1754).

The greater degree of mutual acceptance between Anglicans, Presbyterians, and Protestant Dissenters produced by Evangelicalism was a positive development, yet it failed to address the central issue of the visible division of protestant Christianity in the British Isles and beyond. Evangelical pragmatism was prone to see denominations as platforms for evangelism and sometimes little else. The tendency was to see unity as a purely spiritual matter, rather than one calling for public and institutional expression. From the outset, Evangelicalism failed to develop an adequate doctrine of the church, and this failure was to have serious consequences.

The upper echelons of the Church of England did not welcome the Evangelical Revival with open arms. Many clergy and bishops were contemptuous, if not downright hostile. On returning to London in 1748, after years in America, Whitefield found his following seriously dissipated. Rescue came from Selina, Countess of Huntingdon (1707-91). The support she provided resulted in the planting of an array of churches in England, Wales, and (eventually) Sierra Leone, known as the "Countess of Huntingdon's Connection." Neither the Wesley brothers nor the Countess contemplated the founding of new denominations. They desired to work in and through the Church of England. The Connection itself became a separate entity, thanks to a mixture of inflexibility and hostility exhibited in the Spa Fields court decisions of 1780, in which the rights of patronage played an obstructionist role, and forced the Countess to become a reluctant Dissenter. The Connection constitutes one of the antecedents of the Free Church of England, established in the nineteenth century.

That Evangelicalism, in the early days, was often referred to as Methodism is a mark of John Wesley's early influence and of the *method* of prescriptive spiritual exercises and conduct that marked the ethos of the Holy Club. Initially, the Methodist Societies founded by Wesley and his disciples were voluntarily aligned with the Church of England. That posture became less convincing in the face of official ecclesiastical opposition to the revival. Wesley eventually recognized that the Methodist movement would develop separately, and he legitimized this by his *Deed of Declaration* and first ordination of clergy (Wesley not being a bishop) in 1784. The die was cast. After Wesley's death, his following fractured into an array of connections. Eventually there emerged three main Methodist denominations in England: the Wesleyan Methodist, the Primitive Methodists, and the United Methodists.

A Lack of Initial Clarity Portends a Future of Doctrinal Confusion

Evangelicalism in England suffered serious *doctrinal* division from the outset. Whitefield's doctrine of salvation was essentially that of late Puritan Pietism. He was in accord with the old Puritan mainstream, not so much in his methods, but certainly in his views on election, on the necessity of a prior work of the Spirit in the hearts of those who repent and believe, and on the perseverance of the saints. It was generally appreciated that both Edwards and Whitefield concurred with the view of the necessary priority of divine grace in human salvation as articulated against the Remonstrant followers of Arminius by the counter-Remonstrant party back in the days of the Synod of Dort, although they would have been more familiar with the articulation of this teaching in the Westminster Confession of Faith and the Savoy Declaration. These doctrines of grace were a central teaching of the Protestant Reformation. Articles X and XVII of the *Thirty Nine Articles* of the Church of England are wholly consistent with this standpoint. John Wesley, it should be remembered, was a son of the high church school within the Church of England, which, from the mid-seventeenth century onwards, wore more or less subtle Arminian colors. As has been observed, the strange warming of Wesley's heart in 1738 did not entail for him the full adoption of the Reformation view on the central issue of the necessary priority of divine grace.

This deviation from teaching central to the Reformation became indisputably clear in Wesley's sermon on "Free Grace" (1739), which was further buttressed by his sermon on "Christian Perfection" (1741). The publication of these sermons widened the division that had been initiated by them. Among other things, Wesley claimed that the "free grace" of the Reformers and their successors—including men such as Edwards and Whitefield—tended towards an antinomianism that was marked by loose behavior arising from the presumption of elect status. Wesley believed that what he understood as Calvinism functioned as a license for unholy behavior. Arguably, this teaching of Wesley and his successors opened the door to multiple variants of Evangelicalism, some of them committed to notions of *individual human autonomy*, long since repudiated by historic Christianity. It was from this Wesleyan-Arminian-Perfectionist strand that Evangelicalism eventually produced its immensely influential "holiness," "higher life," "Pentecostal," and "charismatic" variants.

For his part, Whitefield responded with his published letter to Wesley: "In Answer to his Sermon entitled Free Grace" (1741). Wesley was unconvinced. The original Methodism fractured into those who took the Wesleyan-Arminian standpoint and those who took the basic view of the Protestant Reformation. The latter, agreeing with Whitefield on the question at hand, eventually coalesced as the evangelical party within the Church of England. What was termed the Calvinistic Controversy flared again from 1769 onwards, and this time the principal protagonists were John Wesley himself and the redoubtable Augustus Montague Toplady (1740–78), the stalwart champion of Calvinism. Toplady, author of the hymn "Rock of Ages," was on strong ground in his highly charged works on *The Church of England Vindicated from the Charge of Arminianism* (1769) and *Historic Proof of the Doctrinal Calvinism of the Church of England* (1774). The tone of this further round of exchanges did not always reflect well on the participants and seems not to have changed the views of any of the principal protagonists.

John and Charles Wesley did not buckle under the pressure. The (Wesleyan) *Arminian Magazine* first appeared in 1778. Few evangelicals in the early twenty-first century now adhere to Wesley's exact form of perfectionism. However, it has been immensely influential. Its roots lay in Wesley's initial high-church orientation. From this source came strong Platonic influences. Sayings such as "Be perfect as your heavenly Father is perfect" (Matt 5:48 NRSV) were interpreted to teach that we are called to fully exhibit certain divine attributes; to ascend ever higher ("higher, higher, much, much higher" as the "praise and worship" song has it) *up* the great chain of being—as contemplated by Platonists—towards an absorption into the greatest of all beings, even God himself. The Wesleyan influence is to be seen at work in the eventual emergence of a variety of "higher Christian life" movements in which characteristically Platonic, elevated, and otherworldly attitudes came to expression. Such an orientation tends to fight shy of structural reformation; in its subordination to a non-Christian philosophical standpoint it points to the perils of aligning the gospel with thinking that lacks a biblical starting-point. It shows what can happen when Christian thinking and living loses sight of biblical teaching concerning the order of creation. Matthew 5:48 does not call upon us to be God as God is God. In the Bible, "perfection" signifies completion. Our calling is to be complete and wholehearted participants in the covenant that the Father has made with us in Jesus Christ.

Many, but not all, members of the early evangelical party in the Church of England were inclined to the reformed or Calvinistic side of this discussion, but there were always exceptions, of whom John Fletcher of Madeley (1729–85) was one of the most notable, he being viewed at one stage as John Wesley's natural successor. The emerging ethos of evangelical Anglicanism dictated that any overly conspicuous Calvinism (of the five points variety) should be contained and mitigated. The tone was eventually set by the mediating position of Charles Simeon of Cambridge (1759–1836)—an approach that has been characterized as "Calvinist on one's knees and Arminian on one's feet." The deep-running tendency of Evangelicalism has generally been towards a less thoroughly examined Wesleyan-style Arminianism. Not only did this open the way to "holiness" movements of a "perfectionist" kind, but it also rendered Evangelicalism increasingly susceptible to the notion that revivals could be generated by human organization, endeavor, artifice, and ingenuity. The ongoing quest was for the latest technique, method, or formula whereby revival could be instigated and then exploited. In due course this amounted to evangelization by manipulation through managed consent. Once this point had been reached, the way was open to an ever more opportunistic pragmatism, and inevitably it would be said that, if this, that, or the other was done in a "revival" context, then it was therefore "of the Lord." Those evangelicals critical of such tendencies, and willing to struggle against the tide, are liable to face the charge that they are lacking in faith and vision.

None of this should blind us to the truth that the leading figures of the first and second generations of the evangelical party in the Church of England included men of exceptional quality, such as William Grimshaw of Haworth (1708–63), Samuel Walker of Truro (1714–61), William Romaine the London preacher (1714–95), the idiosyncratic John Berridge (1716–93), and the ecclesiastical historian Joseph Milner (1744–97). At its best, early

Evangelicalism was magnificent. With conspicuous energy, men sought to breathe life into the generally moribund parish system of the English church. Alongside them must be mentioned Hannah Moore (1745-1833), who pioneered the distribution of tracts, and the Wesleyan Hannah Ball (1734-92), who along with Robert Raikes (1736-1811), developed Sunday School education for children.

Evangelicalism developed differently in Wales. There, Daniel Rowlands (1713-90) was pressured into nonconformity by Anglican intolerance. That exclusiveness meant that the revival in Wales often assumed a counter-Anglicizing posture, and so had a formative impact on the emergence of modern Welsh nationalism. Next to Rowlands stands the author of "Guide me O Thou Great Jehovah," William Williams (Pantycelyn) (1717-91), and Howell Harris (1714-73), the controversial lay organizer of the Welsh Calvinistic Methodists, who owed much to the Countess of Huntingdon's Connection. Somewhat later, the Welsh Calvinistic Methodists nurtured the famed preacher John Elias (1774-1841).

The Second and Third Generations

In England, a bridge between the first and second generations of evangelicals was provided by men such as John Newton (1725-1807), the preacher and hymn-writer to whom we owe "Amazing grace," William Cowper (1731-1800), the poet who gave us "God moves in a mysterious way / His wonders to perform," and the independent preacher Rowland Hill (1744-1833). The second generation was conspicuous for challenging the moribund state of the church and complacency of the aristocratic elite. Titles such as *The Complete Duty of Man* (1763) by Henry Venn (1725-97); *An Estimate of the Religion of the Fashionable World, by one of the Laity* (1791), by Hannah Moore; and *A Practical View of the Prevailing Religious System of Professed Christians in the Higher and Middle Classes in This Country Contrasted with Real Christianity* (1797) by William Wilberforce (1759-1833) defy the reader to evade their challenge.

Anglican evangelicals established the Eclectic Society in 1783 to discuss matters of mutual concern. The Church Missionary Society was founded in 1799. Wherever human dignity is affirmed, both Quakers and Moravians ought to be honored, if only because they were in the anti-slavery field before most evangelicals. However, it took the persistence of Wilberforce, Henry Thornton (1760-1815), and others of the so-called Clapham Sect (the term seems to have gained currency in the 1840s), and their willingness to work with a diverse range of people of good will, to abolish first the slave trade (1807) and eventually the institution of slavery itself within the British Empire (1833). These were developments of world-historical importance and are among the greatest achievements of Evangelicalism.

After this immense triumph the primacy of activism over doctrinal understanding and the claims of in-depth reflection began to exact an inevitable toll. Even as some prominent evangelicals attained episcopal office—Henry Ryder (1777-1836) was the first evangelical bishop—a certain loss of cohesion becomes evident. As the Church Missionary Society and its dissenting emulators, such as the London Missionary Society, and also, eventually, the China Inland Mission and Sudan Inland Mission, strove to open up vast areas of the globe to the evangelical message, the movement in Great Britain encountered many challenges but lacked the intellectual resources to surmount them adequately.

This was the era of Hugh McNeile (1795-1879), the Ulster-born leader of Evangelicalism within the Church of England. A "true blue" Tory (here also the legacy of Wesley may be discerned), and formidable polemicist, he opposed Roman Catholic Emancipation (1829), supported Wilberforce, and effectively delivered Liverpool to the Tory party. The Evangelicalism of this era was not so exclusively internalized as to foreswear all public good works. McNeile endorsed the immense labors of Anthony Ashley-Cooper, the Seventh Earl of Shaftesbury (1801-85), in the reform of working conditions in British factories and mines. These were the kind of changes already called for by the Moravian-educated Richard Oastler (1789-1861). The changes wrought by Shaftesbury and his supporters were profoundly beneficial to the laboring masses of the nation, yet also deeply conservative in character. The whole orientation was towards the preservation of the established order. Such tendencies had already been evident in the premiership of Spencer Percival (1762-1812). The reforms called for were generally ameliorative—thereby effectively preserving the existing heavily stratified socio-economic culture. Evangelicals were persistently active in checking a range of social evils but always with the effect of preserving rather than reforming the class system. It is not surprising that they lost contact with the laboring masses. Evangelicals found structural change hard to contemplate, and intellectual challenges hard to address. The nineteenth century came with both in abundance.

7

MULTIPLE CONFUSIONS AND CHALLENGES

The "Intellectual Deficit" and Early Liberalism as a Still Distant Threat

The greatest challenge that evangelicals failed to surmount in the nineteenth century was the rise of liberalism. Of course, the term "liberalism" has more than one meaning. It can mean (1) an insistence on human autonomy expressed individually and collectively across human culture that can amount to a declaration (acknowledged or otherwise) of human independence from God. It can also mean (2) advocacy and support for an open society opposed to authoritarianism and totalitarianism within which a diversity of alternative religious convictions may be lived out with mutual respect, if not agreement. The heirs of the Calvinistic Reformation eventually supported liberalism of the *second* variety, only because their initial agendas were thwarted by the preponderance of countervailing powers arrayed against them. In other words, *under the force of circumstances*, the Calvinistic Reformation eventually came to function as a force working towards a more open, or free society.

However, liberalism in the first sense stands for a commitment to *human autonomy*; the notion that individual human beings are in each generation rightly subject only to such laws or norms of conduct as they shall determine. This autonomy-affirming version of liberalism was given great impetus by the thinking of the Enlightenment as expressed in the French

Revolution (1789-94). This liberalism opposed authoritarianism and paternalism, *but did so on a basis of human autonomy and the presumed religious neutrality of reason.* That evangelicals found such thinking uncongenial is not surprising. It is simply not the picture of humankind and the human condition that is so candidly presented in the Bible. Arguably, this variety of liberalism amounts to a fully secularized Arminianism—now with man as his own deliverer in a purely material universe. However, evangelical inclinations towards Arminianism, not least amongst Wesleyan-influenced groupings, coupled with Moravian-acquired aversions towards ideas and theoretical analysis, made the rise of liberalism intractably difficult for evangelicals to address. Its tendencies towards individualism, and propensity to preach the gospel *as if to autonomous creatures*, meant that Evangelicalism was more entangled in liberal assumptions than evangelicals generally appreciated. They could declaim mightily against unbelief, but their intellectual deficit meant that they were unable to discuss complex questions with sufficient cogency and failed to discern the degree to which they were caught up in what they were seeking to address.

In the early nineteenth century, however, the full impact of theological liberalism was not the *most immediately apparent* threat to the evangelical party in the Church of England. This came from the Oxford Movement, which called for an increased orientation towards the traditions and practices of the *ancient Catholic Church* and chafed at parliamentary control over the Church of England. Led by John Henry Newman (1801-90), Henry Edward Manning (1808-92), John Keble (1792-1866), and Edward Pusey (1800-82), this movement soon developed conspicuously *Roman Catholic* tendencies. Architectural changes, sacerdotal vestments, elaborate ritual, and the language of transubstantiation were all illegally reintroduced into the life of the Church of England in ways that alarmed evangelicals and would have scandalized earlier generations of High Churchmen.

Known as the Oxford Movement, and sometimes referred to as Tractarianism (after the tracts it issued), this development challenged the whole basis upon which evangelicals claimed to have a legitimate place in the Church of England. The compromises that were insisted on by Elizabeth at the time of the Elizabethan Settlement (1558), and reinforced by the Act of Supremacy (1662), were occasionally experienced as distressing by evangelicals, and some secessions from the Church of England had from time to time taken place. However, the vast majority of Anglican evangelicals remained firmly within the established church, arguing that although its polity might not be the best, it nevertheless remained officially protestant and certainly was not hopelessly lost in apostasy. However, for some this stance became increasingly tenuous as Tractarianism at the parish level rendered contestable the usual claims for the historic Protestantism of the Reformed English Church. In response, the "Parker Society for the Publication of the Works of the Fathers and Early Writers of the Reformed English Church," named after Matthew Parker (1504-75) the first Elizabethan Archbishop of Canterbury, was established in 1840, and between 1841 and 1855 published the collected writings of the English reformers in fifty-four volumes.

Moreover, even as Evangelicalism in England began to struggle with the challenges presented by Tractarianism, its own character was changing. It lacked sufficient cultural insight into itself, and it was being more influenced by changes in the dominant culture than it realized—by cultural pessimism among conservatives confronting the rise of liberalism, and a hankering for a lost, pure, simple, and pre-industrial past that was such a central feature of Romanticism. Many of the settled understandings of historic Protestantism were now contested and set aside. This took place in three distinct areas. The first was the place (if any) of the charismatic gifts of the Spirit in the latter-day church. The second concerned the right response to apostasy as represented by Tractarianism—was secession the answer? The third concerned what is to be expected *prior* to the return of Christ—the Second Advent. What were the signs of the times? Were the alleged apostasy of the national church and presumed restoration of the *charismata*, or miraculous gifts of the Spirit, themselves signs of the times? In the British Isles, evangelicals were preoccupied with all three questions *before* questions of biological evolution and the critical-historical approach to biblical texts—often accompanied by a pronounced *theological* liberalism—also forced their way onto the agenda.

Historically, Protestantism had generally viewed the gifts of the Spirit as pertaining to the era of the apostles only, and to have *ceased* with the termination of the ministry of the twelve apostles, or possibly upon the demise of those who received the charismata during the apostolic era. This standpoint is now often referred to as *cessationism*. The term is regrettable and misleading, being discouragingly negative. Cessationism should *not* be misrepresented as disbelief in the Holy Spirit, and neither does it entail that Christians may no longer speak with prophetic prescience, nor does it amount to a disavowal of the miraculous. Generations of Protestants had taught that such charismata were rendered increasingly redundant since the consolidation of the New Testament canon, a process that was eventually recognized and ratified by the church at the time of the Council of Nicaea in 325. In this they had a number of the church fathers, including John Chrysostom (347-407), on their side. Some now repudiated this view emphatically.

Doctrinal clarification of questions relating to the Second Advent had not been a priority for the leaders of the Protestant Reformation, although many came to regard the Pope as the Antichrist. Later Protestantism, not least the Puritans and their admirers, had often been post-millennial in general orientation. The key issue hinges on the relationship between the return of Christ, the Second Advent, and the thousand years ("millennium") reign of Christ with his saints mentioned explicitly only in one passage in the highly symbolic Book of Revelation (Rev 20:1-6). In short, "post-millennialism" maintains that the return of Christ will take place *after* ("post-") the millennial era, whereas "premillennialism" holds that the return of Christ will take place before ("pre-") the millennial era. The "a-millennial" standpoint maintains that the millennium is not to be understood literally.

Moreover, a-millennialism favors a historically contextualized *preterist* interpretation of Revelation, in which the greater part of the book speaks specifically to its first century setting, and out of that context to succeeding generations. By contrast, premillennialism is *futurist* in its approach — projecting a more or less literal interpretation of the depicted apocalyptic scenes into the future. In the third and fourth decades of the nineteenth century, post-millennialism went into serious decline. Its place was taken by premillennialism. This latter approach, especially in its dispensational form, has over many generations drawn a significant proportion of evangelicals into seemingly endless speculations based on the assumption that pending events of contemporary history are presented in curiously veiled terms in the books of the Bible, particularly Daniel and Revelation.

Pentecostalism and Dispensationalism

The two men central to these momentous changes in evangelical thinking were Edward Irving (1792–1834), and John Nelson Darby (1800–82). Their influence has inserted a considerable doctrinal distance between many contemporary evangelicals and their Reformation roots. Irving was from Scotland and licensed to preach in the Church of Scotland. Darby was ordained into the ministry of the (Anglican) Church of Ireland in 1825. While Irving's light shone brightly but briefly, Darby was the one who gradually, and eventually massively, influenced Evangelicalism from the mid-nineteenth to mid-twentieth century. Thereafter, interest in Irving returned — especially with the further rise of Pentecostalism and the charismatic movement from the 1960s onwards. In a culture disturbed by the uprooting wrought by industrialization and revolution, both men longed to return to their notions of the "Golden Age" of pure faith and practice exemplified in the apostolic era. This longing was suffused with the feelings and sensibilities of Romanticism, in their case receiving a churchly focus. Purity and authenticity were to be achieved by putting the clock back.

Edward Irving was a product of the evangelical party in the Church of Scotland. He came to London in 1822. There he published *The Coming of the Messiah in Glory and Majesty* (1827)—a work purporting to be by one Juan Josafat Ben-Ezra, but in truth by a Jesuit priest named Manuel de Lacunza (1731–1801). In endorsing this work, Irving was advocating a version of premillennial thinking atypical of protestant eschatology up to the early nineteenth century. Nevertheless, he gained an influential disciple in Henry Drummond (1786–1860). In the later 1820s, Drummond organized a series of conferences at his Surrey residence, Albury Park, to explore the claims of premillennialism. Hugh McNeile moderated these discussions, and many influential evangelical leaders participated. Further conferences on prophecy and eschatology took place during the 1830s at Powerscourt in County Wicklow, Ireland.

In the context provided by his premillennialism, Irving became convinced that the now imminent "latter days" would be marked by a restoration of the charismata, or miraculous gifts, such as speaking in tongues and prophecy. Irving launched his premillennial opinions in Edinburgh in 1828. Thereafter, the novelty of his opinions and conduct worked against him. This was not immediately obvious to Irving. Certain of his followers in Scotland are said to have received the gift of tongues in 1830, which Irving certainly thought were actual human languages. In this circle the "baptism of the Holy Spirit" came to be distinguished from the impartation of spiritual life by the Holy Spirit in regeneration. On occasions, tongue-speaking reduced his congregation's public worship to something like anarchy. Eventually, Irving found himself displaced by those who exhibited the gifts. In due course, one Robert Baxter, an early recipient of the gifts, repudiated his earlier claims in his *Narrative of Facts* (1883). Through all of this, Irving's Christology remained highly problematic: he believed in the sinfulness of Christ's human nature. Irving was eventually deposed from the ministry of the Church of Scotland, and he lost the support of Hugh McNeile. Irving's followers eventually formed the Catholic Apostolic Church. After Irving's death, his reputation and the denomination itself lapsed into obscurity.

The Premillennial Dispensationalism of John Nelson Darby

John Nelson Darby acquired his premillennialism, and not least the notion of a "special rapture" of the saints, from the proto-Pentecostal charismatic circle associated with Irving. Darby became utterly disillusioned with the (Anglican) Church of Ireland; he saw Tractarianism as a portent of coming apostasy and came to view existing denominations as almost or actual apostate entities. Darby became part of the early Brethren movement, dating from 1830 (Dublin) and 1831 (Plymouth). His view of the church and sense of the deepening apostasy of existing Protestantism underpinned his eschatology. The assemblies established by the founders of the Brethren were for those "coming out" of the allegedly apostate churches. Darby did not found this movement, but he left a profound mark upon it, contributing not a little to its distinctive style of divisiveness, as his subsequent controversy with Benjamin Wills Newton (1807–99) made clear. Darby traveled widely—as if to emulate Zinzendorf—on the European continent as well as to North America, assiduously disseminating his particular version of premillennialism, known as *dispensationalism*.

Darby's dispensationalist version of premillennialism was based on a novel way of reading the Bible. While it purportedly endorsed the conventional grammatico-historical method of interpreting Scripture, it brought to this task a rigorous literalism. The Bible was regarded as always plain, and a plain interpretation was therefore always called for, and for him that always meant a literal interpretation. Even prophetic language was to be interpreted literally—including passages of high symbolism. This approach resulted in a highly contestable division between Israel and the Church of the New Testament. Different terminology, it was held, *must* represent different entities and realities. There was no place here for idiom or nuance. Under this impulse some have sought to contrast "the kingdom of heaven" in Matthew with "the kingdom of God" in Luke. On the basis of its literalism a succession of "dispensations" was discerned in Scripture whereby God relates successively to humankind on one distinct basis after another—hence "dispensations." Without this supposed insight, it was confidently asserted that the Scriptures cannot be "rightly divided" (2 Tim 2:15).

It is not unknown for latter-day dispensationalists to insinuate that those who do not adopt their literalist interpretative standpoint are not taking the Bible seriously and might not be true believers. While dispensationalists are confident that they have studied the Bible with the most scrupulous care, the prior question concerns the assumptions that they have brought to their studies. The dispensational outlook has become entrenched among a large proportion of evangelicals for well over a century. Once formulated and absorbed, its findings are experienced as self-ratifying by its committed advocates. Darby posited that the promises made to Israel in the Old Testament were *not* fulfilled in the New Testament church (as the Reformers had taught), but remained unfulfilled and therefore still awaited a literal and physical fulfillment. Moreover, he asserted that the Christian church was a "mystery parenthesis," only brought about by the Jewish rejection of the Messiah. The kingdom of God was in effect postponed as a result of this rejection. The present "church age"—supposedly unanticipated in the Old Testament—will be concluded at the time of the "rapture" when Christ will return and collect his true church and take them to heaven, which Darby understood in ethereal terms.

According to dispensationalists, this event will be secret. Only authentic Christians will experience it—those "left behind" will simply discern that "true believers" were now missing. This "secret rapture" would be followed by a seven-year "great tribulation." It is only in this immensely traumatic period that a remnant of the "true Israel" receives the gospel of the Kingdom, thereby leading to the actual millennial reign of Christ over a Jewish kingdom ("the kingdom of God") in Jerusalem. In dispensationalism, *this* will be the fulfillment of Old Testament prophecy, *not* the incarnation, ministry, death, resurrection and ascension of Jesus Christ and the empowering of his people to preach the good news of the coming of his kingdom. On the contrary, the dispensationalist anticipates an eventual "coming of the kingdom" in anachronistically Davidic terms, even to the restoration of the temple with a functioning sacrificial system. This dispensationalist version of premillennialism contemplates *two* peoples of God—a gentile church of the redeemed dwelling in an ethereal heaven and a restored Israel dwelling in material prosperity on earth.

The passage on which the dispensationalist "secret rapture" doctrine is based on is 1 Thessalonians 4:16-17, which speaks of the appearing (*parousia*) of Christ. The two groups being considered by Paul in this passage are (1) believers who have died "in Christ" and (2) believers who are living on earth at the time of Christ's return. For many centuries Christians had understood this passage in these terms. However, dispensationalism places immense weight on its gloss on the words "caught up" (Latin: *raptura*, meaning "carried away"), asserting that Christ does not actually return to earth, but takes them ("raptures them") to heaven, leaving everyone else to face the great tribulation.

The ramifications of this dualistic outlook have been extensive. Evangelicals who have this thinking as part of their mental furniture can be surprised to learn that prior to the mid-nineteenth century most Protestants did not think this way at all. If they thought of a millennium at all, they were inclined to a general post-millennialism, positively anticipating a growing dissemination and understanding of the gospel across the face of the earth, although never without opposition. This broad post-millennialism had reflected and nurtured a steady optimism. However, in spite of its growth and achievements, the evangelical movement came to sense a certain enfeeblement by around the 1840s. Its conservatism made it uncomfortable with cultural change, even as industrialization and urbanization had an increasing impact on nineteenth-century Great Britain. Even though many evangelicals worked for a wide variety of improving causes, the prevalence of wickedness of one sort or another did not seem to abate, and there developed an inclination to shun the challenges of the temporal by focusing on the eternal as anticipated by the "last things."

The ramifications have been serious. Millions of evangelicals (although definitely not all) have given up on creation and culture. Their prime focus is not on being faithful servants of Jesus Christ in every area of life, but on being "rapture ready." If necessary, "prophetic clocks" will be devised, started, stopped, and re-started, as required to make the system work, as the immense dispensationalist literature on Daniel 9:24–27 makes clear. Popular premillennial dispensationalist writing is strewn with false predictions of the pending date of "the rapture." The media noise made by those concerned, coupled with the repeated confounding of prediction after prediction, serves to provide the secular and skeptical media of the western world—and the biblically illiterate masses they influence—with ready-made excuses not to take the Christian message seriously.

Struggles in England

In 1836 English evangelicals set up the Church Pastoral Aid Society (CPAS). The CPAS sought to guarantee a lasting place for evangelicals within the Anglican parish network, especially in the new urban and industrial areas, by acquiring the patronage rights in selected parishes and thereby ensuring the appointment of evangelical clergy.

However, tendencies within Evangelicalism towards other-worldliness, and their "intellectual-deficit" generally, disadvantaged evangelicals seriously when it came to grappling with that whole nexus of socio-economic issues raised by debates on the condition of England. The strong orientation of evangelicals towards feeling, their deep-seated conservatism, and their general wariness of culture and theory, increasingly took their toll. They could be prodigiously active, but in the nineteenth century the tide was running against them. The evangelical William Goode (1801–68) cogently challenged the assertions and policies of the Anglo-Catholic disciples of the Tractarians, but it was of no avail. Although evangelicals might win these literary altercations with Anglo-Catholics—even court cases on occasions—they found themselves unable to stem the growth of the movement. Evangelicals had presumed that the Church of England was in some sense "theirs"—but that presumption was now powerfully contested.

It is noteworthy that at this time among the evangelical leadership in the Church of England, not least amongst the "Recordites," (who were deeply conservative in church and state), there were those who, having *rejected* Irving's deviations and Darby's ecclesiology, nevertheless tended to move towards a generally premillennial viewpoint. This viewpoint was congruent with an increasing sense of cultural pessimism. The tendency to see humanly wrought cultural change as religiously neutral—provided moral precepts were not contravened—strongly inhibited the attainment of what was unquestionably required: biblically directed insight into the religious impulses directing and animating the emergence of modern society. Intense activism and good intentions could not negate the consequences of shallow understanding and a lack of structural insight.

Evangelical conversion could certainly impart a sense of responsibility and diligence where once there had been lassitude and indolence. Indeed, at one level it might be said that the evangelical successors of Whitefield and the Wesley brothers changed the *face* of Great Britain—but ultimately they did little to change the *religious direction* being taken by British culture. Evangelicalism might endue men and women with a deep sense of duty, but "doing one's duty" alone is insufficient. It can represent a failure to be Christianly distinct. For example, in the great expansion of popular education that took place in later nineteenth-century Great Britain, there were many evangelicals who high-mindedly swelled the ranks of the teachers. However, there is little evidence that they taught the curriculum with any sense of *the importance of a biblically directed starting-point* for their instruction in either the arts or the sciences. All the diligence with which they might encourage Bible study stood to be seriously undermined by the rationalistic and materialistic assumptions with which almost everything else was increasingly taught. Commitment and probity, combined with a high sense of duty, could not overcome the intellectual deficit.

The Disruption in Scotland

If any body of informed Christians in Great Britain exhibited both spiritual and intellectual stamina, it was the Scots. In Scotland, however, old issues of high principle were to rend the church asunder in a conflict between the presumed rights of patronage and the responsibilities of congregations to elect their office-bearers. Here we may detect echoes of the Erastus-Withers controversy in Heidelberg centuries earlier. Patronage had been restored in Scotland by the Stuarts in 1660, abolished in 1690 after the Glorious Revolution and reimposed under the terms of the Church Patronage (Scotland) Act of 1711. The Church of Scotland entered a ten years conflict period in 1834. The issue was patronage, which the majority evangelical party in the General Assembly had sought to negate by passing the Veto Act of 1834. In other words, in Scotland the evangelicals, led by Thomas Chalmers (1780-1847) and Robert Smith Candlish (1806-73), stood for the rights and responsibilities of the congregation to appoint a minister, over against the intrusion of an appointee by a patron.

The issues were brought to a head by the Auchterarder case of 1834. When the (civil *not ecclesiastical*) Court of Session upheld the case of the patron's appointee, sharply contradicting the national kirk's self-understanding as enshrined in the Westminster Standards, the scene was set for a raft of complex jurisdictional situations that many Presbyterians found constitutionally intolerable and even more burdensome spiritually. The rejection of the Scottish evangelical *Claim, Declaration and Protest* by the British parliament was the prelude to the "great disruption," which finally came on May 18, 1843, when the evangelical party, having now lost its majority in the General Assembly, physically quit that body and established the Free Church of Scotland. The signing of the *Act of Separation* and *Deed of Demission* by the founders of the Free Church is memorialized in the famous painting by David Octavius Hill (1802-70).

The Free Church did not repudiate the establishment principle and the idea of a national church, but it did reject the argument that these *necessarily* entailed ecclesiastical subordination to the national legislature in matters the church deemed to be of spiritual import. The leaders of the Free Church included men of exceptional caliber, such as William Cunningham (1805-61), James Bannerman (1807-68), and James Buchanan (1804-70), and the geologist Hugh Miller (1802-56). In later years the tone changed as this generation passed and Robert Rainy (1826-1906) asserted his leadership. One of his objectives was a union with the descendants of earlier secession churches. Also, it should not be forgotten that following the disruption a substantial number of evangelicals remained *within* the Church of Scotland.

The "Church of Scotland Evangelical Network" represents their contemporary successors. Lay patronage was finally abolished by the Church Patronage (Scotland) Act of 1874. The union of Free Church and other secession churches was accomplished by the formation of the United Free Church of Scotland in 1900. The latter was reunited with the Church of Scotland in 1929. However, a minority of Free Church folk remained stalwart, and when they lost their extensive property claims in the Court of Sessions, they appealed to the House of Lords in Westminster, which in 1904 reversed the lower court decision in favor of the continuing body.

A Massive Expansion in the New World

Almost all of the formative features of Evangelicalism in North America may be traced to the British Isles—including a strong tendency towards denominational multiplication. However, in the USA, these influences from the old world interacted and re-combined in new ways, and the consequences were made apparent on a scale that was vast in comparison with the narrow confines of the British Isles. Before 1776, Congregationalism (especially in New England), Presbyterianism, and Anglicanism were pre-eminent in colonial church life. The majority of the leaders on the colonial side of the war of independence were deists rather than evangelicals. George Washington was a deist and a Freemason. That said, most evangelicals in the former colonies supported, or at least accepted, the outcome of the conflict.

After 1789 the Baptists and Methodists came to the fore in the USA. The Wesleyan style Arminianism of the perpetually revival-minded Methodists influenced all denominational traditions during the course of the nineteenth century, not excluding the Presbyterians. In the USA, the Methodist Episcopal Church was founded in 1784 by Thomas Coke (1747–1814) and was pioneered by perhaps the greatest circuit rider of all time, Francis Asbury (1745–1816). They launched *The Arminian Magazine* in America in 1789. The individualism of the Baptists and the belief in human autonomy tacitly presupposed by the Wesleyan version of Arminianism was so pervasive that it set the tone of American public life and culture. The *polity* of the USA might be of Presbyterian structure—with its greater and lesser legislative bodies—but its *ethos* of self-help and individual achievement was Arminian to the core. These tendencies were to put Presbyterianism in the shade and almost eclipsed the Anglicans, who were now referred to as Episcopalians.

In the USA the volatility inherent in the revivalist *modus operandi*— which its advocates could always represent as a spiritual virtue—merged with the fluidity and tension of the ever-moving western frontier. The stabilizing tendencies of protestant denominational confessionalism (especially among Presbyterians committed to the Westminster Standards) were likely to come into conflict with the emotive fervor increasingly characteristic of revivalism. In the wake of the Great Awakening and the effective assertion of national independence, these forces were to contend for dominance within American Protestantism. It was in such a context that the spiritual successors of Jonathan Edwards—represented by figures such as Joseph Bellamy (1719-90), Samuel Hopkins (1721-1803) and Timothy Dwight (1752-1817)—strove to set the tone. This school deserves careful attention. In the tradition of Edwards, it aspired to uphold the priority of grace and also to facilitate Calvinistic participation in revivalist endeavors. It feared spiritual deadness and viewed shallow notions of conversion with deep apprehension. It sought to address the concerns already present in the reflections of Edwards. These were not limited to "old lights" of the Charles Chauncy (1705-87) variety, which shaded off into Unitarianism, but included the reservations of those who advocated a more church oriented and confessionalist stance, such as Ezra Styles (1727-95), Moses Mather (1719-1806), and later William Sprague (1795-1876) and John Williamson Nevin (1803-86). The early nineteenth century in the northern USA witnessed an array of leaders—among them Edward Griffin (1770-1837), Edward Payson (1783-1827), Asahel Nettleton (1783-1843), Bennet Tyler (1783-1858), and Gardiner Spring (1785-1873)—who certainly did not see themselves as enemies of authentic renewal, but who were strongly disposed to question the methods and results of "revivalism."

Yet the future was not to be with these men, but with extreme "new lights," willing to castigate those who did not surrender to their revivalist proclivities—an outlook already typified by men such as the zealous David Brainerd (1718-47) and the somewhat unstable James Davenport (1716-57). Congregationalism was divided along the lines represented by Bennet Tyler and Nathaniel Taylor (1786-1858). Presbyterianism was also fractured; Gilbert Tennent's *On the Danger of an Unconverted Ministry* (1740) had heralded an early division between "old school" and "new school" streams. Many leaders—particularly those associated with Princeton Seminary—such as Archibald Alexander (1772-1851) and Ashbel Green (1762-1848), found themselves participating in, and more especially responding critically to, the so-called Second Great Awakening movements running from about 1792 to 1825. At this time of massive growth, the "old school" was overshadowed by the advocates and exponents of "new measures," which were used to manipulate hearers (not least by playing upon their emotions) so as to engender their positive response to the message. A buoyant "Yankee know-how" set the pace.

These techniques were based upon a set of prior assumptions: that receiving and believing the gospel is a *human decision* that does not require a prior work of the Holy Spirit. The older teaching had been clear: humankind was dependent on a prior work of the Holy Spirit if men and women were ever to "repent and believe" the gospel in a genuine way. Those who are spiritually dead cannot spiritually self-regenerate (Eph 2:1-10). The teaching of Paul, that humankind is *entirely dependent* on the grace of God, also in its repenting, was now increasingly obscured. How was it that this central insight into the human condition became seriously obscured and came to be replaced by what has been called decisionism—the idea that "you can now decide for Christ" unaided? The answer is that this decisionism became the central evangelistic technique of evangelical *revivalism*; it arose from the failure of Evangelicalism to contemplate the actual human condition from a biblically directed standpoint. Inadequate insight and pragmatic opportunism functioned in combination.

How did this transpire? It is not wholly explained by the influence of Wesleyan style Arminianism across America. It simply will not do to blame everything on John Wesley. Arguably, this tendency lay implicit in the entire revivalist *modus operandi*. In this respect it may be traced also in some measure to Jonathan Edwards, who for all his caution, struggled to persuade himself and others that his commitment to the Awakening was compatible with his version of Calvinism. Through the writings of Andrew Fuller (1754-1815), the stance of Edwards came to influence Baptists on both sides of the Atlantic. Edwards's successors in New England amplified and developed the distinction he had already made between a presumed natural ability to repent and a moral incapacity to do so. By the time we are confronted with the full teachings of Nathaniel Taylor, the initial dichotomy between "natural" and "moral" is made sufficiently pliable to open the way to an Evangelicalism that overtly assumed *human autonomy*, rather than the Reformation understanding of human bondage to sin and dependence on the grace of God. Folks might now "help themselves" to salvation. The problem with Edwards's initial distinction arose from the legacy of scholasticism as it permeated his understanding of man and salvation. It impeded any contrary tendency in his thinking to adopt a biblically directed standpoint towards the contemporary philosophical writers from whom he sought stimulus and insight.

A further consideration is that from the later eighteenth century onwards, the Scottish school of common sense philosophy became the assumed frame of reference for North American Protestantism. The Scotsmen

Thomas Reid (1710-96) and Dugald Stewart (1753-1828) developed this philosophy in response to the skepticism of David Hume (1711-76). It accorded well with the outlook of Francis Bacon and was advocated by Thomas Witherspoon (1723-94) when he was President of the College of New Jersey. This common sense philosophy posited that all adult humans, when sane and sober, had been endowed with a *common sense* of reality, irrespective of their operative religious standpoint. In a result wholly unintended by Reid—who was no evangelical Christian—this philosophical outlook in the thinking of Edwards's successors facilitated the magnification of humankind's supposed natural capacities, while it mitigated against what Edwards had insisted was humankind's moral incapacity (unless facilitated by the Holy Spirit) to repent and believe the gospel.

Of course, it is not improper to distinguish between humankind having been created to reflect, represent, and enjoy communion with its Creator, and its fallen state of being at enmity with its Creator and living in willful disobedience. Problems do arise when these two are improperly held apart and understood as being tied to supposed distinctions between "natural" and "moral" capacities that originate in dualistic anthropologies, not rooted in a biblical view of man. This kind of thinking failed to realize the radical centrality of the human heart in the biblical picture. In the Bible, our obedient or disobedient response to the Word of God always proceeds from the heart, *which is radically central*. The heart is not to be reduced to a reference point for conscious emotions. Confusions notwithstanding, the discipleship commended in Scripture always tends towards whole*heart*edness.

Nathaniel Taylor and his associates were pivotal figures in legitimizing the kind of Evangelicalism that came to dominate in the twentieth century. The reality is that those of Jonathan Edwards's mind, who had sought to marry their notion of Calvinism with that of revival, were never in command of the situation. They have been the slowest ships at the rear of the evangelical convoy. In the vanguard in America the Methodists, with their Arminian type Wesleyan understanding of man and the gospel, set the pace and determined the direction. Alongside the Methodists were the Baptists, with their strongly individualistic orientation. The more other denominations sought to catch up, the more they found their classical emphases compromised.

Accordingly, during the course of the nineteenth century, the road was opened to the development and utilization of the extensive array of sensate and manipulative techniques that we have come to associate with *revivalism*. These "new measures," as they were called, included the "altar call," the "anxious seat," and protracted, pressured "gospel appeals"—all of which may be seen as presuming to usurp the office of the Holy Spirit in drawing people to Christ. These practices arose and gained widespread acceptance because Evangelicalism—thanks to the combined legacies of protestant scholasticism and the Wesleyan version of Arminianism—had come to accept a view of man that had lost sight of the biblical teaching that as creatures we are *wholly dependent on our Creator*. Thus it was that Evangelicalism wove into the fabric of its life and practices the presumption of human autonomy to a degree that made salvation itself contingent upon human volition.

In the South, events in the Kentucky-Tennessee region, especially as exemplified by the Cane Ridge Revival (1801), anticipated the direction taken by Evangelicalism in the nineteenth century. Here the "camp meeting" came to the fore, and tendencies towards sheer emotionalism were much more fully manifested than previously. Eventually even the Calvinistic Presbyterianism of the Westminster Standards, in the giddy exuberance of revivalist excess, could morph into the declared Arminianism of the Cumberland Presbyterian Church. The Disciples of Christ, founded by Alexander Campbell (1788-1866), also have their roots in this period. At Cane Ridge, the Wesleyan preacher Peter Cartwright (1785-1872) stands as the representative figure. In the camp meeting setting he exploited the altar call technique relentlessly. Such Methodists had no compunction over the new measures—which were wholly compatible with their Arminian anthropology—although they were liable to be challenged in Presbyterian and Congregationalist settings where something of the older Calvinistic understanding still held sway. The net result was that revivalism was much more likely to divide traditions with roots closer to the Reformation than the Wesleyans themselves. From these developments the Churches of Christ in North America and Australia are derived. They were "restorationist" in that they purported to restore apostolic practice and resisted creedal statements as post-apostolic and divisive.

The life and teaching of Charles Grandison Finney (1792-1875) signaled a further step down the revivalist route to opportunist manipulation. Even though Finney was ostensibly a Presbyterian, his teaching, definitively stated in his *Lectures on Revivals of Religion* (1835 and extensively reprinted) exhibited a deep-seated Arminianism, profoundly in tune with the self-help individualism that was coming to dominate American culture. His sermon "Make Yourselves a New Heart," given at Boston in 1831, exemplified the tendency. Finney was in no way an unlettered enthusiast from the back blocks. He knew what he was doing. He articulated his standpoint in his *Systematic Theology* (1847-8). His gospel presumed, and was pitched to, supposedly autonomous man—the master of his own destiny. For Finney, revival is not a time of renewal granted by the Holy Spirit, so much as something to be consciously and deliberately generated and promoted by an array of techniques and methods. Finney was deliberate and informed, drawing maximally on Edwards's notion of natural ability, as expanded by Taylor, in order to articulate a profoundly Arminian position that bordered on the ancient error of Pelagianism.

Across America there are numerous Christians who have not given in to the distortions and outright heresies that have grown up around them. Yet we must recognize that the American spirit, with its entrepreneurial inventiveness and abounding *self*-confidence has proved fecund in the production of clear departures from the historic Christian faith. From the USA have come Mormonism and the Jehovah's Witnesses. These are both well beyond the evangelical pale. The Seventh Day Adventists, with their roots in evangelical millennialism, are much closer. These entities arose out of the same fermenting instability that pervades much of American Evangelicalism. Wisdom is required. It would be wrong to say that "no good thing can come from America" or to deny that the old world has its share of error, but as each new teaching, or technique, or scheme emanates from the USA, and is promoted globally, Christians across the rest of the world should proceed with discernment and an abundance of caution.

In 1838 controversy over innovations split American Presbyterians into "new school" and "old school" entities. These were not to be reunited again until 1871. The thinking and example of Finney became highly influential. His influence spread to the British Isles. In America, the renowned preacher Lyman Beecher (1775–1863) was inclined towards the new measures and broke with Tyler and Nettleton as a consequence. The second quarter of the nineteenth century saw the emergence of an increasingly pragmatic and populist Evangelicalism of Arminian orientation. The prodigious activism of large numbers of evangelists and churches ensured that an Evangelicalism of this complexion became the default Christianity of the American people. Mention Christianity to the average non-Catholic, non-Orthodox American, and it is this kind of Evangelicalism that automatically comes to mind.

In matters of institutional church polity, American evangelicals typically interpreted the Bible in terms of a mix of the regulative and exemplary standpoints. These approaches could not, however, resolve the issue of slavery, which drew the nation into civil war in 1861, ostensibly on the question of states' rights. The regulative and exemplary approaches to Scripture could be used to justify slavery, as was done in the South. The survival and triumph of the Union under Abraham Lincoln (1809–65) consolidated the immense internal strength that was to emerge in the twentieth century as the American superpower, whose wealthy middle-class evangelicals, especially their millionaire businessmen cohort, were to shape and dominate

English-speaking Evangelicalism worldwide. This process was discernibly underway in the concluding decades of the nineteenth century. American wealth was supremely important in the process, as was the spiritual exhaustion of Great Britain in the wake of the Great War.

8

EVANGELICALISM WRESTLES WITH LIBERALISM

An Array of Multiple Challenges

Evangelicalism was always a house divided. As the nineteenth century unfolded, Evangelicalism manifested itself not simply as a house divided, but as a multiplicity of divided houses. Organizations such as the Evangelical Alliance (founded 1846) strove to attain mutual understanding and acceptance among evangelicals—although by this stage, slavery could be an issue between the British and some of their American brethren. From this point onwards, the priorities expressed by Bebbington's quadrilateral were to prove increasingly inadequate. In addition, at this juncture the initiative within English-speaking Evangelicalism passed to the New World, as the USA emerged as a power of trans-continental proportions following the Louisiana Purchase (1803). This made available a vast area for revivalist evangelical enterprise and experimentation as Evangelicalism in all its diversity expanded across North America.

Yet by 1900, Evangelicalism was fighting to retain the initiative in many areas and had lost it in many others, especially in Great Britain. These mounting difficulties may be attributed to what we have called its intellectual deficit, as manifested in its increasingly diffident attitude towards public culture and scientific thought. In Great Britain these challenges were fourfold. Firstly, there was the massive urbanization and industrialization of life from the 1830s onwards. Large numbers, moving from an over-populated countryside into the burgeoning urban-industrial concentrations, lost contact with the rural parish church system to which their forebears had been bound for centuries. In England both Established Church and Dissenting Chapel were poorly equipped in the face of such massive socio-economic changes. The 1851 census of England and Wales greatly shocked respectable opinion by showing how many of those drawn into the new cities were living without any active churchly affiliation. Christianity had lost effective contact with the greater proportion of the laboring masses in the great new industrial centers. The contemporary secularization of British life is no new phenomenon—it has been centuries in the making.

Secondly, there was the lasting impact of the Oxford Movement. While certain of the Tractarians, such as Manning and Newman, eventually became Roman Catholics, many remained within the Church of England, to form a new kind of Ritualist party, offering teaching and conducting worship as if the Reformation had hardly happened at all. Some sort of clash between this party and evangelicals was seemingly inevitable, and the Gorham Case of 1847–50 provided a *cause célèbre*. After protracted judicial-procedural convolutions the evangelical clergyman George C. Gorham (1787–1857) triumphed over his High Church enemies, but not before he and his supporters were obliged to take the matter to the Judicial Committee of the Privy Council. The latter is not a specifically ecclesiastical body, and it is significant that in this case the evangelical position could only be upheld by resorting to mechanisms reflective of the state control of the Church of England. Subsequent evangelical attempts to prosecute Ritualists (now often termed Anglo-Catholics) for ecclesiastical delinquency backfired. Evangelicals might win specific arguments, but they found themselves losing within the established church.

Thirdly, in 1859, Charles Darwin (1809–82) and Alfred R. Wallace (1823–1913) made public their theories concerning "the evolution of species by natural selection." Their theories did not arise, as some later evangelicals have imagined, from a purposeful intention to destroy the Christian religion. Their work arose out of meticulous observations in the field and from explanatory inadequacies present in contemporaneous notions of design. Certainly, by the mid-nineteenth century many thoughtful readers of the Bible no longer accepted the view that the earth was only some six to ten thousand years old. Initially, better-informed Evangelicals were not ready to categorically repudiate Darwin's *Origin of Species* (1859). The later story might have been very different if figures such as Thomas H. Huxley (1825–95) and later Herbert Spencer (1820–1903) had not succeeded in appropriating and utilizing Darwin's propositions as evolution*ism*, and as a presumed justification of their own agnosticism. Of course, evangelical discomfort levels did increase with the later appearance of Darwin's *Descent of Man* (1871), but the real strife was to come decades later as evangelicals became even more literalist in their readings of Scripture and fundamentalist in outlook, under the twin pressures of dispensationalist hermeneutics and the challenges represented by the critical-historical analysis of the biblical texts.

The Challenge of Critical-historical Scholarship

This fourth challenge—the critical-historical analysis of biblical texts—was the most problematic development for evangelicals. Simultaneously, it addressed "their" Bible in ways that challenged their tendencies towards decontextualized literalism and repeatedly exposed their intellectual deficit. There were certainly early harbingers of this development—in Benedict Spinoza's (1632–77) protests against (Christian) scholasticism and in the writings of Richard Simon (1638–1712). Somewhat later, the Frenchman Jean Astruc (1684–1766), in his analysis of Genesis, argued that the use of different divine names indicated multiple underlying sources. The great change came with *the rise of historical consciousness* that took place in Europe from the later eighteenth century onwards. As discussed by Friedrich Meinecke (1862–1954), this movement achieved its most scholarly articulation in the state universities of German-speaking Protestantism. Here the intense studies of the Hebrew and cognate texts by Edouard G. E. Reuss (1804–91), Karl Heinrich Graf (1815–69) and Julius Wellhausen (1844–1918) resulted in views of the sources, composition, and dating of the Old Testament narrative books that seemed to shatter traditional views of their reliability and trustworthiness.

The Reformation advocacy of an open Bible resulted in a Bible wide open to investigation by all. Whatever else may be said, in the first instance the critical-historical analysis of biblical texts arose in response to the issues raised *within* the texts themselves. At the same time, the Old Testament positively invites historical analysis as it draws us into its storytelling. The immense difficulty with the critical-historical method was *not* intrinsic to the critical-historical method *as such*, but with the wholly naturalistic *philosophical starting-point* utilized by many of its leading practitioners. This Enlightenment-derived stance inevitably resulted in a construing of narratives and other texts not as divine revelation, but as merely the record of the developing religious consciousness towards monotheism of an ancient Semitic people. Conclusions of this order were not derived *from* the texts.

They were *read into* the texts thanks to the Enlightenment-derived, liberal starting-point adopted at the outset by such interpreters.

In this context the "Graf-Wellhausen hypothesis" concerning the multiple sources and relatively late date of the Pentateuch became widely influential. Although the hypothesis was challenged in the twentieth century by authorities such as Moshe David Cassuto (1883–1951) and Roger N. Whybray (1923–97), it is now generally recognized that there is sufficient evidence of multiple authorship and redactor activity to render the traditionalist view of exclusive Mosaic authorship untenable.

For many evangelicals the implications of the critical-historical approach were shattering. The application of its philological and textual techniques applied not only to the entire Old Testament but also to the New Testament. Here the process gained momentum with the work of Johann Jakob Griesbach (1745–1812) on the relationship between the synoptic gospels. Later, Ferdinand Christian Baur (1792–1860), founder of the Tübingen School, influenced by Georg Wilhelm Friedrich Hegel (1770–1831), posited a Christianity arising from the dialectical interaction of Jewish and Pauline standpoints. The ultimate challenge came in the work of Baur's disciple David Friedrich Strauss (1808–74), whose *Life of Jesus Critically Examined* (1835) was repudiated by the Hegelians and anathematized by the conservatives. Strauss combined detailed textual analysis with a relentless, rationalistic skepticism. His tendentious *Life of Jesus* was translated and published in English by the novelist George Eliot (1819–80) in 1846, but generally the penetration of such "advanced" German ideas in the English-speaking world was still relatively slow at the mid-point of the nineteenth century.

Only by about 1890 in the British Isles and by around 1920 at the latest in North America had educated opinion generally come to the conclusion that the conventional evangelical understanding of the Bible was now seriously discredited. This seemed to be confirmed by the scholarship of Hebraists such as Samuel Rolles Driver (1846–1914) and those who followed in their wake, such as Arthur Samuel Peake (1865–1929). By the 1920s, many evangelicals were perilously close to repudiating intellectual integrity in the name of faith, while Modernists (as they came to be called) were at, or over, the brink of repudiating the faith in the name of intellectual integrity and the presumed "assured results" of critical-historical analysis. Evangelicalism's fear of modernism reinforced and entrenched its conservative and static views of Scripture that by the end of the decade was widely known as fundamentalism.

Although in the nineteenth century this Anglo-American "fundamentalist (or conservative) versus modernist" confrontation was not yet so sharply drawn, a large proportion of German-speaking Protestants adopted positions consonant with an enlightenment-derived, liberal starting-point. Initially with Friedrich D. E. Schleiermacher's (1768–1834) *On Religion: Speeches to its Cultured Despisers* (1799), and continuing in the work of theologians such as Johan Gottfried Eichhorn (1752–1827), Wilhelm Gesenius (1786–1842), Heinrich Ewald (1803–75), Johannes Weiss (1863–1914), Johann Wilhelm Herrmann (1846–1922), Adolf von Harnack (1851–1930), and Hermann Gunkel (1862–1932), a reconstructed theology was offered that in terms of historic Christian belief was no gospel at all. Ernst Troeltsch (1865–1923) wrestled inconclusively with the relativizing and leveling implications of *Historismus*, which after the Great War were viewed by many as intractably problematic.

However, the misappropriations of the historical outlook occasioned by the adoption of a rationalistic and naturalistic *religious* starting-point by theological liberalism should not blind us to the truth that the Bible is profoundly historical in outlook. In the Bible, the Exodus narrative itself displaces any cyclical view of reality and orients us towards a linear view of the historical process, characterized by *unfolding covenantal promises*, notwithstanding judgments, trials, and tribulations. Under such circumstances it ought not to surprise us if many an Old Testament text provides evidence of the handiwork of redactors and editors—indeed, it would be much more surprising, even suspicious, if such evidence were absent. The apostles were deeply historical in their outlook. Without question, and however immediate their eschatological expectations may have been initially, the birth, death, resurrection, and ascension of Jesus the Messiah were understood by them as not only incapable of repetition but as changing the very texture of reality and pointing to the eventual and complete realization of the divine purpose. This is not a static vision, and certainly not oriented towards some past Golden Age. In the post-Apostolic centuries, the dynamic of a coming of the kingdom was lost sight of. The institutional church supposedly "unchanged and unchanging" emerged as an alternative. This development may be attributed, at least partly, to the infusion of Platonic and Hellenistic a-historical thinking, which obscured the importance of the Old Testament's view of creation and historical change shaped by the unfolding purposes of a covenant-keeping God.

The commitment of the Reformation to *Sola Scriptura* ought to have driven Protestantism to a genuinely historical study of the biblical texts. However, such a development was undermined by the early reversion to static and a-historically fixed presentations of doctrinal truth based on the *philosophia aristotelico-scholastica*. This scholasticism, with its orientation towards logically honed static symmetry, was never entirely absent from the mental furniture of the Reformers and, as has been discussed, became dominant in the seventeenth century. Much evangelical doctrinal understanding has amounted to a distillation and simplification of that a-historical, theological schematization. Evangelicalism, therefore, was temperamentally indisposed to address the questions that inevitably arose with the profound deepening of the European (and especially German) historical consciousness during the eighteenth and nineteenth centuries. This "historical movement" arose as an antithetical response to earlier theological scholasticism and the rational system-building of the Enlightenment philosophers. It had little concern for the abstract and universal and focused intensely on the individual, the concrete, and the particular. In biblical studies, dating, context, sources and provenance emerged as prime concerns.

Moreover, when the critical-historical movement impacted biblical studies—as it did from the outset—evangelicals were prone to be last in considering the implications when they should have been first. In the so-called Quest for the Historical Jesus, from Herman Samuel Reimarus (1694–1768) to Georg Friedrich Eduard William Wrede (1859–1906)—as considered by Albert Schweitzer (1875–1965), and the subsequent New Quest enunciated by Ernst Käsemann (1906–98) in 1956,[1] evangelical Christians should have been conspicuous at the forefront of the discussion. They were not. Great opportunities were missed. Their intellectual deficit and general fear of scholarship well into the twentieth century resulted in all too many evangelicals indulging in obscurantism in the name of faith, evading or misrepresenting the questions, using the outlandishness of some writers to dismiss the entire project, or pronouncing dogmatic anathemas from the sidelines.

In German Protestantism, Friedrich Wilhelm Krummacher (1796–1868) maintained a pre-critical pietism, Ernst Wilhelm Hengstenberg (1802–69) withstood the tide, and somewhat later Carl Friedrich Keil (1807–88) and Franz Delitzsch (1813–90) produced a commentary on the Old Testament that, although now dated, exemplified what should have been obvious: that competent scholarship was not synonymous with the adoption of an Enlightenment-rationalistic starting-point. Yet it must be acknowledged that in the English-speaking world the critical-historical movement, with its intense commitment to textual analysis, outmatched what the average evangelical preacher could offer, and what the average congregation

---

1. Schweitzer, *The Quest of the Historical Jesus*; Robinson, *A New Quest for the Historical Jesus*.

could immediately absorb. As a straightforward appeal to Scripture was now no longer—at least in the case of the educated—straightforward, these challenges threw into stark relief the weaknesses arising from the intellectual deficit.

In Great Britain there was no way this expanding body of reflection would stay under wraps, and the implications became apparent with the publication of *Essays and Reviews* (1860). The contributors were the spiritual descendants of the latitudinarians, and the collection was highly influential, for decades outselling Darwin's *Origin of Species*. Furthermore, *Essays and Reviews* included a contribution on the ancient near-eastern cosmology as exhibited in the book of Genesis, thereby confirming the connection between the critical-historical analysis of Scripture and the question of the origins and antiquity of man. These issues arose in the area where "heart over head" Evangelicalism proved all too weak; in fields where extra-biblical evidence, requiring philosophical awareness and scientific scrupulousness for their analysis, now increased its challenges to traditional evangelical interpretations of Scripture. That this was no transient episode was promptly confirmed in the writings of the redoubtable John William Colenso (1814–83), the Anglican Bishop of Natal, whose *Critical Examination of the Pentateuch* (1862 onwards) made telling use of the circumstantial inconsistencies and numerical difficulties of the extant texts.

The Rise of Holiness Movements

Evangelicalism, however, continued on its path, even as it seemed that the ground beneath it was giving way. The events surrounding the Businessman's Revival of 1857–8 in New York, and the 1859 Ulster Revival, which spread to other parts of the British Isles, brought many into the Christian fold. Strong revivalist fervor was exhibited among the armies of the Confederacy during the American Civil War—not that this seems to have induced any significant repentance concerning the injustices and cruelties attaching to the "peculiar institution" of slavery. As it was, the eventual triumph of the North represented not only the victory of progress and capitalism over slavery, but for the time being over the forces of conservatism to which many evangelicals were attached. However, while the North won the war by weight of men and material, much of the subsequent spiritual history of the USA suggests that the South—with its many evangelicals—continues to this day to aspire to win the peace.

In the later 1860s and into the 1880s the initiative lay in the northern states, and latterly in the prairie states of the Mid-West. Here the watchwords were improvement and progress, and amongst evangelicals, already deeply oriented towards spiritual individualism and an Arminian understanding of the way of salvation and the Christian life, the themes of improvement and progress assumed the form of a mounting emphasis on *individual* holiness and perfection. These tendencies had their roots in the Methodist tradition, as John Fletcher of Madeley's *Checks to Antinomianism* (1771–5) confirms. The promotion of personal holiness arose not least among those who sensed a growing spiritual weakness in the face of the increasingly secular materialism of American society. Faced with new challenges, the inclination was always to revamp the old techniques and formulas. One of the enduring marks of Evangelicalism is the persistence of its revivalist fixation. The first "National Camp Meeting for the Promotion of Holiness" was held in New Jersey in 1867, and the movement spread across the nation by the 1870s. Holiness Associations abounded. In these settings the writings of Phoebe Palmer (1807–74), especially *The Way of Holiness* (1843) and the periodical *The Guide to Holiness* were disseminated. The movement soon permeated all protestant denominations. For example, significant advocates included William Edwin Boardman (1810–86), a Presbyterian and author of *The Higher Christian Life* (1858), and the Quaker, Hannah Whitall Smith (1832–1911), author of *The Christian's Secret of a Happy Life* (1875).

These activists all visited England, confirming that this was the juncture at which American Evangelicalism begins to be more influential in the British Isles than the other way round. A "Convention for the Promotion of Holiness" was held in Brighton, England, in 1875, which directly influenced Thomas D. Harford-Battersby (1822–83) to initiate the Keswick Convention in his home parish. The motto was "All One in Christ Jesus," and for decades its message was gospel for most British evangelicals. Only those few anchored in the older puritan and reformed views of sanctification stood aside—such as Bishop John Charles Ryle (1816–1900) and the great Baptist preacher Charles Haddon Spurgeon (1834–92). The emphasis of Keswick speakers was on personal "victory over sin," with "full surrender" leading to the "life of faith." These teachings were widely disseminated through the writings of Frederick B. Meyer (1847–1929) and given prestige by figures such as Bishop Handley Moule (1841–1920). Keswick had emulators across the globe, such as the Belgrave Heights Convention in Victoria, Australia.

The Keswick Holiness outlook may be described as otherworldly—with its talk of a "higher Christian life" and "mountaintop experiences." However, on closer inspection, its otherworldliness proves to be illusory. Its preferred piety of "quiet times," supplemented with weekend spiritual retreats, sometimes called conferences, and other expectations, presumed the prior enjoyment of a standard of living beyond the means of the laboring masses in the burgeoning industrial conurbations. For the so-called lower classes, including those who labored long and hard, often in poor health and poorly paid, in the mines, mills, and factories of industrial Britain, the Keswick style of Evangelicalism offered no effective deliverance. It subtly presumed the enjoyment of at least comfortable middle-class circumstances. The "social gospel," eventually advocated by men such as Hugh Price Hughes (1847–1902) in Great Britain and Walter Rauschenbusch (1861–1918) in the USA, arose to address the problems of industrialization and urbanization. As Evangelicalism's earlier commitment to reform drained away, concerns about social conditions and economic justice tended to be dismissed by it as "not the gospel." After trying the more interventionist liberalism of the Newcastle Programme of 1891, which called for Home Rule for Ireland and disestablishment of the (Anglican) Church in Wales, many in Great Britain who were moved by the social question gravitated towards Fabian Socialism (first organized as "The Fellowship of the New Life")—carrying the socio-economical, ethical legacies of Methodism with them.

Even as evangelical views of holiness became increasingly otherworldly and drew upon an already deeply entrenched individualism, the growing influence of premillennial dispensationalist views reinforced and validated the already strong evangelical disposition towards social and political conservatism. In this outlook, everything was going downhill, and change would almost certainly be change for the worse. For many British evangelicals, confirmation of such an outlook came when High Church Anglican and Liberal Prime Minister William Ewart Gladstone (1809–98), to the dismay of many British Protestants, took up the question of Home Rule for Ireland in 1886 and again in 1894. Cries of "Home Rule means Rome Rule" were raised and galvanized more than protestant Ulster. Such concerns could draw upwardly mobile Protestant Nonconformists into the Conservative political fold. The Irish question divided the Liberal Party. By the end of the nineteenth century the political allegiances of almost all British evangelicals were towards the Tories, or Conservatives. Following the leadership of Benjamin Disraeli (1804–81), the Tories became the party of imperial expansion. Returned to government in 1895, they pursued an aggressive policy in South Africa that precipitated the second Anglo-Boer War of 1899–1902.

The Rise of Dispensationalism and the Era of Moody and Sankey

The morality of international relations, and not least the painful ambiguities of imperialism, received much less attention from late nineteenth-century evangelicals than did the ongoing promotion of premillennial views of eschatology, especially in its dispensationalist elaboration—with its expectation of a sudden departure of true believers from earth at "the secret rapture" prior to a "great tribulation." Initially, the promotion of premillennial dispensationalism was hard going for Darby and his supporters, not least because of the great disappointment experienced by the followers of William Miller (1782–1849) of New York, when the return of Christ he had predicted for 1844 did not take place. The premillennial cause was divided between those who accepted the dispensationalist version promoted by Darby and those who did not. Horatius Bonar (1808–89) launched and edited the *Quarterly Journal of Prophecy* in 1849. He was premillennial but criticized the dispensational version of premillennialism. His most astute critic was neither dispensationalist nor a-millennial but the post-millennial Patrick Fairbairn (1805–74). When Darby attacked the existing denominational structures, he caused great offense to the evangelicals therein, including those who were premillennial, such as Ryle and Spurgeon. However, by accepting and promoting the premillennial view, and the cultural outlook that it implied, many evangelicals effectively opened the door to a widespread evangelical acceptance of the dispensational version of premillennialism. In the USA, publication of the *Prophetic Times* (1863 onwards) fanned interest across all major denominations, and considerable further momentum was achieved through the Niagara Bible Conferences, founded by the Presbyterian James Hall Brookes (1830–97) and in which figures such as George C. Needham (1840–1902) and William J. Erdman (1834–1923) played significant roles.

During this period the most celebrated star in the evangelical firmament was the lay evangelist Dwight L. Moody (1837–99). He made his reputation as a revivalist-style preacher when visiting England in 1872. In association with musician Ira D. Sankey (1840–1908), he revisited Great Britain for an extended campaign in 1873–5. Their impact was long lasting—Sankey's *Sacred Songs and Solos* only becoming *passé* in the 1960s. In Moody and Sankey evangelism we see the methodology of orchestrated revivalism, derived from Cane Ridge and formulated by Finney, brought to a new level of organization, and oriented to the conditions of large urban-industrial centers. Great verbal pressure was used to gain decisions; the "altar call" and the "mercy seat" fully utilized, with choirs singing emotively Charlotte Elliott's (1789–1871) "Just as I am, without one plea" to smooth the path. A man of undoubted earnestness and sincerity, Moody appeared a-political on the platform but was a staunch Republican in private. His relationships with business interests assumed without question the middle-class attitudes of his day and place. He opposed the formation of labor unions. In Great Britain, which he revisited in 1881–83, Moody was well received by figures such as Andrew A. Bonar (1810–92), although his utilization of new measures such as the "altar call" and "inquiry rooms" attracted the sharp critique of the redoubtable Presbyterian John Kennedy of Dingwall (1819–84).

Never in any precise sense Calvinistic, or a perfectionist of the Wesleyan variety, Moody presented himself as a simple Christian while embracing a mode of otherworldliness that accorded with his premillennial beliefs and "personal holiness" priorities. His revivalist promotions rested upon a traditional use of Scripture, coupled with a disposition towards calculated spontaneity. He founded the Bible Institute in Chicago in 1886. It opened in 1889 and was later renamed The Moody Bible Institute. The tone was set by figures such as Rubin A. Torrey (1856–1928). Torrey visited Great Britain and Australia. In 1912 he became dean of the new West Coast counterpart to the Moody Bible Institute: the Bible Institute of Los Angeles, later BIOLA University.

However, by the turn of the century it was less possible to ignore the challenges posed by the higher critical biblical scholarship. In 1881 the Free Church of Scotland tried William Robertson Smith (1846–94) for heresy, for statements made in *The Old Testament in the Jewish Church* (1881). In 1887 Spurgeon raised the alarm at the growing influence of the higher critical approach to Scripture among the English Free Churches. This Down-Grade Controversy was instructive. Spurgeon declaimed in the name of faith and doctrine, but he lacked the philosophical insight into the prolegomenal issues necessary to formulate an effective critique. It would take more than the reaffirmation of older confessional standards and rhetorical side-swipes to confront the issues arising from the critical-historical method when deployed from a purely rationalistic starting-point. The evangelical intellectual deficit was now on full display. Those evangelicals who understood the issues, and who confronted them candidly, could find themselves in heart-wrenching struggles to retain their faith. The son of John Charles Ryle, Herbert Edward Ryle (1856–1925), adopted the higher critical standpoint. Some defections from the evangelical ranks were reluctantly made, with anguish and misgiving, because the imperatives of intellectual honesty were undeniable, and a faith based on conscious obscurantism became untenable.

In the nineteenth century evangelicals became pre-eminently preoccupied on three fronts: overseas missions, the higher life of holiness, and an increasing disposition towards premillennial dispensationalist views of the Second Advent. This was the great age of old-style missions. They followed the early lead of the Church Missionary Society (1799) and the London Missionary Society (1818). Charles Hudson Taylor (1832–1905) established the China Inland Mission (1872), receiving the support of the Cambridge Seven in 1885, including the tenacious Charles Thomas Studd (1860–1931), who went on to found the Worldwide Evangelization Crusade (1913), and whose work was continued by Norman Percy Grubb (1895–1993). Victorian evangelicals and their American counterparts exhibited great enterprise and tenacity in these endeavors. Let no one disparage those who labored earnestly and hard, sometimes in the most discouraging and dangerous of circumstances, but it must be recorded that the missionaries took all of the divisions and distortions of their Evangelicalism and projected them across Africa, Asia, Latin America, and the Pacific. Anglo-American style pietistic Evangelicalism has become influential across large parts of Africa, and in countries as diverse as South Korea and the Philippines. Moreover, while some were not as culturally insensitive as others have argued, it was all too easy for English-speaking missionaries to assume that the socio-economic norms of upper-middle-class respectability in northern Europe and North America constituted a specifically Christian standard for all humankind. Accordingly, they carried into new situations their priorities of personal holiness and an array of negative attitudes towards culture.

Over the decades the consequences were manifold. In one direction, they included the phenomenon of the culture-shocked missionaries home on successive furloughs being repeatedly stunned by the moral decay they encountered at home. In the other direction, indigenous converts were discouraged, sometimes categorically, from taking part in colonial politics—sometimes with appalling consequences, as when independence eventually arrived and there was no politically-competent, indigenous leadership available because the missionaries had depreciated all political activity as worldly and therefore tainted.

The Emergence of Contemporary Pentecostalism

In the USA, official Methodism became increasingly concerned about the newly specific manner in which holiness advocates were utilizing terms such as "filled with the Holy Ghost," and the "baptism of the Holy Spirit." These seemed to challenge the traditional Wesleyan-Methodist holiness teaching.

The matter came to a head in 1894–5 and resulted in the formation of the Church of the Nazarene (1895) and a host of additional splintering entities, especially across the South and Mid-West. Among these was the Fire-Baptized Holiness Church of God in the Americas, founded by Benjamin Hardin Irwin (b. 1854) in Iowa (1895). Irwin was much influenced by the writings of Charles Wesley and Fletcher of Madeley. This denomination, one of many divergent holiness strands across America, is significant because it provided the context within which Charles Fox Parham (1873–1929) acquired the doctrine of a "baptism of the Holy Spirit," *distinct* from the "full sanctification" hitherto promoted by strict holiness advocates. Parham was involved in the Topeka, Kansas, revival of 1901, and the distinguishing feature of his doctrine was that *glossolalia* (speaking in tongues) was *the* definitive evidence of having been "baptized in the Spirit."

These events transpired amidst a rising tide of rural populism that brought to prominence the redoubtable William Jennings Bryan (1860–1925). At this time the claim was made that the "tongues" experienced were *actual languages* as in the New Testament itself. Parham's influence was complemented by the work of William Joseph Seymour (1870–1922). Seymour played a central role in the much-vaunted Azusa Street Revival in Los Angeles in 1905–9. It is from these events that many trace the emergence of the organizations of twentieth-century Pentecostalism, including the Elim Churches and the Assemblies of God, along with countless offshoots, including multiple Christian Revival Centers.

The dramatic Welsh Revival of 1904–6 ran parallel to these developments. This revival generated misgivings about Pentecostalism that non-Pentecostal evangelicals have never been able to dismiss completely, or Pentecostals adequately to answer. As Jessie Pen-Lewis's (1861–1927) *War on the Saints* (1912) exemplifies, a hankering after signs and ecstatic experience can plunge those concerned into delusional conditions and disturbed states that detach them from the clear and plain teachings of Scripture. The edition of this work subsequently published by the Christian Literature Crusade (1964) was significantly abridged so as to omit the more excessive passages, but indications of a pronounced orientation towards subjectivism remained. Following this revival one of its leading exponents, Evan Roberts (1878–1951) languished and died a wrecked man. The advocates of the revival insisted that it was an authentic movement of the Holy Spirit, one that had somehow been subverted by Satan and demonic forces. However, authentic renewal is not brought about with psyched-up, beat-up, compulsive singing and a wide repertoire of pulpit histrionics. But concerns already raised in the nineteenth century by writers who could not be pronounced "spiritually dead," were ignored in the twentieth century. Within

Evangelicalism generally (but not at every single point), a near obsession with individual experience has repeatedly led to wrong conduct overriding or sidelining sound teaching. In many evangelical-charismatic settings the self-referential "personal testimony" is a prime vehicle of spiritual self-promotion.

The Elim Churches, and the Elim Fellowship, while both Pentecostal, were not of the same origin. The former (also later known as the Elim Four Square Gospel Alliance) arose in Ireland in 1915 under the initial leadership of George Jeffreys (1889–1962), who was decisively influenced by the Welsh Revival of 1904–6. The Elim Fellowship was set up in New York in 1924. Both were to be dwarfed by the Assemblies of God (AOG) Pentecostal denomination, formed in 1914 in the wake of the Azuza Street Revival.

Many pivotal questions concerning events at Azuza Street were never convincingly answered. When the prominent holiness-minded Methodist evangelist William Baxter Godbey (1833–1920), who was no mean linguist, visited Azusa Street in 1909, he seems to have convinced those present that *he* had received the "baptism of the Holy Spirit" by reciting Latin *that he already knew*. This and other evidence confirms that the "tongues" exhibited at Azusa Street were then thought to be actual extant languages, although subsequent mission field experience did not sustain this assumption. In other words, they were deluded. Certainly, the "tongues" spoken in Acts 2 (to use the seventeenth-century terminology of the Authorized / King James Version) were actual contemporaneous human *languages*, as the context shows. Indeed, when this version of the Bible declares itself to be "Translated out of the Original Tongues," the reference is to specific and actual languages (in this case Hebrew, Aramaic, and Greek). A "tongue" is an actual language, but as non-anatomical usages of the word have become anachronistic, it has become all too easy for those reading the term in the Bible to conclude that what is intended is something other than an actual language.

Holiness stalwarts such as Rubin A. Torrey in America, or George Campbell Morgan (1863–1945) in England, entertained grave doubts about Azusa Street, in part on the basis of claims made by eyewitness Frank Bartleman (1871–1935). The Brethren writer Henry Allen Ironside (1876–1951) took a similar view. In England, the Keswick movement, which was also supported by many followers of the Brethren, continued to teach a "sanctified higher life" without using the term "baptism of the Holy Spirit" in a specifically Pentecostal manner, and without the expectation of an impartation of specific "gifts of the Spirit." From the beginning of the twentieth century, an organized and intense Pentecostalism functioned largely in its own separate world, apart from other evangelicals, until it jumped the denominational barriers as the Charismatic Movement in the 1960s.

The Advent of the Scofield Bible

In Great Britain, from the 1890s, the (non-Anglican Protestant) "Free Churches" were corroded from within by their failure to effectively address the philosophical standpoints foundational to the use of the higher critical methods that they had embraced in the name of intellectual honesty. They came to express a well-intentioned ethos of general goodwill that inadequately confronted the human condition and could not offer the deliverance craved by humankind. The result was a gradual emptying of the Free Church denominations of England and Wales, which in some cases suffered additionally from their understandable alignments with party-political Liberalism—especially as the latter fell from power and fractured as a result of the Great War and its aftermath. From 1919 onwards, it was the evangelical Anglicans who, although a definite minority within the Church of England, nevertheless dominated the evangelical scene nationally, with various Brethren groups, Baptists, and some others in their train. The Keswick outlook dominated the scene. Within the Church of England, evangelicals survived in closely guarded enclaves. The evangelical sense of being besieged was understandably increased as Anglo-Catholic and liberal thinking achieved a *rapprochement* in the papers edited by Charles Gore (1853–1932) and published as *Lux Mundi* (1889).

In the USA, it was in the context of the Niagara Bible Conferences that James Hall Brookes embraced dispensational premillennialism. He had a strong influence on a man who was for a time Moody's pastor, the fervent dispensationalist Cyrus I. Scofield (1843–1921). Scofield articulated his position in *Rightly Dividing the Word of Truth* (1896). He was the author of one of the most influential evangelical publications of the twentieth century—the *Scofield Reference Bible*. The annotations there provided presented (for many readers conclusively) a fully-fledged dispensational system that was to structure the interpretation of the Bible, and therefore the general outlook, of many English-speaking evangelicals around the world.

The *Scofield Reference Bible* was first published in 1909 and received its definitive revision in 1917. It contrasted with and for many years outsold the earlier *Thompson Chain Reference Bible* (1908). Scofield's culturally pessimistic, dispensational outlook appealed to many during a time of tension, anxiety, and warfare. One of the great centers of dispensational thought and publication, Dallas Theological Seminary, was founded in 1924 by Scofield's disciple, Lewis Sperry Chafer (1871–1952), with the tradition faithfully continued by John F. Walvoord (1910–2002) and Charles Caldwell Ryrie.

The Impact of the Princeton Professoriate

At this point it is necessary also to consider the immense influence on Evangelicalism generally of the nineteenth-century bastion of conservative Presbyterianism—Princeton Theological Seminary, Princeton, New Jersey. There have been recurrent debates amongst evangelical historians about the character of Evangelicalism itself. Is it basically reformed, or Wesleyan? Certainly, those who were self-consciously Calvinist (Edwards, Whitefield) as well as those who were Arminian (such as the Wesley brothers) were centrally involved at its inception. Both sides fell *within* Bebbington's quadrilateral of priorities. It was during the nineteenth century that it became increasingly apparent, however, that the intrinsic character of Evangelicalism, especially in its more revivalist orientations, inclined towards the Wesleyan-Arminian side, with its decision-oriented evangelistic strategies. However, this state of affairs has been partly masked by the fact that when confronted by the higher critical approach to the Bible, and suffering from what we have termed its intellectual deficit, Evangelicalism turned to its reformed side, specifically the Presbyterian professors of Princeton Theological Seminary, *not* for their championship of reformed scholastic theology but for their teaching on the inspiration and authority of Scripture.

Archibald Alexander was founding professor of Princeton Theological Seminary, whose remarkable lineage of successors included Charles Hodge (1797–1878), Archibald Alexander Hodge (1823–86), Benjamin Breckinridge Warfield (1851–1921), and Francis Landey Patton (1843–1932). If mid-to-late nineteenth and early twentieth-century Anglo-American Evangelicalism had an intellectual elite, it was these men. Along with Robert Dick Wilson (1856–1930) and John Gresham Machen (1881–1937), they constituted what we might call the Princeton professoriate. They provided twentieth-century Evangelicalism with a particular view of the inspiration and authority of the Scriptures that was widely influential but not free of problems.

In considering the Princeton professoriate, two points need to be kept in view. First, their general philosophical orientation was that of Scottish Common Sense Realism. The impact of Reid's "philosophy of common sense" ought not to be overstated nor underestimated. It would be wrong to envisage the Princeton professoriate as consciously following the dictates of Reid and his school at every step on the exegetical, expository, and didactic way. It is better to envisage it as providing an outer framework of assumptions, and it is these assumptions that are problematic. For example, one of the results of this outlook was the widespread assumption that things and relationships are "just seen" rather than as unavoidably interpreted: in other words, "seen as" contextually and from one *religious* standpoint or another. In this respect Common Sense Realism reinforced the deep-seated tendency of Anglo-American thought towards Baconian style empiricism.

Second, the Princeton professoriate consciously held the scholastic theology of Francis Turretin in the highest regard. Turretin was to them what Aquinas was to Roman Catholics. Through this lineage the *philosophia aristotelico-scholastica* enjoyed prime ordering status at Princeton—it should not be forgotten that Turretin had maintained that even the vowel points of the Hebrew Bible were divinely inspired. Accordingly, the Princeton professoriate construed the Scriptures as providing propositional data that, when *logically* ordered, resulted in a timeless system of truth hidden within Scripture unless made explicit by the systematic theologian. For them, Turretin exemplified the systematic theology already embedded in Holy Writ. We are in the presence of this kind of thinking when we encounter such language as "the system of doctrine contained in Scripture."

Archibald Alexander set precedent at Princeton by making Turretin's *Institutes* (1679) the set text in dogmatics. It was only replaced by Charles Hodge's *Systematic Theology* (1871–3) in 1872. This work was a latter-day rearticulation and adaptation of Turretin's work, which had been reprinted in a Scottish (Latin) edition as recently as 1847. When the professors of Princeton Seminary formulated their view of the inspiration of Scripture, they were not only, as they saw matters, defending the Bible; they were in practice formulating a standpoint that that would facilitate and legitimize its continued utilization for *their* kind of scholastic systematic theology. Charles Hodge envisaged the Scriptures as divinely inspired texts that could be mined for data that could logically, and therefore scientifically, be assembled into a rationally-consistent architectonic system of truth. Archibald Alexander's agenda had been to confront the deism of his day with "common sense" appeals to the presumed truth of the Scriptures. His *Evidences of Christianity* (1836) taught that the Bible was exempt from error, but without the rigidity that was to characterize his successors. The rising concern over higher critical views of Scripture was more specifically registered in the writings of Charles Hodge. Initially, he insisted that what the Bible says is what God says, not merely literally but in a manner starkly literalist and without any recognition of the limited and accommodative character of words. Such a view seems to come perilously close to dictation, with the human author functioning as little more than a passive conduit. In later life Charles Hodge was obliged to admit to difficulties, even as he sought to minimize the discrepancies encountered within the biblical texts themselves.

Archibald Alexander Hodge, author of *The Confession of Faith* (1869), took up his duties at Princeton in 1877. In his writing, the pressures to which Charles Hodge were subject came to far more explicit expression. In 1860 A. A. Hodge had insisted on a full and perfect *infallibility* of every part of the Scriptures. However, it became increasingly difficult to adhere to this position over the next two decades. By the time he published his *Outlines of Theology* (1879 edition), he had retreated to insisting on the infallible accuracy only of the "original autograph copies"—now long since lost! Henceforth, A. A. Hodge and his colleague B. B. Warfield continued to assert that inconsistencies between the biblical texts and contemporary historical and scientific knowledge were only apparent and not actual.

However, their ultimate position was that of the infallibility of the original *autographia*. They now asserted that, in order to demonstrate the non-infallibility of the Scriptures it would be necessary to show that an alleged error also occurred in the same original *autographia*. As a solution to the issues raised by the application of higher critical methods in the scrutiny of the extant biblical texts, this was a pseudo-solution both artificial and contrived. It was nevertheless a key feature of the view of biblical inspiration that large numbers of evangelicals were to adopt in the twentieth century, many of whose doctrinal beliefs were a long way indeed from the Princeton version of Calvinism as expressed in the Westminster Standards. Furthermore, the notion of infallibility embraced by many evangelicals included features of what was subsequently referred to as inerrancy.

By the later nineteenth century, leading Presbyterians in the USA were well aware of the issues raised by higher criticism; but it was the trial of William Robertson Smith and his departure from the Free Church of Scotland that served to concentrate their minds wonderfully. The advocates of higher critical approaches, led by Charles A. Briggs (1841–1913) and Henry Preserved Smith (1847–1927) presented their case, and the professoriate of Princeton offered their responses, in a succession of articles in the *Presbyterian Review* published between 1881 and 1883. The entire sequence of articles repays close analysis. Even though Warfield skillfully upheld the standpoint of the Princeton professoriate, a greater caution on his part is evident in comparison with his predecessors. While Henry Preserved Smith found Warfield's viewpoint inconsistent with the texture and tenor of the actual biblical texts, Briggs challenged and Warfield defended the consistency of the Princeton professoriate's specific view of biblical inspiration with the teaching of the Westminster Standards. This drove Warfield to produce *The Westminster Assembly and its Work* (1908) in response. In practice, the Princeton professoriate placed a post-mid-seventeenth-century construction on the Westminster Confession.

When the Princeton professoriate—specifically A. A. Hodge—wrote of the Scriptures as "the only infallible rule of faith and practice," they were moving beyond the bounds of the Westminster Confession of Faith, which in its first chapter "Of the Holy Scripture" only uses the term "infallible" once, and in connection with the rule of interpreting Scripture with Scripture itself (Chapter I: 9). In practice, when the Princeton professoriate talked about the Bible as an "infallible rule," it was *inerrancy* that they had in view. At best, this was a possible reading of the Confession, but not a necessary one. For the time being, the initiative lay with the conservative and scholastic forces supportive of the Princeton standpoint. Action was taken against both Smith and Briggs in the courts of the church. Smith later became a Congregational minister. In 1893, Briggs, then of Union Theological Seminary, New York, was tried for various heresies, including questioning the full Mosaic authorship of the Pentateuch and upholding the case for a Deutero-Isaiah. He became an Episcopal priest in 1899. The twentieth century would be different. It would prove increasingly inappropriate to use early modern confessional statements as a means of disciplining those who were articulating important questions arising from the findings of contemporary science and scholarship.

Meanwhile, the evangelical use of the Bible continued to ignore the issues raised by critical-historical scholarship. Even as problems arising from the findings of critical-historical scholarship grew in intensity—like a mighty storm building on the prairies—the most conspicuous star in the revivalist firmament was Billy Sunday (1862–1935). In Sunday, when compared to Moody, we encounter a certain coarseness of style—even bellicose crudity, as he pressured his listeners to shake his hand and hit the "sawdust trail" of Christian living. Like Finney, he disregarded older views of the human condition and predicament and presumed that men and women could facilitate their own salvation. The act of stepping forward at the crucial point in the proceedings was tantamount to a public confession of faith that secured salvation. Yet it fell to Sunday to strive in an era confronted by conditions not so readily answered by the conventional prescriptions of rugged individualism and optimistic self-reliance. It seems that not a few ministers supported him in their quest to boost their own church revenues. Sunday's star reached its apogee in 1918. Thereafter, he tended to focus more on the South, where he could still retain a following.

Even without the fundamentalist-modernist confrontation, as it came to be termed, evangelical revivalism was going to have to develop new techniques and strategies for the twentieth century era of mass communication. Yet it was not merely a matter of technique. It never is. It might be argued that Evangelicalism in the USA in the 1910s and 1920s was coming to a fuller realization that it was no longer central to American culture. Perhaps more penetratingly, however, the truth is that it was confronting the more sobering reality that it had never truly commanded the culture at all—at best it only exerted a significant leverage at some pivotal points. Although there has been a measure of interaction, American culture has for a long time exerted a greater formative impact on American Evangelicalism than vice versa.

The Fundamentals

If any one event signaled that the gloves were off between evangelicals and the advocates of critical-historical biblical scholarship, it was the publication of the twelve volume series *The Fundamentals: A Testimony to the Truth*, between 1910 and 1915. In other words, they appeared between the initial publication of the *Scofield Reference Bible* and its definitive edition in 1917. The Texan oil millionaire brothers Lyman and Milton Stewart funded the publication and distribution of *The Fundamentals* to thousands of ministers, missionaries and educators. The series contained contributions from sixty-four evangelical authorities on the theological questions of the day. These included liberal theology and its approach to Scripture.

The term "fundamentalist" is derived from this series of publications. British and antipodean evangelicals rarely adopted the term, not least because they did not wish to be associated with the excesses of certain of their American counterparts. From about 1910 onwards, the clash between conservative fundamentalists and liberal modernists diversely impacted all major American denominational traditions. In view of the subsequent reputation of *fundamentalism* (a term that arose in the early 1920s), it is necessary to state that the authors of *The Fundamentals* were neither incompetent nor obscurantist. They saw themselves as defending historic Christianity from its doctrinal restatement at the hands of liberalism. However, during the 1920s and 1930s, the term fundamentalist, and those who designated themselves fundamentalists, increasingly embraced positions of ecclesiastical separatism—requiring institutional separation from denominations that accepted non-fundamentalists—along with various strong anti-scientific and anti-intellectual tendencies.

Not all in America who would self-identify as fundamentalists would see the Bible as encyclopedically and infallibly addressing *all* questions, but they tended to be strongly committed to a literal interpretation of all biblical texts irrespective of genre. That notion was a cornerstone of the premillennial dispensationalist outlook. On closer examination, not all of the contributors to *The Fundamentals* were rigid literalists. The primary focus of *The Fundamentals* was on upholding the inspiration and authority of Scripture, but what lay behind this objective was the preservation of Scripture that could serve as the basis for their favored interpretation. While protestant scholasticism and dispensationalism presented widely divergent systems, they both looked to the Princeton view of infallibility to underpin their positions.

The Presbyterian Conflict

The most significant of these confrontations took place within the northern Presbyterian body. The influence of Union Theological Seminary, New York, was viewed with disquiet by the old school Princeton professoriate, and they also worried about the absorption of groups into the main Presbyterian body that were far less rigorous as to their adherence to the Westminster Standards. The resulting concerns gave rise to the five points set down as required of office-bearers in 1910: the infallibility of the Bible, the virgin birth of Christ, his atoning death as a substitution for human sin, his bodily resurrection, and the authenticity of his miracles. In truth, the making of such stipulations pointed to a deeper reality—the conservative tide was on the ebb. The challenge came in the form of Harry Emerson Fosdick's (1878–1969) sermon "Shall the Fundamentalists Win?" preached on May 21, 1922. He received the support of prominent liberals, such as Henry Sloane Coffin (1877–1954). Fosdick's apprehensions had been fuelled during a recent visit to the East Asian missionary field, where he had encountered intense organization on the part of premillennial fundamentalist missionaries against their liberal counterparts. Fosdick received a firm rebuttal in *Shall Unbelief Win?: A Reply to Dr. Fosdick* (1922) by Clarence Edward Macartney (1879–1957).

The Auburn Affirmation (1923), issued in opposition to the continued use of the 1910 five points, came as a direct challenge to the conservatives, although it was some time yet before matters were to come to a breaking point. In the meantime, the world was treated to the staged farce of the July 1925 trial of John T. Scopes (1900–70) at Dayton, Tennessee. This episode was at once the grand culmination of the crusade against evolution conducted by William Jennings Bryan, and the subsequent ruination of his public reputation. It also tended to confirm the public's perception that all fundamentalists were academically inept and scientifically inadequate. All too often they were, but the man who emerged as their leader completely defied such a description. J. Gresham Machen was a man of classical learning, an astute scholar and able writer, who as to adroitness and acumen stood head and shoulders above many of the fundamentalists of his day, for many of whom the dispensational system had become the norm. He adhered to the covenant theology of seventeenth-century reformed orthodoxy and had no sympathy for premillennial dogmatism of the dispensationalist variety. His books on *The Origin of Paul's Religion* (1921) and *The Virgin Birth of Christ* (1930) have more than stood the test of time. In the confrontation with theological modernism, his *Christianity and Liberalism* (1923) and *What is Faith?* (1925) explained what was at stake. Although not without problems of its own, his *Christianity and Liberalism* stands as one of the great twentieth-century defenses of historic Christianity.

The issues in play were unquestionably central to the Christian religion. Theological liberalism reinterpreted Christian doctrine in terms of the assumptions of Enlightenment rationalism. In so doing it emptied Christian teachings of their authentic meaning and substituted alternatives that, when put to the test, amounted to little more than moralistic sentiment and good intentions. This was not the faith and teaching of apostles, prophets, martyrs, and reformers. In the words of Helmut Richard Niebuhr (1894–1962), himself no reactionary fundamentalist, in liberal theology we encounter: "A God without wrath [who] brought men without sin into a kingdom without judgment through the ministrations of a Christ without a cross."[2] The kingdom of God was purportedly postponed by the dispensationalists (to make way for the "mystery parenthesis" of the church) and misconstrued by theological liberals in terms of increasingly secularized programs of social action. Yet, sadly, when we scrutinize the arguments offered by Machen in response we find he repeatedly utilizes the concept of the *supernatural* (over against the *natural*), thereby testifying to his dependence on scholasticism. This was a serious point of vulnerability. The right case can be argued in the wrong way. It would have been better to distinguish between the *divine*, and the *creaturely*. Machen's defense of historic Christianity exhibited serious deficiencies. The intellectual deficit of Evangelicalism was evident even in him.

Richard Niebuhr, along with his brother K. P. Reinhold Niebuhr (1872–1971), and Hans Wilhelm Frei (1922–88) are occasionally referred to as among the "Yale school" of post-liberal theologians, who have in turn influenced figures such as Brevard S. Childs (1923–2007) and Stanley Hauerwas. These writers were in significant measure influenced by the new voice that at this time sounded forth from reformed Switzerland: Karl Barth (1886–1968). It is not without irony that as the fundamentalist versus modernist confrontation was raging in "roaring twenties" America, back

---

2. Niebuhr, *The Kingdom of God in America*, Fiftieth Anniversary Edition, 193.

in Europe the carnage, cruelty, and suffering of the Great War and its aftermath had already sounded the death-knell of those Enlightenment-inspired liberal views of human nature and rationality (and the inevitability of "progress") that had underlain the now passé nineteenth-century liberal dilution of protestant Christianity.

Barth's *Epistle to the Romans* (revised 1922) heralded a new era. While not disavowing all higher critical scholarship, Barth encouraged his fellow Protestants to consider once again the teachings of the reformers. His *The Word of God in the Word of Man* (1928) rendered his thought more accessible to the mass of English-language readers. Following the rise of the Nazi movement, in the *Barmen Declaration* (1934), Barth was among those who warned Germany and the world of what was happening. The *Darmstadt Statement* of 1947 confessed the consequences.

The testimony of Barth and his associates against fascism merits the respect of all. However, Barth proved to be something of a false dawn: his "neo-Orthodox" theology pivoted on a radically nominalist distinction between *Geschichte* and *Historie* that left the challenge of Enlightenment-oriented, higher critical thinking insufficiently addressed. The historical method, or, rather, the issues provoked by the Enlightenment philosophical assumptions with which the method was all too often used, remained unconfronted and therefore unresolved. Sadly, this amounted to an evasion and not a resolution. Barth's nominalism, powerfully evident in his strident critique of "natural theology," effectively precluded the articulation of a biblically directed worldview. Yet those who are tempted to dismiss all German Protestantism as the source of our woes must reflect on the example of the life, teaching, and death of Dietrich Bonhoeffer (1906–45).

In the USA, the reorganization of Princeton Seminary precipitated the 1929 withdrawal of Machen and his followers from Princeton to found an alternative institution: Westminster Theological Seminary, Philadelphia, Pennsylvania. Their attempt to establish a contra-liberal "Independent Board of Presbyterian Foreign Missions" was repudiated by the denomination, and when they refused to comply, they were deposed from office. In 1936 they set up a new denominational entity: The Presbyterian Church of America (PCA). There were always misgivings. A new denomination had never been Machen's first choice, and the outcomes were not what were originally intended.

In such polarized times, great figures, such as Geerhardus Johannes Vos (1862–1949), grew silent. Never a modernist, Vos was not in accord with the closed defensiveness of fundamentalism or the scholasticism on which it rested. Clarence E. Macartney, who had stood with Machen and his followers in the early days, shrank from what seemed to be the schismatic consequences of separation and remained in the main northern Presbyterian entity. Reformed and Presbyterian denominations tend to be led from their seminaries, and this was especially the case with the PCA, because the Westminster Theological Seminary was established first, before the PCA. Here men who were to influence Evangelicalism for much of the mid-twentieth century, such as Oswald T. Allis (1880–1973), Ned Bernard Stonehouse (1902–62), Edward J. Young (1907–68), and John Murray (1898–1975), taught and published. In the longer term their work was to foster a limited return to a-millennialism, as exemplified by William B. Hendriksen's (1900–82) widely influential *More than Conquerors* (1939).

However, Machen's followers, although united in their adherence to the Westminster Standards, were conspicuously divided on other matters close to the fundamentalist heart. In 1939 the PCA was obliged to adopt another name and resolved on the Orthodox Presbyterian Church (OPC). However, this was not before the seceding body suffered a further split: in 1937 those committed to premillennialism and the more abstemious practices of fundamentalism followed a group including Alan A. MacRae (1902–77), Carl T. McIntire (1906–2002), and J. Oliver Buswell (1895–1977)—at that time President of Wheaton College—in forming the Bible Presbyterian Church. They established Faith Theological Seminary at Wilmington, Delaware. This split within the split was a *partial* revisiting of the "old school" versus "new school" antipathies of the previous century. In 1936 Carl McIntire founded the militantly separatist *Christian Beacon*. An early graduate of this fundamentalist and premillennial Presbyterian institution was the young Francis A. Schaeffer (1912–84), a highly influential figure in later years.

9

NEO-EVANGELICALISM AND THE GREAT CRUSADE

Some Legacies of the Great War

John Charles Ryle died in 1900 in England. Subsequently, the leadership of the evangelical party in the Church of England was bereft of his clarity and insight. In the early twentieth century the overall complexion of the English national church was far from what evangelicals wished to see. The minority status and marginal position of the evangelical party was all too clear. The presentation of a revised *Book of Common Prayer* with controversial concessions to Anglo-Catholic practice brought on a new crisis. The measure was finally defeated in 1928, but not without the support of Scottish Presbyterian and Welsh Nonconformist members in the House of Commons. The British victory in the Great War was conspicuously pyrrhic. Great Britain emerged from the conflict seriously weakened. The land and its people were spiritually emaciated. The hollowed-out doctrinal offerings of theological liberalism offered stones, not bread, to a grieving people. High moral sentiment is no substitute for grace abounding. The surviving pockets of evangelical pietism offered little more than a mix of escapism and obscurantism. After 1919 it became clear that global pre-eminence now lay with the United States. The Christianity on offer in Great Britain seemed no match for the times. Evangelicals enveloped in the personal-holiness pietism of the Keswick convention and the spiritual legacies of the Moody and Sankey visits were in no position to bind up the nation's wounds.

Yet some important voices did emerge, including some that were way beyond the pale of an introverted Evangelicalism, even as the scene darkened ominously in the 1930s. The scholarly nonconformist Bernard Lord Manning (1892–1941) called for a return to classical orthodoxy and exhorted his countrymen to reconsider the writings of John Calvin. Closer to the evangelical fold were Henry Atherton (1875–1933), who was awed by the breadth of vision and comprehensive thinking of Calvinists in the Netherlands, and Arthur Pink (1886–1952), who, though intensely separatist and working in almost complete isolation, was to challenge the doctrinal superficiality of later generations through his writings.

Scotland remained bruised by the divisions of 1843 and 1900, and Wales languished in the ambiguous aftermath of the events of 1904–6. After 1919, there was little energy and even less money for full-scale separatist denominational developments. The Fellowship of Independent Evangelical Churches (FIEC), founded by Edward Joshua Poole Connor (1872–1962), dates from 1922 and has tended to attract independent Baptist and Congregationalist congregations. Poole Connor's revivalist and separatist orientation are evident in his *Evangelical Unity* (1942) and *Evangelicalism in England* (1952). He was involved in the establishment of the separatist British Evangelical Council in 1952. Some non-denominational and specifically separatist ventures were undertaken. The Student Christian Movement (SCM), founded at Cambridge in 1889, split in 1910 with the founding of the Cambridge Inter-Collegiate Christian Union (CICCU). The work of CICCU was central to the establishment of the staunchly evangelical Inter-Varsity Fellowship (IVF) in 1928. For decades SCM and IVF—the latter as Evangelical Unions or Christian Unions—confronted one another across university campuses. The SCM took to publishing the latest findings from Germany, while the IVF published the work of British evangelicals, as well as selectively from the output of their American contemporaries, not least those teaching at Westminster Theological Seminary, Philadelphia. A comparable situation emerged in the field of missions when the Bible Churchman's Missionary Society (BCMS) separated from the Church Missionary Society in 1922. BCMS became Crosslinks in 1992. The IVF and BCMS were not without their ambiguities. They were organizations separated (from SCM and CMS respectively), even as they received support from evangelicals, many of whom steadfastly declined to quit their mixed mainline denominations. The American fundamentalist versus modernist controversy was not without ramifications in other parts of the English-speaking world. In Canada, for example, Thomas Todhunter Shields (1873–1955) upheld biblical inerrancy and established the separatist Union of Regular Baptist Churches.

In Great Britain during the twentieth century there remained a broad sense of "Christian civilization," to use Winston S. Churchill's phrase of 1940, a notion that implied a tolerant latter-day version of Christendom that included evangelicals, but that was not exclusively of them or for them. The USA was different. The breach of 1776 had a profound effect on civic culture on both sides of the Atlantic. Arguably, as Great Britain lost contact with too much of its future and so became overly bound to tradition, America became overly oriented to the future and too prone to embrace change while discounting the stabilizing ballast provided by tradition. Furthermore, in the USA it was Evangelicalism itself that had imparted a *common and unifying spirituality* to the scattered colonial communities prior to independence. For over two hundred years since 1776 the common default notion of Christianity for non-Catholic Americans was a general Evangelicalism decidedly weighted in the direction of Baptist individualism, Wesleyan self help, and "how to get saved" activism. Evangelicals in America could more readily *assume* a certain proprietorial right over the national culture. In a certain sense they saw it as inherently theirs—even if they had lost it, for the time being, to the modernists by the late 1920s. Many American evangelicals have convinced themselves that the founders of the United States were mostly sincere Christians. As a result, a sense of having now lost the commanding position in the culture can repeatedly fuel strong "take back America" rhetoric and initiatives. In historical fact, the dominant tendency amongst the signatories to the Declaration of Independence (1776) was deism, the Scots-born Presbyterian minister John Witherspoon being a notable exception.

By contrast, in England, evangelicals tended to see themselves as participants rather than proprietors—if they thought seriously about their relationship to their national culture at all. Throughout the darkening 1930s and critical 1940s there was a certain lifting of the spiritual tempo in England, in spite of, not because of, the condition of the churches. A deeper spiritual tide was turning. Those who spoke with a prophetic voice were for the most part *not* evangelicals. In 1930 the businessman Albert Henry Ross (1861–1950), writing under the pseudonym of Frank Morison, published his remarkable *Who Moved the Stone?* Initially skeptical, Ross became, by stringent research, convinced of the bodily resurrection of Jesus Christ. And there were two other lay writers whose work was to have colossal impact in following decades—it is enough simply to mention their names: Dorothy Leigh Sayers (1893–1957) and Clive Staples Lewis (1898–1963). Also in this era of war and austerity John B. Phillips began to produce his paraphrases of the New Testament, starting with *Letters to the Young Churches* (1947). The full New Testament came later (1958). These English developments may

The Emergence of Neo-Evangelicalism

What happened to these promising developments in England was that although they flowered during the trials and austerities of a second great conflict, they were nevertheless partly absorbed and partly overridden by what was to come from America after the war—a new wave of crusading fundamentalist Evangelicalism. This movement was made possible by a wave of new initiatives postdating the nadir represented by the Scopes Trial. In America the fundamentalist-modernist controversies of the 1920s and 1930s cast belief in the Biblical message on the side of obscurantism, demagoguery, and the prejudices and ignorance of the inadequately educated. The plenary inspiration of the Bible was dogmatically affirmed, while those who asked the difficult questions could be slated as doubters or backsliders. In their fervor, some latter-day fundamentalists went beyond the positions more carefully articulated by the authors of *The Fundamentals*. In their super-naturalist questioning of naturalism, they tended to be suspicious of all science, attempting to cling to not a *truly literary* but emphatically *literalistic* understanding of Gen 1–11, notwithstanding the mounting evidence to the contrary. In cultural and political matters they were staunchly to the Right. They were well capable of harnessing modern communication technologies when it came to preaching their highly individualistic version of the gospel. Such evangelicals may be seen as offering a particularly strident early version of fundamentalist Evangelicalism, in which the tendency towards intellectual and cultural barrenness came to conspicuous expression.

In America, although the mainline denominations now lay in modernist hands, the fundamentalists, while pushed to the periphery, refused to lie down and die. They adopted a *separatist* posture towards the large mainline denominations—"come out from among them, and be ye separate" (2 Cor 6:17 KJV) was the cry. For example, the Baptist Bible Union formed in 1923 to oppose modernism had by 1932 changed its name to the General Association of Regular Baptists and become a separate denominational entity. In the 1920s and 1930s fundamentalist mission-driven activity was not abandoned, and many a Bible College was started. The ardent Southern Baptist separatist John R. Rice (1895–1980) founded *The Sword of the Lord* in 1924. For a time Rice was associated with fellow-Texan fundamentalist John Frank Norris (1877–1952), who might be misleadingly described as colorful, or more accurately as a disgrace, and who was most probably criminal in certain of his activities. He brought discredit to the cause, as did Amy Semple McPherson (1890–1944). She founded the International Church of the Four Square Gospel in 1927, just one year after some questionable, yet unexplained conduct. Norris, McPherson, and the Scopes trial provided material for writers such as Sinclair Lewis (1885–1951) and H. L. Mencken (1880–1956) and films such as *Elmer Gantry* and *Inherit the Wind* (both 1960). It is not surprising that back in England, evangelicals tended to shun the term fundamentalist, not because they necessarily disagreed with such views of the Bible but in order to evade association with American excesses.

Also in this era, Bob Jones (1883–1968), of Wesleyan-Holiness parentage, spurred on by the humiliation at Dayton and the encouragement of Bryan, set up the stridently fundamentalist Bob Jones College in 1927, which became the Bob Jones University in 1947 on relocation to Greenville, South Carolina. The name of the institution says a lot. Our contemporary cult of the celebrity owes almost as much to militant, fundamentalist revivalism as it does to the entertainment industry. Carl T. McIntire was ever diligent and episodically argumentative in the separatist cause, establishing the separatist American Council of Christian Churches (1941) and later the International Council of Christian Churches (1948). Marginalized fundamentalism became ever more conspicuous for its *individual entrepreneurialism*. Not only was this to open the way back to mass attention, in due course it also primed the emergence of what came to be known as neo-Evangelicalism.

The separate "evangelicals only" para-church organizations that emerged from the 1920s to the 1940s were portentous. They were the means by which fundamentalist evangelicals regrouped and recovered from the nadir of the 1920s. The regrouping produced what the literature, as well as their critics, eventually referred to as neo-Evangelicalism. This supposedly *new* kind of Evangelicalism aspired to distance itself from the negativism of separatist fundamentalism, while resisting modernism. It was more open than the militantly separatist fundamentalism of the 1920s, and under some circumstances ready to co-operate with non-evangelicals. With this new departure there was always the question of how far Neo-Evangelicalism itself would or could move without exceeding the limits of Evangelicalism itself, or losing its support base, or both. Of course, none of this was as new as it might seem. English and Scottish evangelicals had already coexisted with non-evangelicals for two centuries.

Initially, the two pivotal neo-evangelical figures were Charles Edward Fuller (1887–1968), who for years conducted the much loved Old Fashioned Revival Hour radio program in the United States, and Harold John Ockenga

(1905–85), pastor of Park Street Church in Boston, Massachusetts, from 1936 to 1969, who was trained at the Westminster Theological Seminary, Philadelphia. Along with leaders such as Clarence Macartney, they held an aversion to "come-out-ism," notwithstanding the respect in which they held Machen's memory. By the late 1930s, Fuller and Ockenga had come to the conclusion that separatism should *not* be made a necessary additional plank on the evangelical platform. They were influenced in part by their perception that separatist fundamentalism had become excessively shaped by its own penchant for emphatic repudiations, in part by a sense that the spiritual tide was starting to turn in their favor, and also that there were a lot more Bible-believing Christians "out there" in mainline denominations than they initially suspected. Encouraged by the example of the New England Fellowship, founded in 1929 by J. Elwin Wright (1890–1973), Wright and Ockenga established the National Assembly of Evangelicals (NAE) in 1942. This body was unacceptable to McIntire and his separatist associates because it received into membership evangelical denominations as well as individual evangelicals in mainline or other such mixed denominations. What the NAE would not do is accept denominations as members if they were affiliated with the mainline Federal Council of Churches.

Billy Graham and Crusading Neo-Evangelicalism

The rising spiritual tide detected by the neo-evangelicals in the late 1930s was especially exemplified in the emergent Youth for Christ rallies. The Youth for Christ movement started in the USA around 1940, and British Youth for Christ was in action by the summer of 1945. It brought to public attention a raft of new evangelists, including Jack Wyrtzen (1913–96) known for his wartime Word of Life rallies in New York City, Torrey Maynard Johnson (1909–2002) who eventually became first President of Youth for Christ, and Marvin Rosell, preacher at the trend-setting Youth for Christ Victory Rally in Chicago in October 1944. That Youth for Christ style rallies were immensely successful is beyond dispute. The word revival was inevitably in play. It is often forgotten that although this was the era of big-band dance music, the teenage youth of countless fundamentalist households were forbidden dancing, the movies, and much more besides. The rallies provided opportunities to meet and mix with members of the opposite sex that even the strictest fundamentalist parents could not forbid. Their children attended in droves. Onto this scene came the Canadian Charles Bradley Templeton (1915–2001) and the man who was to become the preaching prince of the new evangelicals: William Franklin Graham.

Billy Graham's parents were separatist Presbyterians. He became a Southern Baptist in 1934, when he experienced conversion under the revivalist preaching of Mordecai Ham (1877–1961). Graham was educated at the strictly evangelical Wheaton College. He first achieved prominence at Youth for Christ rallies. He visited Great Britain with Johnson and Templeton in 1946, and again in 1947–8. Graham collaborated with Templeton in the founding of Youth for Christ International at Winona Lake, Indiana, in July 1945. Graham was to be the greatest and most influential exponent of "mass rally altar call evangelism" in the second half of the twentieth century.

From the outset of this new phase in the history of Evangelicalism, its intellectual deficit was evident. Templeton had established his reputation in Toronto by the late 1940s, but he became concerned by what he perceived as the superficiality of revivalist-style evangelism. Amid the hype, a sense of shallowness gnawed away at him. He concluded that responsible evangelism now required considerably more than a rhetorical aptitude for utilizing Bible passages and turns of phrase in the contrived atmosphere of a mass rally. It became clear to him that preaching required an in-depth understanding of the Bible and its teaching. Templeton was disposed to think that this was, or ought to be, the case with Graham also. Templeton entered Princeton Seminary in the fall of 1948. Templeton discussed his concerns with Graham. Templeton could not ignore the reality that while neo-Evangelicalism had repudiated separatism, it remained deeply fundamentalist in its biblical literalism. Graham was a premillennial dispensationalist—for him there could be no other way. The issues Templeton found himself unable to dismiss included the status of the creation narratives at the opening of Genesis and the biological origins of humankind.

Alas, Graham could only reply with conventional dogmatic assertions from the fundamentalist repertoire, and personal affirmations of the power of "the Bible says" declarations in the pulpit. The required reading of Scripture was not simply literary, but *literalistic*, and to question such a reading was to question God—end of story. For Templeton this amounted to a blind and unthinking obedience that was tantamount to spiritual disobedience. His rebuke to Graham is reported thus:

> "Bill, you cannot refuse to think. To do that is to die intellectually. You cannot disobey Christ's great commandment to love God 'with all thy heart and all thy soul *and all thy mind!*' . . . Not to think is a sin against your Creator. You can't stop thinking. That's intellectual suicide."[1]

---

1. Martin, *The Billy Graham Story*, 110–112; Frady, *Billy Graham*, 181–182.

Graham was bereft of serious answers to serious questions. The resolution of his subsequent turmoil came with a dogmatic reaffirmation of biblical authenticity and reliability, but without a cogent and coherent response to the issues Templeton was raising. Here, once again, we see the intellectual deficit in evidence. Years of fundamentalist obscurantism had taken their toll. When the Scottish Old Testament scholar George Adam Smith (1856–1942) had visited the aging Moody in 1899, he found him unable to grasp the gravity of the issues raised by the historical critical analysis of the biblical texts. Half a century later, by far the greater part of Evangelicalism was no further forward—including the rising Billy Graham. Sadly, Princeton Seminary could not give Templeton the clarity he was seeking either, and he eventually disavowed the faith. The intellectual deficit can and does have serious pastoral consequences. The neo-evangelical movement briefly considered a Christian university in North America, but true to form, the project lapsed.

Graham ignored the intellectual issues as he went on to his Los Angeles revival meetings in 1949 and founded the Billy Graham Evangelistic Association in 1950. Thereafter there seemed to be no stopping him. His reputation was further boosted by extended Crusades in London (1954, twelve weeks) and New York (1957, sixteen weeks). There were Crusades in Australia and New Zealand. In all there were to be over forty major evangelistic campaigns in America and around the world. His anti-communist fervor brought the support of right-wing nationalist newspaper mogul William Randolph Hearst (1863–1951). In his prime, Graham was an impressive figure—tall, handsome, with a grand head of wavy hair, piercing eyes, all with a relentlessly insistent platform eloquence that could play on fear and guilt with intense persuasiveness. In a cultural context never free of the fear of global thermo-nuclear destruction, Graham's dark prognostications concerning the future owed much to his underlying premillennial dispensationalism. And with it came the employment of an extensive array of perception-shaping, attitude-forming, response-generating techniques including stirring music ("Just as I am," "How great Thou art,") performed by George Beverley Shea (1909–2013) and massed choirs, a stream of periodical and occasional publications, and a radio program: "The Hour of Decision." All was designed to elicit decisions for Christ. The methods used merit careful comparison with the techniques of manufactured consent, developed in the United States earlier in the century. The invitation system was routinely employed. In 1954 Graham was on the cover of *Time* magazine. His style of crusade evangelism rode the rising tide of American global influence. For a time, all seemed grist to its mill. When the Billy Graham Crusade came to town, pastors either had to go with the flow, or be locked out of the action. The dominance of the US dollar at that time rendered much of the non-communist world highly accessible. In crest-fallen British, and post-colonial Australian and New Zealand settings, an American accent could of itself sound commandingly authoritative. Graham was less successful on the European continent, where his customary techniques could be eerily redolent of the 1930s Nuremberg rallies.

Graham was the master of a passing phenomenon; he was the only crusade-style evangelist to survive as a big-time operator well into the age of television. The tendency was towards the tele-evangelist of the late twentieth century. And here let honor be given where it is due: Graham acted early and decisively to suppress any tendency towards questionable financial practices in the BGEA, and by all accounts he was scrupulous when it came to upholding his marriage vows. This cannot be said for others. Yet whenever Graham delivered his stock-in-trade "the Bible says . . ." he knew that there were big questions on the relationship between biblical teaching and extra-biblical evidence that he was unwilling or unable to discuss in depth.

The actual impact of the Graham crusades remains open to question. The number of totally unchurched people reached and influenced seems to have been decidedly limited. Many who were bussed to crusade meetings already had some previous local church connection. Furthermore, a good proportion of decisions for Christ were by persons seeking to reaffirm a prior but possibly somewhat lapsed commitment. The overall impact was transient. Crime figures might drop for a time, but deeper, culture-wide, deleterious trends were not halted or reversed. There was no great crusade-ignited revival.

On the contrary, the stark truth is that shortly after the great 1954 Harringay Crusade the massive downturn in attendance at public worship in Great Britain commenced with a vengeance. Two further crusades in 1964–5 were of minimal impact. By that time many in England had come to equate Christianity with Billy Graham—and that was the end of the discussion. Since the 1960s, and in spite of some highly active segments, English Christianity has been in retreat. The evangelical mix of fundamentalism and private piety (sometimes laced with high doses of anti-intellectualism) has proved incapable of addressing the mounting challenges. By the beginning of the twenty-first century senior evangelicals might recollect the Graham crusades with a certain wistful nostalgia, but there are hard questions about them that need to be asked and answered.

The Pasadena Saga

Meanwhile, in the USA, Charles Fuller had long pondered Evangelicalism's intellectual deficit, although he did so in pre-eminently theological terms. In 1947, with Ockenga and others, he established Fuller Theological Seminary at a salubrious location in Pasadena, California. To varying degrees the group had been influenced by Gordon Haddon Clark (1902-85). At Wheaton College he had persistently challenged fundamentalist-inclined students to avoid obscurantism and take ideas seriously. The founders of Fuller held the reputation of "old Princeton" in high esteem, even envisaging Fuller as a successor, but without the baggage that came with Westminster Theological Seminary scholasticism and separatism. It sought to influence mainline Protestantism with its broader brand of Evangelicalism. Also involved in establishing Fuller was Carl Ferdinand Howard Henry (1913-2003), who at this time published *The Uneasy Conscience of Modern Fundamentalism* (1947), in which he challenged the abdication of fundamentalism from questions of humanitarian and civic concern. In effect, he called for a return to the much earlier tradition of evangelical social ethics. Carl Henry edited *Christianity Today* from 1956 to 1968. The publication functioned as the new Evangelicalism's response to the mainline *Christian Century*.

The stance of Fuller Theological Seminary was decidedly evangelical while forthrightly non-separatist. There was ongoing friction with separatist evangelicals who were convinced that they detected the putrid stench of spiritual compromise. Edward John Carnell (1919-67) was appointed President of Fuller in 1957. In *The Case for Orthodox Theology* (1959) he repudiated fundamentalism and attacked Gresham Machen as a separatist. Controversy was inevitable. John R. Rice, editor of the separatist *The Sword of the Lord,* was scathing. Militant separatists such as Carl McIntire rarely passed up opportunities to apply condemnatory pressure on the fledgling institution. Bob Jones withdrew his support.

The early Fuller faculty was diverse. In addition to Carnell himself, George Eldon Ladd (1911-82) was most conspicuous in aspiring to demonstrate that neo-evangelicals could debate the issues with modernists with integrity, acumen, candor, and faith abounding. The early faculty also included Old Testament specialist David Allan Hubbard (1927-96), apologetics writer Wilbur Moorehead Smith (1894-1976), the still separatist-minded Charles Woodbridge (1902-1980), and Harold Lindsell (1913-98). All were premillennial in their eschatology. To these and others was added Béla Vassady (1902-92) of Hungarian reformed origins, who had translated Barth into Hungarian. The circumstances of Fuller were exceedingly fraught, especially for those attempting to grapple with modernist biblical scholarship while adhering to versions of the "old Princeton" notion of inerrancy.

In the case of Carnell, he found the occasionally acerbic responses to his own forthright language hard to endure. When Barth visited Chicago in April 1962, Carnell managed to ask him a question that did not endorse inerrancy—which in turn inevitably provided further ammunition for his separatist-fundamentalist critics. Indeed, at this time Cornelius Van Til (1895-1987), of Westminster Theological Seminary, Philadelphia, played the role of Elisha to Gresham Machen's Elijah, by mounting a crusade against Barth as the initiator of a new modernism in his *Christianity and Barthianism* (1962)—the title being an allusion to Machen's *Christianity and Liberalism* (1923). Fuller was not a Barthian institution, but in addition to Vassady, the Englishman Geoffrey Bromiley (1915-2009), who translated much of Barth into English, was on the faculty from 1958 onwards. Moreover, and as if to build a case against the institution, Charles Fuller's son Daniel had studied for years in Switzerland under Barth himself. These associations militated against the trenchant avowals of inerrancy made by Lindsell and Woodbridge.

Matters came to a head on Black Saturday, December 1, 1962.[2] The immediate issues included Hubbard's rejection of the Mosaic authorship of the full Pentateuch, the dating of Daniel, and Daniel Fuller's insistence that there were technical errors and inexactitudes in the biblical texts. The founder's son was careful to assert that while the Bible does not err in what it reveals, this lack of error does not extend to the cosmological assumptions, chronological ordering, and historical details provided by the authors. Moreover, he drove the point home by emphasizing that these issues would not be resolved even if we had recourse to the original autographs so central to the standpoint of the nineteenth-century Princeton professoriate.

Here was an uncomfortable doctrine—for fundamentalists. It takes the realities of the biblical texts, and shows them to be incompatible with the central fundamentalist *shibboleth* of inerrancy. It does not set aside the historic Christian belief in the inspiration and authority of Scripture. It does, however, require an adequate contextualization of the biblical texts. It requires that the canonical texts be regarded as being of divine inspiration *and human composition*. And it requires recognition that the Scriptures, not being God, are therefore *creaturely*. Certainly, many evangelicals have formally disavowed bibliolatry, but they have not always avoided it in practice. As if to order, within a year of the 1962 crisis at Fuller Seminary, Richard

2. Marsden, *Reforming Fundamentalism*, 197-248.

Hofstadter (1916–70) published his *Anti-Intellectualism in American Life* (1963).

Carnell, already encountering serious health difficulties, relinquished the Presidency, and died in 1967 in tragic circumstances. In the wake of Black Saturday, Ockenga and his circle turned to Graham for leadership, but as with Templeton he proved to be less than adequate. Hubbard eventually assumed the Presidency of the seminary. This was a tipping-point, and expressions of conservative disaffection were inevitable. Wilbur Morehead Smith—author of *Therefore Stand* (1945)—resigned from Fuller in 1963. Harold Lindsell resigned in 1964 and became the editor of *Christianity Today* in 1968. Meanwhile, Ladd was deeply affected by the critical reception accorded his *Jesus and the Kingdom* (1964), from which he never fully recovered, and eventually sank into alcoholism. The experiences of Carnell and Ladd serve to confirm the challenges for Bible-believing Christians when seeking to make a mark with the intellectual-academic mainstream for much of the twentieth century. Above all, they lacked the grounding in philosophical prolegomena required to effectively interact with astute, articulate and well-informed critics.

English Divisions

To many evangelicals it seemed best to stick with the position articulated by "old Princeton," also eloquently restated by the faculty of Westminster Theological Seminary, Philadelphia, in their symposium *The Infallible Word* (1946). Graham may have been a neo-evangelical, but on the subject of the Bible he was an old-style fundamentalist. He always maintained close connections with British counterparts. He greatly admired the Ulsterman, J. Edwin Orr (1912–87), a NAE cofounder, and his extensive worldwide evangelistic campaigns between 1931 and 1962. He was close to the Welsh revivalist preacher Thomas B. Rees (1911–70) and the African-born son of British missionaries, Stephen F. Olford (1918–2004). Evangelists such as Alan Redpath (1907–89) operated on both sides of the ocean. The trans-Atlantic dimension is never to be ignored.

Mainline churchly opinion in England viewed Graham as problematically fundamentalist, especially in the wake of his 1954 Crusade and 1955 CICCU mission to the University of Cambridge. This is the background to A. G. Herbert's *Fundamentalism and the Church of God* (1957). The response came from a rising English evangelical, James I. Packer, in the form of *Fundamentalism and the Word of God* (1958). This was a polemically astute restatement of the "old Princeton" standpoint and remains one of the key texts for understanding twentieth-century Evangelicalism. At the time, Packer was a Church of England clergyman teaching at Tyndale Hall, Bristol, England, where some students nicknamed him "infallible Jim."

Packer had already had a significant impact on English Evangelicalism with an article in which he criticized the Keswick view of sanctification.[3] In short, Packer rejected the teachings of the holiness movement in favor of those of reformed theology. His ecclesiology was contra-separatist and ecumenically inclusive, with a willingness to receive Anglo-Catholics as affirmers of the ancient creeds—as expressed in his editing of *All in Each Place* (1965).

Packer was one of those gathered around the London-based Free Church preacher David Martyn Lloyd-Jones (1899–1981). Puritanism was their common inspiration. The key to understanding Lloyd-Jones—"the Doctor"—was that he was Welsh, Calvinistic, and Methodist. His pastorate at Westminster Chapel, London, extended from 1939 to 1968. From 1956 to 1969 he oversaw annual Puritan and Reformed Study Conferences at Westminster Chapel. Parallel with this development was the establishment of the Banner of Truth Trust, under the leadership of Iain H. Murray in 1957. Initially based in London, and later in Edinburgh, "The Banner" has pursued a publishing agenda that, while it has eschewed many of the superficialities of contemporary Evangelicalism, exhibited an anachronistic appropriation and melding of seventeenth-century Puritan ecclesiology, eighteenth-century Great Awakening Evangelicalism, and nineteenth-century Princeton theology.

The Westminster Central Hall Confrontation

Separatist-minded Free Church evangelicals, of whom Lloyd-Jones was by far the most conspicuous, and others who were committed to evangelical participation in the mainline Church of England, such as Packer, originally supported this tendency, which might be termed neo-Puritan. The mix was unstable. The misgivings of the separatists towards the ecumenical movement exerted a definite pressure on the evangelical Anglicans participating in the Puritan and Reformed Study Conferences. At the same time, it seemed that the old nonconformist denominations of England were on the verge of collapse.

On the Anglican evangelical side, the 1950s had witnessed the rise to prominence of John R. W. Stott (1921–2011), the crisply eloquent Rector of

---

3. Packer, "Keswick," 153–167.

All Souls Langham Place in the West End of London, from 1950 onwards. Stott was among those instrumental in bringing Billy Graham to England in 1954. If Graham was the arch-evangelist, Stott was the arch-pastor of neo-Evangelicalism. At least by the late 1950s he was widely considered to be the unofficial leader of the evangelical party in the Church of England. Matters between the separatists and the evangelical Anglicans came to a head at a public meeting of the Evangelical Alliance held at Westminster Central Hall in London on October 18, 1966. There, Lloyd-Jones, in effect, called upon Anglican evangelicals to quit their position within the established church and to join with their non-Anglican evangelical brethren. How this was to be achieved was unclear. Stott, in the chair, resisted this appeal and asserted that Lloyd-Jones's separatist proposal was unscriptural. There was considerable unease as the meeting wound down. The tension was palpable and the body language eloquent. Nothing was resolved. English Evangelicalism was never the same thereafter.[4]

Evangelicals had long talked of their spiritual unity. Lloyd-Jones's call arose from his deep apprehensions as to the direction of the renewed ecumenical movement since the World Council of Churches 1948 meeting in Amsterdam. However, he came to the meeting with an inadequate ecclesiology. While he was clear that parallel denominational structures are without scriptural basis, little structural and insufficient historical insight was displayed concerning the relationship between the church as the people of God, and its various institutional expressions. The possible outcome of Lloyd-Jones's exhortations, if widely heeded, would have been a separatist evangelical body alongside Anglican and other Free Church entities. When considering these matters, it is worth recalling that the main body of sixteenth and seventeenth-century English Puritans were *not* separatists, and in 1660 they did *not* immediately quit the Church of England upon the restoration of episcopacy, and had sought to work constructively within the English Church until they were maneuvered out in 1662.

After the events of late 1966, the Anglican evangelicals proceeded to intensify and consolidate their participation in the full life of the Church of England, as their decisions at Keele (1967) and Nottingham (1977) confirmed. However, many in the Anglican evangelical rank and file were less than adequately equipped to participate fully. Nevertheless, it is important to observe that in Great Britain evangelical biblical scholarship at last began to achieve significant scholarly depth in New Testament studies. The leaders included F. F. Bruce (1910–90), Donald Guthrie (1915–92), John Wenham

---

4. For diverse retrospectives on this episode, see Murray, *D. Martyn Lloyd-Jones*, 513–528; Brencher, *Martyn Lloyd-Jones*, 92–95; Trueman, "J.I. Packer," 119–126; and Atherstone, *Engaging*, 261–292.

(1913–96), and Richard Thomas France. A long way has been travelled since F. F. Bruce published *The New Testament Documents. Are They Reliable?* (1943). Tyndale House in Cambridge, established in 1944, played an important role in this development. From England, recent decades have seen the publication of superb studies by the historian Richard Bauckham, and the impressive output of Nicholas Thomas (N.T.) Wright, including *Surprised by Hope* (2008) and especially *The Resurrection of the Son of God* (2003), arguably the most important book on the resurrection produced in a century. Alongside these must be placed the contributions of the James Dunn, a minister of the Church of Scotland, and the Methodist Ian H. Marshall. Comparable figures on the other side of the Atlantic include Craig A. Evans, Craig Blomberg, Ben Witherington III and Craig S. Keener.

The work of these scholars largely post-dates the 1962 crisis at Fuller and represents a significant advance on what was on offer half a century ago. Alas, the actual condition of Evangelicalism on the ground is far below what might be inferred from the best evangelical literature on the New Testament. John Stott famously stated that evangelicals were "Bible people and gospel people." Arguably, the problem of the evangelical rank and file (in pulpit and pew) remains that they don't know how to read the Bible, and function with a seriously *reduced and truncated* version of the gospel. In all this, the intellectual deficit of Evangelicalism, also in the fields of scientific endeavor and cultural expression, has become increasingly evident.

10

AFTER THE GREAT CRUSADE

A Babel of Discordant Voices

After the great wave of Graham crusades, English-speaking Evangelicalism exhibited increasingly volatile and disparate tendencies. Some would interpret the resulting ferment as the pains and stresses of spiritual growth. Without doubt there were those who did grow in grace and understanding, but a sustained analysis of the years following the World Congress on Evangelism (Berlin, 1966) and the First International Congress on World Evangelization (Lausanne, 1974) reveals a tangle of multiple and recurrent interrelated controversies and crises. Evangelicalism has been incapable of resolving its own inner conflicts. It is seriously deficient in bringing an integral Christian message to the barren materialism and deepening secularity so characteristic of the spiritual wastelands of contemporary western civilization. The Graham crusades may have shored up the faith of many, perhaps for a generation, but they could not resolve the deeper issues at the heart of Evangelicalism.

This array of unresolved inner conflicts includes: problems over what may or may not be meant by the terms infallibility and inerrancy when applied to the Bible; continued contention concerning the correct interpretation of Genesis 1–11; the question of the age of the earth and the causes and rate of deposition of the sedimentary strata in the geological column; issues raised by successive theories concerning the appearance, distribution, variegation and extinction of plant and animal species—in short, evolution—and more recently the status of assertions concerning intelligent design, and, for good measure, the question of how evangelicals ought to address and relate to contemporary culture.

Contemporary evangelical controversies about the age of the cosmos and evolution exhibit a sad lack of insight into the dynamic character of the order of creation. Evangelicalism's inability to formulate a biblically directed understanding of human culture is marked by an ugly inclination in the direction of right-wing authoritarianism and the counter-historical flowering of the charismatic movement with its unsubstantiated claims and questionable "wealth gospel" proclivities. Especially in the burgeoning charismatic sector of Evangelicalism, new waves of premillennial dispensationalism have flourished, to the point where for many evangelicals, Christian Zionism and its priorities have become a hallmark of soundness.

It is no exaggeration to say that contemporary Evangelicalism is in serious trouble because a great many evangelicals have come to seriously misread the Bible. This has been the case since the birth of Evangelicalism to the extent that it was already marked by a pronounced *individualism*, but is particularly so where the *premillennial dispensationalism* of Darby, Scofield, and their successors holds sway. Evangelicals under the spell of this teaching have *misrepresented* and *postponed* the kingdom of God. Having misconstrued the New Testament, they are convinced that the good news of the kingdom of God is not for them—and as far as they are concerned not for the rest of us either. This is the result of reading the Bible with an improper literalism and through the distorted lenses of dispensationalism.

The Continuing "Battle for the Bible"

Protestantism had generally asserted the infallibility of the canonical Scriptures, and by this term it had sought to acknowledge and receive the Scriptures as wholly trustworthy in the doctrine that they impart and that humankind is called to receive. In this sense the term *infallible* should present no difficulties to the Christian, in that the Scriptures *never fail* to teach us rightly of God our Creator, the creaturely status of all that is, apart from God himself, our human condition and predicament, of the deliverance provided by Jesus Christ, of the Holy Spirit, and so forth. However, the infallibility terminology can become problematic when pressed to the point of anachronistically imposing on Scripture latter-day notions of scientific accuracy. The Scriptures nowhere avow such notions themselves, which is hardly surprising, for the kind of analysis of the order of creation known to us as *scientific* was only in its infancy when the Scriptures were written. In relation to modern science, the biblical texts are not anti-scientific—they are pre-scientific. In some measure infallibility suffered by association with Papal Infallibility, as promulgated by Vatican I in 1870, involving the purported infallibility of the Roman pontiff when speaking *ex cathedra* on matters of faith and morals. However, apart from this development, infallibility was not tight enough for the Princeton professoriate in the later nineteenth century, since what they were really insisting on was *inerrancy*. However, in the later twentieth century, as competent evangelical scholars addressed the details of the biblical texts, and the more they compared texts with texts, along with extra-biblical textual and other evidence, the harder it became to live comfortably with the precepts of "old Princeton" affirmations of inerrancy. While some saw inerrancy as a bulwark, others found it to be a prescriptive barrier to understanding the texts themselves.

Even as the Graham Crusades were getting underway, the evangelical waters were being much disturbed by controversies surrounding the appearance of the Revised Standard Version (RSV) of the Bible, eventually published by the National Council of Churches (NT in 1946, OT in 1952, modified in 1962). Many evangelicals took strong exception to the RSV translation of messianic verses (such as Gen 49:10; Isa 7:14; Mic 5:2). The debate on the RSV draws our attention to the close orientation of protestant scholasticism to the "received text" (*Textus Receptus*) established in the wake of Erasmus of Rotterdam's groundbreaking work by Beza and his successors. The full history of the *Textus Receptus*, (the term itself dates from an edition of 1633), its formation, advocacy, criticism, and especially its relationship to the now less readily received Byzantine text, is beyond the scope of this study. It is sufficient to say that since the immensely painstaking work of Johann Jakob Griesbach in distinguishing the Alexandrian, Western, and Byzantine texts, and the subsequent appearance of B. F. Westcott (1825–1901) and F. J. A. Hort's (1828–92) *The New Testament in the Original Greek* (1881), it has been as good as impossible to insist on the exclusive use of the *Textus Receptus* without a measure of obscurantism.

Increasing awareness that the *Textus Receptus* no longer constituted a reliable basis for a trustworthy English translation prompted the production of the Revised Version (NT in 1881, OT in 1885). Evangelical organizations such as the Trinitarian Bible Society (founded 1831) have supported a *Textus Receptus* based text in order to retain passages such as the "Johannine Comma" (I John 5:7–8) against translations based on the United Bible Society texts. Discontent with the RSV spurred on the production of the New American Standard Bible (NASB), based on the earlier Revised Version, and the New International Version (NIV). The orientation of the latter towards inerrancy is evident in its rendition of passages such as Matthew

13:32. Discontent with the NIV helped to produce a slew of King James Version updates. Unease about Americanisms in the RSV helped generate the New English Bible (NT in 1961, OT in 1970). It was later (1989) revised and republished as the Revised English Bible (REB). The less idiosyncratic RSV-based English Standard Version (ESV) of 1971 has proved more acceptable. The RSV was revised as the New Revised Standard Version (NRSV) in 1989, the NASB was revised in 1995, and the NIV in 2011. For some, this complex history confirms the superiority of the Authorized Version (AV), but it is often not appreciated that the text of this version received considerable editorial revision in the 1760s.

Most contemporary evangelicals use modern English versions of the Bible. Donald A. Carson's *The King James Version Debate: A Plea for Realism* (1979) challenged King James Version diehards by reminding evangelicals that they were committed to the Reformation principle of the Bible in the language of the people, and not to an eighteenth-century revision of an early seventeenth-century text. At the same time, publishing houses catering to American-style evangelical proclivities have sought to maximize sales by vigorously using the techniques of market segmentation. Consequently, along with a great array of devotional bric-à-brac, known as "Jesus junk," the average evangelical retail store is well stocked with specially produced Bibles for soul-winners, end-times buffs, amateur archeologists, men, women, youth leaders, young people, and in some locations American patriots. The degree to which culturally naïve evangelicals are open to market place manipulation should not be underestimated. Contemporary evangelicals are much more likely to read the Bible individually, rather than corporately as members of the Body of Christ.

After Black Saturday in 1962, fundamentalist-inclined evangelicals were much more prone to want to add inerrancy to infallibility, believing that the addition of inerrancy would reduce to near zero the wiggle room habitually sought by doubters, waverers, temporizers and defectors. Harold Lindsell sounded the trumpet with his *The Battle for the Bible* (1976). The "International Council on Biblical Inerrancy" (ICBI) was constituted in 1977 and held its first summit in Chicago in 1978. Lindsell subsequently published *The Bible in the Balance* (1979). Norman L. Geisler edited the papers read at the summit as *Inerrancy* (1980). Not least, all of this was designed to hold the line at the requirement of the Evangelical Theological Society (ETS), founded in 1949, that its members *annually* affirm that the Bible was "inerrant in the autographs." Here again the influence of the old Princeton professoriate is readily apparent. They had, in effect, argued for an inerrant Bible that no longer exists, as the original autographs are long lost.

The Chicago summit promulgated *The Chicago Statement on Biblical Inerrancy* (1978). Not everyone self-defining as conservative evangelical was ready to concur. The temperature rose appreciably with the publication of *The Authority and Interpretation of the Bible: An Historical Approach* (1979), by Jack B. Rogers (1915-2005) and Donald McKim. Rogers had previously published *Scripture in the Westminster Confession* (1966). Both men were Presbyterians and Reformation historians. Arguably they overstated their case at certain points, also in respect of the extent to which the Princeton professoriate had at all points *deliberately* based their theological formulations on the precepts of Scottish Common Sense philosophy. The emphatic statements of Rogers and McKim left them open to strong critical responses, and these were duly provided by James I. Packer, in *Beyond the Battle for the Bible* (1980), and John D. Woodbridge in *Biblical Authority* (1982).

The conversation did not develop in the manner that Rogers and McKim desired. At times they must have felt themselves bombarded by the heavy artillery of inerrancy. Yet two features of the Rogers and McKim thesis ought not to be forgotten. First, they recognized the dependence of theological reflection on epistemological assumptions open to philosophical analysis—which in turn points to the need for the articulation of an authentically Christian philosophy. Second, they commended to evangelicals the *non-liberal and non-fundamentalist* understanding of biblical authority exemplified in the series Studies in Dogmatics by the Dutch theologian Gerrit Cornelis Berkouwer (1903-96), whose work on *De Heilige Schrift* Rogers had edited and translated as *Holy Scripture* (1975). Berkouwer was indebted to the doctrinal legacy of Abraham Kuyper (1837-1920) and Herman Bavinck (1854-1921) of the Free University, Amsterdam.

In the USA of the 1980s, evangelicals were disinclined to learn what the thinking of Reformation-minded Christians from the Netherlands and elsewhere might have to teach them. They pressed forward with their inerrancy crusade. However, the concept of inerrancy continued to collide with the discontinuities exhibited within the extant biblical tests. Fine bold declarations had to be qualified in the face of problems and anomalies. For example: Who killed Goliath?[1] A second summit issued *The Chicago State-*

---

1. Was it David (1 Sam 17:49-51) or Elhanan (2 Sam 21:19)? If there was only one Goliath then he is reported as having been slain by two different men. Or were there *two* Goliaths, namely Goliath the Philistine (1 Sam 17:23) and Goliath the Gittite (2 Sam 21:19)? But were there *really* two Goliaths? A certain edge is lent to this question by the Chronicler, who apparently wants to circumvent a perceived incompatibility between the two texts by stating that it was Lahmi a *brother of Goliath* who was slain by Elhanan (1 Chr 20:5). Of course, this leaves us with a further question—precisely who did Elhanan slay, "the shaft of whose spear was like a weaver's beam"? Was it Goliath the Gittite or his brother Lahmi? The KJV sought to resolve these problems by importing

ment on Biblical Hermeneutics (1982), the relevant papers were published as *Hermeneutics, Inerrancy and the Bible* (1984). One of the editors was Robert D. Preus (1924–95), who played a central role in opposing historical critical scholarship within the Lutheran Church-Missouri Synod. Defending inerrancy prompted a high level of literary production in short order. Composite publications abounded. While McKim edited *The Authoritative Word* (1983), the other side came forth with *Scripture and Truth* (1983) and *Hermeneutics, Authority and Canon* (1986), both edited by Donald A. Carson and John D. Woodbridge. *The Chicago Statement on Biblical Application*, the third statement in the sequence, came in 1986. The relevant papers were edited by Kenneth S. Kantzer and published as *Applying the Scriptures* (1987). The ICBI records now repose in the archives of Dallas Theological Seminary, a bastion of premillennial dispensationalism.

Among evangelicals, pressure to conform to the Chicago statements affirmed by both reformed scholastics and premillennial dispensationalists has generated a *non-liberal and non-fundamentalist* literature on biblical authority that has not always received the attention that it deserves. In this category are Harry R. Boer's (1913–1999) *The Bible and Higher Criticism* (republished 1981) and Carl E. Armerding's *The Old Testament and Criticism* (1983). It was during this period that the work of two rising evangelical historians shed light on the troubles Evangelicalism now endured. They were George M. Marsden and Mark A. Noll. Marsden published *Fundamentalism and American Culture* (1980), *Reforming Fundamentalism: Fuller Seminary and the New Evangelicalism* (1987), and edited *Evangelicalism and Modern America* (1984). Shortly thereafter Noll's valuable *Between Faith and Criticism* (1986) appeared. However, these elucidations of the influence of the "old Princeton" thinking on inspiration, and particularly inerrancy and its implications for evangelical biblical scholarship, still tended to assume the validity of Evangelicalism's self-understanding, and were arguably written too much from within the circle of its assumptions about itself. The continued adherence of the Evangelical Theological Society to its inerrancy formula was not all that was at stake—for the defenders of biblical inerrancy, Evangelicalism of *any* sort was at stake.

The pressures of that era are well illustrated by the protracted struggle that took place within the Southern Baptist Convention (SBC)—the largest protestant denomination in the USA. There an early focus of attention was on *The Message of Genesis: A Theological Interpretation* (1961), by Ralph H. Elliott (1921–2012), who was dismissed from Midwestern Baptist

---

the Chronicler's reference to a "brother of Goliath" into its rendition of 2 Sam 21:19. The RSV, NRSV, and NIV avoid this strategy.

Theological Seminary, Kansas City, Missouri, for refusing to "voluntarily" allow the suppression of his book. Avoidance of a scrupulous consideration of the issues presented by Genesis 1–11, literalism and infallibility was all too prevalent. The tensions and insecurities generated by this affair, coupled with other issues relating to the Pentateuch, and unresolved issues concerning seminary training, combined to produce a context favoring a conservative reaction. Over some two decades fundamentalist opinion within the SBC was fostered, organized, and mobilized by figures such as Wallie Amos Criswell (1909–2002), Paige Patterson, R. Albert Mohler, and H. Paul Pressler. The success of this orchestrated conservative resurgence from 1979 onwards resulted in the SBC functioning as a fundamentalist bastion. As the reverberations continue, it should be recognized that questions concerning how the Bible is to be interpreted are never genuinely resolved by the outcome of orchestrated ecclesiastical power plays. The losers might be banished and their works suppressed, but the basic questions remain.

The Churchman-Anvil Affair

In Great Britain, James Barr (1924–2006) threw the fat into the fire with the publication of *Fundamentalism* (1977). Barr distressed the British evangelical leadership by declaring them to be fundamentalists. Notwithstanding diverse inaccuracies, Barr was correct on this point: many British evangelicals were fundamentalists in their understanding of biblical inerrancy. However, they did not include most of the better British evangelical biblical scholars, who could see the point of at least some of Barr's assertions, but could justifiably claim that they did not apply to themselves personally. A little later, at the 1981 Anglican Evangelical Assembly in London, James Dunn read a paper entitled "The Authority of Scripture: According to Scripture," which was published the following year as a two-part article in *The Churchman*.[2] Dunn challenged the "old Princeton" doctrine as championed by Packer and the Chicago statements by questioning the construction placed on the proof texts usually adduced in support of inerrancy, and with reference to the overall tenor and character of the canonical texts themselves.

The article exacerbated the strained relationship between the Church Society, the publishers of *The Churchman*, and its editorial board. The following year the Society dismissed and replaced the Board, the displaced

---

2. Dunn, "Authority," 104–122; 201–225. For a response, see Nicole, "Inspiration," 198–215; 7–27; 198–208. See also the earlier exchange between J.I. Packer and R.T. France. Of particular interest is France's discussion of 1 Cor 10:4. See Packer, "Hermeneutics" and France, "Inerrancy," 3–12 and 12–18 respectively.

party eventually launching an alternative publication named *Anvil*. As in the case of the SBC, the power plays of ecclesiastical maneuvering could not of themselves resolve questions of principle and scholarship, only who might control what platform at a given time. John Stott was unable to prevent a rupture. The Churchman-Anvil affair confirmed that some evangelicals were much more fundamentalist, in the sense of being committed to inerrancy, than others. Barr's assertion that English evangelicals were more fundamentalist than they were disposed to acknowledge was of greater validity when applied to the pro-inerrancy end of the evangelical spectrum than to the other. It was not until Harriet A. Harris published her *Fundamentalism and Evangelicals* (1998) that the much-needed elucidation of the relationship between the two could be said to have begun in earnest. Overall, in comparison with Barr, Harris offered a much better-informed discussion and was altogether more astute in her assessments.

Continuing American Turbulence

American Evangelicalism generally remains committed to inerrancy. The inerrancy doctrine is the necessary prerequisite without which the adherents of the reformed-scholastic and premillennial dispensationalist systems are unable to argue for the authoritative "Bible-based" status of their respective standpoints. Beyond these groupings, the tide has been moving *away* from inerrancy. There is a pattern of better evangelical biblical scholars producing important work in contested fields, only to be challenged as defectors and revisionists and sometimes dislodged from their teaching positions if deemed recalcitrant. The provenance and context of the Book of Daniel remains a veritable battleground. While this book, and a certain way of reading it, remains pivotal for premillennial dispensationalists, Genesis 1–11 also continues to be contentious.

The publication of *Inspiration and Incarnation: Evangelicals and the Problem of the Old Testament* (2005) by Peter Enns evoked memories of the experience of Ralph H. Elliott more than four decades earlier. Gregory K. Beale offered an early response in *The Erosion of Inerrancy in Evangelicalism: Responding to New Challenges to Biblical Authority* (2008). After a protracted process, in 2008 the board of Westminster Theological Seminary, Philadelphia, obliged Enns to quit. Much of the discussion was framed in terms of consistency with the Westminster Standards—so in this case confessionalism was also in play. Enns subsequently published *The Evolution of Adam: What the Bible Does and Doesn't Say about Human Origins* (2012).

The inconvenient truth was that challenges to inerrancy were arising from among evangelicals who took the Bible very seriously. The position enshrined in the Chicago statements, if its postulates were to be preserved, seemed to require that *believing* biblical scholarship, on the texts and contexts of Scripture, be called to an artificial halt always at the point where the inerrancy doctrine was liable to be compromised. In effect, inerrancy inhibited a deepening of understanding. Such matters were addressed at the Wheaton Theology Conference in 2001. The resulting papers, edited by Vincent E. Bacote as *Evangelicals and Scripture: Tradition, Authority and Hermeneutics* (2004), included serious criticisms of the inerrancy postulate. Subsequently, A. T. B. McGowan published *The Divine Authenticity of Scripture: Retrieving an Evangelical Heritage* (2007), wherein evangelicals again had their attention drawn to the work of important authors from the Netherlands: Bavinck, Berkouwer, and the New Testament scholar Herman Ridderbos (1909–2007). These writers took the inspiration and authority of Scripture very seriously, but adopted a more organic understanding of biblical inspiration than that of "old Princeton."

Of course, the champions of "old Princeton" are always ready to assert that without inerrancy everything else goes, but amid the heady rhetoric there have always been mainline evangelicals ready to argue otherwise, such as James Orr (1844–1913) and Donald G. Bloesch (1928–2010). Among those associated with Westminster Theological Seminary, the legacy of Geerhardus Vos pointed beyond the confines of "old Princeton" and the same may be said of the work of Meredith G. Kline (1922–2007). Following the Enns affair, Jonathan J. Yeo published *Plundering the Egyptians: The Old Testament and Historical Criticism at Westminster Theological Seminary (1929–1998)* (2010). This study indicated that even the faculty of Westminster could not remain permanently impervious to broader developments in Old Testament scholarship. Moreover, in recent years, researchers such as Carlos R. Bovell have explored the deleterious psycho-spiritual consequences of requiring young Christians to adhere to a position of such dubious tenability. After all, faith and repentance are the true preludes to Christian discipleship—not intellectual obscurantism.

Many evangelicals have found it very hard to face up to the creaturely status of the Bible. The Bible is not God—it is not divine. In terms of the Nicene Creed, it is not a person of the Triune Godhead. Inspired by the Holy Spirit, and of divine authority, yes—but unquestionably a product of human composition and transmission. A synchronous reading of the Samuel-Kings and Chronicles sequences in the Old Testament, or of the four gospels in the New Testament, leaves the scrupulous reader well aware of the humanity, partiality and perspectival standpoint of the various authors.

The discontinuities and inconsistencies are part of that picture and do not require contrived explanations based on special pleading. In all of this it is necessary for Christians to recognize that they have received the Scriptures that the Holy Spirit has been pleased to provide.

The truth of the Bible does not reside in any absolute rational-literary consistency. The "hear and do the Word" impact of the Scriptures in the lives of those who believe takes place as the Holy Spirit, indwelling God's people, directs us to respond obediently to the instruction of the Holy Spirit speaking in Scripture. In contemporary Evangelicalism the Word and Spirit are liable to be driven apart. The authority of the written Word can be misconstrued in rational-logical terms without reference to the Holy Spirit, while the work of the Holy Spirit can be misconstrued in irrational-emotive terms without reference to the written Word. The consequences of the latter became increasingly apparent in the largest growing grouping within mid-twentieth-century Evangelicalism: the Pentecostal and charismatic movements.

Creation and Creationism: Evolution and Evolutionism

As the intra-evangelical debate on inerrancy was entering its most recent phase, John H. Walton published *The Lost World of Genesis One* (2009), in which he presented the case for a "cosmic temple view" of Gen 1:1–2:3. This view is of considerable cogency, and merits serious attention, as does *The Lost World of Adam and Eve* (2015). These are literarily sensitive without being literalist and make textual and contextual sense. Regrettably, such work stands in stark contrast to the literalist tendency in much evangelical—and especially fundamentalist and charismatic—thinking over the last half-century. Indeed, this period has witnessed the rise among evangelicals of a new and sometimes aggressive "creationism."

By creationism we do not, of course, mean the belief that God is the Creator of all things. That has always been the Christian confession. By creationism we mean the belief that "the heavens and the earth," were created a mere six to twelve thousand years ago in the course of six days, each of twenty-four hours of sixty minutes. Famously, in calculations he offered in 1654, James Ussher (1581–1656) came up with the date of October 26, 4004 BC for the creation of the cosmos. As is now obvious to most people, Ussher made a number of erroneous assumptions, including interpreting the genealogical listings of Genesis 4 and 11 as precise chronologies rather than as indications of general lineage.

In the course of geological exploration and reflection from the seventeenth to the mid-nineteenth centuries, it became very clear that the earth was very much older than had hitherto been assumed. The rise of the geological sciences was not driven by any intention to challenge biblical teaching but in order to increase scientific understanding. There was no sinister plot to sideline the Bible; rather, the patient investigation of extensive sedimentary strata yielded results that had a persuasive strength of their own. Christians of undoubted conviction were often involved in such scientific endeavors. Hugh Miller, author of *The Old Red Sandstone* (1841), *Footprints of the Creator* (1849), and *The Testimony of the Rocks* (1857), is a frequently cited example. As a result, in the nineteenth century, many reflective readers of Scripture—even if they lacked adequate insight into the ancient near-eastern context of Genesis 1–11—concluded that these Scriptures should be read in a literary and possibly metaphorical or poetic manner, and not as an antithetical alternative to the findings of scientific research. Cumulative astronomical findings were to confirm the wisdom of this approach.

Of course, the question of the great age of the earth is not to be confounded with the theories propounded in 1859 by Charles Darwin and Alfred Russel Wallace concerning the evolution of species by natural selection. However, as the work of James R. Moore and David N. Livingstone has shown, although there were apprehensions and questions, most Bible-believing Protestants did not repudiate the notion of evolutionary processes as envisaged in Darwin's *Origin of Species* (1859). Certainly, among many Christians, questions pertaining to the relationship, distribution, diversification, and extinction of species were not declared illegitimate. At the same time, it was clear that geology and especially paleontology inevitably posed questions as to how their findings related to Genesis 1–11.

The notion of "non-overlapping *magisteria*" is sometimes used in this context. It asserts, in nominalist fashion, that Bible and science function in two *separate* realms that have no contact with each other. This tendency, which was much earlier present in Francis Bacon, has been advocated more recently by Stephen Jay Gould (1941–2002). This, however, simply will not do—if only because the Bible constantly talks to us about God *and* his creation. Unless they clung to the literal six days of twenty-four hours reading, most Christians in the century following 1859 opted for some version of "concordism"—in which the days of Genesis were viewed as a chronological sequence, with each day representing a period of time of considerable duration. In England, the *Victoria Institute, or Philosophical Society of Great Britain* (founded 1865) was initially wary of evolutionary thinking, but it eventually became more receptive. Not all later evangelicals forgot that in an earlier era men such as B. B. Warfield had wrestled with the issues in a manner that scrupulously honored the cogency of the scientific method. The *American Scientific Affiliation* (founded 1941) eventually exhibited a change in orientation similar to that of the *Victoria Institute*. The same mature standpoint is also evident, for example, in the work of the *Institute for the Study of Christianity in an Age of Science and Technology* (ISCAST) in Australia. Once God was envisaged as using evolutionary methods, it seemed that theistic evolution could be readily accommodated within the framework already provided by "day-age" style concordism. It is possible to view concordism as an apologetic strategy designed to salvage the Bible from what might otherwise prove to be the destructive force of science. Much evangelical literature, including *The Christian View of Science and Scripture* (1954) by Bernard Ramm (1916–92), reflects this outlook. However, arguably the concordist view did not fully honor the text itself. A careful reading of the "days of creation" (an expression not used in the text) at the start of Genesis indicates that the days are not strictly chronological. Rather, days one and four, two and five, and three and six stand in a non-chronological complementary relationship with each other. An authentically literary, rather than literalist, reading is required.

In the longer run, the issues raised by Darwin served to expose what we have termed Evangelicalism's creational and intellectual deficits. The waters were further muddied by the appearance of a class of historiography written to assert the thesis that Christianity and science are and always have been in an antithetical relationship—in effect, in a state of continual warfare—and that, in the nineteenth century, science had finally and irrevocably triumphed. Foremost in this school were John William Draper (1811–82), author of *History of the Conflict between Religion and Science* (1875), and Andrew Dickson White (1832–1918), who published *A History of the Warfare of Science with Theology in Christendom* (1896). The militant atheists, or "atheists with attitude" of the early twenty-first century, and their fundamentalist-creationist counterparts, continue to wage the same conflict. Both are prone to present themselves as the only consistent and tenable alternative to the other. In reality, they represent false alternatives that need to be resisted.

Much of the evangelical writing on evolution has failed to make sufficiently clear the distinction between evolution as a phenomenon recognizable in the fossil record, about which various scientific theories may be formulated, and evolution*ism* as an (unscientific) dogma which takes the phenomenon and turns it into an absolute principle upon which everything else depends. This distinction between evolution as a phenomenon and evolution*ism* is pivotal. Whether Darwin ever supplied a sufficient explanation for the phenomena he discussed is definitely open to question. Certainly,

Darwin worked without the benefit of the work of Gregor Johann Mendel (1822–64), whose work in genetics became known only posthumously. Certainly, both he and Mendel would have been enthralled by developments in genetics following the isolation and identification of nucleic acids by the Swiss biologist Johannes Friedrich Miescher (1844–95), known to us as Deoxyribonucleic acid (DNA). The beautifully complex double-helix molecular structure of DNA was comprehensively described in the work of James D. Watson, Francis H. C. Crick, (1916–2004), and Rosalind E. Franklin (1920–58) in the 1950s.

Subsequent work in this field, on both mitochondrial DNA (mtDNA) in females and the successive and divergent markers on the Y-chromosome in males has resulted in a convincing mapping of the genetic connection of all extant ethnic groups and suggests that Homo Sapiens has lived on earth for some 7,500 generations, originally in East Africa. The three major out-of-Africa ethnic branches have been designated "Abel," "Cain," and "Seth," the latter having the most extensive sub-branches. The relevant investigative techniques have elucidated some long-standing puzzles concerning the relationship of diverse human ethnicities and uncovered some intriguing phenomena. For example, we are told that Jewish males having the surname Cohen (meaning "priest") are predominantly the descendants of a single Hebrew male some 106 generations ago, which approximates to the time of Aaron of the tribe of Levi and the institution of the Levitical priesthood (Exod 6:16–20).[3]

The Genesis Flood and Intelligent Design

Even as these remarkable developments were taking place in the field of genetics, including the work of the Human Genome Project, many evangelicals, especially those committed to fundamentalist styles of literalism, reasserted a position much closer to that of James Ussher. John C. Whitcomb and Henry M. Morris (1918–2006) provided many fundamentalist evangelicals with what they were looking for in *The Genesis Flood: The Biblical Record and its Scientific Implications* (1961). This work ascribed the successive sedimentary deposits of the geological column almost entirely to Noah's flood (Gen 6–9). *The Genesis Flood* was replete with misrepresentations, some of which were lucidly exposed by J. R. Van de Fliert (1919–2001).[4]

Morris and Whitcomb's attempted revival of global "flood geology" (also known as "diluvialism") owed much to the polemical writings of

3. Olson, *Mapping*, 108–109.
4. Van de Fliert, "Fundamentalism," 5–27; "Bible," 34–39.

Seventh Day Adventist author George McCready Price (1870–1963). The Creation Research Society, set up around 1963, promoted the resurgence of "young earth" creationism, as did the Institute for Creation Research, founded by Morris in 1972. Since that time the American fundamentalist public has been treated to the offerings of the Creation Museum, at Petersburg, Kentucky, run by Kenneth Alfred Ham's Answers in Genesis organization. A counterpart operates at Portsmouth, England. Back in Kentucky a Noah's Ark replica theme park is in contemplation. This latter-day flood-geology is promoted with aggressive marketing and entrepreneurial flair.

The young earth and flood-geology standpoint is supported pre-eminently by those evangelicals best described as fundamentalist in terms of their orientation towards a literal reading of all parts of Scripture, and the assumption that the Bible speaks with scientific precision on all matters it addresses. The congruence here with premillennial dispensationalist hermeneutics is not coincidental. The insistence on a literarily insensitive literalism in respect of biblical passages addressing the end times finds its complementary counterpart in an identical insistence in respect to those passages addressing origins and the deluge in Genesis 1–11. To abandon the one would be to jeopardize the other. In other words, it would be hermeneutically inconsistent to adopt a literarily sensitive and culturally contextualized reading of Genesis 1–11 and not to adopt the same posture towards the books of Daniel and Revelation.

Of greater cogency than the effusions of young-earth creationists has been the work of those who have advocated intelligent design (ID). They have included Philip E. Johnson, Michael J. Denton, Michael Behe, Stephen C. Meyer, and William Dembski. In many respects this development harks back to the sort of thinking that preceded Darwin, and that he found so explanatorily deficient, especially in the Galapagos Islands. It brings to mind the thinking of William Paley (1743–1805), in his *Natural Theology; or, Evidences of the Existence and Attributes of the Deity* (1802). For Paley, the organic complexity of living creatures, including humans, implied the creative agency of an intelligent designing mind.

However, a great many of the illustrations in such arguments from design employ pocket watches, mouse-traps, and so forth—in other words, humanly fabricated mechanisms. This is understandable, but it points to a serious difficulty. From our knowledge of humankind we can easily infer that mousetraps and pocket watches are the results of human design and fabrication. However, such analogies run into multiple difficulties when applied to God and nature—the latter term here meaning the entire order of creation, distinct from all that is attributable to human contrivance and practice. The prime difficulty with such argumentation is that it presumes that we are capable of entering the mind of God, as it were, to know how God thinks and intelligently designs complex organisms so as to recognize in them the hallmarks of his handiwork. The intention here may be to affirm God as the Creator of all things, including all living creatures, but the execution of the intention apparently presumes something like a platonic "great chain of [intelligent] being"—with God and man on the same rational continuum. Such ID thinking does not sufficiently take into account that the God of the Bible is *not* a creature at all—nor that our thinking is inevitably creaturely. Neither does it take into consideration and draw opposite conclusions from those phenomena that appear to us utterly random and unpredictable. Furthermore, ID thinking can all too easily lend itself to quasi-deist notions of an otherwise autonomous creation into which the Intelligent Designer occasionally inserts himself as and when required. Of course, it is worth asking: What is ID theory for? If the answer is to prove the existence of God, then ID fails because the God revealed in the Bible is the Creator of all things, including the laws of logic, to which he is *not* subject.

Yet it is undeniable that the arguments and examples utilized by ID proponents have nevertheless served a useful function by exposing the inadequacies of the explanatory models used in many discussions of evolutionary phenomena. This is especially so in cases where the presumption of given outcomes being the result of chance have been scrutinized in terms of prevailing views of mathematical probability. In many calculations the "chances" that complex organisms are the result of "self-organization" are so prodigiously remote as to lack all credibility. The dual interactive mechanisms of random mutation and natural selection can now be seen as lacking *sufficient* cogency when it comes to explaining biological change at the species level. The origin of life is at another level entirely.

Of course, much hinges on what is meant by evolution. If it is seen as a process upon which all organic life exclusively depends, and that requires nothing more than the existence of matter and the operations of chance, then we are in the presence not simply of a theory of evolution but much more: *a dogma of evolutionism*. In some measure the opposition to ID from contemporary Neo-Darwinians has arisen from the challenges ID has presented to their religiously-espoused evolution*ism*. The term "evolution" itself has become increasingly problematic. The arguments used to present conventional neo-Darwinian theory call out for the kind of philosophical analysis that will expose the functioning of basically religious assumptions that remain in some measure effectively masked by the use of seemingly neutral, descriptive terminology. The paleontological evidence presented in immense sequences of sedimentary strata does at certain junctures indicate dramatic species change, but the same sedimentary strata also exhibit vast extended periods of species stability.

Arguably, we live at a time in the development of the biological sciences as innovative and challenging as that of physics in the era of Albert Einstein (1879–1955) and Erwin Schrödinger (1887–1961), or after Kurt Gödel (1906–78) in mathematics. The "Punctuated equilibrium" proposals presented by Stephen Jay Gould and the "quantum evolution conjecture" formulated by George G. Simpson (1902–84) are straws in the wind. As it becomes clearer that the heavily reductionist naturalism that has generally dominated the biological sciences is untenable, the last thing that Christians needed to commit themselves to was a reversion to a crude biblical literalism coupled with "creation science" and "flood geology." That, however, is the path down which many fundamentalist evangelicals have travelled since the 1960s, in spite of the endeavors of writers such as Michael R. Johnson, Douglas Spanner, and Davis A. Young.

Presenting itself as "Bible-based," such fundamentalism exhibits a closing of the mind before increasingly evident realities. In its most extreme form, the Bible becomes an alternative to all scientific research and understanding—as if all research were superfluous—though few live this viewpoint out with any consistency. Even as the dogmatic adherents to naturalistic materialism are distressed by discussions on just how problematic are assumptions of the supposed self-organization of living organisms, the immense body of geological and astronomical evidence supportive of the old earth viewpoint equally distresses evangelical fundamentalists. Moreover, just as the implausibility of the notion that life "just happened" is becoming increasingly evident, those who insist on reading Genesis 1–11 as if it were in some sense a scientific account have effectively written themselves out of the discussion. The evangelical intellectual deficit has once again been in evidence.

A highly questionable literalism influenced too many (but not all, and there are some important exceptions) evangelicals to assume that the Genesis narratives bind us to notions of absolute fixity—although even they can hardly deny the operation of Allen's and Bergmann's rules respecting human physiological adaptation to climatic conditions. The work of Jesus Christ on the cross is finished (John 19:30), but we have yet to see its full consequences (1 Cor 2:9). Similarly the work of creation is finished (Gen 2:1), but it is not for us to presume to set limits on the versatility of the Creator, and we have yet to witness the full unfolding of the divine purpose for the creation. The great sweep of the Bible teaches us to anticipate a new (not another) heaven and earth (Rev 21:1). The coming of the kingdom orients us away from *fixity* (with its various static and conservative connotations), towards wholesome and all-fulfilling change (Acts 3:21; 1 Cor 15:24-28). The accomplished work of the cross encompasses the full renewal of creation (Rom 8:18-25).

The Charismatic Movement

One of the greatest strongholds of creationism in the twentieth century has been the charismatic movement. In the years following the Topeka revival of 1901 and Los Angeles Azusa Street Revival of the same era, Pentecostals, with their distinctive "second blessing" claims concerning the baptism of the Holy Spirit and speaking in tongues, were mostly confined to their own distinctive denominational structures, such as the AOG.

The picture changed significantly in the 1960s with the emergence of the charismatic movement. In this movement, Pentecostalism jumped the existing denominational boundaries and entered the mainline denominations. Episcopalians and Lutherans were at the forefront of this development. In the United States, Dennis Bennett (1917-91) in Van Nuys, California, and Graham Pulkingham (1926-93) in Houston, Texas were early exponents. In the case of Pulkingham, the influence of David Wilkerson (1931-2011), author of *The Cross and the Switchblade* (1963), was decisive. Spurred on by the exhortations of veteran, Yorkshire-born Pentecostal preacher Smith Wigglesworth (1859-1947), the South African David du Plessis (1905-87)—sometimes dubbed "Mr. Pentecost"—developed wide ecumenical connections in order to commend Pentecostalism to the mainline denominations.

In England, the leaders were Colin Urquhart, author of *When the Spirit Comes* (1974), and Michael Harper (1931-2010), at one time curate at All Souls Langham Place during the era of John Stott. Stott rejected Harper's position in his *The Baptism and Fullness of the Holy Spirit* (1964). Harper quit All Souls, and advocated his cause in *Third Force in the Body of Christ* and *As at the Beginning* (both 1965). Harper converted to Eastern Orthodoxy in 1995. In the longer term, David Watson (1933-84) became the most prominent charismatic among the Anglican evangelicals. In the decade when the Banner of Truth publishing organization aspired to have a major impact on evangelicals in a puritan and reformed direction, it found itself in competition with the charismatic movement, and it was the latter that made the more obvious progress. Amongst British evangelicals the legacy of pietistic, "higher life" attitudes was heavily ingrained, and this favored the spread of the charismatics.

The role of D. M. Lloyd-Jones was not free from ambiguity, because he was a careful advocate of the charismatic "baptism of the Holy Spirit"—unlike many Puritan and Reformed evangelicals who held the cessationist views of writers such as B. B. Warfield. Here we may see Lloyd-Jones's Welsh revivalism gaining the ascendancy over his latter-day Puritanism. During his 1927–38 ministry at Sandfields in Wales, Lloyd-Jones hoped to see his style of pietistic neo-Puritanism initiate a renewal of Welsh national culture. It did not happen. It would take more than an earnest pietism to renew national culture in a land caught in the socio-economic grip of long-term industrial decline. Lloyd-Jones's pietism rendered him incapable of contemplating a more integral alternative and drew him down paths too reminiscent of the Welsh Revival of 1904–5. The *dénouement* came in the ministry of his successor, Kentucky-born Robert T. Kendall at Westminster Chapel from 1977 to 2002. At this time charismatic doctrine and practice eclipsed the older ways of Protestant Dissenting Pietism. Kendall strongly supported as a genuine prophet the now discredited Paul Cain. The much-touted revival never took place. Such episodes have a way of leaving serious spiritual wreckage in their wake.

In the mid-twentieth century, Pentecostalism in the United States was dominated by figures such as William M. Branham (1909–65) and Granville (Oral) Roberts (1918–2009). Branham claimed to have received various angelic visions and is widely credited with an extensive "divine healing" ministry. He repudiated the conventional Trinitarian doctrine, arguing that Father, Son and Holy Spirit were but three manifestations (not persons) of the one God (monistic theism). Accordingly, baptism was not to be in the name of the Father, Son, and Holy Spirit, but in Jesus Christ only. In *An Exposition of the Seven Church Ages* (1950) he followed the "Church Age" schema of the Scofield Bible, leaving open the possibility that he, Branham, might be the seventh angel to the seventh and final church. A marked tendency towards spiritual *hubris* was to become a recurrent feature of this wing of Evangelicalism.

Never to be outdone, Oral Roberts claimed to have received repeated visions of Christ—sometimes of super-sized dimensions. He too offered a "healing ministry," and both men promoted earlier versions of what subsequently became known as the "prosperity gospel." An Oral Roberts University was established at Tulsa, Oklahoma, in 1963. In some respects Roberts was ahead of Graham when it came to communications technique. It was the Oral Roberts Evangelistic Association that led the way into the post-Graham, post-mass-evangelistic crusade era by developing the new field of tele-evangelism. Television, with its rapid scene-changes required to prevent viewer boredom, facilitated a blending of the sensational and superficial, along with a hypnotic-like dulling of the critical faculties, and was tailor-made for the grandiloquent orations (and, not least, eschatological speculations) of the enterprising tele-evangelist.

By the late twentieth century the names of the leading performers were familiar in North America and beyond. They included Jerry L. Falwell (1933–2007), of the SBC, leader of the Moral Majority and founder of Liberty University; D. James Kennedy (1930–2007), of Coral Ridge Presbyterian Church, Fort Lauderdale, Florida; Alpha Rex Emmanuel Humbard (1919–2007), of the Cathedral of Tomorrow; Robert H. Schuller, founder of the now defunct Crystal Cathedral; M. G. "Pat" Robertson, of The 700 Club; John C. Hagee, of Cornerstone Mega Church, San Antonio, Texas and Christians United for Israel; T. B. "Benny" Hinn, promoter of Miracle Crusades; Joel Scott Osteen, of Lakewood Church, Houston, Texas; Jack Van Impe, of Jack Van Impe Presents; Heidi Baker, of Catch the Fire TV of Toronto; Todd Bentley, of Lakeland Revival; James and Tammy Faye (1942–2007) Bakker of the PTL [Praise the Lord] Television Network and Heritage USA theme park; Perry Stone, of the Voice of Evangelism; and Jimmy Lee Swaggart, of Jimmy Swaggart Ministries. The cult of the celebrity personality is undeniably operative here.

These and other such ministries most probably came to maximum impact in the final decades of the twentieth century. They tended to exhibit an array of persistent characteristics, although these were not uniformly present in all instances. These included protracted worship styles that verged on entertainment, sometimes with rock concert features, a doctrinal orientation towards charismatic teachings and proclivities, including in some cases the prosperity gospel—in which believers are exhorted to "name it and claim it"; a pro-Zionist advocacy of premillennial rapture eschatology; tacit endorsement (at the very least) of contemporary capitalist market place economics, coupled with a highly entrepreneurial approach to Christian ministry; and (in the USA) a presumed orientation towards the Republican Party and willingness to display the emblems of American patriotism along with affirmations of American exceptionalism.

The "Latter Rain Movement" and the "New Apostolic Reformation"

The "latter rain" movement arose in the late 1940s to 1960s among Pentecostals influenced by Branham. It arose at Sharon Bible College in North Battleford, Saskatchewan, Canada. It exhibited a strong *counter-historical* orientation. Without repudiating rapture teaching, it side-stepped dispensationalism, and adopted an "ultra-restorationist" posture, which included the full reinstitution or *restoration* of the apostolic and prophetic office in the church *as if this were the first century*. The contention was that these actual offices could be, should be, and were now being restored among those who advanced this teaching. Predictably enough, those who were now proclaimed apostles or prophets expected that due deference should be accorded their leading status.

This Pentecostal-charismatic Third Wave has been widely and diversely influential, also in an array of mainline and other non-Pentecostal denominations. The diverse manifestations include the "laughing revival"—the so-called Toronto Blessing promoted by the now widely discredited Rodney Howard Browne. Arguably, however, the two central figures in the Third Wave are John Wimber (1934–97) and C. Peter Wagner. Both men had taught at Fuller Theological Seminary. Wimber's emphasis was on "power evangelism." At some points the "Kingdom Now" emphasis of third-wave thinking aligns with fringe movements such as Theonomy and Christian Reconstruction, which displayed a strong post-millennial orientation, and an insistence that the full rigors of the Old Testament laws are applicable to the whole of contemporary society. The fullest expression of this latter standpoint is to be found in *The Institutes of Biblical Law* (1973), by Rousas John Rushdoony (1916–2001), leader of the California-based Christian Reconstructionist movement. The latter aspired to a theocratic America, based on a literal and a-historical reading of the biblical (including Old Testament) texts. Their literalist hermeneutic, when applied to the Bible, was synchronous with their "strict constructionist" interpretation of the US Constitution, requiring a minimalist Federal Government and the dismantling of social security programs. A great deal of evangelical participation in the Tea Party movement is attributable to a mingling and melding of fundamentalist, dispensationalist, neo-Pentecostal, and Christian Reconstructionist influences.

The influence of Wimber and Wagner has been widespread, penetrating to almost all evangelical congregations across and beyond the English-speaking world. As a result, Pentecostal-charismatic styles of "praise and worship" have become prevalent. The position on spiritual gifts, and prophecy, adopted by Wayne Grudem in his *The Gift of Prophecy in the New Testament and Today* (1988), and supported by John Piper paved the way for third-wave charismatic influences to enter even Presbyterian and Reformed settings where such teaching had previously been rejected as inconsistent with the final word, as represented by the completed canon of biblical books.

Evangelicals have long been prone to seek one spiritual nostrum after another, from the "Four Spiritual Laws" of Bill Bright (1921–2003), and the

"Sit, Walk, Stand" of Watchman Nee (1903–72), through Bill McCartney's Promise Keepers, on to Bruce Wilkinson's "Prayer of Jabez," and down to Rick Warren's *The Purpose Driven Life* (2002). Each in turn ends up on the scrap heap of fads, with only core devotees remaining, as room is made for the next grand promotion. The Pentecostal-charismatic variant of Evangelicalism is particularly prone to this tendency because it self-validates by defining and presenting itself as *the* agency of purportedly ongoing revival. Consistent with this claim, there are always present within the effervescent mix of Pentecostal-charismatic Evangelicalism elements ready to innovate—"mutate" might be a better term—in order to self-promote as the leading edge of the still to arrive but ever anticipated revival.

Wagner advanced the thesis that the apostolic and prophetic offices of the New Testament ought to be a continuing feature of contemporary Christianity. This has become known as the New Apostolic Reformation (NAR), and has been promoted by Wagner himself, along with William (Bill) Hamon, David Cannistraci, and Hector Torres. Although it is not clear that its "new apostles" can legitimately claim to have seen the risen Christ (1 Cor 15:8), this movement asserts the restoration in the modern church of the apostolic office of New Testament times. It is significant that committed Pentecostal writers, such as H. Vinson Synan, have expressed reservations about this movement.[5] Its claims are unquestionably consistent with the counter-historical desire to recover a Golden Age primitivism, engendered by many evangelicals of a fundamentalist, Bible-based orientation. It remains to be seen if the *hubris* evident in NAR claims will prompt from among its own adherents a long overdue, searching analysis of the peculiar claims of the Pentecostal-charismatic side of Evangelicalism.

Few Third Wave Pentecostal-charismatic evangelicals, including those of NAR persuasion, are sufficiently aware of the historical trajectory of their own sub-groups. Hardly any within the movement are ready and able to reflect critically and scrupulously on the claims of their version of Evangelicalism. Typically, their interpretations of their experiences are considered normative. The problematic claims of classical Pentecostals and evangelical charismatics alike have been challenged by some bold evangelicals, even though this risks being charged with lack of faith, of being "unspiritual" or "carnal," and among those who have "a form of godliness," but who "deny the power thereof" (2 Tim 3:5 KJV). It might even be insinuated that critics are Enlightenment-inspired liberals who do not believe there is a Holy Spirit. Such conversations can become highly charged.

---

5. Synan, *Eye-Witness*, 181–186.

There are four more reasons why older varieties of evangelicals have found it difficult to address the challenging claims made by the Pentecostal-charismatic wing. First, although there are clear exceptions, Evangelicalism generally lacks the doctrinal clarity required to address the issues with cogency and lucidity. Second, an Evangelicalism that has for more than a century become habituated to pragmatic accommodation to the prevailing culture "for the sake of the gospel" now finds it extraordinarily difficult to take a principled stand against the more egregious Pentecostal-charismatic examples of the selfsame tendency. Third, in many congregational situations non-charismatic ministers fear that if they address charismatic claims and practices too directly they will upset the local congregational apple cart and lose members and their financial contributions, perhaps to charismatic-style mega churches. Finally, the evangelical intellectual deficit is again on display. Few evangelicals know enough of the history of Christianity to adequately understand their present predicament.

A Need for Critical Discernment

Difficulties notwithstanding, it is high time for the peculiar doctrines, claims, and practices of the Pentecostal-charismatic movement to be scrutinized with rigor. The protestant reformers, when they called for an inventory of all the supposed relics across Europe (just how many pieces of the cross were there?), were accused of impiety, even of atheism, but those accusations rightly did not stop them from *seeking the truth*. Should contemporary evangelicals be committed to anything less? The Pentecostal-charismatic understanding of Pentecost, the *charismata* (including tongues, prophecy and healing), and the apostolic office are distorted by an a-historical approach to the Bible and an implicit downgrading of the Old Testament. If that is a prevalent characteristic of much Evangelicalism overall, its consequences are most severely apparent in its Pentecostal-charismatic wing. Although we still await a full discussion of the outstanding questions, the following considerations should be sufficient to indicate that a fundamental reconsideration is required.

First, in the Bible, exceptional miracles, signs, and wonders are almost completely restricted to three great phases in the redemptive history of God's covenant people: Exodus-Judges, Elijah and Elisha, and the ministry of Jesus Christ and his apostles. These three epochs are represented by those present on the mount of transfiguration—Moses, Elijah, and Jesus—in an episode recorded by Matthew, Mark and Luke and recalled in 2 Peter 1:16–18. For the rest of the historical experience of God's people such miracles, signs, and wonders have *not* been the norm.

Second, the New Testament knows nothing of a two-stage Christian experience, in which a second stage is inaugurated by a "Holy Spirit baptism" marked by "speaking in tongues." This is a notion imposed on Scripture, and although it uses biblical expressions, it is not intrinsic to Scripture. Moreover, the tongues of the New Testament are *actual languages*, not private-devotional or public-worship burble-speak. The production and repetition of segmental phonemes, often borrowed from general linguistic usage, to produce more or less ecstatic vocalizations has its parallels in pagan practice but has no scripturally sanctioned place in Christian devotion or worship. At Pentecost, speaking in tongues (which there meant speaking in actual intelligible human languages) eloquently proclaimed the reversal of Babel— the gathering together of all peoples in, through, and under the risen Christ.

Third, many Pentecostal-charismatic claims to "miraculous healing" remain unverified. They fail to meet the criteria presented in the gospels: being permanent, without relapses, and comprehensive, including the full and evidentially verifiable restoration of major body parts, including limbs. The Pentecostal-charismatic grapevine continually pulses with news of purported healings, but is seriously lacking in stringent authentication to a standard that would meet the legitimate requirements of medical science or the evidentiary standards of courts of law. Of course, to ask for these standards and requirements to be met is to court the charge of being carnal and lacking in faith, but we should not be fooled: it is time that churches that purport to offer bodily healing are held to account on the basis of the biblical criteria, and that frauds and charlatans be exposed and repudiated. The public reputation of Jesus Christ requires nothing less.

Fourth, the Pentecostal-charismatic side of Evangelicalism claims to have recovered in its midst the ancient gift of prophecy. In the same quarters there is a serious lack of clarity as to how this purported recovery relates to the post-Apostolic closure of the canon of Scripture. Unquestionably, there were prophets in New Testament times, such as Agabus (Acts 11:28; 21:10–14) and, of course, they functioned alongside apostles at a time when the Old Testament writings were the only Bible the church had, simply because at that juncture, the New Testament was, of course, still in the process of composition.

Moreover, the New Testament never speaks of prophecy in a way that represents a substantive break from prophecy in the Old Testament. The full *moral* weight of the Old Testament condemnations of *false prophets* (see, for example Deut 13:1–5; 18:20–22; Jer 14:13–16; 23:16–32) would therefore apply into the apostolic era. The reality is that the purported prophecies of the Pentecostal-charismatic variety fall conspicuously short of the biblical standard, which affirms that an erroneous prophet is a false prophet. As might be expected, certain Pentecostal-charismatic advocates try to evade the point of these assertions by saying that tongues and prophecy among them today are *not the same* as those of the New Testament era, but this evasion amounts to an unacknowledged retraction—it is an admission that their purported tongues and prophecy are *not* actually consistent with biblical teaching and practice. The result is a serious delusion, because it implies possession of (or at least access to) human utterance imparting new revelation. The streams of Evangelicalism most subject to this delusion are those which draw upon the legacy of the Anabaptists, with their a-historical and literalist way of understanding biblical authority and their concomitant assumption that we are still living in the era of the apostles and prophets. The reality is otherwise, and by every biblical standard the Anabaptists Melchior Hoffman and Jan Mathias were false prophets.

Fifth, in the wake of the NAR, it is necessary to address the claim that from out of its inner ferment the Pentecostal-charismatic movement has been the means of actually restoring the apostolic office of the New Testament era. In some respects the NAR is at least consistent with other Pentecostal-charismatic claims and serves to render even more apparent the core implications of the wider movement. Those not carried along by the tide may be forgiven for choking on the sheer presumptuousness of the proposition that the movement "in these latter days" is providing the church with persons of comparable stature to James, John, Peter and Paul—all of whom had seen the risen Christ and received their office directly from him (note especially Gal 1:17; 1 Cor 15:7-9; 2 Cor 11:13).

By contrast, Paul taught that the church was "founded upon" apostles and prophets—in the way that a building is erected on its foundations, the point being that the building rests *upon* its foundations but does not consist wholly *of* its foundations (Eph 2:20; 3:5). The entire Pentecostal-charismatic movement persistently flounders before two complementary historical realities: (1) The first century church had apostles and prophets, but no canonical New Testament, and (2) in subsequent centuries the church has a canonical New Testament, but is without apostles and prophets. All of which is not to deny that Christians are always called by the Holy Spirit to be *both apostolic and prophetic*.

The standpoint outlined above is sometimes referred to as cessationism. It has strong support among both patristic and Reformation authors. Nevertheless, it is a regrettably negative and potentially misleading term. A term such as "apostolically-foundational" might be preferable. Asserting that the church was built *upon* the testimony and teaching of apostles and prophets whose office has now ceased, along with the associated charismata, does *not* entail that the person and work of the Holy Spirit are denied, or that he has ceased to provide outstanding, gifted men and women to the church of Christ. Neither does it mean that remarkable experiences of healing and restoration are not now occasionally granted. Unquestionably, there are those who can testify to such mercies without affectation or embellishment. Christians are right to believe that the Holy Spirit remains sovereign and will do what he pleases, however exceptional. It is wisdom to be neither presumptuous nor unbelieving.

New Wave Premillennial Dispensationalism: "Christian Zionism"

Among premillennial dispensationalists, expectancy as to the immanence of the "secret rapture" could always be fuelled by developments in the Middle East following the collapse of the Ottoman Empire. The Balfour Declaration, made by Great Britain and favoring "the establishment in Palestine of a national home for the Jewish people" (December 2, 1917); the subsequent entry of General Edmund Allenby (1861–1936) into Jerusalem in a manner that acknowledged its holy status (December 11, 1917); the end of the British Mandate and proclamation by David Ben-Gurion (1886–1973) of an independent State of Israel (May 14, 1948) and its prompt recognition by the USA; and the stunning triumphs of Israeli armed forces in the Six Day War (June 5–10, 1967), served to fuel the flames of anticipatory fervor among those committed to the system. If ardent dispensationalists were somewhat ambivalent concerning the circumstances of the British Mandate, they were much encouraged by Israeli independence and the triumphs of Israeli arms. Dispensationalists were quick to see demonstrations of Israeli strength as vindications of their standpoint. They convinced themselves that they were on the right track; they understood how and why God was at work.

Christian sympathy for the Jewish people and an Israeli state cannot be divorced from our post-holocaust knowledge of the hideous, vile, despicable, lamentable, and criminal record of European anti-Semitism. We must include its Medieval and post-Medieval "Christian" manifestations, as well as its more recent genetic-ethnic forms as demonstrated by the Nazi and comparable totalitarian regimes. Western support for Israel is driven at least in part by a sense of guilt, arising from partial responsibility (by omission or commission) for these past atrocities. This said, it is *not* anti-Semitic to observe that successive Israeli administrations have not been above utilizing that sense of guilt for their own purposes.

It is all too easy to be shaped by that to which we have been most deeply opposed and has done us the greatest harm. In truth, the post 1948 Israeli Defense Forces, more than any other, have demonstrated a prowess in the techniques of *Blitzkrieg* for which the *Wehrmacht* was feared and renowned. Furthermore, successive Israeli governments (which unquestionably face serious challenges) have been all too willing to confine and ghettoize entire populations in occupied territories and dehumanize them. It is small wonder that they rebel violently. Many Christians, including some evangelicals, are alert to these injustices, but for committed premillennial dispensationalists—their Christian Zionism credentials ever on display—the cause of Israel must be upheld regardless, whatever the teachings of the Prince of Peace (Matt 5:3–11).

The events of 1967, and the manner in which Middle East tensions embroiled both superpowers, when combined with dark apprehensions about the future held by conservatively inclined Christians, constituted an immense market-place opportunity for a literature of eschatological speculation, graphically written and cast in the dispensationalist mold. The "need" was resoundingly met with Hal Lindsey's best-selling *The Late Great Planet Earth* (1970). Greatly assisted by the growth of the charismatic movement, and undergirded by successive generations of discourse shaped by the Scofield Bible, the era produced a multiplicity of literary and film productions, including the fiction writings of Tim LaHaye and Jerry Jenkins and the related "left behind" movies. Millions of evangelicals are convinced these products reflect biblical truth. They are enthralled if not actually enraptured.

The nature of the system requires its followers to be constantly reinstructed by the movement's ever-vocal advocates. While Hal Lindsey set the pace, figures such as Jerry Falwell, John Hagee, Derek Prince, and Pat Robertson were prominent. Constant reinstruction is required by the system's false literalism and commitment to Israel-related pro*gnostic*ations. As conditions change, those supposedly indubitable prognostications, in all their dramatic detail, must be constantly revised. Russia, the European Union, Islam, Iraq, Iran, and China are assigned differing roles in the approach to Armageddon, depending on the most recent turn of events. For example, adjustments must be made to the master scenario when the Soviet Union is replaced by the Russian Federation—or when Iran becomes the prime Middle East enemy instead of Iraq. Lindsey's publication record reveals a career-long program of assiduous self-revision. *The Late Great Planet Earth* is subsequently recast as *The Final Battle* (1994); *There's A New World Coming* (1973) becomes *The Apocalypse Code* (1997), and *The 1980's: Countdown to Armageddon* (1981) becomes *Planet Earth 2000 AD* (1994). In content such works manage to be at once sensationalist and banal. They invite us into a realm of interpretative surrealism, as when the reader is urged to envisage the locusts of biblical imagery as military helicopters. So much for a literal interpretation!

However, wrong doctrine can have deadly consequences. The renewed vigor of premillennial dispensationalism at the end of the twentieth century, itself fueled by the rise of Pentecostalism and the charismatic movement, imparted an unmistakable "foreign policy" orientation to fundamentalist evangelical movements such as Pat Robertson's Moral Majority. In such settings it was persistently urged that the foreign policy of the USA ought always to be a pro-Israeli policy, come what may. The result is a Christian Zionism in which support for Israeli policies and conduct is automatic, irrespective of the rights of Arab peoples, be they Christian or Islamic. Coupled with the already immense leverage enjoyed by the Zionist lobby within the United States, Christian Zionism has influenced the foreign policies pursued by both Republican and Democratic White Houses. The message goes forth in mega-churches and on the shows of numerous tele-evangelists. The Christian Zionist stance is clear in the "Jews for Jesus" organization led by David Brickner, and blatant at the International Christian Embassy of Jerusalem. All this is reinforced by Christian Zionist tourism to Israel—with bus tours that hide much of the truth from willing patrons who are all too ready to believe what they are told. The Christian Zionist movement is unjust in what it represents and dangerous in what it encourages. It represents a policy of injustice towards many thousands of Arabs. With its encouragement of building a (third) temple on the Temple Mount site of the present Al-Aqsa Mosque, and relocation of the US Embassy to Jerusalem, such Zionism helps propel both the USA and Israel down confrontational paths that could lead to fearful conflagrations. In other words, all that literalistic talk of a pending Armageddon could become self-fulfilling.

The premillennial, dispensationalist-inspired willingness of the Christian Right in the USA to urge upon the nation warlike policies in the Middle East is particularly serious for the rest of the world because of the Christian Right's significant role within the Republican Party. Of course, governments remain responsible for their actions. The "statesmen" responsible for the wrong-headedness of the US response to the crimes of 9/11 and the 2003 invasion of Iraq may have taken their actions, with all their loss of life and limb, without the constant urgings of Christian Zionists, which some other Christians strenuously opposed, but the Christian Zionists nevertheless helped to advance a policy among the population at large that any authentically prophetic voice would have opposed strenuously.

11

EVANGELICAL DISTRESS AND AN INTEGRAL ALTERNATIVE

A Problematic Legacy

Contemporary evangelical Christianity is in deep trouble. Its immense diversity is not of the wholesome variety but expresses its own complex, unresolved, and inter-related confusions. Each subgroup is disposed to view others with a degree of suspicion. It is not merely that the evangelical trumpet gives an uncertain sound. Rather, multiple dissonant trumpets combine to bring forth one screeching discord after another. For those seeking the truth, contemporary Evangelicalism offers its own uncertain cacophony.

Yet in spite of everything, men and women of the highest caliber may be found serving in its ranks. The best evangelicals have rightly reminded the protestant part of the Christian church of truths—such as belief in the bodily resurrection of Jesus Christ—without which no one can credibly claim to be Christian. However, even as they look askance at the seemingly limitless ability of "liberal" Protestantism to make "courageous" concession after concession to the secularizing, rationalistic materialism that pervades the contemporary West, they are complacently insensitive to the degree to which they themselves have become subject to, and are pervaded by, the self-same tendencies. In certain respects the circumstances of contemporary evangelicals are the most egregious, for while they have presented themselves as the pre-eminent advocates of biblical Christianity to church and people alike, it is just at this point that they have fallen short so grievously.

In thought, word, and deed they have *reduced* the gospel to something much less than the good news concerning the kingdom of God.

Christianity is either world-formative or it is formed by the world. Once this is grasped, an adequate elucidation of the contemporary situation can commence. The Christianity that we have inherited, also in its protestant expressions, has been very largely shaped by the world, it is—in a word—worldly. So, what, exactly, does the term world mean in this context? The term certainly appears in the New Testament, but here we immediately encounter a serious problem. In most evangelical, more or less fundamentalist, more or less Pentecostal-charismatic churches the standard of pulpit exposition of Scripture is woefully inadequate. In addition, while there are worthy evangelical publishers, many Christian bookshops can only survive by sales of sentimental-devotional and apocalyptic-speculative titles.

Their practice reflects current conditions: those who stock serious literature often feel obliged to place it on the shelves at the back of the store. The result is that the average person is hard pressed to exercise discernment amidst the plethora of opinions on offer. The world-wide-web is loaded with misdirection for the unwary. The result is that at the congregational and personal level many evangelicals are confused and perplexed about large areas of New Testament teaching, while for too many the Old Testament is virtually unknown territory.

Clarity is therefore at a premium, and when terms such as world and worldly are used, it is necessary to use them in a manner consistent with their New Testament usage. When read in context it becomes clear that these terms are used in the English-language Bible in two distinct ways. Firstly, the world of human culture is distorted and deformed because of humankind's sinfulness, disobedience, and wickedness. Confronting this, Paul says: "Do not conform any longer to the pattern of this world" (Rom 12:2 NIV). This is the world that Paul is contemplating when he writes of "the basic principles of this world" (Col 2:20 NIV). This world is what Christians are up against. The disciples of Jesus Christ are *not* called to be "other-worldly" in an out-of-the-world sense, but distinctly present, in thought, word, deed, and life, *in* the world, as a new humanity anticipating the full coming of the kingdom of God. This points to a *second* sense of the term world in the New Testament, as in "God so loved the cosmos" (John 3:16). Here the cosmic scope of Christ's redeeming work is in view, securing the eventual restoration of all things (Acts 3:21; 1 Cor 15:20–28; 2 Cor 5:18–19).

Such teaching implies and requires precisely what Evangelicalism has failed to develop: a *biblically directed* understanding of the cosmos and the religious meaning of human culture. Here we should reiterate a distinction already made: *biblically directed* is not to be confused with Bible-based. The latter is much favoured by evangelicals, especially those of a more distinctly fundamentalist orientation. The Bible-based approach, with its strong preference for proof texts, and when applied consistently, requires of us today that we adhere to the world picture (*Weltbild*) of the original biblical writers, while the *biblically directed* understanding of scriptural authority recognises that the teaching of the Scriptures transcends the circumstances of its original inspired composition. It applies biblical first principles to our understanding of cosmos and culture, without binding us, for example, to a three-tier picture of the universe (as in Exod 20:4), geo-centricity, or an earth that is only six to ten thousand years old. It also enables us to apply biblical principles and insight to entities such as universities and hospitals, business corporations, and labour unions to which *explicit* reference could not be made in Scripture. Its own biblicism, its Bible-based approach, has actually impeded Evangelicalism from developing and applying to all of life a *biblically directed* world and life view.

This is important, because we always have a world and life view, and if Christians are not living out of a Christian world and life view then they are (at least partly) living out of an alternative, non-Christian view. One could say that their cultural and intellectual sanctification has hardly begun, and is perhaps actually impeded by the church-culture with which they are familiar. Here we are close to uncovering the systemic weakness of Evangelicalism. It cannot walk straight because it staggers between two incompatible opinions (1 Kgs 18:21). In this respect much of the Evangelicalism of our day *lacks integrity*. It is not *integral*. It lacks wholeness and is therefore to some degree unwholesome. It may profess to preach the gospel, but it does so in a presumed spiritual realm that, contrary to the clear teaching of the New Testament, leaves cosmos and culture somehow beyond the kingly rule of Jesus Christ, and a vast range of human activities as somehow outside the scope of Christian discipleship. Such activities are viewed as secular or material and "not the gospel," and therefore as dangerous distractions from evangelism itself. Evangelicalism is certainly not the only part of the broader Christian church to have functioned with such a dualistic outlook, but in its case the inner contradiction is more conspicuous because of its constant *claim* to be scriptural. And this deep-seated dualism by no means leaves evangelism itself untouched. In an era of deepening secularism, in which evangelistic endeavor can be akin to "plowing concrete," the reduced gospel of much contemporary Evangelicalism simply does not grip the rails.

In the long history of Christianity, Christian theologians have repeatedly used Platonism as the philosophical basis for Christian doctrine. One of the most telling barbs thrown at Christianity in the modern era is that of the neo-pagan prophet-philosopher Friedrich Nietzsche (1844–1900), who asserted that "Christianity is Platonism for the people."[1] Nietzsche is too close to the truth for comfort. The legacy of a wide and pervasive Platonism is why so many Christians even today can only contemplate an ethereal heaven for their immortal souls. They share Plato's aversion towards matter, even though biblical religion exhibits a wholesome, down-to-earth character. Here also we find a key to deep-seated Christian difficulties with human physicality—and not least sexuality. Such Platonic Christians—and among them, countless evangelicals seeking some version of the "higher life," are not at all clear why Psalm 104 or Proverbs 30 and similar passages should be in the Bible at all! They have forgotten that Christ did not come to save us from being creatures but to save us from our sins (Matt 1:21).

The creation is good. Contrary to what is heard from many an evangelical pulpit, when Christ said "My kingdom is not of this world" (John 18:36 NIV), he was *not* saying that his kingdom had nothing to do with this world; rather that it was *not* founded on any worldly principle, and his servants are not to behave in a worldly fashion (in the sense warned against in Rom 12:2). While the coming of the kingdom brings division on earth (Matt 10:34), those who have entered the kingdom are *not* to draw the sword on its behalf as if they were defending an earthly jurisdiction or worldly cause (Matt 26:51–52). Certainly, the kingdom is spiritual. It is spiritually discerned (Matt 13:11; John 3:3), and neither is it positioned in a particular locality (Luke 17:20–21). It is to be proclaimed by the people of God (Luke 9:2, 60). It is everlasting (Dan 2:44; Luke 1:33; Rev 11:15). The risen Christ, to whom has been given all authority in heaven and earth (Matt 28:18), over the course of forty days instructed the Apostles *concerning the kingdom of God* (Acts 1:3). The kingdom of God is his sovereign rule over the entire creation, including all human culture. Therefore, while the kingdom is not grounded in any worldly principle or place, *it has everything to do with life as it is lived on the face of the earth*. Any inclination towards an improper, ethereal spiritualization of the kingdom is overthrown by the clear meaning of "Your kingdom come, Your will be done, on earth as it is in heaven" (Matt 6:10 NRSV).

However, without an integral "all of life" world view, Christianity, evangelicals included, inevitably adopts a part-Christian, part non-Christian posture that suffuses all of life with a multiplicity of dualistic contradictions and a wide array of spiritually-corrosive, syncretistic consequences. Arguably, this has happened in the history of Christianity as its original full-orbed "all of life" message of the good news of the kingdom of God was

---

1. *Basic Writings of Nietzsche* (edited by Kaufmann), 193.

reduced to the dimensions of the church as an institution and to individual, personal salvation. This *reductionist* tendency will be discussed further shortly.

Enthralled to Christian Zionism and Neo-liberal Corporate Capitalism

The case can be made for saying that the church is constantly called to shun both syncretism and sectarianism. If Protestantism has widely failed on both counts, its evangelical segments have often been in the vanguard of failure. Evangelicalism has contributed significantly to the fragmentation of Protestantism, although it is not the only culprit. Sectarianism has abounded among evangelicals to the point where across the English-speaking world there are many hundreds if not thousands of evangelical denominational structures, often endeavoring to establish duplicate colleges, schools, missions, and other such projects.

Syncretism abounds amongst evangelicals. Rather than be salt and light for the world, much contemporary Evangelicalism functions as its own biggest distraction. It is obsessed with eschatological speculation rooted in the premillennial, dispensationalist misuse of Scripture. It largely shares in the Pentecostal-charismatic failure to read Scripture in Bible-consistent, covenantal-redemptive-historical terms. It has even led some to presume to reinstall the office of Apostle. It has undergone widespread capitulation—in and beyond "health and wealth" teachings—to contemporary neo-liberal modes of individualism and materialism.

These points need to be unpacked further. Their consequences are often poorly appreciated. The dominant influence of premillennial dispensational eschatology entrenches a pro-Israel, Christian Zionist outlook that closes the hearts and minds of its adherents to the cries for peace and justice that rise from the dispossessed. Of course, those who point to unjust Israeli actions can so easily and falsely be labeled as anti-Semitic. Nevertheless, this misguided support for Zionism amongst evangelicals has imperiled the position of many Christian churches and organizations across the Arab-speaking world. The fate of the Arabs who profess Christ in these regions seems to be of little consequence to those whose outlook is primarily ruled by Christian Zionism. The latter, of course, is deeply congruent with the overall global posture of the United States, which two decades after the collapse of the Soviet Union remains by far the most heavily armed state on the face of the earth. In short, Christian Zionism arraigns a large segment of English-speaking Evangelicalism on the side of the American global empire. At the heart of that empire is multinational corporate capitalism that since the late 1970s has made a small elite stupendously wealthy while it has relentlessly depressed the circumstances of countless millions within and beyond the western world. And, let it be said, many an ancient prophecy tells us that Almighty God is centrally concerned with how we treat the poor, the bereaved, the handicapped, the bereft, and the marginalized.

It is no coincidence that many vocal Christian Zionists are drawn from among the ranks of Pentecostal-charismatic evangelicals. The groups are not coterminous, but there is a considerable overlap. Both exhibit their greatest strength in the American heartland. Not only in its tendency to promote "name it and claim it" style "health and wealth" teaching, but in its individualism and emphasis on self-affirmation, its love of the sensate and the spectacular, and its susceptibility to the cult of the "star performer" celebrity personality, Pentecostal-charismatic Evangelicalism is much more deeply mired in contemporary secular-materialist corporate culture than it realizes. Its repudiation of liberalism is rendered shallow by its deep complicity in the methods and styles of contemporary corporate culture. Their preachers are platform performers, marketing a range of "spiritual products" to consumers who must be kept in a continual state of animated ready-to-consume-more anticipation. Here we are confronted with the crass worldliness of the supposedly super-spiritual, and the lack of an adequate evangelical understanding of the religious significance of human culture comes home to roost with a vengeance. Evangelicals cannot avoid having one view or another of the character and purpose of human culture. The question needs to be: Is the evangelical view of human culture—including socio-economic life—consonant with, and directed by, the Scriptures?

At this point, contemporary Evangelicalism has largely failed. As might be expected, strategies are offered on all sides. The "emerging church" of Brian McLaren and his associates offers evangelicals its own version of deep, cool and sophisticated syncretism, even as boldly advertised charismatic venues (especially in their mega-church manifestations) offer a high, hot, and noisy syncretism. The predominance of premillennial dispensationalism, and the attitudes it engenders, has helped to induce in a large proportion of English-speaking evangelicals a deep passivity towards the multiple challenges of the twenty-first century. The two exceptions are when trends in the culture directly offend evangelical moral sensibilities (such as abortion and euthanasia), or when the latest developments in the Middle East are construed as having apocalyptic Armageddon-inducing significance.

From innumerable platforms orators harangue their audiences with the question "Are you rapture-ready?" They do not offer a *scripturally directed* exposition of *the integral character of Christian discipleship and its implications for contemporary life*. There is little or no notion among them of a Christian calling to stand for public justice in national and international affairs, to uphold the cause of the poor, the aliens, or refugees at or within our gates. There is no notion of a distinctive Christian calling in all branches of intellectual and cultural endeavor, or even the possibility of a distinctively Christian contribution to the arts and sciences. If Jesus is coming very soon, and if Christians are going to be "raptured" off the face of the earth anyway, why then bother—the inference is—with creation care and environmental responsibility, or with questions of public justice or socio-economic equity? Such evangelicals live out their error that the kingdom of God has been "postponed" and is for Jewish people only. They espouse what is, by biblical standards, a truncated and distorted "gospel."

Contemporaneous with the further rise of this type of Evangelicalism, the public life of the USA and UK has been marked by the almost complete triumph of the socio-economic ideology of neoliberalism. The leading political exponents were British (Conservative) Prime Minister Margaret Thatcher (in office 1979–90), and US (Republican) President Ronald Reagan (in office 1981–89). "Free market economics," as articulated by neoliberalism, was endorsed by many evangelicals on both sides of the Atlantic, among them Brian Griffiths in his *Morality and the Market Place* (1982). He went on to become Vice-President of Goldman Sachs International. The woefully inadequate performance of governments in addressing issues of global warming and environmental degradation is attributable to the overwhelming dominance of this free-market corporate capitalism in public life.

The dominance of corporate capitalism effectively *reduces* everything to its own version of materialism—so that *everything* must be structured according to the ways of the business corporation (corporatization), everything must be viewed as a product or service that may be brought to market (commodification), and anything of value must be capable of being priced in terms of monetary value (monetization). These are the principles and priorities *according to which we are now expected to live*. When viewed in biblical terms, corporate capitalism has become the *ruling idolatry* of our age. The writings of Bob Goudzwaard and others have made this clear, although it is barely discernable to those who only read their Bibles as a devotional guidebook to attaining an individual and ethereal salvation.

The onset of this latest and ruthlessly aggressive iteration of contemporary paganism finds present day Evangelicalism in spiritually compromised disarray. Many evangelicals find it extraordinarily difficult to address such issues. The lack of sufficient biblical understanding among them, combined with strong tendencies to *reduce* the gospel message to individual salvation, coupled with a failure to grasp the religious significance of human culture has produced an Evangelicalism that is up to its neck in spiritual compromise. Evangelicals who just do not see these problems are blinded by the way in which they have reduced the gospel to a form of escapism. In fear of socialism or trade unions, evangelicals habitually default to right-wing politics and corporate capitalism. As a result they end up (at least tacitly) supporting the prevalent idolatry of our times. Such Evangelicalism lacks the structural insight that an integral vision encourages. It can too readily present as adolescent, when it needs to grow up, be mature, re-read the Bible, and take responsibility.

Certainly, these censures do not apply equally to all evangelical subgroups. Its compromised character is variously expressed, but no more conspicuously than in its "Tele-evangelist" and megachurch manifestations. In the latter, the full sensate repertoire of corporate dominated contemporary culture is on display, and the *modus operandi* is followed in a worldwide profusion of emulating Revival Centers and Revival Fellowships. The preacher or pastor is boosted as a kind of spiritual celebrity. The standard of biblical exposition is likely to be abysmal, but delivered with flamboyant arrogance and overbearing rhetoric, emotionally manipulative, sometimes with claims of privately received revelation, rarely devoid of eschatologically-speculative, pro-Israel language, and possibly including market-affirming health and prosperity ("God wants you to be rich") teaching. This "gospel" is aggressively marketed (there is no other word for it) as a spiritual product available on bargain terms.

In such settings, "special offer" spiritual fads may be multimedia marketed one after another. The church "venture" is entrepreneurially managed as a going financial proposition. In "praise and worship" the lusty roar of the congregation is replaced by a plethora of songs and choruses, sometimes repeated with a mantra-like cadence producing a mesmeric effect, the whole performance electronically enhanced with drums, guitar, and the rest, with words and effects conveyed and reinforced by the ubiquitous big screen. It is altogether possible that the proceedings will be led by a sincere sister whose singing will be delivered with an expressive ardor reminiscent of the orgasmic transports depicted by Giovanni Lorenzo Bernini in "The Ecstasy of Saint Theresa." In megachurch settings multiple overhead screens project the words, pan the "audience" and highlight the "performers." This is the only mode of worship known to a growing number of Christian congregations.

Although they fulminate against secular humanism, such megachurch environments represent a profound spiritual conformity to the world, offering, as they do, settings in which spectacle triumphs over understanding and wisdom. The whole "production" amounts to a combination of preacher-plus-ensemble-centered entertainment and highly contrived audience participation. It is designed to achieve maximum penetration in the spiritual market place. Its proponents consider it a "winning strategy"—and the numbers prove it. For those with eyes to see, this subordination to the ways of contemporary culture, particularly in its entertainment, advertising and public relations expressions, is all too obvious.

Yet amidst the hype, and all the electronically amplified cacophonous jangling that contemporary Evangelicalism is capable of inflicting on us—if we let it—there are still those *of all age groups* who realize that there is much more to the Christian calling than this, and who still long to hear "the still small voice" (1 Kgs 19:12 AV). Immense and committed interests apparently hold the present structures in place, but we are wise not to underestimate the flexibility—even fluidity—of the historical process. The *status quo* can appear intransigently solid when in truth it is being ripened for change. The arrival in a market place not far from Wittenberg of that entrepreneurial vendor of grace, John Tetzel (1465–1519), doubtless bore many of the marks of late medieval "spiritual business as usual"—but it was not to be. Of course, in history there are no exact parallels. The Texas of today, for example, is not Saxony half a millennium ago. That said, the parallels between Tetzel and his "special offer indulgences" and today's platform revivalists are greater than many contemporary evangelicals are ready to contemplate. What came in the sixteenth century was neither planned nor predictable: Luther's Ninety Five Theses, the Diet of Worms, and a cascading of events that led to the Protestant Reformation. Whatever happens in our era will certainly not be a rerun of the sixteenth-century Reformation or the eighteenth-century Awakenings. Whether we like it or not, there can be no going back to past eras. Anyway, Christianity now stands in need of an authentic renewal of much greater breadth and depth than the waves of renewal experienced in past centuries.

Francis Schaeffer

At one stage, in the late 1960s and earlier 1970s, it appeared as if a significant trend might emerge among evangelicals that would challenge their strong disposition towards subjective, anti-intellectual emotionalism. Francis "Fran" Schaeffer broke upon the scene with the publication of his *Escape from Reason* (1968). This should be read in conjunction with two of his other works: *The God Who is There* (1968) and *He is There and He is Not Silent* (1972). In the late 1930s Schaeffer had commenced training at Westminster Theological Seminary, Philadelphia, but, of strong premillennial convictions, he transferred to and graduated from Faith Theological Seminary, Wilmington, Delaware. Schaeffer eventually turned out to be startlingly different from the norm, in that he taught evangelicals to take art and philosophy seriously—and some actually listened.

His a-typical development calls for explanation. In 1948 he moved with his wife Edith (1914–2013) to Switzerland. Their purpose was evangelistic, and they eventually set up L'Abri ("The Shelter")—a place of retreat intended to communicate the gospel and a venue for philosophical and cultural discussion. Schaeffer sought to counter the prevailing philosophies of the day with a dogmatic assertion of Christian presuppositions that owed much to the apologetics of the professors of old Princeton. This strategy brought Schaeffer into the realms of philosophy, while the world of art provided him with an immense storehouse of examples. Even though his characterizations of figures such as Thomas Aquinas, Jean-Jacques Rousseau, and Søren Kierkegaard (1813–55) proved problematic, Schaeffer's early writings opened doors to young evangelicals that many of them hardly knew existed. Inadequately educated evangelical pastors, caught way out of their depth, could be heard to mutter: "This is not the gospel." Older evangelical traditions of withdrawal and pietistic restrictions on the scope of Christian discipleship remained dominant.

Less than obvious at the outset was the extent of Schaeffer's intellectual indebtedness to Hans Rookmaaker (1922–77). This became more apparent with the publication of Rookmaaker's *Modern Art and The Death of a Culture* (1970). Rookmaaker's insight into the history of Western art and culture owed much to the profound renewal of Christian philosophical and cross-disciplinary thinking that took place at the Free University, Amsterdam, from the 1920s to the 1960s, of which little was known among evangelicals generally. The Schaeffer episode was transient. He found disciples in writers such as Os Guinness, author of *The Dust of Death* (1973), and more recently Charles Wendell Colson and Nancy Pearcey.

Intellectually, Schaeffer had never really left the United States, and in his later years, with the encouragement of his son Frank Schaeffer, he became involved in the rise of the Christian Right—sometimes in evidence as the Moral Majority. The seminal period for this development covered the presidencies of Jimmy Carter and Ronald Reagan in 1977–81 and 1981–89 respectively. Its roots lay in the US 1971 District Court for the District of Columbia decision in *Green v. Connally* against Bob Jones University, and the catalyst was the 1973 US Supreme Court decision in the *Roe v. Wade* abortion issue. The coalition formed to fight the case for Bob Jones University maintained its momentum by marshaling Roman Catholic and evangelical opposition to *Roe v. Wade*. Frankie assisted his father in launching into the movie-making business. Schaeffer's book plus movie *How Should We Then Live? The Rise and Decline of Western Thought and Culture* (1976) concluded with a rejection of *Roe v. Wade*. Extensive speaking tours ensued. Further titles were forthcoming, amongst them *Whatever Happened to the Human Race?* (1979) and *A Christian Manifesto* (1982). These made Schaeffer the "public intellectual" of the emerging Moral Majority, which helped to put Ronald Reagan in the Oval Office in 1981.

In *The Great Evangelical Disaster* (1984), Schaeffer continued to defend inerrancy in the manner of Cornelius Van Til. Moreover, he continued to uphold his version of "American exceptionalism"—for him the United States was consciously founded on specifically Christian, protestant, and evangelical principles, and therefore is and ought to be regarded as a "Christian nation." Some evangelical historians incisively challenged this standpoint, among them Nathan Hatch, George Marsden and Mark Noll in papers published as *The Search for Christian America* (1983). Yet America as an intrinsically Christian nation was the very notion that Schaeffer wanted to utilize in the culture wars against all forms of liberalism and secular humanism. Marsden and Noll conducted an extensive correspondence with Schaeffer prior to publication, but Schaeffer proved to be intractable. Schaeffer wanted a Christian historiography that would back up his assumptions, and the evangelical historians, who knew better, would not accommodate him. They were right and he was wrong.

Later, Frankie went on to repudiate his part in the rise of the Christian Right and present a less than hagiographic view of his father. He converted to Eastern Orthodoxy in 1990. It was suggested that he had betrayed his father. The Christian Right went on to help put two members of the Bush dynasty into the Oval Office, the terms of George W. Bush being notorious for the deliberate launching of a war of aggression in Iraq (2003) that caused the loss of hundreds of thousands of lives, among them many Christians.

Not all evangelicals were beguiled by the claims and campaigns of the Christian Right. Those of a more Anabaptist orientation, alert to the totalitarian character of "Christian empire," were not so easily fooled. The strong opposition of figures such as Howard Yoder (1927–97) and Stanley Hauerwas to the violent ways of American empire owed something to the influence of Barth and his opposition to German militaristic nationalism. However, their Anabaptist stance served to inhibit any articulation of an authentically Christian *political* alternative. Along with the tendency to think exclusively in terms of the institutional church community, what is missing here is a clear understanding of Christ as king over political life.

Others, with reformed rather than Anabaptist commitments had reflected on the sobering lessons of the Vietnam conflict, notwithstanding the public rhetoric of fervent patriotism relentlessly vented on all sides. Among them, the historian Ronald Wells, then of Calvin College, wrestled with the question of how he might resign as an evangelical without in any way repudiating the Christian faith. Where was he to send his letter of resignation? There was no one to give an authoritative answer. By that stage Evangelicalism was increasingly dissipated by its own tendencies towards anarchy. It became possible to say of it what was once said of ancient Israel: "In those days . . . every man did that which was right in his own eyes" (Judg 21:25 KJV). This happens when a reduced gospel of private, ethereal salvation is preached and the pan-cosmic and pan-cultural kingship of Jesus Christ is slighted. These are hard words, but the problems of contemporary Evangelicalism are not restricted to its extremists but pervade wherever Bebbington's quadrilateral of priorities typically prevail.

The Significance of Hans Rookmaaker and the Free University, Amsterdam

What was problematic in the teaching of Francis Schaeffer was derived from his conservative-evangelical-fundamentalist past and connections in the United States. What was constructively innovative arose pre-eminently from his connection with Rookmaaker. The two men first met in 1948. The turning point in Rookmaaker's life took place in the inauspicious circumstances of his incarceration in a German Prisoner of War camp at Stanislau (now in the Ukraine), where in 1943 he was converted after encountering a Christian thinker named Johan Peter Albertus Mekkes (1898-1987). Mekkes was the author of an extended work on the humanistic theory of the law-state. He was greatly influenced by Herman Dooyeweerd (1894-1977) of the Free University, Amsterdam. Abraham Kuyper founded this institution of Christian higher education in 1880. In short, the Rookmaaker who came into Schaeffer's life was from a trajectory of Christian living, thinking, and public involvement unknown to the vast majority of evangelicals, including their leadership.

Kuyper's initial theological orientation was to liberal Protestantism. He became a Doctor of Theology and was ordained as a minister in the Netherlands Reformed Church in 1862. Starting out as a country pastor, he became committed to traditional Christianity through the influence of a female congregant, Pietje Balthus. In the 1860s Kuyper started to correspond with Guillaume Groen van Prinsterer (1801-76), who had criticized the principles of the French Revolution in his work *Unbelief and Revolution*

(1847). Groen van Prinsterer had developed an *anti-revolutionary* Christian political movement in the Netherlands that was founded upon a Christian critique of liberalism in its theological, philosophical, cultural, and political guises. Kuyper rejected the liberal insistence on human autonomy, but called for an open society opposed to authoritarianism and totalitarianism, within which a diversity of alternative religious convictions might be lived out with mutual respect, sometimes called principled pluralism. In 1872 Kuyper established a newspaper, *The Standard*. By this means he mobilized reformed opinion in the Netherlands. He was elected to parliament in 1874, and wrote *Our Program* in 1876, defining the standpoint of the Anti-Revolutionary Party (ARP) founded in 1879. These efforts were supported by the *kleine luyden*—the everyday folk. Kuyper led the party until his death. The educational funding issue allied Reformed and Roman Catholic Christians against a state-backed and liberal-supported secularization of education.

Kuyper advocated a *non-reductionist* understanding of Christianity. He taught that the sovereignty of God was no mere theological proposition but extended over all creation and human culture, and that everything in our lives flows from the heart and is therefore indicative of our ultimate religious stance. Kuyper talked of "common grace," whereby God sustains all things and without which human culture would not be possible. He also spoke of "the antithesis" between the obedience of faith and the disobedience of unbelief. In so doing, Kuyper was not standing for an us-versus-them scenario, but stressed that the line between belief and unbelief runs through the hearts and lives of believers as well as through human culture with all its institutions and diversity. Finally, he used the terminology of "sphere-sovereignty" to argue that different types of societal structures (such as marriage, family, church, state, business, educational and medical institutions), have specific callings as well as limited competencies. Each has an office to perform to the glory of God. None of these structures is all-competent—not even the church or state. When any sphere seeks to override or usurp the calling and functions of another, confusion and suffering can be expected to ensue. This teaching respected societal diversity and rejected reductionism.

Kuyper's most enduring legacy was the founding of the Free University, Amsterdam. In his opening address he delivered the now famous line: "No single piece of our mental world is to be hermetically sealed off from the rest, and there is not a square inch in the whole terrain of our human existence over which Christ, who is Sovereign over all, does not cry: 'Mine!'"[2] Here was a bold and clearly *anti-reductionist* message. In 1898 Kuyper gave the "Stone Lectures" on Calvinism at Princeton, there spelling out his

---

2. Bratt (editor), *Abraham Kuyper: A Centennial Reader*, 488.

integral vision in greater detail. Previously Kuyper had confronted evangelical, Keswick-style of holiness teaching while visiting Brighton, England, in 1875. He rejected this teaching as shallow and not fully scriptural, and preferred to find spiritual sustenance from sources much closer to the Protestant Reformation. Nevertheless, although he appreciated the "old writers," Kuyper's notion of Calvinistic Christianity was not a rerun of that era, but aspired to be a contemporary and *biblically-directed* rearticulation of the first principles of Calvin's teachings. This line of thinking has sometimes been called Neo-Calvinist.

Some features of Kuyper's teaching have been taken up in North America. Here caution is appropriate, as these developments are not always in line with his thinking. For example, Kuyper's insistence that the state was not omni-competent is not to be equated with minimalist views of the state associated with John Locke and the American right wing. Here Kuyper himself would detect the influence of the Enlightenment. His critique of the consequences of the Enlightenment is abundantly clear in his opening address to the First Christian Social Congress held in the Netherlands in 1891—published in English as *The Problem of Poverty* (1991). Moreover, via Francis Schaeffer, notions such as "world and life view" and "the antithesis" were appropriated by some American evangelicals in ways that Kuyper never contemplated. Kuyper and his successors used them to facilitate understanding and elucidate the spiritual character of complex problems.

The Kuyperian Legacy

Kuyper was a prodigious author and speaker. He was as prolific as Luther. He addressed a broad range of issues primarily in world view terms. Only after Kuyper's demise were his teachings explored and articulated with philosophic rigor. This work was done at the Free University by Dirk Hendrik Theodoor Vollenhoven (1892–1978) and Herman Dooyeweerd, who were brothers-in-law. Vollenhoven was a classicist, while Dooyeweerd's special field was jurisprudence. Both men were philosophers of considerable range and depth. While their thought was not identical, both adopted a critical stance towards any synthesis between biblically directed faith and supposedly neutral thought patterns arising out of Hellenistic thinking. This is why their thought has sometimes been contentious among orthodox theologians.

Their purpose was not to challenge (still less to overthrow) the faith but to refine it of the dross arising from centuries of seeking to accommodate Christian doctrine to pagan philosophy. This involved the reshaping (reformation!) of our understanding of the encyclopedia of the sciences under the direction of biblical first principles. Vollenhoven developed a "problem-historical method" of interrogating the literature of the Western intellectual tradition from the standpoint of biblical teaching on God, law, and cosmos. Dooyeweerd's *De Wijsbegeerte der Wetsidee* (1935-6)—"philosophy of the law idea"—was both foundational and encyclopedic. Central to this project was unmasking the falsehood of the presumed or pretended autonomy of theoretical thought as variously understood in Hellenic philosophy, the scholastic theologians and philosophers of the medieval period, and the Enlightenment-driven thinkers of more recent centuries.

The call was for "the inner reformation of theoretical thought." This entailed a thorough and coherent reshaping, from the foundations upwards, of our understanding of the place and task of each of the special sciences. This reformation was to be *biblically directed* in the sense of founded in scriptural teaching concerning creation, fall, and redemption, but not Bible-based in the fundamentalist sense of requiring proof texts at each step of the discussion, as if the Bible was itself a handbook of philosophy. It respected reality as God-given and was therefore empirical without being empiricist. It was able to address contemporary questions with a structured insight precluded by habitual evangelical approaches. Not a few evangelicals were rightly appreciative of the depth of insight that Rookmaaker could provide, but they were unable to replicate it without abandoning the *reduced* Christianity that they had received from an Evangelicalism that sought to function only within the parameters of Bebbington's quadrilateral of priorities.

Following Kuyper, Dooyeweerd initially presented his philosophic and jurisprudential work as Calvinistic. It was certainly consistent with what we have termed the *directional* understanding of biblical authority that pervades the writings of Calvin. His original articulation took its bearings from the Calvinistic Reformation, but what was developed from that was no mere in-house debate limited to Calvinistic philosophers and reformed church denominations; instead, it was to be of service to all Christians. Moreover, Dooyeweerd's orientation towards systematic coherence never came with the intention of propounding a *closed* philosophical system. In practice, it opened up insight that continues to require interaction with like-minded practitioners in the special sciences. Dooyeweerd's starting-point was "creation, fall and redemption" as the biblically-directed "ground-motive" for all consistently-Christian thinking. Consequently, in his later work, he emphasized that "this philosophy is not to be understood as the exclusive thought of a small clique of Calvinists." He rejected the use of that descriptor, preferring to use the term "Christian philosophy without any further qualification."[3] His mature insight was offered ecumenically to the full household of faith, the entire body of Christ.

Dooyeweerd introduced his thought to an American audience in his 1960 lectures entitled *In the Twilight of Western Thought: Studies in the Pretended Autonomy of Theoretical Thought* (first published in 1962). His English-language *Roots of Western Culture: Pagan, Secular and Christian Options* (1979) is an incomplete but valuable translation of an earlier Dutch work. Dooyeweerd has not always been well served by his English-language translators and publishers. Part of the problem is that he wrote in the manner characteristic of continental European philosophy, which is somewhat impenetrable to many English-language readers. Thankfully, a great deal of what Dooyeweerd has to say has been articulated in clear and lucid English by Roy A. Clouser in *The Myth of Religious Neutrality* (1991, second edition 2005) and *Knowing with the Heart* (1999). Clouser has argued that at pivotal points, this school of Christian thinking not only draws from the leading Protestant Reformers but also has parallels with some of the most incisive thinking of the Cappadocian Fathers. Reformation and Patristic studies should belong together.

Along with Rookmaaker, the earlier followers of Vollenhoven and Dooyeweerd included Andree Troost (1916–2008) in ethics, Klaas Jan Popma (1903–1986) in classics, Hendrik van Riessen (1911–2000) in engineering, Meijer Cornelis Smit (1911–1981) in history, and Sytse Ulbe Zuidema (1908–75) in philosophy. The next generation included Jan Dengerink (1921–2010), Johan van der Hoeven, Henk Geertsema, Marinus Dirk Stafleu, Jacob Klapwijk, Egbert Schuurman, Bob Goudzwaard, Sander Griffioen, and Roelof Kuiper.

In North America this line of thinking was passionately advocated by H. Evan Runner (1916–2002), not least in *The Relation of the Bible to Learning* (1960) and *Scriptural Religion and Political Task* (1961). Runner was a student of Vollenhoven at the Free University. Among the most outstanding representatives in North America are Calvin G. Seerveld in philosophical aesthetics, James W. Skillen in political theory and practice, and Roy A. Clouser in philosophy of religion. Nevertheless, over many decades the Netherlands remained the home base for this school of thought, with a measure of interest and involvement continuing from around the globe, lately in Asia and Latin America.

---

3. Dooyeweerd, *New Critique*, I, 523; 524.

The word "*reformational*" appears to have been introduced into the English-language by Calvin Seerveld to denote this line of thinking.[4] To reiterate, this view is not Bible-based in the old evangelical-fundamentalist sense but *biblically directed*. To use the familiar words of the Psalmist "Your word is a lamp to my feet and a light to my path" (Ps 119:105 NRSV), the word is *not* to be equated *with* the path: the word is a light *on* the path. The picture is of walking forward in obedient discipleship. The Word of God gives *direction*. Accordingly, this outlook came to understand itself not as "Reformed" (past tense) in any restricted theological or denominational sense. It is not forgetful of history and tradition: it takes the apostolic deposit very seriously, but it does not seek to return to any era of the past. It offers its insights ecumenically and invites all to walk forward together by living lives of *integral* discipleship.

The Evangelical Reception of Reformational Thinking

The reception of reformational thinking in North America has taken place pre-eminently (but not exclusively) within the ambit of the Christian Reformed Church of North America (CRCNA). Nevertheless, Runner was not well received at Calvin College, the CRCNA liberal arts college in Grand Rapids, Michigan. The problem was not merely a matter of ethnicity and temperament. Calvin College shared in the long tradition of synthesising reformed doctrine with versions of Platonic philosophy, and his call for an integral, non-dualistic, non-reductionistic approach was not appreciated. This synthesizing tendency is also present in the school of thinking known as Reformed Epistemology.

At the same time, twentieth century North American Reformed theologians often baulked at the prospect of reshaping (reforming!) their dogmatics on an integral basis by discarding the legacies of scholastic-theological accommodation with pagan thought. There has been a strong tendency to take flight in an almost antiquarian confessionalism—as if twenty-first century issues can be settled with a pre-emptive invocation of seventeenth-century confessional statements. There have been notable exceptions to this tendency, including the ecumenist Paul G. Schrotenboer (1922–98) and at Calvin College the theologian Gordon Spykman, as exemplified by his *Reformational Theology* (1994).

Runner was involved in the establishment of the Institute for Christian Studies in Toronto, Canada, but the Institute seems to have never adequately recovered from the premature death of Bernard Zylstra (1934–86).

---

4. Seerveld, *How to Read the Bible*, 39.

Generally speaking, the reformational movement in North America has been confined to a minor place within the CRCNA and its cognate institutions. At the same time it has been important in the development of writers such as Craig Bartholomew, Jonathan Chaplin, Richard Middleton and Brian Walsh, whose influence is growing way beyond the confines of denominational structures. In short, the CRCNA provided a restricted milieu within which reformational thought and action could take initial root but not subsequently flourish. The comparable denominational structures in Australia and New Zealand were less than encouraging. Among the Reformed in the Antipodes, a stringent confessionalism repeatedly stymied reformational developments.

It is not always appreciated that Vollenhoven and Dooyeweerd's first English language publications were in the British journal *The Evangelical Quarterly*.[5] However, the opposition of Oliver Barclay, who became General Secretary of the Inter-Varsity Fellowship (IVF)—later Universities and Christian Colleges Fellowship (UCCF)—after organizational pioneer Douglas Johnson (1904–91), largely thwarted further influence in Great Britain. Barclay was influenced by two natural scientists like himself: Donald MacCrimmon MacKay (1922–87), author of *Clockwork Image: Christian Perspective on Science* (1974), and Reijer Hooykaas (1904–96), who argued his case in *Christian Faith and the Freedom of Science* (1957), and *Religion and the Rise of Modern Science* (1972). Hooykaas and Mackay were close friends. Together they resisted the reformational critique of the presumed autonomy of all theoretical thought, including that of the physical sciences.

By the end of 1948 it appears that the IVF leadership had decided that the correct path was Baconian empiricism, with its ideal of "value free" and supposedly "neutral" scientific statements. In a manner typical of empiricism, the importance of any substantive philosophical investigation into the necessary structure of scientific thought was downplayed, as were the deistic implications of much Baconian scientific language. The standpoint adopted by the IVF leadership accorded well with the uncritical empiricism of many Anglo-Americans. It forgets that things are never "just seen," but always "seen as." Such empiricism resonated with the endemic evangelical depreciation of thinking, philosophy, literature (other than its own), the humanities, and the social sciences. All these were suspect. This was all before the 1960s when Thomas S. Kuhn (1922–96) called into question the Baconian account of scientific change. By then the IVF (later UCCF) die

---

5. Vollenhoven, "Significance," 128–160; 398–427; Dooyeweerd, "Introduction," 42–51.

was already cast. A later publication by Oliver Barclay exhibits embarrassing misrepresentations and misunderstandings of the reformational approach.[6]

In the British Isles and beyond, the outlook of Barclay was partly attributable to, and reinforced by, the pietism of Lloyd-Jones. Since 1958, British evangelicals of reformed soteriological orientation have drawn encouragement from the publications of the "Banner of Truth Trust." Its offerings have provided a historiography of Evangelicalism deeply critical of Arminianism and its derivatives, including the "invitation system" of the Graham crusades. In "Banner" publications, reformational thinking has rarely if ever been given much scope. It does not speak the Banner's language—and hence is deeply suspect. In this respect, Banner publications reflect accurately the tone set by Lloyd-Jones. "The Doctor" could acknowledge the significance of Groen Van Prinsterer and the greatness of Kuyper.[7] However, reformational thinking was another matter. In his biography of Lloyd-Jones, Iain Murray offers the following curious passage:

> Another injurious influence . . . he [Lloyd-Jones] traced to the teaching of Herman Dooyeweerd of Holland, 'in many ways the greatest living philosopher.' Out of his teaching a school had grown up whose great message is the implementation of the cultural mandate of Genesis 1:27, with the aim of bringing the world in every respect under 'the Lordship of Christ.' Those of this view criticized evangelicals for being too concerned about personal salvation. The Christian is to go out and capture every realm: schools, politics, economics, trade unions . . .[8]

It is not clear why such influence is "injurious." Is an anti-Christian philosophy preferred? Is salvation only personal and private? That is not what the Scriptures teach. They teach that Jesus Christ *is* Lord, not that Christians make him so! Are Christians here expected to opt for anti-Christian alternatives (there being no neutral standpoint) in cultural life, in education, in politics, in socio-economic affairs, and so forth? Can they do that in the name of Jesus Christ—after Jesus has taught them that they cannot serve two masters? It is hard to escape the conclusion, even allowing for the fact that Iain H. Murray is here reporting on Lloyd-Jones, that this is a denigration of Herman Dooyeweerd and reformational thinking by innuendo that is driven by a *reductionist* pietism. Yet such statements can be highly

---

6. Barclay, *The Intellect and Beyond*, 153–157; published in the UK as *Developing a Christian Mind*. A revised edition edited by Geoffrey Stoner omitted the offending section.

7. Lloyd-Jones, *The Puritans*, 330–333.

8. Murray, *D. Martyn Lloyd-Jones*, 619.

influential, shaping the attitude of Christians long after they have forgotten the specific passage, or the actual words by which they were decisively influenced.

The intellectual deficits and exegetical deficiencies of such Evangelicalism is well on display when Paul's words: "See to it that no one takes you captive through hollow and deceptive philosophy, which depends on human tradition and the basic principles of this world rather than on Christ" (Col 2:8 NIV) are taken as repudiating *all* philosophical endeavor; when in truth Paul is warning against all theorizing that does *not* obediently recognize the kingship of Christ over all creation, our own thinking not excluded.

The tragedy of such Evangelicalism is that it has persistently entrenched itself within a reduced version of the biblical message. On those rare occasions when it has addressed the reformational alternative it has all too often betrayed its own reductionist tendencies and tellingly misrepresented it as aiming at some sort of cultural domination for itself, when it genuinely aspires to serve all humankind as it first endeavors to serve and testify to the risen Christ in all things. Put simply, Christian discipleship is an all-of-life-encompassing calling—and no evangelical leaders, whatever their prestige and however revered, are entitled to abridge or curtail the calling of Jesus to all of his people and in all things to: "Follow me!"

12

IS AUTHENTIC RENEWAL POSSIBLE?

Reductionism as the Core Problem of Christianity and Evangelicalism

A central problem in the history of Christianity is that of *reductionism*. Moreover, at this stage in our discussion it can be established that *Evangelicalism is a reduction of a reduction*. The first great reduction was accomplished well over a millennium ago. In the wake of Constantine, Eusebius, and Theodosius, the true meaning of the good news concerning the kingdom of God was lost sight of as the Christian religion became *reduced* to its institutional ecclesiastical expression. It is instructive to consider what happened to Christian understandings of the kingdom of God in this context. It is not altogether absent from the Nicene Creed but appears at the end of the following extract:

> For us and for our salvation he came down from heaven, was incarnate of the Holy Spirit and the Virgin Mary and became truly human. For our sake he was crucified under Pontius Pilate; he suffered death and was buried. On the third day he rose again in accordance with the Scriptures; he ascended into heaven and is seated at the right hand of the Father. He will come again in glory to judge the living and the dead and his kingdom will have no end.

The positioning here of the only reference to "his kingdom" seems to imply, but does not necessitate, *a kingdom that is only a future reality*. This may perhaps be related to a tendency in the post-apostolic church to read the Apocalypse in a static (arguably Hellenic) fashion, rather than in the dynamic manner characteristic of much earlier Jewish thought. If the millennium in the Book of Revelation is equated with the kingdom of God, and if the millennium is then viewed as a literal epoch taking place *after* the Second Advent, that might account for the location of the only reference to the "kingdom" in the Nicene Creed. This is perhaps indicative of how, in post-apostolic thinking, "gospel" and "kingdom" gradually became disconnected.

The message of Christ was: "the time is fulfilled" and "the kingdom of God is at hand—repent . . . and believe the gospel" (Mark 1:15; Matt 4:17 KJV). He declared: "I must proclaim the good news of the kingdom of God . . . for I was sent for this purpose" (Luke 4:43 NRSV). How powerful is the change if we venture to insert a single line (here in italics) into the text of the Nicene Creed, as follows:

> For us and for our salvation he came down from heaven, was incarnate of the Holy Spirit and the Virgin Mary and became truly human. *He proclaimed the good news of the kingdom of God.* For our sake he was crucified under Pontius Pilate; he suffered death and was buried. On the third day he rose again in accordance with the Scriptures; he ascended into heaven and is seated at the right hand of the Father. He will come again in glory to judge the living and the dead and his kingdom will have no end.

Faced with the multiple confusions of contemporary Evangelicalism, especially in its Pentecostal-charismatic wing, and the aching rootlessness of so much contemporary life, it is understandable that Thomas C. Oden has advocated, in *The Rebirth of Orthodoxy* (2003), a sober return to a core Christianity identified in principle and articulated by Vincentius of Lérins (d. 445), as that which is believed *ubique, semper, omnibus*—everywhere, at all times and by all. The rub, here, of course, is that while this "Canon of Vincentius" might be invoked to repel what is new and false, it does not serve us well when it comes to recovering what is central but was lost sight of—such as the all-encompassing proclamation of the kingdom of God so conspicuous in the New Testament. In other words, the "Canon of Vincentius" does not allow for the reality that many Christians in many places and over an extended period had lost sight of the kingdom of God in its full meaning, largely *reducing* it to churchly life.

We are on firmer ground with the principle set forth in Chapter 17 of the Second Helvetic Confession (1566): "It [the church] does not err as long as it rests upon the rock Christ, and upon the foundation of the prophets and apostles."[1] This is the true "Apostolic deposit" that is to be upheld and guarded (2 Tim 1:13–14; Jude 3). The apostolic deposit is not in safe hands where the kingdom of God is reduced to the church or completely excluded.

As the centuries passed, the full formalization of the medieval "cradle to the grave" sacramental system narrowed things down further to processes and procedures that guaranteed *to the individual believer* an eventual eternal life. Alas, the Protestant Reformation did not sufficiently penetrate the fabric of western Christendom to address these issues adequately. Evangelicalism's "reduction of the reduction" simply offered a protestant alternative to the medieval sacramental system. Among many Protestants the tendency has been to equate the kingdom of God with the church as an institution. For example, the Orthodox Presbyterian Church, in its *Form of Church Government*, states: "Jesus Christ . . . hath erected in this world a kingdom, which is his church."[2]

Wording of this sort is truly problematic. The kingdom of God is not among us thanks to the presence of the church, but the presence of the church as the people of God is a result of the coming of the kingdom as proclaimed by Jesus and his apostles. Once this point is grasped we can see that a life of consistent, comprehensive, and integral discipleship extends way beyond churchly boundaries. Those church leaders who think it is the task of the church to provide an oasis of spirituality amidst the wastelands of secularism and deserts of materialism have utterly missed the point of the gospel; they have lost sight of the coming of the kingdom of God. The roots of this problem go back at least to the distant days of Constantine, Eusebius, and Theodosius. This is why it is necessary to take the long historical view when addressing the problem of Evangelicalism, as a key feature of that problem is not only the reductionism that Evangelicalism inherited from earlier centuries (that reduced everything to the church and missions), but provided the starting-point for the *further reductionism* in which Evangelicalism is complicit, namely the reduction of the gospel to the requirements for inner, individual, and personal salvation.

The phenomenon of clericalism is but one manifestation of the consequences of reducing the kingdom to the institutional church. Endowed with the authority of churchly ordination, and educated in the ways of sacred

---

1. *Reformed Confessions* (edited by Cochrane), 263.

2. *The Standards of Government Discipline and Worship of the Orthodox Presbyterian Church*, 4.

theology (in contrast to supposedly "secular" sciences), the priest or minister becomes (supposedly) an authority on *all things* Christian, rather than an office-bearer specifically administering the word and sacraments. The result is cramping and secularizing. When Christians strive to understand the meaning of Scripture for the physical sciences, or as directive for Christian political engagement, or for the conduct of educational or medical institutions, they are liable to come up against the presumed insight and leadership monopoly of the clergy, and the more theologically conservative the latter, the more they will seek to subordinate all Christian thought and practice to ecclesiastically-wrought confessional standards and their preferred versions of dogmatic theology. This will not work, because everything is not churchly, and not everything in reality can be reduced to the ecclesiastical.

The followers of Kuyper showed considerable structural insight when they wrote the following in connection with their Christian political endeavours: "While recognizing the Church's calling to proclaim the message of the Word of God as it applies to all of life . . . Government and people must learn to understand on their own, in the light of Holy Scripture, what this message means for the political life of every age."[3] Here is wisdom: it is the calling and task of the church as an institution to preach the Word of God, applying it to the whole of life. It is the calling and task of the citizenry to hear the Word preached, and to understand its meaning also with specific reference to public life and the public legal order. This is an approach that does not seek a return to any form of theocratic Christendom, and neither does it abandon the public square to the forces of secularism and materialism.

Evangelicalism as a Further Reduction of the Earlier Reduction

Evangelicalism typically takes this reduction of the kingdom to the institutional church a reductionist step further. As stated, *Evangelicalism is a reduction of a reduction.* We have seen that Bebbington's quadrilateral of evangelical priorities captures most persuasively the evangelical attitude, which does not only *reduce* all to the churchly, but *further reduces everything* to the issue of individual salvation: Bible, cross, missions and conversion all exist for this purpose. It is hardly surprising that many in the wider church complain that evangelicals have little church consciousness—it is because

---

3. *Statement of the Principles and General Political Program of the Anti-Revolutionary Party*, I: 2.

they so stress the "invisible church" of all true believers that they too often pay insufficient attention to wider church affairs.

If we consult the doctrinal basis of the Universities and Colleges Christian Fellowship (UCCF), in the United Kingdom—or its counterparts in in the USA (InterVarsity Christian Fellowship) or Australia (Australian Fellowship of Evangelical Students) the marks of *reductionism* are again clear. And we should indeed consult them, because these organizations are the spiritual nursery of much contemporary Evangelicalism. These statements affirm certain foundational Christian teachings of the Christian religion, and they are right to do so, but there is not a single reference to the kingdom of God—*the gospel as the gospel of the kingdom has no place in these statements*. The suggestion has been made that the omission was necessary in order to gain the support of students and others who espoused the teachings of premillennial dispensationalism. If so, this serves to further highlight how evangelical confusions seriously abridge and distort Evangelicalism's testimony to the full gospel message. In these doctrinal basis statements the focus is almost entirely on the salvation of individual sinners. The Second Advent is expected, but there is no reference to a new heaven and a new earth. The indwelling of the Spirit in believers is mentioned, but—even in a student organization—there is no reference to any calling to structure scholarly and scientific thought in terms of a biblically directed world and life view. Once again, salvation amounts to a Christ-facilitated individual escape to an ethereal heaven.

Not only does this perspective miss the mark by failing to acknowledge the call of Christ to follow him in labors intrinsic to the special sciences, it also implies that the lordship of Jesus Christ does not touch the greater part of intellectual as well as daily life generally. It thereby tacitly condones the secularization of western science, scholarship, and culture. Spokespersons for such organizations may say that the "other stuff" is not central, but in so saying they betray how their outlook is structured by their own reductionism. In truth, they have no biblical grounds to restrict Christ's kingship or abridge the comprehensiveness of his call to "Follow me!" in all things.

Even if it requires something like spiritual open-heart surgery without anesthetics, the leadership and members of such bodies need to reflect with the utmost gravity on what they are doing. While academic honesty and regular devotions are enjoined, they seem to have neither time nor inclination for "the inner reformation of theoretical thought" or for integral Christian thinking and living in every area of life. As the pressures of life increase, the now graduated adherents of this reduced gospel suffer a considerable attrition rate in their middle years, even as it enables others to draw the inference that Christianity is a form of individual escapism that has little or nothing to say about life as generally lived on the face of the earth. In practice, this evangelical reductionism may contain just enough of the gospel to successfully inoculate hearers against ever taking the kingdom of God seriously.

An Integral and Constructive Alternative to Reductionism

These are serious issues, but Evangelicalism's own self-criticism will continue to be inadequate if it remains circumscribed by the reductionist parameters recognized by Bebbington's quadrilateral of priorities. Arguably, the "ground motive" (meaning its foundational and directional basis) of an *integral* Christian approach, specifically "creation, fall, and redemption through Jesus Christ in the communion of the Holy Spirit" —provides Evangelicalism with a powerfully *anti-reductionist* alternative.[4] This approach is all-encompassing in its scope and consonant with the ancient creeds of the faith as well as the best teaching of the Reformation.

Such a *reformational* outlook sees continuing reformation as a calling that applies to the whole of life—and not limited to the church, or church and missions, or church, missions, and family. It does not confine discipleship to devotions, pious fellowship, church, and missions. It applies to our understanding of the entire order of creation and encompasses every aspect of our lives—it includes art, literature, drama, music, science, scholarship, engineering, philosophy, education, medicine, agriculture, manufacturing, trade, commerce, law, and politics. It is not interested in gaining acceptance by allowing an apostate or neo-pagan culture to shape our thought and deeds according to its requirements. It is not interested in any attempted conjoining of the supposedly sacred with the presumably secular. It seeks an integrally Christian standpoint that is free from false dichotomies. Simultaneously, it delights in the rich diversity present within the order of creation, even as it sees in every lawful expression of human culture an opportunity to honor the living God and be of service to humankind.

For this perspective to become the standard among Christians a great deal will need to change. Of course, it is not we who inaugurate and establish the kingdom of God. Ours is the task of preaching the good news of the kingdom in its fullness, of receiving and living out that integral message in every part of our lives—in thought, word, and deed (1 Cor 10:31). To dismiss this as a species of idealism is to miss the point: what is being

---

4. Dooyeweerd, *Roots*, 28.

considered here is what it means for the people of God to be the wholehearted disciples of Jesus Christ.

Some may ask if a convergence of evangelical and reformational outlooks is possible. Certainly both adhere to the foundational teachings of the Christian faith. At times it can seem as if Evangelicalism is capable of appropriating features of the reformational standpoint and partially absorbing them within its characteristic quadrilateral of priorities. However, such an appropriation is liable to be superficial because it is only piecemeal. Evangelical activism in the field of education is a case in point. Those inspired by the vision of Kuyper for education have long been engaged in establishing and maintaining Christian schools and institutions of higher learning. Genuine Christian education across the encyclopedia of the sciences—at all levels, and therefore beyond the restrictive parameters of the theological seminary—is a wonderful thing, honoring to God, training young people and adults alike to serve Jesus Christ in all areas of life. However, when evangelicals expressing a characteristically evangelical outlook embark upon such educational endeavors, they have tended to do so for basically reactionary purposes—such as avoiding developments prevalent in state-run institutions. Evangelical schools of this variety tend to become, perhaps inevitably, enterprises that tacitly promote socio-economic elitism and possibly also intellectual obscurantism as well. Such schools and colleges can favor the rich and further disadvantage the poor. This truth needs to be faced. In spite of impressive "mission statements" and the like, such institutions can be Christian in name but ruled more by the priorities and propensities identified by Max Weber than the integral Christian vision envisaged by Abraham Kuyper.

As long as Evangelicalism binds itself to reductionist notions of what it means to submit to the authority of Scripture, and reads the latter principally in terms of individual salvation, it will remain incapable of bringing the full gospel of the kingdom to the totality of life, and inevitably it will miss the point of genuinely Christian education. And that integral vision is what the increasingly bereft and desperate masses across and beyond the English-speaking world are hungry for—if they did but know it. The failure of reductionist versions of Christianity to grip the rails of reality is increasingly evident. It is widely perceived as escapist. Reductionist Christianity is being weighed in the balance and found wanting.

A reformational posture in no way involves abandoning belief in the inspiration and authority of Scripture, but understands that the written word gives *direction* in all things. It brings a whole-hearted, all-of-life quality to discipleship, and equips God's people to be Christ's ambassadors across the full range of human existence. Some might decry this as the sacralization of the secular, or the secularization of the sacred, but that is to introduce false dichotomies, extrinsic to the Bible. The present reality is that the *double reductionism* of Evangelicalism is deeply entrenched. It continues to hold many evangelicals in thrall. It blinkers them even as they read their Bibles with earnest sincerity.

Yet for all that, the Spirit continues to speak in Scripture, and there are not a few younger evangelicals across the globe, in a great diversity of sub-groups, who are ill at ease with what they have been bequeathed by preceding generations. In their hearts they know that there has to be more to their lives as Christians. What they are being drawn to is the full meaning of the kingdom of God. If Evangelicalism is ever to grasp this full meaning it must transcend the limitations of its own reductionist character—it must die unto itself—if it is to learn to walk the path of integral discipleship. Otherwise, it will remain incapable of proclaiming the good news of the kingdom with integrity.

When we compare where we are with where we need to be we can be stunned by the yawning chasm between the two. Contemporary Christianity stands in need of something much more radical than the Protestant Reformation of the sixteenth century. Reruns of past evangelistic crusades will not suffice, still less the wow-factor productions of stage-managed megachurches. Evangelicalism needs to grasp the radical difference between an integral renewal and a more superficial revivalism, and to contemplate the serious possibility that presumptuously engineered revivalist behavior might so grieve the Holy Spirit that it actually precludes the integral renewal of which Western Christianity stands in such conspicuous need. It is time to engage in sober reflection.

Our Need for a Continued Renewal of Biblical Scholarship

The availability of the Scriptures varied considerably across late medieval Europe. In England, fear of the followers of Wycliffe led the authorities to greatly restrict the availability of the Scriptures. One of the greatest glories of the English Reformation, aided by the movable type printing press, is that it made the Scriptures available to the people, and this in turn was a great spur towards wider literacy. After the Reformation, as the study of the Scriptures deepened, it became clear that the entire Bible was not always as straightforward as some had initially assumed. There were variant texts giving rise to variant readings. The Samuel-Kings cycle did not always harmonize with the Chronicles. The four gospels were not wholly synchronous.

There also arose questions of dating and authorship, particularly in regards to Moses and the Pentateuch.

Moreover, these latter questions came to the fore in circumstances where their discussion was frequently based on the assumptions of Enlightenment rationalism. At least since the time of Spinoza the church has not had exclusive control of the study and public discussion of Scripture. From the late eighteenth to mid-twentieth centuries, Evangelicalism was at variance with the greater part of northern European biblical scholarship because the latter was dominated by the assumptions of Enlightenment rationalism. However, the tendency of Evangelicalism to depreciate scholarship left it seriously handicapped even in the defense of the Bible itself. Attempts to "draw the line" in the face of liberal Bible scholarship led to intense and sometimes anguished discussions as to exactly what the terms "infallibility" and "inerrancy" might or might not contribute in this context. Evangelicals were right to resist Enlightenment-driven, liberal depreciations of the inspiration and authority of Scripture, but they generally lacked the capacity to challenge it effectively. In particular, they lacked the philosophical rigor needed to address Enlightenment thought at its *religious roots*.

We have stated that the original and second "Quest for the historical Jesus" provided Evangelicalism with immense opportunities that its neglect of scholarship prevented it from taking. Thankfully, the situation had improved considerably by the time of the "third quest" associated with the "Jesus Seminar" established by Robert W. Funk (1926–2005) in 1985, and involving figures such as Marcus Borg and John Dominic Crossan. Evangelical scholarship on Second Temple Judaism, the Gospels, the early church, and Pauline studies has advanced impressively. There is now a far greater evangelical capacity to engage late-liberal New Testament scholarship effectively. In the works of Richard Bauckham and N. T. Wright, for example, the benefits of historical contextualization for enhancing our understanding of the meaning of the Scriptures have been repeatedly demonstrated. At the same time, following the lead of authors including Kenton L. Sparks, Christopher M. Hays and Christopher B. Ansberry, some evangelicals have learned that historically critical approaches to Scripture are not *intrinsically* incompatible with its inspiration and authority. This represents a great stride forward from where Evangelicalism has been in times past and its significance should not be underestimated. The current flowering of evangelical New Testament scholarship was originally spurred on by a need to assert the trustworthiness of the Scriptures. Even an Evangelicalism dominated by an introverted pietism was constrained to defend its sacred texts. However, as these labors proceeded, and especially as they reached a high level of historical-contextual sophistication, the results repeatedly pointed to the full cultural (and not least political) relevance of the Bible, including the New Testament. In the wake of such research and scholarship, it would take a deliberate act of obscurantism to go back to using the Bible exclusively as a private devotions treasure trove from which to derive "pious thoughts for the day."

All Christians should give thanks for the positive contributions that these evangelicals have made to the deepening of our understanding of the New Testament. What has been achieved does not undermine the personal discipleship of believers, but it has served to erode individualistic notions of "the life of faith." Of course, it is not the calling of all Christians to be top-order biblical scholars. That said, it is remarkable how biblically ignorant many evangelical Christians are, especially in an era when so many resources are so readily available to so many. The condition of contemporary Evangelicalism indicates that evangelicals need again to become a people of the written word, while being wisely skeptical of allowing their understanding to be twisted by the reductionist systems that have arisen over the centuries.

The Need for a Blossoming of Biblically Directed Thinking and Action

However, if evangelicals were to further entrench themselves in a "Bible-based" model of scriptural authority, they would find themselves continuing to be unable to understand how the word of God applies to the totality of human life and culture. As has been discussed, Evangelicalism has inherited from the Reformation a diversity of views on exactly how the Bible is authoritative. Each in its own way, the *corrective, regulative* and *exemplary* alternatives have facilitated the retention of dualistic notions that are incompatible with the call of Jesus to serve him as wholehearted disciples in his kingdom.

It is at this point that the more *directional* understanding of biblical authority merits consideration and adoption. The directional approach is not a license to construe the Bible in conformity with contemporary thinking and culture. It is rooted in the teachings of the law, the prophets, and the apostles. At the same time, it is not anchored in past precedent. It is not so much "back to the Bible" as "forward with and in the light of the Bible"—for this approach there is ample evidence even *within* the span of the New Testament canon itself. For example, during his earthly ministry Jesus only hinted at the entrance of gentiles into the kingdom of God. After Pentecost the entire church had to go through the process of receiving Samaritans, proselyte gentiles, and also formerly pagan gentiles as fellow members of the body of Christ. There were certainly many relevant passages of the Old Testament relating to this development, but the early church had to seek the direction of the Holy Spirit through the written word in order to work out in practice what the relevant unchanging principles required in what were dramatically new circumstances. They had to find their way under the direction of the Holy Spirit. This is what the council at Jerusalem was all about (Acts 15:1–29; 21:17–26).

Once Christians get past the proof-texting tendencies of the Bible-based model and understand that the whole Word (*Tota Scriptura*) applies to the whole of life, and that biblically revealed first principles are *directive* for every part of life and every field of human endeavor, they are then in a position to speak integrally to the twenty-first century. For example, one of the most—perhaps *the* most—foundational distinction made in Scripture is between God and his creation. God is non-dependent. The entire order of creation *depends* on its Creator. If we exalt what is creaturely and worship, honor, or serve it as if it were divine, then we are engaging in idolatry. This principle also applies to the fabric of our thinking in all areas of intellectual endeavor. Once this principle is grasped, once it is understood that there is no zone that is religiously neutral, and once it is understood that Christ the king calls for an obedient response in every field of thought and action, then the death-knell of evangelical anti-intellectualism will sound and a restoration of the ancient association of piety, learning, and good works will be forthcoming.

An authentically Christian view of the natural sciences, or the social sciences, or of human history is going to reckon with the *dependent* as well as the interwoven character of all that is creaturely. This key insight imparts a foundational distinctiveness to systematic and coherent Christian reflection across the encyclopedia of the sciences. And this Christian insight is not simply philosophical, scientific, and scholarly. It has important directive—and redirective—implications for practical life in politics, education, medicine, horticulture and agriculture, manufacturing, trade and commerce, and so forth. Such thinking can provide immense insight into our global condition. It can offer what some have called serviceable insight into the multiple interrelated ills that afflict human culture worldwide and that arise from our unbelief, rebelliousness and idolatry. It provides insight without slogans that become clichés. It is an ongoing, communal task. It glorifies God and serves humankind simultaneously (Matt 22:36–40).

In their heart of hearts many Christians long for this kind of thinking, or something very much like this. They are aware that the dominant culture asserts that their belief in Christ is a form of escapism. They know that the "sacred pie in the heavenly sky" style of "preaching the gospel" to which they are generally exposed is not only strangely barren, but dangerously close to the escapism of which they are accused. They know that there is more to Christian teaching than theological systematics. An example is the deeply poignant predicament of those Christians with gifts as writers, dramatists and artists, who wish to dedicate these callings to Christ, but whose churches have no idea how to respond to them. Such things are frequently viewed as worldly and "not the gospel" and so yet again God-given skills are left to wither on the vine. The truth is that God gives his people many gifts, but as presently structured, the institutional church often discourages and wastes where it should encourage and strengthen.

The manner in which many denominations and evangelical organizations currently function stands in the way of such integral, all-of-life blossoming. The presumption that the institutional church must always be the focus of everything Christian functions as a barrier to the kind of integral Christian thinking and living here presented. Here again we see reductionism in action—Christianity is reduced to little more than "Churchianity." Yet contemporary Evangelicalism, as we have observed, presents an immensely mixed picture. Evangelicalism is not wholly dominated by its most problematic tendencies. Not all evangelicals who affirm inerrancy according to the Chicago formulas see it as requiring that the "days" of Genesis be understood as astronomical days of 24 hours, or Noah's flood as having been on a global scale. Crude literalism does not have as absolute a hold over many evangelicals as some of its declaratory statements might lead us to expect. The best evangelical writers are increasingly attuned to the diversity of literary genres represented in the canonical books.

Certainly, some of the best neo-evangelicals of the later twentieth century have sought to distance themselves from the anti-intellectualism of earlier twentieth-century fundamentalism. That was a start, but simply adopting an anti-anti-intellectualism is not enough. A positive approach to the study of the order of creation and human culture in all its facets is what is required—one that gets beyond merely chatting about "Christianity and this, that, and the other." Christians need to reconstitute their understanding of the special sciences from the foundations upward—an integral rather than integrative approach, one that recognizes the wholly dependent status of the creation and the coherence of all things in Christ (2 Cor 5:16–20; Col 1:15–20).

Old-style reductionist Evangelicalism could be quick to reject such talk as "not the gospel." In view of the currently dire condition of Evangelicalism across much of the English-speaking world, it is well worth picking up the other end of the stick. Such an all-of-life Christianity, with Christians publicly and constructively busy as Christians and on a Christian basis in science, education, medicine, farming and manufacturing, trade and commerce—indeed, in all lawful callings—is inevitably evangelistic because in all things it testifies to the hope that is within us. It would speak and *do* the gospel much more effectively than all those evangelistic sermons preached in churches telling us how to get to an ethereal heaven. In the West we are far too prone to view faith as a private conviction rather than as a public calling. We forget that early Christianity was viewed as a dangerously subversive *political* movement! (Acts 17:6–7).

As the twenty-first century opened, it was abundantly clear that the old order of the church as an institution plus missionary activity plus parallel theological endeavors, one that leaves otherwise untouched all other areas of human activity, is a formula for gross ineffectiveness. It bespeaks a stance of spiritual compromise because it concedes to the spirit of the age all that does not fall under the "church, missions, and theology" headings. In the long run we can expect the acids of secularization and materialism to corrode the selfsame church, missions and theology, however self-fortified they may be with doses of conservatism. Then "Ichabod" will be written on the walls of the church (1 Sam 4:21).

The Need for a Grand Renewal of Christian Participation in Public Life

Of course, public life is far wider than politics in the specifically public-legal, party-political, parliamentary-governmental sense of the term. Nevertheless, politics in the sense of on-going debate and action (in and out of the legislature) in respect of public governance cannot be avoided. Those who tell us that they "have no politics" are as mistaken as those who say that their confession of Christ has no political consequences. Such attitudes arise from the reductionism already discussed. The Apostles took the risen Christ's proclamation of his all-encompassing authority seriously (Matt 28:18). When vexed by the enemies of the risen Christ, they made a prayerful appeal to him who is the Sovereign Ruler of all and from whom all authority is derived (Acts 4: 24–30; 5:29). It is within this context that New Testament teaching concerning subjection to the authorities *in all matters lawful* is to be understood (Matt 22:17–21; Rom 13:1–7).

Far too many contemporary evangelicals are deist in their politics (Christ rules not here but in my heart and in heaven) and antinomian (without law) in their practical political, social and economic life. For example, they give themselves permission to engage in unfettered marketplace competition, irrespective of the consequences, and that kind of life is acceptable provided they put money in the plate on Sunday. Such conduct can amount to a latter-day mode of *corban*—where, in self-deception, the conscience is eased as socio-economic responsibilities are ignored, and Christian cultural endeavor goes begging (Mark 7:6–13).

How different was the attitude of church fathers and protestant reformers! How many evangelicals realize the directness with which the good news of the kingdom of God confronts all pagan and apostate presumptions—and therefore the prevalent ideologies of our times? They seem not to know that Polycarp (65–155) was martyred for the simple confession that Christ and not Caesar is Lord.[5] And what of the poor, at home and abroad? They might know that in his *Critique of the Gotha Program* (1875, published 1891) Karl Marx (1818–1883) popularized the saying "From each according to his ability, to each according to his need," but they are mostly unaware that Calvin said something remarkably similar in his Commentary on 2 Corinthians.[6]

As things stand, political involvement is a hotly debated issue among many contemporary evangelicals. Lacking a Christian worldview that is integrally coherent, important political questions only serve to magnify Evangelicalism's multiple confusions. Those who promote neoliberal economic policies are content to find a place in right wing parties. Some promote the notion of a Christian politics because they see it as a means of rescuing "our Christian heritage" and possibly also working towards the statutory imposition of Christianity on society as a whole. Others reject Christian politics altogether because they envisage Christian politics exclusively in terms of attitudes and policies which they rightly reject. Other discussions have focused on whether or not a Christian political party is both sound in principle and feasible in practice. Certainly, in English-speaking jurisdictions, even where a Christian political party is considered to be sound in principle, it is found to be less than feasible in practice in the absence of a proportional representation electoral system. Pressing for just and equitable electoral reform might be the place to start.

As has been observed, among evangelicals there is, for the most part, an active or passive endorsement of economic policies based on neoliberalism,

5. Holmes, *Apostolic Fathers*, 298–333.

6. Calvin on 2 Cor 8:14: "the Lord commends to us this fair proportioning of our resources that we may, in so far as funds allow, help those in difficulties that there may not be some in affluence and some in want." *Calvin's Commentaries: Second Epistle to the Corinthians*, 113. Biéler has stated: "Because of each individual's work and the mutual compensation enjoined by love, we may define in terms of the celebrated formula, 'from each according to his abilities to each according to his needs' the social system God prescribes for human beings so that they may live harmoniously in society." *Calvin's Thought*, 296.

notwithstanding the resulting human and ecological devastation. The prevalence of dualistic attitudes, including those of premillennial dispensationalism, strongly reinforces this outlook. The stance is basically reactionary. Fearful of socialism, they persistently seek to weaken the collective representation of employees while strengthening the hand of employers who demand levels of flexibility that undermine the married and family lives of workers. The notion of a "Christian Labor Association" is for them strangely unfamiliar—if not wildly esoteric. Nevertheless, the Christian Labour Association of Canada has been in operation since 1952.

In contemporary politics, the insistence is upon individual rights rather than upon human dignity and societal wellbeing. What drives this emphasis on rights is an unbiblical and anti-Christian insistence on individual human autonomy—entailing a maximum entitlement to be a law unto one's self. Politically right wing Christians caught up in this neoliberal movement often fail to realize that it fuels the very tendencies that they deeply oppose, such as a "woman's right to choose" to abort her unborn child and the now rapidly developing public support for same-sex "marriage." Both clearly reflect the free-market-driven desire of many to live as autonomous individuals. By aligning themselves with those who have sown the idolatrous ideology of neoliberal economics across public life, such Christians stand to reap a whirlwind of individual, cultural and ecological death and destruction. Such a prospect is now upon us. Consistent with this culture of death is the previously observed tendency of right wing evangelicals to endorse military solutions to international conflicts—especially where Israel is involved. Those evangelicals who have sided with neoliberal, right-wing politics and the ways of corporate capitalism can be expected to oppose any proposal for an integral and coherent, biblically-directed, Christian political option. They will insist that their path of spiritual compromise is *the* Christian way.

There are, thankfully, evangelical Christians who see beyond the spiritual bankruptcy of this outlook and who aspire to a better focused Christian political presence, but they often underestimate the depth and interacting complexity of policy issues that arise one after another. Without an integral Christian framework with which to understand what they are doing, they are liable to find themselves undermined. In the Western intellectual tradition, reflection on the *polis* and its right governance is older than Christianity itself. Moreover, such reflection, over the centuries, has attained a high degree of sophistication, in which different versions of the Christian faith were prime contributors. Furthermore, since the French Revolution (1789), political thought and policy in the West has been dominated by a range of post-Christian ideologies, including liberalism, nationalism, socialism, conservatism, libertarianism, anarchism, dialectical materialism, neoliberalism, and so on. Without an adequate insight into the religiously apostate character of these conflicting spiritual-cultural currents, any attempt at an integrally Christian politics is bound to flounder. Such a venture is not impossible, but it cannot be pursued as a dilettante might take up a hobby. On the contrary, it calls for a leadership and a rank-and-file blessed with considerable wisdom, insight, integrity, patience, and imagination. It also calls for a willingness to suffer.

Those who have reflected on such matters from a reformational standpoint have understood that the calling of the public legal order is the provision of public justice. This has been well articulated in the writings of Jonathan Chaplin, David T. Koyzis, and James W. Skillen. It envisages a distinctively Christian politics that does not function as a pro-Christian or pro-church lobby group, but that seeks to glorify God and serve Jesus Christ by maximizing the provision of public justice for all persons within the jurisdiction. It aims at an equitable compromise between conflicting legitimate interests. It avoids the authoritarianism implied by a return to the ecclesiastically integrated order of Christendom, and it refuses to vacate the public arena because the going is tough. It shows Christians how they can function in the public square not by disavowing or masking their Christian principles, but by actually living them out in a manner that is both radical and constructive. It recognizes that a wide variety of religious standpoints are adhered to within modern national communities. It is comfortable with diversity and stands for "principled pluralism." It promotes religious liberty not because religion is unimportant but because it is so important—regardless of whether this is appreciated by society generally. By heeding the norms of sphere sovereignty and public justice, it seeks to uphold the distinctive character and callings of marital, familial, ecclesiastical, educational, medical, and commercial entities and relationships, promoting a rich mutual flourishing of each and restraining where any one might be usurping its rightful place to achieve an improper and therefore damaging dominance over the others.

So envisaged, Christian politics is a service to Jesus Christ by being a service to all. It opposes absolutisms, and in providing what might be called "cultural breathing space" for all, it also opens up room for Christianity to prosper. It is in no respect triumphalist, it never says: "we always have all the answers in fine detail"—still less "we have the answers at the drop of a hat." It can be expected to face the opposition of those who are committed to the prevalent absolutisms of the day—such as the neoliberalism of contemporary corporate capitalism—and their political enablers. It can expect misrepresentation, sadly also from the pulpit, false allegations, "dirty tricks," and worse.

Such Christian political action would be no "walk in the park." It would stand for a wholesome and constructive (and not destructive) use of the resources of the earth. It would require what obedient discipleship always calls for: a willingness to pick up our cross in following our Lord. It might never achieve a dominant role in government—even where some version of proportional representation was in operation. That would not constitute failure. Its notion of success is to serve Jesus Christ faithfully. It might possibly participate as a coalition partner under a proportional representation system. It would function as salt in the political world (Matt 5:13). The point is to be present and to provide principled policy insight from a standpoint reflective of the peaceable, kingly rule of Jesus Christ over all nations and over all the earth—which the Bible says are his inheritance (Ps 2:8).

It must be acknowledged that much contemporary Evangelicalism is a very long way from such a prospect. The wisdom, insight, integrity, patience, and imagination already mentioned are not often apparent. Yet, God does not leave his people bereft of what they need in order to serve. Christians can stir one another up to good political works by taking a well-informed and critical interest in public affairs. Christians need to address the vast literature on law, politics, and the state from a biblically directed standpoint. They need to consider how the idolatrous ideologies of our times function in political debate and decision-making. Above all, they need to cultivate a political outlook that refuses subservience to these false gods and the "there is no alternative" (TINA) absolutisms that they propagate, and envisage modes of political thought and action that serve everyone by testifying to the kingly rule of Jesus Christ over political life.

Of course, political thought and action are neither everything nor merely ends in themselves. An unambiguously Christian presence is called for across the spectrum of cultural life. Christian higher education is a conspicuous example. Under state-mandated subservience to the requirements of corporate capitalism, the contemporary university is a shadow of its former self and an immense distance from what it ought to be. The need remains for Christian universities to address, research, and teach across the full spectrum of the encyclopedia of the sciences on a biblically directed basis. Without such institutions Christians, and especially Christian students, stand as shorn lambs before the blizzards of crude rationalism and the gales of crass secularism.

The Need for a Full Renewal of Catechetical Instruction and Expository Preaching

Part of the problem is that for far too long many evangelicals have read their Bibles exclusively as a devotional resource. This takes place in the "quiet time." Once the "pious thought" or "special word" for the day has been extracted, the written word is liable to be dispensed with until the next devotional session. It is also worth remembering that, unlike the early church, as well as in the churches of the Reformation, the vast majority of believers today *have never received a course of catechetical instruction in the faith*. In this area large portions of the institutional church have failed abysmally. In some settings of conspicuous irresponsibility, pastors and churches have sent forth young converts to witness to and evangelize others without a shred of catechetical instruction. The churches of the Fathers and the reformers knew better. They catechized the newly converted, thereby giving them a coherent understanding of the faith and so prepared them for a lifetime of discipleship and service. It would be an indication that the tide was turning if ministers and their congregations resolved once again to use their catechism to instruct congregations in the faith they profess.

Such a deepening can be expected to generate a call for better preaching. In many instances, the preaching given from the contemporary protestant pulpit is a disgrace. Repeatedly, among the laity, when the minister is out of earshot, the question is heard: "What *do* they teach them in seminary?" It is a fair question. Theological college training that focuses exclusively on the received theology in its formal and pastoral expressions leaves its graduates without the means of articulating a Christian world and life view—and the result is preaching that fails to address people in the circumstances that they are actually negotiating. Many ministers have received a training that is as much a hindrance as it is beneficial. Sometimes excellence comes in spite of, rather than because of, the training provided. This is not an argument against training or against a learned ministry; rather it is to say that the right kind of training is imperative, training which focuses on the coming of the kingdom in the here and now. Alas, stuck with a reductionist view of the biblical message, one that amounts to presenting a roadmap of the route to be taken for the individual soul to arrive safely in an ethereal heaven, the vast majority of evangelical preachers fall well short of this standard.

In short, many evangelical preachers do not understand how to preach the whole word of God to the whole of life. Here is the root cause of many an excruciating sermon from the evangelical pulpit. The best evangelicals are aware that there is a crisis in the pulpit. A renewal of interest in *expository preaching* in some quarters is an encouraging development. Of course, in so diverse a movement as Evangelicalism, what expository preaching there is varies considerably in quality. Nevertheless, its cultivation should be strongly encouraged, especially in settings where the sermon has degenerated to little more than a pious thought for Sunday delivered with varying degrees of sentimentality. Such public exposition of Scripture involves preaching through entire books of the Bible, passage by passage. This approach can be instructive, challenging and encouraging. In no way does it have to be tedious or boring, but it does require a broad education and effective communication skills on the part of the preacher. To take a congregation through wide portions of the Old and New Testaments, perhaps over years and decades, is an immensely constructive thing to do. At least it has the merit of rescuing the congregation from the minister who is overly preoccupied with a single topic, doctrine, or part of Scripture. The cumulative deficiencies of our era call for a responsible preaching that lifts the faithful beyond "pious thoughts" and that introduces them to the great revelatory sweep of Scripture by way of an accessible expository approach. Congregations should encourage their ministers by calling for preaching of this sort.

Of course, especially where subservience to the cult of personality dictates the abandonment of the pulpit for the liberties of the platform, the designated text can all too easily function as a mere springboard from which the preacher launches forth into flights of impassioned, rhetorical fancy that have little or nothing to do with the biblical passage from which it is drawn. The malformed entrepreneurial structure of the megachurch, revival center enterprise means that "management" is very likely to ignore calls for reformation away from entertainment and towards responsible expository preaching. Those who support such enterprises with their patronage need to consider their position, and the example they are setting others before the face of Almighty God. However, even this is not enough if the expositor is only reinforcing a *reductionist* reading of Scripture. This is why many evangelicals understand the parables of the kingdom exclusively in individual personal terms rather than also in world historical cosmic dimensional terms. Similarly, those evangelicals attracted to classical reformed soteriology are particularly prone to interpret the Pauline epistles in terms of an individualistic soteriology and an ecclesiology restricted to the church in its institutional manifestation.

It is no coincidence that at the time of the reformational renewal of Christian thinking in the Netherlands between the wars, there also arose a *redemptive-historical* "history of the covenant" (*verbondsgeschiedenis*) school of biblical interpretation. Some evangelicals became aware of this standpoint through the *Promise and Deliverance* series by S. G. de Graaf (1889–1955). This approach refused to constrain the text within the reductionist confines of either scholastic theology or still less, latter-day dispensationalist timetabling. It recognized that in the canonical library that we call the Bible, the Holy Spirit has given us an overarching and all-encompassing narrative that tells us what all things are all about. It is nothing less than a revelation of God and his purposes for his creation. It encompasses everything known to astronomical and geological science, all human culture, and much more besides. It narrates God's covenantally-steadfast dealings with his creation and people. It unfailingly points to the kingship and majesty of the risen Christ.

Once Scripture is viewed in these terms, the classic reductionist interpretations start to lose their grip on the hearts and minds of hearers and readers. The Bible ceases to be a series of texts to be mined, construed, and reduced to theological propositions. This does not entail a depreciation of sound doctrine. The "sound words" of right teaching are not slighted (1 Tim 6:3). Nor is the call to individual hearers to repent and believe in any way muted. On the contrary, the overthrow of the classic reductionist interpretations of Scripture opens up vast vistas and great depths of understanding. The full meaning of the ancient creeds of the church becomes apparent. Whole areas of the Bible that have otherwise been misconstrued in line with reductionist-interpretative agendas become pregnant with meaning. The words of Christ, his apostles and prophets resonate with an authority that is at once comprehensive and all-pervasive.

This kind of perspective cannot be readily achieved when functioning within the confined parameters of Bebbington's evangelical quadrilateral of priorities. Yet it is wholly consonant with the ground motive of an *integral* Christian approach, specifically "creation, fall, and redemption through Jesus Christ in the communion of the Holy Spirit." If congregations are seeking a more integral pulpit ministry, in which the whole word is applied directionally to the whole of life then they are seeking a pearl of great price. They are actually seeking the kingdom of God and its righteousness. They would do well to encourage their preachers down this path, not least by praying for and upholding all those who are charged with the ministry of the Word. They do well to remember that the vast majority of preachers remain anchored to the teaching they absorbed in the course of their training. Refocusing can be a difficult exercise, especially in circumstances in which the multitask, week-by-week exigencies of parish ministry can exact a heavy toll. In such circumstances the continuing encouragement of congregations, especially from its elders, can make a decisive difference. At the same time, all this calls for a grand rethinking of ministerial training.

In addition, congregation members can take it upon themselves to deepen their understanding of the Scriptures by way of sustained study and reflection. It is time to turn off the television for longer and bridle the mobile phone! Church members should not only study the Bible for themselves, but also come to understand how diverse philosophies, theologies, and schools of thought have come to structure, and, yes, distort our habitual understanding of one passage after another. As both theological scholasticism and premillennial dispensationalism clamor for acceptance among evangelicals, the merits of the redemptive-historical understanding of Scripture have not always been recognized. However, in more recent times it has been explored and exemplified in the writings of Lesslie Newbigin, Sidney Greydanus, Michael Goheen, Craig G. Bartholomew, and J. Richard Middleton—and it resounds strongly in the work of N. T. Wright.

The Need for a Wholesome Renewal of Public Worship

Only recently has awareness strengthened with regard to the immense damage done to public worship as "third wave" Pentecostal-charismatic influences came to pervade the worship of many churches with the seemingly ubiquitous "praise and worship" group, which "leads" congregations through a succession of songs whose banal superficiality and poor musical quality is underscored by mantra-like repetitions. Many contemporary evangelicals have little or no knowledge of a wholesome and robust Christian worship which, with or without a written liturgy, stands, spiritually and aesthetically, in marked contrast to the rock concert tonalities, vaudeville entertainments, or sugary sweet sentimental refrains currently served up by the contemporary megachurch or revival center. With mixed results many smaller congregations attempt to emulate the larger trendsetters.

The supporters of the style are enraptured while others are left numb, often reduced to mumbling in their places, yet inhibited from expressing concerns lest they be accused of waging "worship wars." Senior members (and not they alone) of who knows how many congregations endure this style because "It's what the young people want"—even though the young themselves are well capable of tiring of such things. They easily spot tacky emulations of secular entertainment. Guitar accompaniment with drums is virtually mandatory. The whole thing only works with electronic amplification and overhead screens. The central focus is on heightening the individual worship experience in a way that tends towards a collective seeking after private forms of spiritual validation and affirmation. Any congregational singing is overridden by the amplified voices and instrumental ensemble of the buoyant "worship group" positioned in front of them. Those who are not "with it" are reduced to mumbling or simply fall mute. Under such impulses many evangelical congregations have travelled a considerable distance from the authentic worship of the ancient church and the Protestant Reformation. Actual participation in worship is declining. What happens now is overly centered on the presumed feelings experienced by the individual rather than on the public worship of Father, Son and Holy Spirit.

In the wake of these devastations *a return to the centrality of the psalms in public worship* should be viewed as a high priority. This is not to say that the psalms should be all that is read or sung in worship, nor is it to advocate a wholesale reversion to the Genevan or Scottish psalters of the sixteenth century. The general Christian consensus is that hymns have their place. That said, it is noteworthy that the robust hymnody of the eighteenth century emerged at a time when the psalms were still very well known and widely used. By comparison, the Evangelicalism of the nineteenth century, as familiarity with the psalms decreased, produced hymns that placed a far greater emphasis on subjective feelings, human emotions, and sentimental expression. In short order, a "safe in the arms of Jesus" thinly veiled eroticism emerged in the songs sung by the pious. Men quit the church in droves. Few ever returned. The turn toward subjective sentimentalism opened the way for the choruses of the early twentieth century and eventually the "praise and worship" compositions of "third wave" Pentecostal-charismatics and their fellow travelers. The earlier downgrade was but a prelude to what now remains widespread, and from which we need to recover.

A return to the centrality of the psalms would be most beneficial. The psalms encompass the entire biblical view of God, of the creation, of humankind as sinners, and as recipients of God's covenant promises. As such they run the full gamut of the believer's life: from death to life, in sorrow and joy, under adversity and with rejoicing, and from condemnation to deliverance. Here we encounter feeling without self-indulgence, and a robust clarity without either insensitivity or escapism. Those who doubt the wisdom of this proposal are invited to engage in a simple exercise. Let them compare the "praise and worship" lyrics that they sang in church last Sunday with the texts of two or three of the psalms. Let them examine themselves. Can they then honestly say, lifting holy hands to Almighty God, that their "praise and worship" lyrics *are superior in any valid respect* to the texts of the psalms? Of course, the response that "Visitors don't understand the psalms" is invalid. Public worship is for the assembled people of God to offer to their Creator and Redeemer. The question of our understanding of the psalms is for the teaching office of the church to address.

The great need is for translations and musical settings of the Psalms that are at once God-honoring and accessible for users in the twenty-first century. Here the cultural, aesthetic, and musical deficit of too much of Evangelicalism stands to impede the restoration of psalmody and the reformation of public worship that we so desperately need. A renewal of Christian art, poetry, and music should be earnestly sought. Those who have the requisite gifts and who are working in this area are to be encouraged. May the Spirit of the LORD be upon them! Meanwhile, congregations functioning without the requisite musical skills and means might consider introducing the responsive congregational *reading* of the psalms as a first step. Such a practice opens up great possibilities. Congregations will find their horizons expanded and their discipleship deepened.

Beyond the specific issue of congregational singing much more needs to be restored to public worship that has been lost thanks to the neglect or abandonment of earlier liturgical or other ordered forms of public worship. For example, those congregations who, perhaps driven by false notions of "freedom from the law" have abandoned the regular recitation of the "ten words" of God for right living are courting antinomianism, whether they intend to or not. The calumny that ordered worship equates to spiritual deadness needs to be exposed once and for all.

The Need for a Grand Renewal of the Church as a Core Institution

Under current conditions it is understandable that many Christians find the matter of church membership problematic. The mainline protestant churches have leaderships that are a decidedly mixed bag—the good, the bad, and the ugly. This observation applies to the episcopate across the Anglican Communion as well as to the moderators and presidents of Presbyterian, Methodist, Baptist, and other bodies. The presence of clergy who deny the bodily resurrection of Jesus Christ is shameful—such "leaders" are conspicuous betrayers of their office, and if they were honest, they would resign forthwith. They undermine the faith and mislead the faithful. Those who have membership and worship in such settings may find themselves called upon to defend the faith *within* the church as well as in the face of a culture that can be hostile or apathetic.

In the face of such scandals, some evangelicals take the separatist route. Their intention is to preserve themselves in doctrinal purity within denominations that they control exclusively, but they can all too easily find themselves languishing in the stagnant backwaters of their own separatism or riven by internal tensions arising from disputes over how tightly the lines of doctrinal orthodoxy are to be drawn. Some are consumed by interminable squabbles over a speculative rapture, while others are caught in a time warp of seventeenth-century scholastic theology. Moreover, however much such entities might aspire to be doctrinal islands distinct from the larger mainline denominations, they are in reality less separate than they assume.

Eastern Orthodoxy and Protestantism alike are on strong doctrinal and historical grounds in their rejection of centuries of ongoing Roman Catholic assertions of Papal supremacy. All three of these great branches of Christianity have been shaped by the reductionism already discussed. The contra-reductionist standpoint associated with reformational thought and action stands in marked contrast to the greater part of Christianity as widely perceived and experienced. It envisages the distinctive presence and communal engagement of Christians *as Christians* across the whole range of legitimate human endeavor before the face of the Lord. As indicated, this great calling includes art, literature, drama, music, the mathematical, natural and cultural sciences, scholarship, engineering, philosophy, education, medicine, agriculture, manufacturing, trade, commerce, law, and politics. Have Christians not for far too long wandered in the wilderness of ecclesiastical and evangelical-reductionist Christianity?

In practice, many Christians have found themselves shifting from one churchly oasis to another across the increasingly parched cultural deserts of Western secularism. As a friend once put it: it is time to "break out and unfold." It is time to blossom in new and long-repressed ways. Of course, what we are used to is easier to contemplate. It is much easier to think of communicating the gospel in terms of the evangelical-reductionist model of saving souls for an ethereal salvation. Yet the full cultural mandate given at creation (Gen 1:26) is neither replaced by, nor conflicts with, our calling to preach the gospel "to every creature under heaven" (Col 1:23 NRSV). The two exhibit an inextricable, mutual coherence.

Yet, when the glory of this calling is glimpsed, it is altogether possible to be weighed down by the wide scope of our mandate. Even after it is recognized that there is a great diversity of giftedness among God's people; that some are called to lead in one or two areas and that all are called to follow and support in many others and that clearly not everyone is called to do everything, even then a cry of despair may still go up as to where the time and resources can be found to express such a pan-cultural, non-reductionist Christian presence. Over-stretched clergy may wilt, burdened pastors wither, and church councils concerned about the cost of utility bills and looming roof repairs simply roll their eyes at the impossibility of it all.

The reality is that this supposed impossibility arises from the extent and character of protestant denominational fragmentation across the English-speaking world, for which Anglican intolerance (towards Puritanism and Methodism) and evangelical separatism (in its multiple variants) must be held pre-eminently (if not exclusively) responsible. The denominational fracturing of the body of Christ produces situations in which Christians may live close to each other across suburbia, unaware of each other's presence because they are caught up, or held down, in the life of divergent denominational traditions. The result is a crippling lack of cohesion in which any clear Christian voice stands to be blurred, distorted, and perhaps drowned out completely. This situation has produced an immense duplication of parallel denominational structures, each with its seminary and related training institutions, administrative architecture run by church bureaucracies, diaconal humanitarian activities, missionary societies, and possibly aligned institutions providing schooling, medical services, and aged care.

Of course, in some contexts denominations have learned to collaborate and sometimes actually amalgamate. Frequently this only takes place under the duress of circumstances. All too often, protestant denominations function as corporate enterprises, with administrative elites in corporate head offices, and each in reality competing against their rivals for a share of the "ecclesiastical market." The entire situation does not exude the aroma of Christ. It stands in disregard of Christ's high-priestly prayer. Many evangelicals have argued that the unity of believers is spiritual and not visible, but that is simply not what the same passage teaches—Christian unity should be evident for the world to see (John 17:23).

In the aggregate, contemporary protestant denominationalism represents a massive duplication-generated misuse of resources. The consequences are scandalous—compare the large number of Bible colleges and seminaries in the English-speaking world with the number of Christian universities offering a full curriculum addressing the encyclopedia of the sciences from a biblically directed standpoint. The lack of the latter helps to explain the almost complete absence of Bible-believing, protestant leaders actually standing up for a Christian standpoint in public life. In short, evangelical *reductionism* comes with its own kind of spiritual blindness—so that where Evangelicalism prevails, these vast and crippling deficiencies are not even noticed but accepted as normal.

By contrast, once the full-orbed character of the gospel of the kingdom of God is grasped, the current arrangements become untenable. At present, attempts to even promote discussion about the possibilities of change are liable to come up against the opposition of those who are heavily invested in the present order. Even in the face of serious decline and multiple self-inflicted injuries, the present order remains entrenched. In the discussions, teachings, and declarations of the churches, the kingdom of God hardly rates a mention—or is reduced to a social welfare program.

Rightly understood, the call of the gospel—which is at once a loving invitation and a royal command—is not to come to church but to seek, find and enter the kingdom of God. How is this message to be preached and lived out?

Certainly, all of this necessitates a profound restructuring in the life and work of protestant churches. Denominational leaderships who see the church as offering a zone of sacred repose amid the pressures and follies of secular and materialistic life have missed the point entirely. Reformation is way beyond their comfort zone. A releasing of resources presently tied up in multidenominational duplication presupposes and would lead to immense changes. For a while this might entail fewer church buildings but a far greater Christian visibility in respect of all those things that do not take place on Sundays. The kingly authority, sympathetic priesthood, and prophetic word of Christ could be much more effectively presented in the thoughts, words, and deeds of his presently divided people. Those who are fearful that all this represents a diminution of the church are laboring under a serious misapprehension. On the contrary, it opens up the prospect that the church, as an institution, will come fully into its own. In no way does this "kingdom vision" deprive the church as an institution of its central place and task. It alone remains the place where the word is to be faithfully preached and the sacraments rightly administered—it is here that the entire people of God congregate for prayer, worship, and fellowship.

However, right now the church as a publicly visible institution looks too much like the hub of a wheel that has only a few broken spokes and no rim at all. This kingdom vision alternative envisages an array of Christian organizations and endeavors—perhaps with some more formally organized than others—across the entire span of human culture, all in their own way following Christ in their distinct callings, thereby constantly building up the church, and being built up by the church, as each and all listen to the Holy Spirit speaking in Scripture. Here a renewed Christian pulpit, preaching the whole word to the whole of life, would really come into its own. Such preaching can lead the church away from both syncretism and sectarianism.

Of course, this is a very great distance from where we are today. Although the internet provides opportunities for global communication, Christians who have recovered something of this kingdom vision might well find themselves isolated in their immediate congregational settings. Such spiritual discontents may ache for something better than lonely isolation. They might be confronted with questions concerning how they are to relate to fellow Christians, who might be up to their ears in eschatological speculation and dispensational timetabling, corporate capitalism and celebrity culture, a deism that disregards our propensity to harm the earth or a Gnosticism that presumes to receive private revelations. All these, and more besides, may be encountered within a single congregation. Certainly, wisdom will indicate how to use genuine opportunities to discuss such matters locally—such topics can be highly charged. It is sad to observe that many evangelical Christians are obsessed with these topics in a manner that far exceeds their commitment to the kingdom of God. What is clear is that we are always at liberty to pray for and love such Christians—against that there is no law. The responsibility to challenge is not to be avoided, but the opportunity to do so personally and in local settings must be earned. Amid the deficiencies and follies of contemporary Evangelicalism, all Christians would do well to say daily, "I believe in the sovereignty of the Holy Spirit."

Authentic Renewal is Impossible for Anyone or any Church to Achieve

Renewal is impossible, in that it is beyond the capacity of any or all Christians to achieve. It is beyond all human accomplishment. Early in the last century, Karl Barth posed the bold question "Can a minister be saved?" His reply was "with men this is impossible; but with God all things *are* possible. *God* may pluck us as a brand out of the fire."[7] He was right, and he was of course alluding to Jesus' response to a searching question put by his disciples (Luke 18:26). The resources for curing the present condition of Christianity—Evangelicalism included—are not to be found *within* our Christianity itself. In just the same way, the answer to the problem of the human condition is not to be found within humanity itself, and the answers to the multiple malformations of human culture are not to be found within our admittedly immense cultural resources.

According to the Bible, the answer lies in the sovereign mercies of Almighty God offered to us in Jesus Christ and the coming of his peaceable kingdom among us. Toward the end of the nineteenth century, Abraham Kuyper, peering with some trepidation into an uncertain future, was right to affirm "The quickening of life comes not from men: it is the prerogative of God . . . Unless God send forth His Spirit, there will be no turn, and fearfully rapid will be the descent of the waters."[8] We are now much further down the inclined plane than in Kuyper's days. In the English-speaking West and beyond, the public standing of the churches as well as the Christianity they represent, is now vastly lower. As matters now stand, no one should be surprised if judgment commences with the house of God (1 Pet 4:17).

Christians must be prepared for a mighty shaking and for every façade to crumble. At the same time, and as they tremble before such a prospect,

7. Barth, *Word of God and the Word of Man*, 126.
8. Kuyper, *Calvinism*, 199.

a growing awareness among diverse Christians that the gospel is *the good news of the kingdom of God and its righteousness* may yet portend momentous changes worldwide. It is possible that an immense hunger for authentic and integral Christian renewal is building among the peoples of the earth. They need to hear that the last, best, and only hope of humankind is not the USA, or "the American dream," or Platonic escapism, or the empty offerings of globalized neoliberal corporate capitalism: it is Jesus Christ and the coming of his peaceable kingdom. A future movement of authentic Christian renewal will not necessarily look like our images of past revivals, and it is altogether possible that Evangelicalism as we have come to know it may have to die to itself in order to bear its most abundant and glorious harvest (John 12:24). Come what may, Jesus Christ remains the same, yesterday, today and forever (Heb 13:8).

GLOSSARY

A-millennial—the view that "the millennium" in the Book of Revelation is to be understood symbolically rather than literally and refers to the time between the first and second advents.

Anabaptist; Anabaptists—meaning originally "re-baptizers," pertains to those especially during and after the Reformation who rejected infant baptism and the authoritarian ways of medieval Christendom, and shunned public life.

Anglican; Anglicanism—pertaining to the Church of England, especially after the Reformation, its daughter churches across the world, and their related institutions.

Antinomian; Antinomianism—alleged or actual belief that because the grace of God is received freely, Christian life and conduct is therefore not subject to the requirements of the moral law.

Arminian; Arminianism—named after Jacob Arminius, adhering to the views of the Remonstrants at the time of the Synod of Dort in affirming human free will, notwithstanding our sinful nature, and the possibility of genuine Christians falling from grace.

Baptist—adhering to the view that baptism ought only to be administered to adult persons professing faith in Christ, and therefore not to their infant offspring. Baptist churches are usually *Congregationalist* (see below) in polity.

Calvinist; Calvinism—named after John Calvin, the term is generally used to refer to historic Reformed Church theology and practices, and attitudes associated therewith, and only occasionally to the actual teachings of Calvin himself.

Cessationist; Cessationism—the view that in the span of redemption history, special signs, including direct divine healing, have been largely confined to the three eras of the exodus from Egypt and entry into the promised land, the era of Elijah and Elisha, and the ministry of Christ and the early apostolic era.

Charismatics; Charismatic movement—persons and organizations advocating the distinctive teachings and practices of *Pentecostalism* (see below) in non-Pentecostal church settings.

Concordism—The view that the Bible and modern scientific findings may be harmonized by viewing the "days" of Genesis as a chronological sequence, with each day representing a period of time of considerable duration.

Confessionalist; Confessionalism—a post-reformation tendency in which churchly confessional statements were used in ecclesiastical and church-related settings as a test of orthodoxy and source of authority over and above Scripture.

Congregationalist; Congregationalism—a mode of church government oriented to the full independence of the local congregation. Accordingly, national or regional assemblies are only consultative, having no authority over local churches.

Dispensationalist; Dispensationalism—the teaching that God has related to humankind according to seven successive "dispensations." The promises of the Old Testament apply to the Israel as the genetic descendants of Abraham and not to the church as the people of God. Israel is "earthly" and the church is "heavenly." The two stand apart.

Episcopal; Episcopalian—church oversight exercised by bishops, possibly in conjunction with ecclesiastical assemblies such as synods. Anglican Churches are episcopal in government.

Eschatology—from the Greek *eschatos*, meaning last, furthest or ultimate; the study of Biblical and subsequent Christian teaching concerning the second advent of Christ and the restoration of all things.

Evangelical; Evangelicalism—see the definition offered in Chapter 1.

Fundamentalist; Fundamentalism—originally "Fundamentalist" pertained to the teachings offered in *The Fundamentals* (1910–15). Subsequently used of and by those advocating a more constrained and rigid view of infallibility (see below) and represented by inerrancy (see below).

Gnostic; Gnosticism—from the Greek *gnosis*, meaning knowledge. Within and in relation to contemporary Christianity, modern Gnosticism is present where the possession of a higher knowledge of spiritual truth is presumed, possibly through the receipt of new divine revelation and or guidance not openly available to the whole people of God in Scripture.

Inerrancy (of Scripture)—may be taken to mean that the Scriptures do not err in what they teach. However, when the concept is used rigorously, inerrancy may assert that the Scriptures are without any error or inaccuracy whatsoever in all technical, numerical, chronological and other such matters.

Infallibility (of Scripture)—meaning that the Scriptures are trustworthy in that they do not fail to teach the truth concerning God, the creation, humankind, and our need for deliverance. However, many who have argued for infallibility have at least implied that it necessarily entails *inerrancy* (see above).

Infralapsarian; Infralapsarianism—the view that the divine decree to permit the fall in Adam of all humankind into sin *logically* precedes the divine decree to elect some to eternal life, and others as reprobates to eternal perdition.

Lutheran; Lutheranism—followers of Martin Luther and his teachings, churches and related institutions arising from the Lutheran Reformation. Generally affirming Luther's critique of the Church of Rome.

Methodist; Methodism (1)—Usually used in respect of the followers of John Wesley, including his *Arminianism* (see above), but not necessarily implying adherence to Wesley's *perfectionist* teachings (see below).

Methodist; Methodism (2)—Sometimes used in respect of the *Welsh Calvinistic Methodists*, who as their name implies did *not* concur with the Arminian (see above) teachings of the Wesleyans. The Welsh usage reflects the early stage of the revival when all evangelicals were likely to be termed "Methodists."

Nonconformity; nonconformists—Protestant churches and individuals in England and Wales who did not conform to, but dissented from, the Church of England as established by law from 1662. Also known as "Protestant Dissenters."

Patronage; patronage system—in ecclesiastical matters a practice or system whereby ministers are appointed to the care of congregations by a local patron or other such appointing agency, rather than by the congregation itself.

Pentecostal; Pentecostalism—evangelicals who believe in a "baptism of the Holy Spirit" as a "second blessing" post-conversion event, and that the charismatic gifts of the earliest apostolic period should be and are present in the contemporary church, and possibly in the restoration of the office of Apostle.

Perfectionism—teaching (particularly in the case of John Wesley) which asserts that Scripture teaches that a presumably "sinless" perfection may be attained in this life. This doctrine is contrary to that taught by the protestant reformers.

Philosophia aristotelico-scholastica—scholastic thinking (including but not only theological) that is based on the philosophical thought (including the logic) of Aristotle and his disciples.

Post-millennial—the belief that the Second Advent of Christ will take place *after* ("post-") the millennium mentioned in the Book of Revelation.

Premillennial—the belief that the Second Advent will take place *before* ("pre-") the millennium mentioned in the Book of Revelation. Some premillennialists are "classical premillennialists," while many today are premillennial *dispensationalists* (see above) believing in a secret *rapture* (see below).

Presbyterian; Presbyterianism—reformed system of church government, including a hierarchy of ecclesiastical assemblies (usually local, regional, national), as eventually practiced by the post-reformation Church of Scotland and its daughter churches across the world.

Prolegomena—the "first words." A term sometimes used with reference to the philosophical discussion of the basis, focus, and methodology of a particular field of study.

Protestant Dissent; Dissenters—English and Welsh Free Churches (Baptist, Congregationalist, and Presbyterian), and their members, first established by Puritans ejected from the Church of England in 1662.

Puritans; Puritanism—advocates of the worship and organizational "further reformation" of the Church of England on Presbyterian, and later Congregational, lines during and following the reign of Elizabeth I.

Rapture—pertains to the teaching of *premillennial* (see above) *dispensationalists* (see above) that the Second Advent will be a two-fold event, the first of which will be a "secret" rapture whereby all saints then on earth will suddenly disappear from view as they are taken to be with Christ.

Reformational—committed to integral and ongoing biblically-directed reformation in all areas of contemporary life in the spirit of the Reformation, without being anachronistic, and to working with others without abandoning Christian beliefs and principles.

Reformed—pertaining to the non-Lutheran churches of the Reformation, with special reference to their doctrinal teachings and ecclesiastical practice. Sometimes used as a synonym for Presbyterian (see above).

Restorationist; Restorationism—the idea that reformative change in church and or society should aim at the restoration of a presumed "correct" ordering of things at some designated previous "Golden Age" in history.

Second Advent—the second coming of Jesus Christ following his Ascension.

Separatist; Separatism—evangelicals, especially fundamentalists, who believe that evangelicals should not be associated with non-evangelicals in so-called mainline denominations, but form separate denominations of their own.

Sola Scriptura—"the Scriptures only"; the principle that only the scriptures contain teaching that is of binding authority concerning Christian belief and conduct. Often used in contradistinction to views vesting ecclesiastical tradition and human reason with autonomous authority.

Soteriology—from the Greek *soteria*, meaning salvation or deliverance; the study of Biblical and subsequent Christian teaching concerning the way of salvation.

Supralapsarian; Supralapsarianism—The view that the divine decree to elect some to eternal life, and others as reprobates to eternal perdition *logically* precedes the divine decree to permit the fall in Adam of all humankind into sin.

Tota Scriptura—"all of the Scriptures"; the principle that the entire canonical Scriptures are of equal authority, in contradistinction to any improper privileging of the New Testament and depreciation of the Hebrew Scriptures.

Wesleyan—following in the tradition of John and Charles Wesley, including his version of Arminianism (see above), but not necessarily his explicitly *perfectionist* teachings (see above).

BIBLIOGRAPHY

Abanes, Richard. *American Militias: Rebellion, Racism and Religion.* Downers Grove, IL: InterVarsity, 1996.
———. *End-Time Visions: The Road to Armageddon.* Nashville: Broadman & Holman, 1998.
Abraham, William J. *Aldersgate and Athens: John Wesley and the Foundations of Christian Belief.* Waco, TX: Baylor University Press, 2010.
———. *Canon and Criterion in Christian Theology: From the Fathers to Feminism.* New York: Oxford University Press, 2002.
———. *Crossing the Threshold of Divine Revelation.* Grand Rapids: Eerdmans, 2006.
———. *The Divine Inspiration of Holy Scripture.* New York: Oxford University Press, 1981.
———. *Divine Revelation and the Limits of Historical Criticism.* New York: Oxford University Press, 1982.
Adams, James E. *Preus of Missouri and the Great Lutheran Civil War.* New York: Harper & Row, 1977.
Aikman, David. *Billy Graham: His Life and Influence.* Nashville: Nelson, 2007.
———. *A Man of Faith: The Spiritual Journey of George W. Bush.* Nashville: Nelson, 2004.
Aland, Kurt and Barbara. *The Text of the New Testament: An Introduction to the Critical Editions and to the Theory and Practice of Modern Textual Criticism.* Grand Rapids: Eerdmans, 1987.
Alleine, Joseph. *An Alarm to the Unconverted.* London: Banner of Truth, 1959.
Allis, Oswald Thompson [a-millennial]. *The Five Books of Moses.* Philadelphia: Presbyterian & Reformed, 1943.
———. *Prophesy and the Church.* Phillipsburg, NJ: Presbyterian & Reformed, 1945.
———. *Revised Version or Revised Bible? A Critique of the Revised Standard Version of the Old Testament (1952).* Philadelphia: Presbyterian & Reformed, 1953.
———. *Revision or New Translation? "The Revised Standard Version of 1946: A Comparative Study.* Philadelphia: Presbyterian & Reformed, 1948.
Alter, Robert. *The Art of Biblical Narrative.* New York: Basic, 1981.
———. *The Art of Biblical Poetry.* New York: Basic, 1985.
———. *The World of Biblical Literature.* New York: Basic, 1992.
Ammerman, Nancy T. *Baptist Battles: Social Change and Religious Conflict in the Southern Baptist Convention.* New Brunswick, NJ: Rutgers University Press, 1990.

———. *Bible Believers: Fundamentalists in the Modern World*. New Brunswick, NJ: Rutgers University Press, 1987.
Amstutz, Mark A. *Evangelicals and American Foreign Policy*. New York: Oxford University Press, 2013.
Anstadt, Peter. *Luther, Zinzendorf and Wesley: An Account of John Wesley's Conversion, Through Hearing Luther's Preface to Saint Paul's Epistle to the Romans Read in a Moravian Prayer Meeting in London, England*. York, PA: Peter Anstadt & Sons, 1895.
Antonides, Harry. *Multinationals and the Peaceable Kingdom*. Toronto, Canada: Clarke, Irwin, 1978.
Armerding, Carl E. *The Old Testament and Criticism*. Grand Rapids: Eerdmans, 1983.
Armstrong, Anthony. *The Church of England, the Methodists and Society 1700–1850*. London: University of London Press, 1973.
Armstrong, Brian G. *Calvinism and the Amyraut Heresy: Protestant Scholasticism and Humanism in Seventeenth-Century France*. Madison, WI: University of Wisconsin Press, 1969.
Atherstone, Andrew. *An Anglican Evangelical Identity Crisis: The Churchman-Anvil Affair of 1981–1984*. London: Latimer, 2008.
Atherstone, Andrew, and David Ceri Jones, eds. *Engaging with Martyn Lloyd-Jones: The Life and Legacy of 'the Doctor.'* Nottingham, UK: Inter-Varsity, 2011.
Aukerman, Dale. *Reckoning with Apocalypse: Terminal Politics and Christian Hope*. New York: Crossroad, 1993.
Ault, James M. *Spirit and Flesh: Life in a Fundamentalist Baptist Church*. New York: Knopf, 2004.
Backus, Irena. *The Reformed Roots of the English New Testament: The Influence of Theodore Beza on the English New Testament*. Alison Park, PA: Pickwick, 1980.
Bacote, Vincent, et al., eds. *Evangelicals and Scripture: Tradition, Authority and Hermeneutics*. Downers Grove, IL: InterVarsity, 2004.
Baird, William. *History of New Testament Research from Jonathan Edwards to Rudolf Bultmann*. Minneapolis: Augsburg Fortress, 2003.
Baker, Robert A. *The Southern Baptist Convention and Its People, 1607–1972*. Nashville: Broadman, 1972.
Balleine, G. R. *A History of the Evangelical Party in the Church of England*. 2nd ed. London: Church Book Room, 1951.
Balmer, Randall. *Blessed Assurance: A History of Evangelicalism in America*. Boston: Beacon, 1999.
———. *The Making of Evangelicalism: From Revivalism to Politics and Beyond*. Waco, TX: Baylor University Press, 2010.
———. *Mine Eyes Have Seen the Glory: A Journey into the Evangelical Subculture in America*. New York: Oxford University Press, 1989.
———. *Redeemer: The Life of Jimmy Carter*. New York: Basic, 2014.
———. *Thy Kingdom Come: How the Religious Right Distorts the Faith and Threatens America—An Evangelical's Lament*. New York: Basic, 2006.
Barclay, Oliver R. *Developing a Christian Mind*. Leicester, UK: Inter-Varsity, 1984. US ed.: *The Intellect and Beyond*. Grand Rapids: Zondervan, 1985.
———. *Evangelicalism in Britain, 1935–1995: A Personal Sketch*. Leicester, UK: Inter-Varsity, 1997.
———. *Whatever Happened to the Jesus Lane Lot?* Leicester, UK: Inter-Varsity, 1977.

Barker, Daniel. *Godless: How an Evangelical Preacher Became One of America's Leading Atheists*. Berkeley: Ulysses, 2008.
Barker, William S., and W. Robert Godfrey, eds. *Theonomy: A Reformed Critique*. Grand Rapids: Zondervan, 1991.
Barkun, Michael. *Crucible of the Millennium: The Burned-Over District of New York in the 1840s*. New York: Syracuse University Press, 1986.
———. *Disaster and the Millennium*. New Haven, CT: Yale University Press, 1974.
Barr, James. *The Bible in the Modern World*. London: SCM, 1973.
———. *Escaping from Fundamentalism*. London: SCM, 1984.
———. *Fundamentalism*. London: SCM, 1977.
———. *The Scope and Authority of the Bible*. Philadelphia: Westminster, 1980.
———. *The Semantics of Biblical Language*. London: Oxford University Press, 1961.
Barrett, Peter. *Science and Theology since Copernicus: The Search for Understanding*. London: T. & T. Clark, 2004.
Barth, Karl. *The Epistle to the Romans*. Translated by Edwyn C. Hoskyns. London: Oxford University Press, 1933.
———. *Protestant Theology in the Nineteenth Century: Its Background and History*. Valley Forge, PA: Judson, 1973.
———. *The Word of God and the Word of Man*. Translated by Sidney A. Weston. London: Hodder & Stoughton, 1928.
Bartholomew, Craig G., and Michael W. Goheen. *The Drama of Scripture*. Grand Rapids: Baker, 2004.
———. *The True Story of the Whole World: Finding Your Place in the Biblical Drama*. Grand Rapids: Faith Alive, 2009.
Bartleman, Frank. *Azusa Street*. New Kensington, PA: Whitaker House, 2000.
Barton, Stephen C., and David Wilkinson. *Reading Genesis after Darwin*. New York: Oxford University Press, 2009.
Bass, Clarence. *Backgrounds to Dispensationalism: Its Historical Genesis and Ecclesiastical Implications*. Grand Rapids: Eerdmans, 1960.
Bauckham, Richard. *The Bible and Ecology: Rediscovering the Community of Creation*. Waco, TX: Baylor University Press, 2010.
———. *The Bible in Politics: How to Read the Bible Politically*. London: SPCK, 1989.
———. *The Climax of Prophecy: Studies on the Book of Revelation*. London: T. & T. Clark, 1993.
———. *Gospel Women: Studies of the Named Women in the Gospels*. Grand Rapids: Eerdmans, 2002.
———. *The Jewish World Around the New Testament*. Tübingen: Mohr Siebeck, 2008.
———. *The Theology of the Book of Revelation*. Cambridge: Cambridge University Press, 1993.
Bauder, Kevin, ed. *Four Views on the Spectrum of Evangelicalism*. Grand Rapids: Zondervan, 2011.
Bawer, Bruce. *Stealing Jesus: How Fundamentalism Betrays Christianity*. New York: Three Rivers, 1997.
Beale, David O. *In Pursuit of Purity: American Fundamentalism since 1850*. Greenville, SC: Bob Jones University Press, 1986.
Beale, G. K. *The Erosion of Inerrancy in Evangelicalism: Responding to New Challenges to Biblical Authority*. Wheaton: Crossway, 2008.

Bean, Lydia. *The Politics of Evangelical Identity: Local Churches and Partisan Divides in the United States and Canada*. Princeton, NJ: Princeton University Press, 2014.

Bebbington, David W. *Baptists Through the Centuries: A History of a Global People*. Waco, TX: Baylor University Press, 2010.

———. *The Dominance of Evangelicalism: The Age of Spurgeon and Moody*. A History of Evangelicalism: People, Movements and Ideas in the English-Speaking World, Vol. III. Downers Grove, IL: InterVarsity, 2005.

———. *Evangelicalism in Modern Britain: A History from the 1730s to the 1980s*. London: Unwin Hyman, 1989.

———. *Holiness in Nineteenth-Century England*. Carlisle, UK: Paternoster, 2000.

———. *The Nonconformist Conscience: Chapel and Politics, 1870-1914*. London: George Allen & Unwin, 1982.

———. *William Ewart Gladstone: Faith and Politics in Victorian Britain*. Library of Religious Biography. Grand Rapids: Eerdmans, 1993

Bebbington, David W., and David Ceri Jones. *Evangelicalism and Fundamentalism in the United Kingdom in the Twentieth Century*. New York: Oxford University Press, 2013.

Becker, Carl Lotus. *The Heavenly City of the Eighteenth-Century Philosophers*. New Haven, CT: Yale University Press, 1932.

Behe, Michael J. *Darwin's Black Box: The Biochemical Challenge to Evolution*. 2nd ed. New York: Free, 2006.

———. *The Edge of Evolution: The Search for the Limits of Darwinism*. New York: Free, 2008.

Belcham, Leigh. *Toronto: The Baby or the Bathwater: Serious Questions about the "Toronto Blessing."* Bromley, UK: Day One, 1995.

Bell, P. M. H. *Disestablishment in Ireland and Wales*. London: SPCK, 1969.

Benedict, Philip. *Christ's Churches Purely Reformed: A Social History of Calvinism*. New Haven, CT: Yale University Press, 2002.

Bennett, Denis J. *Nine O'Clock in the Morning*. Alachua, FL: Bridge-Logos, 1970.

Berding, Kenneth. *What are Spiritual Gifts? Rethinking the Conventional View*. Grand Rapids: Kregel, 2006.

Berkouwer, Gerrit Cornelis. *Holy Scripture*. Translated and edited by Jack B. Rogers. Grand Rapids: Eerdmans, 1975.

———. *Man: The Image of God*. Translated by Dirk W. Jellema. Grand Rapids: Eerdmans, 1962.

Berry, Lloyd E. (Introduction by). *The Geneva Bible: A Facsimile of the 1560 edition*. Madison, WI: University of Wisconsin Press, 1969.

Betjeman, John. *Sweet Songs of Zion*. London: Hodder & Stoughton, 2007.

Bèze, Théodore de. *Correspondance de Théodore de Bèze,* edited by Hippolyte Aubert. Vol. XI. Travaux d'Humanisme et Renaissance. Geneva: Droz, 1983.

Bezzant, Rhys S. *Jonathan Edwards and the Church*. New York: Oxford University Press, 2013.

Biéler, André. *Calvin's Economic and Social Thought*. Geneva: World Alliance of Reformed Churches and WCC, 2005.

Bilezikian, Gilbert. *Beyond Sex Roles: What the Bible Says About a Woman's Place in Church and Family*. 2nd ed. Grand Rapids: Baker, 1985.

Bivins, Jason C. *Religion of Fear: The Politics of Horror in Conservative Evangelicalism*. New York: Oxford University Press, 2008.

Black, Davis Alan, and David R. Beck. *Rethinking the Synoptic Problem*. Grand Rapids: Baker, 2001.

Blanchard, John, et al. *Pop Goes the Gospel*. Welwyn, UK: Evangelical, 1983.

Blomberg, Craig L. *Can We Still Believe the Bible? An Evangelical Engagement with Contemporary Questions*. Grand Rapids: Brazos, 2014.

Blomberg, Craig L., and Sung Wook Chung [Classical Pre-millennialists]. *A Case for Historic Premillennialism: An Alternative to "Left Behind" Eschatology*. Grand Rapids: Baker, 2009.

Bloom, Harold. *The American Religion: The Emergence of the Post-Christian Nation*. New York: Simon & Schuster, 1992.

Blumenthal, Max. *Goliath: Life and Loathing in Greater Israel*. New York: Nation, 2013.

Boer, Harry R. *Above the Battle? The Bible and its Critics*. Grand Rapids: Eerdmans, 1975. Republished as: *The Bible and Higher Criticism*. Grand Rapids: Eerdmans, 1981.

———. *An Ember Still Glowing: Humankind as the Image of God*. Grand Rapids: Eerdmans, 1990.

Boliek, Lynn. *The Resurrection of the Flesh: A Study of a Confessional Phrase*. Grand Rapids: Eerdmans, 1962.

Bolt, Peter G., and Mark D. Thompson, eds. *Donald Robinson: Selected Works*. 3 vols. Sydney: Australian Church Record, 2008.

Bosher, Robert S. *The Making of the Restoration Settlement: The Influence of the Laudians, 1649–1662*. London: Oxford University Press, 1951.

Bothwell, Cecil. *The Prince of War: Billy Graham's Crusade for a Wholly Christian Empire*. Asheville, NC: Brave Ulysses, 2007.

Bouma-Prediger, Steven. *For the Beauty of the Earth: A Christian Vision for Creation Care*. Revised ed. Grand Rapids: Baker, 2010.

Bovell, Carlos R. *By Good and Necessary Consequence: A Preliminary Genealogy of Biblicist Foundationalism*. Eugene, OR: Wipf & Stock, 2009.

———. *Inerrancy and the Spiritual Formation of Younger Evangelicals*. Eugene, OR: Wipf & Stock, 2007.

———. *Rehabilitating Inerrancy in a Culture of Fear*. Eugene, OR: Wipf & Stock, 2012.

Bovell, Carlos R., ed. *Interdisciplinary Perspectives on the Authority of Scripture: Historical, Biblical, and Theoretical Perspectives*. Eugene, OR: Wipf & Stock, 2011.

Bowler, Peter J. *Monkey Trials and Gorilla Sermons: Evolution and Christianity from Darwin to Intelligent Design*. Cambridge, MA: Harvard University Press, 2007.

———. *Reconciling Science and Religion: The Debate in Early Twentieth-Century Britain*. Chicago: University of Chicago Press, 2001.

Boyd, Robin. *The Witness of the Student Christian Movement*. London: SPCK, 2007.

Bradley, Ian C. *The Call to Seriousness: The Evangelical Impact on the Victorians*. London: Macmillan, 1976.

Brake, Donald L. *A Visual History of the English Bible: The Tumultuous Tale of the World's Bestselling Book*. Grand Rapids: Baker, 2008.

Bramadat, Paul A. *The Church on the World's Turf: An Evangelical Christian Group at a Secular University*. New York: Oxford University Press, 2000.

Brand, David C. *Profile of the Last Puritan: Jonathan Edwards, Self-Love, and the Dawn of the Beatific*. New York: Oxford University Press, 1991.

Brand, Hilary and Adrienne Chaplin. *Art and Soul: Signposts for Christians in the Arts*. Downers Grove, IL: InterVarsity, 2001.

Branham, William Marrion [Pre-millennial dispensationalist]. *An Exposition of the Seven Church Ages*. Self published: Oklahoma, 1950.
Bratt, James D. *Abraham Kuyper: Modern Calvinist, Christian Democrat*. Library of Religious Biography. Grand Rapids: Eerdmans, 2013.
Bratt, James D., ed. *Abraham Kuyper: A Centennial Reader*. Grand Rapids: Eerdmans, 1998.
Bready, John Wesley. *England Before and After Wesley: The Evangelical Revival and Social Reform*. London: Hodder & Stoughton, 1938.
Brencher, John. *Martyn Lloyd-Jones (1899–1981) and Twentieth-Century Evangelicalism*. Carlisle, UK: Paternoster, 2002.
Brenneman, Todd M. *Homespun Gospel: The Triumph of Sentimentality in Contemporary American Evangelicalism*. New York: Oxford University Press, 2013.
Brewster, Paul. *Andrew Fuller: Model Theologian-Pastor*. Nashville: Broadmen and Holman, 2010.
Brody, David. *The Teavangelicals: The Inside Story of How the Evangelicals and the Tea Party are Taking Back America*. Grand Rapids: Zondervan, 2012.
Brown, Callum G. *The Death of Christian Britain: Understanding Secularization 1800–2000*. 2nd ed. London: Routledge, 2009.
Brown, Candy Gunther. *Global Pentecostal and Charismatic Healing*. New York: Oxford University Press, 2011.
Brown, Colin, ed. *History, Criticism and Faith: Four Exploratory Studies*. Leicester, UK: Inter-Varsity, 1976.
Brown, Ford K. *Fathers of the Victorians: The Age of Wilberforce*. Cambridge: Cambridge University Press, 1961.
Brown, Peter. *Augustine of Hippo: A Biography*. London: Faber & Faber, 1967.
Brown, Robert E. *Jonathan Edwards and the Bible*. Bloomington: Indiana University Press, 2002.
Brown, Thomas. *Annals of the Disruption; with Extracts from the Narratives of Ministers who Left the Scottish Establishment in 1843*. Edinburgh: MacNiven & Wallace, 1884.
Brown, Walt. *Beginning: Compelling Evidence for Creation and the Flood*. Phoenix, AZ: Center for Scientific Creation, 1995.
Brown, Warren S., et. al. *Whatever Happened to the Soul? Scientific and Theological Portraits of Human Nature*. Minneapolis: Fortress, 1998.
Brown, William P. *The Seven Pillars of Creation: The Bible, Science, and the Ecology of Wonder*. New York: Oxford University Press, 2010.
Bruce, F. F. *The Acts of the Apostles: The Greek Text with Introduction and Commentary*. London: Tyndale, 1956.
———. *In Retrospect: Remembrance of Things Past*. Grand Rapids: Baker, 1994.
———. *The New Testament Documents. Are They Reliable?* London: Inter-Varsity Press, 1943.
Bruijn, Jan de. *Abraham Kuyper: A Pictorial Biography*. Grand Rapids: Eerdmans, 2014.
Bruner, Frederick Dale. *A Theology of the Holy Spirit: The Pentecostal Experience and the New Testament Witness*. Grand Rapids: Eerdmans, 1971.
Brunn, Dave. *One Bible, Many Versions: Are All Translations Created Equal?* Downers Grove, IL: InterVarsity, 2013.
Brunner, Daniel L., et al. *Introducing Evangelical Ecotheology: Foundations in Scripture, Theology, History, and Praxis*. Grand Rapids: Baker, 2014.

Bruns, Roger. *Billy Graham: A Biography*. Westport, CT: Greenwood, 2004.
Bryant, Scott. *The Awakening of the Freewill Baptists: Benjamin Randall and the Founding of an American Religious Tradition*. Macon, GA: Mercer University Press, 2011.
Budgen, Victor. *Charismatics and the Word of God: A Biblical and Historical Perspective on the Charismatic Movement*. Welwyn, UK: Evangelical, 1985.
Bullinger, Ethelbert William [extreme dispensationalist]. *The Foundation of Dispensational Truth*. London: Eyre & Spottiswoode, 1930.
Bunyan, John. *The Entire Works of John Bunyan*, edited by Henry Stebbing. 4 vols. London: James Virtue, 1860.
Burch, Maxie B. *The Evangelical Historians: The Historiography of George Marsden, Nathan Hatch, and Mark Noll*. Lanham, MD: University Press of America, 1996.
Burkee, James C. *Power, Politics, and the Missouri Synod: A Conflict that Changed American Christianity*. Minneapolis: Fortress, 2011.
Burlein, Ann. *Lift High the Cross: Where White Supremacy and the Christian Right Converge*. Durham, NC: Duke University Press, 2002.
Burnside, Jonathan. *God, Justice and Society: Aspects of Law and Legality in the Bible*. Oxford: Oxford University Press, 2011.
Burrows, Roland. *John Wesley in the Reformed Tradition: The Protestant and Puritan Nature of Methodism Rediscovered*. Stoke on Trent, UK: Tentmaker, 2008.
Butterfield, Herbert. *Christianity and History*. London: Bell, 1949.
———. *The Origins of Modern Science, 1300–1800*. London: Bell, 1949.
Caird, George Bradford. *The Language and Imagery of the Bible*. Philadelphia: Westminster, 1980.
Calvin, John. *Institutes of the Christian Religion*, edited by John T. McNeill. Translated by Ford Lewis Battles. 2 vols. Library of Christian Classics. Philadelphia: Westminster, 1960.
———. *John Calvin's Commentaries: The Second Epistle of Paul the Apostle to the Corinthians and the Epistles to Timothy, Titus and Philemon*, edited by David W., and Thomas F. Torrance. Translated by S. M. Smail. Edinburgh: Oliver & Boyd, 1964.
———. *The Selected Works of John Calvin: Tracts and Letters*, edited by Henry Beveridge and Jules Bonnet. 7 vols. Vol. VII translated by Marcus Robert Gilchrist. Philadelphia: Presbyterian Board of Publications, 1858.
Camden, Vera, ed. *Trauma and Transformation: The Political Progress of John Bunyan*. Redwood City, CA: Stanford University Press, 2007.
Cameron, Marcia Helen. *An Enigmatic Life: David Broughton Knox, Father of Contemporary Sydney Anglicanism*. Sydney: Acorn, 2006.
Campbell, Roderick. *Israel and the New Covenant*. Phillipsburg, NJ: Presbyterian & Reformed, 1981.
Campbell, Susan. *Dating Jesus: A Story of Fundamentalism, Feminism and the American Girl*. Boston: Beacon, 2009.
Canfield, Joseph M. *The Incredible Scofield and His Book*. 2nd ed. Vallecito, CA: Ross House, 2005.
Cannistraci, David ["New Apostolic Reformation" advocate]. *Apostles and the Emerging Apostolic Movement*. Delight, AR: Gospel Light, 1998.
Cannon, Mae Else, et al. *Forgive Us: Confessions of a Compromised Faith*. Grand Rapids: Zondervan, 2014.

Capps, Walter H. *The New Religious Right: Piety, Patriotism, and Politics.* Columbia: University of South Carolina Press, 1990.
Carpenter, Joel A. *Revive us Again: The Reawakening of American Fundamentalism.* New York: Oxford University Press, 1997.
Carpenter, Joel A., ed. *Two Reformers of Fundamentalism: Harold John Ockenga and Carl F. H. Henry.* New York: Garland, 1988.
Carson, Donald Arthur. *The King James Version Debate: A Plea for Realism.* Grand Rapids: Baker, 1979.
Carson, Donald Arthur, and John D. Woodbridge, eds. *Hermeneutics, Authority and Canon.* Grand Rapids: Zondervan, 1986.
———. *Scripture and Truth.* Grand Rapids: Zondervan, 1983.
Cartledge, David. *The Apostolic Revolution: The Restoration of Apostles and Prophets in the Assemblies of God in Australia.* Chester Hill, Australia: Paraclete, 2000.
Carwardine, Richard J. *Evangelicals and Politics in Antebellum America.* New Haven, CT: Yale University Press, 1993.
———. *Trans-Atlantic Revivalism: Popular Evangelicalism in Britain and America, 1790–1865.* Westport, CT: Greenwood, 1978.
Case, Jay Riley. *An Unpredictable Gospel: American Evangelicals and World Christianity, 1812–1920.* New York: Oxford University Press, 2013.
Cassuto, Umberto. *The Documentary Hypothesis and the Composition of the Pentateuch.* Translated by Israel Abrahams. Jerusalem: Shalem, 1961.
Catherwood, Christopher. *The Evangelicals: What They Believe, Where They Are, and Their Politics.* Wheaton: Crossway, 2010.
Catherwood, Frederick. *At the Cutting Edge: A Lifetime in Politics, Industry and Faith.* London: Hodder & Stoughton, 1996.
Caudill, Edward. *Intelligently Designed: How Creationists Built the Campaign Against Evolution.* Urbana: University of Illinois Press, 2013.
Chadwick, Owen. *The Secularization of the European Mind in the Nineteenth Century.* Cambridge: Cambridge University Press, 1975.
Chafer, Lewis Sperry [pre-millennial dispensationalist]. *Dispensationalism.* Dallas, TX: Dallas Seminary, 1951.
———. *The Kingdom in History and Prophecy.* Chicago: Revel, 1915.
Chafets, Zev. *A Match Made in Heaven: American Jews, Christian Zionists, and One Man's Exploration of the Weird and Wonderful Judeo-Evangelical Alliance.* New York: Harper Collins, 2007.
Chai, Leon. *Jonathan Edwards and the Limits of Enlightenment Philosophy.* New York: Oxford University Press, 1998.
Chaplin, Jonathan. *Herman Dooyeweerd: Christian Philosopher of State and Civil Society.* Notre Dame, IN: University of Notre Dame Press, 2011.
Chaplin, Jonathan, and Robert Joustra, eds. *God and Global Order: The Power of Religion in American Foreign Policy.* Waco, TX: Baylor University Press, 2010.
Chapman, Alister. *Godly Ambition: John Stott and the Evangelical Movement.* New York: Oxford University Press, 2012.
Church, John Edward. *Quest for the Highest: An Autobiographical Account of the East African Revival.* Exeter, UK: Paternoster, 1981.
Cinnamond, Andrew. "The Reformed Treasures of the Parker Society." *Churchman* 122/3 (2008) 221–242.

Clabaugh, Gary K. *Thunder on the Right: The Protestant Fundamentalists*. Chicago: Nelson-Hall, 1974.
Clark, Harold Willard. *Crusader for Creation, the Life and Work of George McCready Price*. Oakland, CA: Pacific, 1966.
Clark, Victoria. *Allies for Armageddon: The Rise of Christian Zionism*. New Haven, CT: Yale University Press, 2007.
Clifford, Alan C. *Atonement and Justification: English Evangelical Theology, 1640–1790*. Oxford: Oxford University Press, 1990
———. *The Good Doctor: Philip Doddridge of Northampton, A Tercentenary Tribute*. Norwich, UK: Charenton, 2002.
Clouse, Robert G., ed. *The Meaning of the Millennium: Four Views*. Downers Grove, IL: InterVarsity, 1977.
Clouser, Roy A. *Knowing with the Heart: Religious Experience and Belief in God*. Downers Grove, IL: InterVarsity, 1999.
———. *The Myth of Religious Neutrality: An Essay on the Hidden Role of Religious Belief in Theories*. 2nd ed. Notre Dame, IN: University of Notre Dame Press, 2005.
Coad, Frederick Roy. *A History of the Brethren Movement*. Exeter, UK: Paternoster, 1968.
———. *A History of the Brethren Movement: Its Origins, Its Worldwide Development and Its Significance for the Present Day*. Vancouver, Canada: Regent College, 2001.
Cochrane, Arthur, ed. *Reformed Confessions of the Sixteenth Century*. London: SCM, 1966.
Cockshut, A. O. J. *Anglican Attitudes: A Study of Victorian Religious Controversies*. London: Collins, 1959.
Coe, Bufford W. *John Wesley and Marriage*. Bethlehem, PA: Lehigh University Press, 1996.
Cohick, Lynn H. *Women in the World of the Earliest Christians: Illuminating Ancient Ways of Life*. Grand Rapids: Baker, 2009.
Cohn, Norman. *Cosmos, Chaos, and the World to Come: The Ancient Roots of Apocalyptic Faith*. New Haven, CT: Yale University Press, 1993.
Collins, C. John. *Science and Faith: Friends or Foes?* Wheaton: Crossway, 2003.
Collins, Francis Sellers. *The Language of God: A Scientist Presents Evidence for Belief*. New York: Free, 2007.
Collins, Kenneth J. *The Evangelical Moment: The Promise of an American Religion*. Grand Rapids: Baker, 2005.
———. *Power, Politics and the Fragmentation of Evangelicalism: From the Scopes Trial to the Obama Administration*. Downers Grove, IL: InterVarsity, 2012.
Collinson, Patrick. *Archbishop Grindal, 1519–1583: The Struggle for a Reformed Church*. London: Jonathan Cape, 1979.
———. *The Elizabethan Puritan Movement*. London: Jonathan Cape, 1967.
Conn, Harvie M., ed. *Inerrancy and Hermeneutic: A Tradition, A Challenge, A Debate*. Grand Rapids: Baker, 1988.
Coomes, Anne. *Festo Kivengere: A Biography*. Eastbourne, UK: Monarch, 1990.
Cooper, John W. *Body, Soul, and Life Everlasting: Biblical Anthropology and the Monism-Dualism Debate*. Grand Rapids: Eerdmans, 2000.
Cooper, Kate, and Jeremy Gregory, eds. *Revival and Resurgence in Christian History*. Woodbridge, UK: Boydell & Brewer, 2008.

Cothen, Grady C. *What Happened to the Southern Baptist Convention?: A Memoir of the Controversy.* Revised ed. Macon, GA: Smyth & Helwys, 1993.
Cox, William E. [a-millennial]. *An Examination of Dispensationalism.* Philadelphia: Presbyterian & Reformed, 1963.
———. *Why I Left Schofieldism.* Philadelphia: Presbyterian & Reformed, 1975.
Cranston, Maurice. *Jean-Jacques: The Early Life and Work of Jean-Jacques Rousseau, 1712-1754.* New York: Norton, 1983.
———. *The Noble Savage: Jean Jacques Rousseau, 1754-1762.* Chicago: University of Chicago Press, 1991.
———. *The Solitary Self: Jean-Jacques Rousseau in Exile and Adversity.* Chicago: University of Chicago Press, 1997.
Crawford, Michael. *Thunder on the Right: The "New Right" and the Politics of Resentment.* New York: Pantheon, 1980.
Crisp, Oliver D. *Jonathan Edwards among the Theologians.* Grand Rapids: Eerdmans, 2015.
Crisp, Oliver D., and Douglas A. Sweeney, eds. *After Jonathan Edwards: The Courses of the New England Theology.* New York: Oxford University Press, 2012.
Cromwell, Oliver. *Letters and Speeches of Oliver Cromwell with Elucidations by Thomas Carlyle,* edited by S. C. Lomas. 3 vols. London: Dent, 1904.
Cross, Whitney R. *The Burned-Over District: The Social and Intellectual History of Enthusiastic Religion in Western New York, 1800-1850.* Ithaca, NY: Cornell University Press, 1950.
Crutchfield, Larry. *The Origins of Dispensationalism: The Darby Factor.* Lanham, MD: University Press of America, 1991.
Dallimore, Arnold. *George Whitefield: The Life and Times of the Great Evangelist of the Eighteenth-Century Revival.* 2 vols. Edinburgh: Banner of Truth, 1970, 1980.
———. *The Life of Edward Irving: The Fore-Runner of the Charismatic Movement.* Edinburgh: Banner of Truth, 1983.
———. *Spurgeon: A New Biography.* Edinburgh: Banner of Truth, 1985.
Daniell, David. *The Bible in English: Its History and Influence.* New Haven, CT: Yale University Press, 2003.
Danker, Frederick W. *No Room in the Brotherhood: The Preus-Otten Purge of Missouri.* St. Louis, MO: Clayton, 1977.
Dann, G. Elijah. *Leaving Fundamentalism: Personal Stories.* Waterloo, Canada: Wilfrid Laurier University Press, 2008.
Davenport, Stewart. *Friends of the Unrighteous Mammon, Northern Christians and Market Capitalism, 1815-1860.* Chicago: University of Chicago Press, 2008.
Davies, G. C. B. *The Early Cornish Evangelicals 1735-60: a Study of Walker of Truro and Others.* London: SPCK, 1951.
Davies, Michael. *Graceful Reading: Theology and Narrative in the Works of John Bunyan.* Oxford: Oxford University Press, 2002.
Davis, Stephen T. *The Debate About the Bible.* Philadelphia: Westminster, 1977.
Dayton, Donald W. *Discovering an Evangelical Heritage.* New York: Harper & Row, 1976.
———. "Donald Dayton Replies." *Christian Scholar's Review* 7 (1977) 207-211.
———. "Rejoinder to Historiography Discussion." *Christian Scholar's Review* 23 (1993) 62-71.

———. "'The Search for the Historical Evangelicalism': George Marsden's History of Fuller Seminary as a Case Study." *Christian Scholar's Review* 23 (1993) 12–33.
———. *Theological Roots of Pentecostalism*. Grand Rapids: Zondervan, 1987.
De Graaf, Simon Gerrit. *Promise and Deliverance*, Vol. 1: *From Creation to the Conquest of Canaan*; Vol. 2: *The Failure of Israel's Theocracy*; Vol. 3: *Christ's Ministry and Death*; Vol. 4: *Christ and the Nations*. St. Catharines, Canada: Paideia, 1977–81.
D'Elia, John A. *A Place at the Table: George Eldon Ladd and the Rehabilitation of Evangelical Scholarship in America*. New York: Oxford University Press, 2008.
Delotavo, Alan J. *Back to the Original Church: The Secret Behind Church Movements*. Eugene, OR: Wipf & Stock, 2010.
———. *Contemporary Evangelicalism and the Restoration of the Prototypal Church*. Eugene, OR: Wipf & Stock 2007.
DeMar, Gary. *Last Days of Madness*. Revised ed. Atlanta, GA: American Vision, 1994.
Dembski, William A. *The Design Revolution: Answering the Toughest Questions about Intelligent Design*. Downers Grove IL: InterVarsity, 2004.
Denton, Michael. *Evolution: A Theory in Crisis*. Bethesda, MD: Alder & Alder, 1986.
———. *Nature's Destiny: How the Laws of Biology Reveal Purpose in the Universe*. New York: Free, 2002.
DeWitt, Calvin B. *Caring for Creation: Responsible Stewardship of God's Handiwork*. Grand Rapids: Baker, 1998.
Dilulio, John J. *Godly Republic: A Centrist Blueprint for America's Faith-Based Future*. Berkeley: University of California Press, 2007.
Dochuk, Darren. *From Bible Belt to Sun Belt: Plain-Folk Religion, Grassroots Politics, and the Rise of Evangelical Conservatism*. New York: Norton, 2010.
Dochuk, Darren, et al., eds. *American Evangelicalism: George Marsden and the State of American Religious History*. Notre Dame, IN: University of Notre Dame Press, 2014.
Dockery, David, et al., eds. *Southern Baptists: Evangelicals and the Future of Denominationalism*. Nashville: Broadmen & Holman, 2011.
Doddridge, Philip. *The Rise and Progress of Religion in the Soul: Illustrated In A Course Of Serious And Practical Addresses, Suited To Persons Of Every Character And Circumstance With A Devout Meditation And Prayer*. Orlando FL: Soli Deo Gloria, 2005.
Dollar, George W. *A History of Fundamentalism in America*. Greenville, SC: Bob Jones University Press, 1973.
Donaldson, Alistair W. *The Last Days of Dispensationalism: A Scholarly Critique of Popular Misconceptions*. Eugene, OR, Wipf & Stock, 2011.
Doner, C. V. *The Late Great Evangelical Church: How an Age-Old Heresy is Killing the Modern-day Church and how it still can be saved*. Lincoln, NE: Oakdown, 2007.
Dooyeweerd, Herman. *In the Twilight of Western Thought: Studies in the Pretended Autonomy of Theoretical Thought*. Philadelphia: Presbyterian & Reformed, 1960.
———. "Introduction to a Transcendental Criticism of Philosophical Thought." *Evangelical Quarterly* 19/1 (January 1947) 42–51.
———. *A New Critique of Theoretical Thought*. 4 vols. Nutley, NJ: Presbyterian & Reformed, 1954–58.
———. *The Roots of Western Culture: Pagan, Secular, and Christian Options*. Toronto, Canada: Wedge, 1979.

Dorsett, Lyle. *A Passion for God: The Spiritual Journey of A.W Tozer.* Chicago: Moody, 2008.
Drane, John. *The McDonaldization of the Church: Consumer Culture and the Church's Future.* Macon , GA: Smyth & Helwys, 2001.
Draney, Daniel, and James Bradley. *When Streams Diverge: John Murdoch MacInnis and the Origins of Protestant Fundamentalism in Los Angeles.* Eugene, OR: Wipf & Stock, 2008.
Draper, Jonathan A., ed. *The Eye of the Storm: Bishop John William Colenso and the Crisis of Biblical Interpretation.* Pietermaritzburg, South Africa: Cluster, 2003.
Drummond, Andrew L. *German Protestantism since Luther.* London: Epworth, 1951.
Drummond, Andrew L., and James Bulloch. *The Church in Late Victorian Scotland, 1874-1900.* Edinburgh: Saint Andrews, 1978.
———. *The Church in Victorian Scotland, 1843-1874.* Edinburgh: Saint Andrews, 1975.
———. *The Scottish Church: The Age of the Moderates, 1688-1843.* Edinburgh: Saint Andrews, 1973.
Drummond, Lewis A. *The Canvas Cathedral: A Complete History of Evangelism from the Apostle Paul to Billy Graham.* Nashville: Thomas Nelson, 2003.
———. *Eight Keys to Biblical Revival: The Saga of Scriptural Spiritual Awakenings, How They Shaped the Great Revivals of the Past, and Their Powerful Implications.* Grand Rapids: Bethany, 1994.
———. *The Evangelist: The Worldwide Impact of Billy Graham.* Nashville: Thomas Nelson, 2001.
———. *The Life and Ministry of Charles G. Finney.* Grand Rapids: Bethany House, 1985.
Drummond, Lewis A., and Betty Drummond. *Women of Awakenings: The Historic Contribution of Women to Revival Movements.* Grand Rapids: Kregel, 1997.
Duckworth, Jenny and Justin. *Against the Tide: Towards the Kingdom.* Eugene, OR: Wipf & Stock, 2011.
Dudley-Smith, Timothy. *John Stott: A Global ministry—A Biography: The Later Years.* Downers Grove, IL: InterVarsity, 2001.
———. *John Stott: The Making of a Leader—A Biography of the Early Years.* Downers Grove, IL: InterVarsity, 2001.
Duin, Julia. *Days of Fire and Glory: The Rise and Fall of a Charismatic Community.* Baltimore, MD: Crossland, 2009.
———. *Quitting Church: Why the Faithful are Fleeing and What to Do about it.* Grand Rapids: Baker, 2008.
Dungan, David Laird. *A History of the Synoptic Problem: The Canon, the Text, the Composition, and the Interpretation of the Gospels.* New York: Doubleday, 1999.
Dunn, James D. G. "The Authority of Scripture According to Scripture." *Churchman* 96 (1982) 104-22 and 201-25.
———. *Baptism in the Holy Spirit: A Re-Examination of the New Testament Teaching on the Gift of the Spirit in Relation to Pentecostalism Today.* 2nd ed. London: SCM, 2010.
———. *The Living Word.* 2nd ed. Minneapolis: Fortress, 2009.
Du Plessis, David Johannes. *The Spirit Bade Me Go.* Alachua, FL: Bridge Logos, 2009.
DuPont, Carolyn Renee. *Mississippi Praying: Southern White Evangelicals and the Civil Rights Movement, 1945-1975.* Albany: New York University Press, 2013.
Duriez, Colin. *Francis Schaeffer: An Authentic Life.* Wheaton: Crossway, 2008.

Ebeling, Gerhard. *Word and Faith.* Philadelphia: Fortress, 1963.
Edwards, Jonathan. *The Works of Jonathan Edwards*, edited by Edward Hickman. 2 vols. London: Westley & Davis, 1834.
———. *The Yale Edition of the Works of Jonathan Edwards*, edited by Paul Ramsey and Perry Miller. 26 vols. New Haven, CT: Yale University Press, 1957 onwards.
Edwards, Maldwyn. *After Wesley, A Study of the Social and Political Influence of Methodism in the Middle Period, 1791–1849.* London: Epworth, 1935.
———. *John Wesley and the Eighteenth Century: A Study of His Social and Political Influence.* London: George Allen and Unwin, 1933. Revised, London: Epworth, 1955.
———. *Methodism and England: A Study of Methodism in its Social and Political Aspects during the period 1850–1932.* London: Epworth, 1943.
Elliott, Ralph H. *The Genesis Controversy and Continuity in Southern Baptist Chaos—A Eulogy for a Great Tradition.* Macon, GA: Mercer University Press, 1992.
Elliott Binns, Leonard. *The Evangelical Movement in the English Church.* London: Methuen, 1928.
Ellis, Edward Earle. *Christ and the Future in New Testament History.* Leiden: Brill, 2001.
———. *History and Interpretation in New Testament Perspective.* Williston, VT: SBL, 2001.
———. *The Making of the New Testament Documents.* Williston, VT: SBL, 2009.
Ellul, Jacques. *The Subversion of Christianity.* Grand Rapids: Eerdmans, 1986.
Engel, Katherine Carté. *Religion and Profit: Moravians in Early America.* Philadelphia: University of Pennsylvania Press, 2008.
Enns, Peter. *The Evolution of Adam: What the Bible Does and Doesn't Say About Human Origins.* Grand Rapids: Brazos, 2012.
———. *Inspiration and Incarnation: Evangelicals and the Problem of the Old Testament.* Grand Rapids: Baker, 2007.
Erickson, Millard J. *The Evangelical Left: Encountering Postconservative Evangelical Theology.* Grand Rapids: Baker, 1997.
Escott, Harry. *Isaac Watts, Hymnographer.* London: Independent, 1962.
Espinosa, Gaston J. *William J. Seymour and the Origins of Global Pentecostalism: A Biography and Documentary History.* Durham, NC: Duke University Press, 2014.
Etherington, Norman. *Missions and Empire.* London: Oxford University Press, 2008.
Eusebius of Caesarea. *Eusebius' Ecclesiastical History: Complete and Unabridged*, translated and introduced by C. F. Cruse. Peabody, MA: Hendrickson, 1993.
Evans, Eifion. *Bread of Heaven: The Life and Work of William Williams, Pantycelyn.* Bridgend, UK: Bryntirion, 2011.
———. *Daniel Rowland and the Great Evangelical Awakening in Wales.* Edinburgh: Banner of Truth, 1985.
Evensen, Bruce J. *God's Man for the Gilded Age: D.L. Moody and the Rise of Modern Mass Evangelism.* New York: Oxford University Press, 2003.
Falk, Darrel R. *Coming to Peace with Science: Bridging the Worlds between Faith and Biology.* Downers Grove, IL: InterVarsity, 2004.
Falwell, Gerry L. *The Fundamentalist Phenomenon: the Resurgence of Conservative Christianity.* New York: Doubleday, 1981.
Fant, David J. *A. W. Tozer: A Twentieth Century Prophet.* Harrisburg, PA: Christian, 1964.
Farley, Ian D. *J. C Ryle: First Bishop of Liverpool.* Carlisle, UK: Paternoster, 2001.

Fawcett, Arthur. *The Cambuslang Revival: The Scottish Evangelical Revival of the Eighteenth Century*. London: Banner of Truth, 1971.
Fea, John. *Was America Founded As a Christian Nation? A Historical Introduction*. Louisville, KY: Westminster John Knox, 2011.
Fenwick, John R. K. *The Free Church of England: The History and Promise of an Anglican Tradition*. London: T. & T Clark, 2004.
Ferrell, Lori Anne. *The Bible and the People*. New Haven, CT: Yale University Press, 2008.
Ferris, Paul. *The Church of England*. London: Victor Gollancz, 1962.
Fielder, Geraint. *Lord of The Years: Sixty Years of Student Witness. The Story of the Inter-Varsity Fellowship, Universities and Colleges Christian Fellowship, 1928–1988*. Leicester, UK: Inter-Varsity, 1988.
Finstuen, Andrew S. *Original Sin and Everyday Protestants: The Theology of Reinhold Niebuhr, Billy Graham, and Paul Tillich in an Age of Anxiety*. Chapel Hill: University of North Carolina Press, 2009.
Flew, Robert Newton. *The Idea of Perfection in Christian Theology: An Historical Study of the Christian Ideal for the Present Life*. London: Oxford University Press, 1934.
Flippen, J. Brooks. *Jimmy Carter, the Politics of Family, and the Rise of the Religious Right*. Athens: University of Georgia Press, 2011.
Foege, Alec. *The Empire God Built: Inside Pat Robertson's Media Machine*. New York: John Wiley, 1996.
Follett, Richard R. *Evangelicalism, Penal Theory and the Politics of Criminal Law Reform in England, 1808–30*. Basingstoke, UK: Palgrave Macmillan, 2001.
Fountain, David Guy. *Contending for the Faith: E. J. Poole-Connor—A 'Prophet' Amidst the Sweeping Changes in English Evangelicalism*. Revised ed. London: Wakeman, 2005.
———. *Isaac Watts Remembered*. Worthing, UK: Henry E. Walter, 1974.
Fowler, Thomas B., and Daniel Kuebler. *The Evolution Controversy: A Survey of Competing Theories*. Grand Rapids: Baker, 2007.
Frady, Marshall. *Billy Graham: A Parable of American Righteousness*. New York: Simon and Schuster, 2006.
Frame, Thomas. *Anglicans in Australia*. Sydney: University of New South Wales Press, 2007.
France, Richard Thomas. *Divine Government: God's Kingship in the Gospel of Mark*. Vancouver, Canada: Regent, 2003.
———. "Inerrancy and New Testament Exegesis." *Themelios* 1 (1975) 12–18.
———. *Jesus and the Old Testament: His Application of Old Testament Passages to Himself and His Mission*. London: Tyndale, 1971.
———. *Women in the Church's Ministry: A Test Case for Biblical Hermeneutics*. Carlisle, UK: Paternoster, 1995.
Frank, Douglas W. *Less than Conquerors: How Evangelicals Entered the Twentieth Century*. Grand Rapids: Eerdmans, 1986.
Frankl, Razelle. *Televangelism: The Marketing of Popular Religion*. Carbondale: Southern Illinois University Press, 1987.
Freeman, Arthur J. *An Ecumenical Theology of the Heart: The Theology of Count Nicholas Ludwig von Zinzendorf*. Winston Salem, NC: Moravian Church of America, 1998.
Frei, Hans W. *The Eclipse of Biblical Narrative: A Study in Eighteenth and Nineteenth Century Hermeneutics*. New Haven, CT: Yale University Press, 1974.

Frykholm, Amy Johnson. *Rapture Culture: Left Behind in Evangelical America*. New York: Oxford University Press, 2004.
Fuller, Daniel P. *Gospel and Law: Contrast or Continuum? The Hermeneutics of Dispensationalism and Covenant Theology*. Grand Rapids: Eerdmans, 1980.
Fuller, Robert C. *Naming the Antichrist: The History of an American Obsession*. New York: Oxford University Press, 1995.
Furneaux, Robin. *William Wilberforce*. London: Hamish Hamilton, 1974.
Gaffin, Richard B. *Perspectives on Pentecost: New Testament Teaching on the Gifts of the Holy Spirit*. Phillipsburg, NJ: Presbyterian & Reformed, 1979.
Gagnon, Robert A. J. *The Bible and Homosexual Practice: Texts and Hermeneutics*. Nashville: Abingdon, 2002.
Ganiel, Gladys M. *Evangelicalism and Conflict in Northern Ireland*. New York: Palgrave Macmillan, 2008.
Ganis, Monica. *Under the Influence: California's Intoxicating Spiritual and Cultural Impact on America*. Grand Rapids: Brazos, 2010.
Garff, Joakim. *Søren Kierkegaard: A Biography*. Princeton, NJ: Princeton University Press, 2005.
Garnett, Jane, and Colin Matthew, eds. *Revival and Religion since 1700: Essays for John Walsh*. London: Hambledon, 1993.
Gasaway, Brantley W. *Progressive Evangelicals and the Pursuit of Social Justice*. Chapel Hill: University of North Carolina Press, 2014.
Gasper, Louis. *The Fundamentalist Movement, 1930–1956*. The Hague: Mouton, 1963.
Gasque, Laurel. *Art and the Christian Mind: The Life and Work of H. R. Rookmaaker*. Wheaton: Crossway, 2005.
Gatiss, Lee. *The Tragedy of 1662: The Ejection and Persecution of the Puritans*. London: Latimer, 2007.
Gay, Craig M. *With Liberty and Justice for Whom? The Recent Evangelical Debate over Capitalism*. Grand Rapids: Eerdmans, 1991.
Geisler, Norman L., ed. *Biblical Inerrancy: An Analysis of its Philosophical Roots*. Grand Rapids: Zondervan, 1981.
———. *Inerrancy*. Grand Rapids: Zondervan, 1979.
Genovese, Eugene. *A Consuming Fire: The Fall of the Confederacy in the Mind of the White Christian South*. Athens: University of Georgia Press, 2009.
Genovese, Eugene, and Elizabeth Fox-Genovese. *The Mind of the Master Class: History and Faith in the Southern Slaveholders' Worldview*. New York: Cambridge University Press, 2005.
George, Timothy, ed. *J. I. Packer and the Evangelical Future: The Impact of His Life and Thought*. Grand Rapids: Baker, 2009.
Gerstner, John H. *A Primer on Dispensationalism*. Philadelphia: Presbyterian & Reformed, 1982.
———. *Wrongly Dividing the Word of Truth, A Critique of Dispensationalism*. Brentwood, TN: Wolgemuth & Hyatt, 1991.
Gersztyn, Bob. *Jesus Rocks the World: The Definitive History of Contemporary Christian Music*. 2 Vols. New York: Praeger, 2013.
Gibbs, Nancy, and Michael Duffy. *The Preacher and the Presidents: Billy Graham in the White House*. New York: Center Street, 2007.
Gill, Frederick Cyril. *The Romantic Movement and Methodism*. London: Epworth, 1937.

Gillespie, Michele, and Robert Beachy, eds. *Pious Pursuits: German Moravians in the Atlantic World*. New York: Berghahn, 2007.
Gillies, John. *Memoirs of the Life of the Reverend George Whitefield*. London: Edward and Charles Dilly, 1772.
Gillquist, Peter E. *Becoming Orthodox: A Journey to the Ancient Christian Faith*. Brentwood, TN: Wolgemuth & Hyatt, 1989.
Gish, Duane Tolbert. *Creation Scientists Answer Their Critics*. Dallas, TX: Institute for Creation Research, 1993.
———. *Evidence Against Evolution*. Carol Stream, IL: Tyndale, 1972.
———. *Evolution: The Challenge of the Fossil Record*. Green Forest, AR: Master, 1995.
———. *Evolution, the fossils say no!* Green Forest, AR: Master, 1973.
———. *Evolution: The Fossils Still Say No!* Green Forest, AR: Master, 1979.
Gloege, Timothy. *Guaranteed Pure: The Moody Bible Institute, Business, and the Making of Modern Evangelicalism*. Chapel Hill: University of North Carolina Press, 2015.
Glover, Willis B. *Evangelical Nonconformity and Higher Criticism in the Nineteenth Century*. London: Independent, 1954.
Goheen, Michael W., and Craig G. Bartholomew. *Living at the Crossroads: An Introduction to Christian Worldview*. Grand Rapids: Baker, 2008.
Goldman, Shalom L. *Zeal for Zion: Christians, Jews, and the Idea of the Promised Land*. Chapel Hill: University of North Carolina Press, 2009.
Goldsworthy, Graeme. *According to Plan: The Unfolding Revelation of God in the Bible*. Downers Grove, IL: InterVarsity, 2002.
———. *Gospel and Kingdom: A Christian's Guide to the Old Testament*. San Francisco: Harper & Row, 1983.
———. *Gospel and Wisdom: Israel's Wisdom Literature in the Christian Life*. Exeter, UK: Paternoster, 1997.
———. *The Gospel in Revelation: Gospel and Apocalypse*. Exeter, UK: Paternoster, 1994.
Goudzwaard, Bob. *Capitalism and Progress: A Diagnosis of Western Society*. Toronto, Canada: Wedge and Grand Rapids: Eerdmans, 1979.
———. *Idols of Our Time*. Downers Grove, IL: InterVarsity, 1981.
Goudzwaard, Bob, and Harry de Lange. *Beyond Poverty and Affluence: Toward an Economy of Care*. Geneva: WCC and Grand Rapids: Eerdmans, 1995.
Goudzwaard, Bob, et al., *Globalization and the Kingdom of God*, edited by James W. Skillen. Grand Rapids: Baker, 2001.
Goudzwaard, Bob, et al., *Hope in Troubled Times: A New Vision for Confronting Global Crises*. Grand Rapids: Baker, 2007.
Grabbe, Hans-Jürgen, ed. *Halle Pietism, Colonial North America and the Young United States*. Stuttgart: Franz Steiner, 2008.
Graham, William Franklin. *America's Hour of Decision*. Wheaton: Van Kampen, 1951.
———. *Just As I Am—The Autobiography of Billy Graham*. San Francisco: Harper Collins, 1991.
Grass, Timothy. *F.F. Bruce: A Life*. Grand Rapids: Eerdmans, 2012.
Gray, Denis. *Spencer Perceval: The Evangelical Prime Minister 1762–1812*. Manchester, UK: Manchester University Press, 1963.
Grayson, Carter. *Anglican Evangelicals: Protestant Secessions from the Via Media, c. 1800–1850*. Oxford: Oxford University Press, 2001.
Greaves, Richard L. *Glimpses of Glory: John Bunyan and English Dissent*. Redwood City, CA: Stanford University Press, 2002.

———. *John Bunyan and English Nonconformity*. London: Hambledon, 2003.
Greeley, Andrew, and Michael Hoult. *The Truth About Conservative Christians: What They Think and What They Believe*. Chicago: University of Chicago Press, 2006.
Green, S. J. D. *The Passing of Protestant England: Secularisation and Social Change c.1920–1960*. Cambridge: Cambridge University Press, 2011.
Green, Steven K. *Inventing a Christian America: The Myth of the Religious Founding*. New York: Oxford University Press, 2015.
Greenlee, James G., and Charles M. Johnston. *Good Citizens: British Missionaries and Imperial States, 1870–1918*. Montreal, Canada: McGill-Queen's University Press, 1999.
Gregory, Joel. *Too Great a Temptation: The Seductive Power of America's Super Church*. Fort Worth, TX: Summit, 1994.
Gregory, Joel, et al., *The Proceedings of the Conference on Biblical Inerrancy*. Nashville: Broadman & Holman, 1987.
Greidanus, Sidney. *The Modern Preacher and the Ancient Text: Interpreting and Preaching Biblical Literature*. Grand Rapids: Eerdmans, 1988.
———. *Preaching Christ from Ecclesiastes: Foundations for Expository Sermons*. Grand Rapids: Eerdmans, 2010.
———. *Preaching Christ from Genesis: Foundations for Expository Sermons*. Grand Rapids: Eerdmans, 2007.
———. *Preaching Christ from the Old Testament*. Grand Rapids: Eerdmans, 1999.
———. *Sola Scriptura: Problems and Principles in Preaching Historical Texts*. Kampen, The Netherlands: Kok, 1970.
Grenz, Stanley. *The Millennial Maze*. Downers Grove, IL: InterVarsity, 1992.
Grey, John. *Black Mass: Apocalyptic Religion and the Death of Utopia*. New York: Farrar, Straus & Giroux, 2007.
Gribben, Crawford. *Evangelical Millennialism in the Trans-Atlantic World, 1500–2000*. New York: Palgrave Macmillan, 2010.
Griffiths, Brian. *Morality and the Market Place*. London: Hodder & Stoughton, 1982.
Grigg, John A. *The Lives of David Brainerd: The Making of an American Evangelical Icon*. New York: Oxford University Press, 2009.
Grudem, Wayne. *The Gift of Prophesy in the New Testament and Today*. Westchester, IL: Crossway, 1988.
Grudem, Wayne, ed. *Are Miraculous Gifts for Today?* Grand Rapids: Zondervan, 1996.
Guelzo, Allen G. *For the Union of Evangelical Christendom: The Irony of the Reformed Episcopalians*. University Park: Pennsylvania University Press, 1994.
Guinness, Oz. *Fit Bodies, Fat Minds: Why Evangelicals Don't Think and What to Do About It*. London: Hodder & Stoughton, 1995.
Gundlach, Bradley J. *Process and Providence: The Evolution Question at Princeton, 1845–1929*. Grand Rapids: Eerdmans, 2013.
Gundry, Robert Horton. *First the Antichrist: Why Christ Won't Come Before the Antichrist Does*. Grand Rapids: Baker, 1997.
Gutjahr, Paul C. *Charles Hodge: Guardian of American Orthodoxy*. New York: Oxford University Press, 2011.
Haan, Roelf. *The Economics of Honor: Biblical Reflections on Money and Prosperity*. Grand Rapids: Eerdmans, 2009.

Haarsma, Deborah B., and Loren D. Haarsma. *Origins: Christian Perspectives on Creation, Evolution, and Intelligent Design*. 2nd ed. Grand Rapids: Faith Alive, 2011.
Haddon, Jeffrey K., and Anson Shupe. *Televangelism, Power and Politics on God's Frontier*. New York: Henry Holt, 1988.
Haddon, Jeffrey K., and Charles E. Swann. *Prime Time Preachers: The Rising Power of Televangelism*. Reading, MA: Addison-Wesley, 1981.
Hagee, John [premillennial dispensationalist]. *In Defense of Israel*. Lake Mary, FL: Frontline, 2007.
Hague, William. *William Wilberforce: The Life of the Great Anti-Slave Trade Campaigner*. London: Harper Collins, 2007.
Halevy, Elie. *The Birth of Methodism in England*, edited by Bernard Semmel. Chicago: University of Chicago Press, 1971.
Ham, Ken. *The Lie: Evolution*. San Diego, CA: Master, 1987.
Hamilton, Ian. *The Erosion of Calvinist Orthodoxy: Seceders and Subscription in Scottish Presbyterianism*. Edinburgh: Rutherford, 1990.
Hamon, William ["New Apostolic Reformation" advocate]. *Apostles, Prophets and the Coming Moves of God: God's End-Time Plans for His Church and Planet Earth*. Shippensburg, PA: Destiny Image, 1997.
Hankins, Barry. *American Evangelicals: A Contemporary History of a Mainstream Religious Movement*. Lanham, MD: Rowman & Littlefield, 2008.
———. *Francis Schaeffer and the Shaping of Evangelical America*. Grand Rapids: Eerdmans, 2008.
———. *God's Rascal: J. Frank Norris and the Beginnings of Southern Fundamentalism*. Lexington: University Press of Kentucky, 1996.
———. *Jesus and Gin: Evangelicalism, the Roaring Twenties and Today's Culture Wars*. New York: Palgrave Macmillan, 2010.
———. *Uneasy in Babylon: Southern Baptist Conservatives and American Culture*. Tuscaloosa: University of Alabama Press, 2002.
Hankins, Barry, ed. *Evangelicalism and Fundamentalism: A Documentary Reader*. New York: New York University Press, 2008.
Hannah, John D. *An Uncommon Union: Dallas Theological Seminary and American Evangelicalism*. Grand Rapids: Zondervan, 2009.
Hannah, John D., ed. *Inerrancy and the Church*. Chicago: Moody, 1984.
Harbison, E. Harris. *The Christian Scholar in the Age of the Reformation*. New York: Charles Scribner's Sons, 1956.
———. *Christianity and History*. Princeton, NJ: Princeton University Press, 1964.
Harding, Alan. *The Countess of Huntingdon's Connection*. Oxford: Oxford University Press, 2003.
Harper, Michael. *As at the Beginning*. London: Hodder & Stoughton, 1966.
———. *Third Force in the Body of Christ*. London: Fountain, 1965.
Harrell, David Edwin. *All Things are Possible: The Healing and Charismatic Revivals in Modern America*. Bloomington: Indiana University Press, 1975.
———. *Oral Roberts: An American Life*. Bloomington: Indiana University Press, 1985.
———. *Pat Robertson: A Life and Legacy*. Grand Rapids: Eerdmans, 2010.
Harris, Harriet A. *Fundamentalism and Evangelicals*. Oxford: Oxford University Press, 1998.

Harrison, J. F. C. *The Second Coming: Popular Millenarianism, 1780–1850*. Brunswick, NJ: Rutgers University Press, 1979.
Harrisville, Roy A., and Walter Sundberg. *The Bible in Modern Culture: Theology and Historical-Critical Method from Spinoza to Käsemann*. Grand Rapids: Eerdmans, 1995.
Hart, Darryl G. *Deconstructing Evangelicalism: Conservative Protestantism in the Age of Billy Graham*. Grand Rapids: Baker, 2004.
———. *Defending the Faith: J. Gresham Machen and the Crisis of Conservative Protestantism in Modern America*. Baltimore, MD: Johns Hopkins University Press, 1994.
———. *From Billy Graham to Sarah Palin: Evangelicals and the Betrayal of American Conservatism*. Grand Rapids: Eerdmans, 2011.
———. *John Williamson Nevin: High-Church Calvinist*. Phillipsburg, NJ: Presbyterian & Reformed, 2005.
———. *That Old-Time Religion in Modern America: Evangelical Protestantism in the Twentieth Century*. Lanham, MD: Dee, 2003.
Hart, Darryl G., ed. *Reckoning with the Past: Historical Essays on American Evangelicalism from the Institute for the Study of American Evangelicals*. Grand Rapids: Baker, 1995.
Hassett, Miranda K. *Anglican Communion in Crisis: How Episcopal Dissidents and their African Allies Are Reshaping Anglicanism*. Princeton, NJ: Princeton University Press, 2007.
Hatch, Nathan O. *The Democratization of American Christianity*. New Haven, CT: Yale University Press, 1989.
Hauerwas, Stanley. *War and the American Difference: Theological Reflections on Violence and National Identity*. Grand Rapids: Baker, 2011.
Haykin, Michael A. G., and Kenneth J. Stewart. *The Advent of Evangelicalism: Exploring Historical Continuities*. Nashville: Broadmen & Holman, 2008.
Hays, Christopher M., and Christopher B. Ansberry, eds. *Evangelical Faith and the Challenge of Historical Criticism*. Grand Rapids: Baker, 2013.
Hazard, Paul. *The European Mind: (1680–1715)*. London: Hollis & Carter, 1953.
———. *European Thought in the Eighteenth Century: From Montesquieu to Lessing*. London: Hollis & Carter, 1954.
Hefley, James C. *The Truth in Crisis I: The Controversy in the Southern Baptist Convention*. De Soto, TX: Criterion, 1986. *The Truth in Crisis II: Bringing the Controversy Up to Date*; *The Truth in Crisis III: The Controversy in the Southern Baptist Convention*; *The Truth in Crisis IV: The Controversy in the Southern Baptist Convention*; *The Truth in Crisis V: The Winning Edge*; and *VI: The Conservative Resurgence in the Southern Baptist Convention*. Garland, TX: Hannibal, 1987–91.
Hefner, Robert William, and Peter L. Berger, eds. *Global Pentecostalism in the 21st Century*. Bloomington: Indiana University Press, 2013.
Heideman, Eugene P. *The Practice of Piety: The Theology of the Midwestern Reformed Church in America*. Grand Rapids: Eerdmans, 2009.
Heitzenrater, Richard P. *The Elusive Mr. Wesley*. 2nd ed. Nashville: Abingdon, 2003.
———. *Wesley and the People called Methodists*. Nashville: Abingdon, 1995.
Helseth, Paul Kjoss. *Right Reason and the Princeton Mind: An Unorthodox Proposal*. Phillipsburg, NJ: Presbyterian & Reformed, 2010.

Hempton, David. *Evangelical Disenchantment: Nine Portraits of Faith and Doubt.* New Haven, CT: Yale University Press, 2008.
———. *Methodism and Politics in British Society, 1750–1850.* London: Hutchinson, 1984.
———. *Methodism: Empire of the Spirit.* New Haven, CT: Yale University Press, 2005.
Hendriksen, William [a-millennial]. *Israel in Prophesy.* Grand Rapids: Baker, 1974.
———. *More than Conquerors: An Interpretation of the Book of Revelation.* Grand Rapids: Baker, 1939.
Hennell, Michael. *John Venn and the Clapham Sect.* London: Lutterworth, 1958.
Henry, Carl F. H. *Confessions of a Theologian.* Waco, TX: Word, 1988.
———. *God, Revelation and Authority.* 6 Vols. Wheaton: Crossway, 1999.
———. *The Uneasy Conscience of Modern Fundamentalism.* Grand Rapids: Eerdmans, 1947.
Henzel, Robert N. *Darby, Dualism, and the Decline of Dispensationalism.* Tucson, AZ: Fenestra, 2003.
Herbert, Arthur Gabriel. *Fundamentalism and the Church of God.* London: SCM, 1957.
Hession, Roy. *My Calvary Road.* London: CLC, 1978.
Hession, Roy and Revel. *The Calvary Road.* London: CLC, 1950.
Hilton, Boyd. *The Age of Atonement: The Influence of Evangelicalism on Social and Economic Thought, 1785–1865.* Oxford: Oxford University Press, 1986.
———. *A Mad, Bad and Dangerous People? England 1783–1846.* London: Oxford University Press, 2006.
Hindmarsh, Bruce. *The Evangelical Conversion Narrative: Spiritual Autobiography in Early Modern England.* New York: Oxford University Press, 2008.
———. *John Newton and the English Evangelical Tradition: Between the Conversions of Wesley and Wilberforce.* Oxford: Oxford University Press, 1996.
Hochschild, Adam. *Bury the Chains: The British Struggle to Abolish Slavery.* London: Macmillan, 2005.
Hodgkins, Christopher. *Reforming Empire: Protestant Colonialism and Conscience in British Literature.* Columbia: University of Missouri Press, 2002.
Hoekema, Anthony [a-millennial]. *The Bible and the Future.* Grand Rapids: Eerdmans, 1979.
Hoezee, Scott. *Remember Creation: God's World of Wonder and Delight.* Grand Rapids: Eerdmans, 1998.
Hofstadter, Richard. *Anti-Intellectualism in American Life.* New York: Knopf, 1963.
———. *The Paranoid Style in American Politics and Other Essays.* New York: Vintage, 1967.
Hogue, Andrew P. *Stumping God: Reagan, Carter, and the Invention of a Political Faith.* Waco, TX: Baylor University Press, 2012.
Hollenweger, Walter J. *The Pentecostals.* London: SCM, 1972.
Holman, Robert. *F. B. Meyer: If I had a Hundred Lives.* Fearn, UK: Christian Focus, 2007.
Holmes, Michael W., ed., and translator. *The Apostolic Fathers: Greek Texts and English Translations.* 3rd ed. Grand Rapids: Baker, 2007.
Holwerda, David E. *Jesus and Israel: One Covenant or Two?* Grand Rapids: Eerdmans, 1995.
Hooykaas, Reijer. *Philosophia Libera: Christian Faith and the Freedom of Science.* London: Tyndale, 1957.

———. *Religion and the Rise of Modern Science*. Edinburgh: Scottish Academic, 1972.
Hopkins, Hugh Evan. *Charles Simeon of Cambridge*. London: Hodder & Stoughton, 1977.
Horton, Michael Scott. *Christless Christianity: The Alternative Gospel of the American Church*. Grand Rapids: Baker, 2008.
———. "Is Evangelicalism Reformed or Wesleyan?" *Christian Scholar's Review* 31 (2001) 131–55.
———. *Made in America: The Shaping of Modern American Evangelicalism*. Grand Rapids: Baker, 1991.
Howard, Thomas Albert. *God and the Atlantic: America, Europe, and the Religious Divide*. New York: Oxford University Press, 2011.
Howse, Ernest Marshall. *Saints in Politics: The "Clapham Sect" and the Growth of Freedom*. London: George Allen & Unwin, 1952.
Hughes, Archibald. *A New Heaven and a New Earth: An Introductory Study of the Coming of the Lord Jesus Christ and the Eternal Inheritance*. London: Marshall, Morgan & Scott, 1958.
Hulse, Erroll [post-millennial]. *Billy Graham: The Pastor's Dilemma*. Hounslow, UK: Maurice Allen, 1966.
———. *The Restoration of Israel*. Worthing, UK: Walter, 1968.
Hunt, Keith and Gladys. *For Christ and the University: The Story of Intervarsity Christian Fellowship—USA, 1940–1990*. Downers Grove, IL: InterVarsity, 1991.
Hunter, James Davison. *American Evangelicalism: Conservative Religion and the Quandary of Modernity*. Brunswick, NJ: Rutgers University Press, 1983.
———. *Culture Wars: The Struggle to Define America*. New York: Basic, 1991.
———. *Evangelicalism: The Coming Generation*. Chicago: University of Chicago Press, 1987.
———. *To Change the World: The Irony, Tragedy, and Possibility of Christianity in the Late Modern World*. New York: Oxford University Press, 2010.
Hutton, Joseph Edmund. *A History of the Moravian Church*. 2nd ed., London: Moravian Publication Office, 1909.
Hylson-Smith, Kenneth. *Evangelicals in the Church of England, 1734–1984*. Edinburgh: T. & T. Clark, 1988.
Inglis, Kenneth Stanley. *Churches and the Working Classes in Victorian England*. London: Routledge & Kegan Paul, 1963.
Ironside, Henry Allen. [pre-millennial dispensationalist]. *The Great Parenthesis*. Grand Rapids: Zondervan, 1943
———. *Lectures on Daniel the Prophet*. New York: Loizeaux, 1920.
Isichei, Elizabeth. *A History of Christianity in Africa: From Antiquity to the Present*. Grand Rapids: Eerdmans, 1995.
Jacobs, A. J. *The Year of Living Biblically: One Man's Humble Quest to Follow the Bible as Literally as Possible*. New York: Simon & Schuster, 2007.
Jamieson, Alan. *A Churchless Faith: Faith Journeys Beyond the Churches*. Wellington, New Zealand: Garside, 2000; London: SPCK, 2002.
Jebb, Stanley. *No Laughing Matter: The "Toronto" Phenomenon and its Implications*. Bromley, UK: Day One, 1995.
Jensen, Michael P. *Sydney Anglicanism: An Apology*. Eugene, OR: Wipf and Stock, 2012.
Johnson, Galen. *Prisoner of Conscience: John Bunyan on Self, Community and Christian Faith*. Milton Keynes, UK: Paternoster, 2007.

Johnson, Michael R. *Genesis, Geology and Catastrophism: A Critique of Creationist Science and Biblical Literalism*. Exeter, UK: Paternoster, 1988.
Johnson, Phillip E. *Darwin on Trial*. Downers Grove, IL: InterVarsity, 1991.
Johnston, E. A. *George Whitfield: A Definitive Biography*. 2 vols. Stoke on Trent, UK: Tentmaker, 2008.
Johnstone, William, ed. *William Robertson Smith: Essays in Reassessment*. Sheffield, UK: Sheffield Academic, 1995.
Jones, David Ceri. *Glorious Work in the World: Welsh Methodism and the International Evangelical Revival, 1735–1750*. Cardiff: University of Wales Press, 2004.
Jones, David Ceri, et al. *The Elect Methodists: Calvinistic Methodism in England and Wales, 1735–1811*. Cardiff: University of Wales Press, 2012.
Jones, Peter d'A. *The Christian Socialist Revival, 1770–1914: Religion, Class, and Social Conscience in Late-Victorian England*. Princeton, NJ: Princeton University Press, 1968.
Jorstad, Erling. *Being Religious in America: The Deepening Crisis over Public Faith*. Nashville: Abingdon, 1986.
———. *The Politics of Doomsday: Fundamentalists of the Far Right*. Nashville: Abingdon, 1970.
———. *The Politics of Moralism: The New Christian Right in American Life*. Minneapolis: Augsburg, 1981.
———. *Popular Religion in America: The Evangelical Voice*. Westport, CT: Greenwood, 1993.
Judd, Stephen. *Sydney Anglicans: A History of the Diocese*. Sydney: Anglican Information Office, 1987.
Kantzer, Kenneth S., ed. *Applying the Scriptures*. Grand Rapids: Zondervan, 1987.
Kaplan, Esther. *With God on Their Side: How Christian Fundamentalists trampled Science, Policy, and Democracy in George W. Bush's White House*. New York: New, 2004.
Katz, David S. *God's Last Words: Reading the English Bible from the Reformation to Fundamentalism*. New Haven, CT: Yale University Press, 2004.
Kaufmann, Walter, ed. *Basic Writings of Nietzsche*. New York: Modern Library, 1992.
Kay, William K. *Pentecostals in Britain*. Carlisle, UK: Paternoster, 2000.
Kay, William K., and Anne Dryer, eds. *Pentecostal and Charismatic Studies: A Reader*. London: SCM, 2004.
Kaye, Bruce N. *Conflict and the Practice of Christian Faith: The Anglican Experiment*. Sydney: Cascade, 2009.
———. *Re-inventing Anglicanism: A Vision of Confidence, Community and Engagement in Anglican Christianity*. Sydney: Church, 2004.
———. *Wonderfully and Confessedly Strange: Australian Essays in Anglican Ecclesiology*. Adelaide, Australia: Australasian Theological Forum, 2007.
Kendall, Robert T. *Holy Fire: A Balanced, Biblical Look at the Holy Spirit's Work in Our Lives*. Lake Mary, FL: Charisma, 2014.
———. *In Pursuit of His Glory*. Lake Mary, FL: Charisma, 2004.
Kengor, Paul. *God and George W. Bush: A Spiritual Life*. New York: Harper, 2004.
Kent, John H. S. *The End of the Line? The Development of Christian Theology in the Last Two Centuries*. London: SCM, 1982.
Kidd, Thomas S. *George Whitefield: America's Spiritual Founding Father*. New Haven, CT: Yale University Press, 2014.

———. *God of Liberty: A Religious History of the American Revolution*. New York: Basic, 2012.
———. *The Great Awakening: The Roots of Evangelical Christianity in Colonial America*. New Haven, CT: Yale University Press, 2007.
Kik, Marcellus J. [post-millennial]. *Matthew Twenty-Four: An Exposition*. Philadelphia: Presbyterian & Reformed, 1948.
———. *Revelation Twenty: An Exposition*. Philadelphia: Presbyterian & Reformed, 1955.
Kilde, Jeanne Halgren. *When Church Becomes Theatre: The Transformation of Evangelical Architecture and Worship in Nineteenth-Century America*. New York: Oxford University Press, 2005.
King, John. *The Evangelicals*. London: Hodder & Stoughton, 1969.
Kitchen, K. A. *Ancient Orient and Old Testament*. London: Tyndale, 1966.
———. *On the Reliability of the Old Testament*. Grand Rapids: Eerdmans, 2003.
Klauber, Martin I. *Between Reformed Scholasticism and Pan-Protestantism: Jean Alphonse Turretin (1671–1737) and Enlightened Orthodoxy in the Academy of Geneva*. Selinsgrove, PA: Susquehanna University Press, 1994.
Kline, Meredith G. *By Oath Consigned: A Reinterpretation of the Covenant Signs of Circumcision and Baptism*. Grand Rapids: Eerdmans, 1968.
———. *Glory in Our Midst: A Biblical-Theological Reading of Zechariah's Night Visions*. Eugene, OR: Wipf & Stock, 2001.
———. *God, Heaven and Har Magedon: A Covenantal Tale of Cosmos and Telos*. Eugene, OR: Wipf & Stock, 2006.
———. *Images of the Spirit*. Grand Rapids: Baker, 1980.
———. *The Structure of Biblical Authority*. Grand Rapids: Eerdmans, 1972.
———. *Treaty of the Great King: The Covenant Structure of Deuteronomy: Studies and Commentary*. Grand Rapids: Eerdmans, 1963.
Knox, John. *The Works of John Knox*, edited by David Laing. 6 vols. Edinburgh: James Thin, 1845.
Koss, Stephen. *Nonconformity in Modern British Politics*. London: Batsford, 1975.
Koyzis, David T. *Political Visions and Illusions: A Survey and Christian Critique of Contemporary Ideologies*. Downers Grove, IL: InterVarsity, 2003.
———. *We Answer to Another: Authority, Office, and the Image of God*. Eugene, OR: Pickwick, 2014.
Krattenmaker, Thomas. *The Evangelicals You Don't Know: Introducing the Next Generation of Christians*. Lanham, MD: Rowman & Littlefield, 2013.
Kraus, Clyde Norman. *Dispensationalism in America: Its Rise and Development*. Richmond, VA: Knox, 1958.
Kroeger, Richard Clark, and Catherine Clark Kroeger. *I Suffer Not a Woman: Rethinking I Timothy 2: 11–15 in Light of Ancient Evidence*. Grand Rapids: Baker, 1992.
Kruse, Kevin M. *One Nation Under God: How Corporate America Invented Christian America*. New York: Basic, 2015.
Kuhn, Karl Allen. *The Kingdom according to Luke and Acts: A Social, Literary, and Theological Introduction*. Grand Rapids: Baker, 2015.
Kuhn, Thomas S. *The Structure of Scientific Revolutions*. 2nd ed. Chicago: University of Chicago Press, 1970.
Kuyper, Abraham. *Lectures on Calvinism*. Grand Rapids: Eerdmans, 1931.
———. *The Problem of Poverty*, edited by James W. Skillen. Grand Rapids: Baker, 1991.

———. *The Work of the Holy Spirit*. New York: Funk and Wagnalls, 1898.
Kyle, Richard. *Evangelicalism: An Americanized Christianity*. New Brunswick, NJ: Transaction, 2006.
Laats, Adam. *Fundamentalism and Education in the Scopes Era: God, Darwin, and the Roots of America's Culture Wars*. New York: Palgrave Macmillan, 2010.
Lachman, David. *The Marrow Controversy, 1718–1723: An Historical and Theological Analysis*. Edinburgh: Rutherford, 1988.
Ladd, George Eldon [Classical Pre-millennial]. *Crucial Questions about the Kingdom of God*. Grand Rapids: Eerdmans, 1952.
———. *The Gospel of the Kingdom: Scriptural Studies in the Kingdom of God*. Grand Rapids: Eerdmans, 1959.
———. *Jesus and the Kingdom: The Eschatology of Biblical Realism*. New York: Harper & Row, 1964.
———. *Presence of the Future: The Eschatology of Biblical Realism*. Grand Rapids: Eerdmans, 1974.
LaHaye, Tim. *The Beginning of the End*. Carol Stream, IL: Tyndale, 1972.
LaHaye, Tim, and Jerry B. Jenkins. *Left Behind: A Novel of the Earth's Last Days*. Carol Stream, IL: Tyndale, 1995.
Lambert, Frank. *Inventing the Great Awakening*. Princeton, NJ: Princeton University Press, 1999.
———. *"Pedlar in Divinity": George Whitefield and the Transatlantic Revivals, 1737–1770*. Princeton, NJ: Princeton University Press, 1994.
Lamoureux, Denis O. *Evolutionary Creation: A Christian Approach to Evolution*. Eugene, OR: Wipf and Stock, 2008.
Lange, Stuart M. *A Rising Tide: Evangelical Christianity in New Zealand, 1930–1965*. Dunedin, New Zealand: Otago University Press, 2013.
Larkin, William J. *Culture and Biblical Hermeneutics: Interpreting and Applying the Authoritative Word in a Relativistic Age*. Grand Rapids: Baker, 1988.
Larsen, Timothy. "Defining and Locating Evangelicalism." In *The Cambridge Companion to Evangelical Theology*, edited by Timothy Larsen and Daniel T. Treier, 1–14. Cambridge: Cambridge University Press, 2007.
Larson, Edward J. *The Creation / Evolution Debate: Historical Perspectives*. Athens, GA: University of Georgia Press, 2007.
———. *Summer for the Gods: The Scopes Trial and America's Continuing Debate over Science and Religion*. New York: Basic, 2006.
Laurence, Anne, et al., eds. *John Bunyan and his England*. London: Hambledon, 2003.
Law, William. *A Serious Call to a Devout and Holy Life, Adapted to the State and Condition of all Orders of Christians*. London: William Innes, 1729.
Lawrence, David. *Heaven . . . It's Not the End of The World: The Biblical Promise of a New Earth*. London: Scripture Union, 1995.
Lee, Philip J. *Against the Protestant Gnostics*. New York: Oxford University Press, 1987.
Lee, Shayne, and Phillip Luke Sinitiere. *Holy Mavericks: Evangelical Innovators and the Spiritual Marketplace*. New York: New York University Press, 2009.
Lennox, John C. *God's Undertaker: Has Science Buried God?* Oxford: Lion, 2007.
Leonard, Bill J. *The Challenge of Being Baptist: Owning a Scandalous Past and an Uncertain Future*. Waco, TX: Baylor University Press, 2010.
Levenson, John D. *The Hebrew Bible, the Old Testament, and Historical Criticism: Jews and Christians in Biblical Studies*. Louisville, KY: Westminster John Knox, 1993.

Lewis, Clive Staples. *The Great Divorce: A Dream*. London: Geoffrey Bles, 1946.
―――. *Mere Christianity*. London: Geoffrey Bles, 1953.
―――. *Surprised by Joy*. London: Geoffrey Bles, 1955.
Lewis, Donald M. *The Origins of Christian Zionism: Lord Shaftesbury and Evangelical Support for a Jewish Homeland*. Cambridge: Cambridge University Press, 2009.
Lewis, Donald M., and Richard V. Pierard, eds. *Global Evangelicalism: Theology, History and Culture in Regional Perspective*. Downers Grove, IL: InterVarsity, 2015.
Lienesch, Michael. *In the Beginning: Fundamentalism, The Scopes Trial, and the Making of the Antievolution Movement*. Chapel Hill: University of North Carolina Press, 2009.
―――. *Redeeming America: Piety and Politics in the New Christian Right*. Chapel Hill: University of North Carolina Press, 1993.
Lindberg, David C., and Ronald L. Numbers, eds. *God and Nature: Historical Essays on the Encounter between Christianity and Science*. Berkeley, CA: University of California Press, 1986.
―――. *When Science and Christianity Meet*. Chicago: University of Chicago Press, 2003.
Lindsay, Michael D. *Faith in the Halls of Power: How Evangelicals Joined the American Elite*. New York: Oxford University Press, 2007.
Lindsell, Harold. *The Battle for the Bible*. Grand Rapids: Zondervan, 1976.
―――. *The Bible in the Balance*. Grand Rapids: Zondervan, 1979.
―――. *Park Street Prophet: A Life of Harold John Ockenga*. Wheaton: Van Kampen, 1951.
Lindsey, Hal [pre-millennial dispensationalist]. *The Apocalypse Code*. Palos Verdes, CA: Bantam, Doubleday, Dell, 1997.
―――. *The Final Battle*. Palos Verdes, CA: Western Front, 1995.
―――. *The 1980's: Countdown to Armageddon*. New York: Doubleday, Dell, 1981.
―――. *Planet Earth 2000 AD*. Palos Verdes, CA: Western Front, 1994.
―――. *Satan is Alive and Well on Planet Earth*. Grand Rapids: Zondervan, 1972.
―――. *The Terminal Generation*. New York: Doubleday, Dell, 1977.
―――. *There's A New World Coming: "A Prophetic Odyssey."* Ventura, CA: Vision House, 1973.
Lindsey, Hal, with C. C. Carlson [pre-millennial dispensationalists]. *The Late Great Planet Earth*. Grand Rapids: Zondervan, 1970; London: Marshall, Morgan & Scott, 1971.
Little, Bruce A. *Francis Schaeffer: A Mind and Heart for God*. Phillipsburg, NJ: Presbyterian & Reformed, 2010.
Little, Thomas J. *The Origins of Southern Evangelicalism: Religion, Revival, and the Southern Carolina Low Country, 1670–1760*. Columbia: University of South Carolina Press, 2013.
Livingstone, David N. *Adam's Ancestors: Race, Religion, and the Politics of Human Origins*. Baltimore, MD: Johns Hopkins University Press, 2008.
―――. *Darwin's Forgotten Defenders: The Encounter Between Evangelical Theology and Evolutionary Thought*. Grand Rapids: Eerdmans, 1987.
―――. *Dealing With Darwin: Place, Politics, and Rhetoric in Religious Engagements with Evolution*. Baltimore, MD: Johns Hopkins University Press, 2014.
Livingstone, David N., et al., eds. *Evangelicals and Science in Historical Perspective*. New York: Oxford University Press, 1999.

Lloyd, Gareth. *Charles Wesley and the Struggle for Methodist Identity*. New York: Oxford University Press, 2007.
Lloyd, Mark. *Pioneers of Prime Time Religion: Jerry Falwell, Rex Humbard, Oral Roberts*. Dubuque, IA: Kendall Hunt, 1988.
Lloyd-Jones, D. M. *Knowing the Times*. Edinburgh: Banner of Truth, 1989.
———. *The Puritans: their Origins and Successors*. Edinburgh: Banner of Truth, 1987.
Loane, Marcus Lawrence. *Archbishop Mowll: The Biography of Howard West Kilvinton Mowll, Archbishop of Sydney and Primate of Australia*. London: Hodder & Stoughton, 1960.
———. *Cambridge and the Evangelical Succession*. London: Lutterworth, 1952.
———. *John Charles Ryle, 1816–1900: A Short Biography*. London: James Clarke, 1953.
———. *Oxford and the Evangelical Succession*. London: Lutterworth, 1950.
Loftus, John W. *Why I Became an Atheist: A Former Preacher Rejects Christianity*. Amherst, NY: Prometheus, 2008.
———. *Why I Rejected Christianity: A Former Apologist Explains*. Victoria, Canada: Trafford, 2007.
Long, Kathryn Theresa. *The Revival of 1857–58: Interpreting an American Religious Awakening*. New York: Oxford University Press, 1998.
Long, Michael G., ed. *The Legacy of Billy Graham: Critical Reflections on America's Greatest Evangelist*. Louisville, KY: Westminster John Knox, 2008.
Longfield, Bradley J. *The Presbyterian Controversy: Fundamentalists, Modernists and Moderates*. New York: Oxford University Press, 1991.
Lovejoy, Arthur Oncken. *The Great Chain of Being: A Study of the History of an Idea*. Cambridge, MA: Harvard University Press, 1936.
Lovelace, Richard F. *The American Pietism of Cotton Mather: Origins of American Evangelicalism*. Grand Rapids: Eerdmans, 1979.
———. *Dynamics of Spiritual Life: An Evangelical Theology of Renewal*. Exeter, UK: Paternoster, 1981.
Lubenow, Marvin L. *Bones of Contention: A Creationist Assessment of Human Fossils*. Revised ed. Grand Rapids: Baker, 2004.
Lynerd, Benjamin J. *Republican Theology: The Civil Religion of American Evangelicals*. New York: Oxford University Press, 2015.
MacArthur, John F. *Charismatic Chaos*. Grand Rapids: Zondervan, 1992.
———. *Strange Fire: The Danger of Offending the Holy Spirit with Counterfeit Worship*. Nashville: Thomas Nelson, 2013.
Macartney, Clarence Edward Noble. *Shall unbelief win?: A Reply to Dr. Fosdick (For the Faith)*. Philadelphia: Hanf, 1922.
Machen, J. Gresham. *The Christian View of Man*. London: Banner of Truth, 1965.
———. *Christianity and Liberalism*. Grand Rapids: Eerdmans, 1923.
———. *The Origin of Paul's Religion*. New York: Macmillan, 1921.
———. *The Virgin Birth of Christ*. New York: Harper, 1930.
Machin, G. I. T. *Politics and the Churches in Great Britain 1832 to 1868*. London: Oxford University Press, 1977.
Mack, Phyllis. *Heart Religion in the British Enlightenment: Gender and Emotion in Early Methodism*. New York: Cambridge University Press, 2008.
MacKay, Donald MacCrimmon. *Clockwork Image: Christian Perspective on Science*. Leicester, UK: Inter-Varsity, 1974.
MacKenzie, Robert. *John Brown of Haddington*. London: Hodder & Stoughton, 1964.

Macleod, John. *Scottish Theology in Relation to Church History.* Edinburgh: Free Church of Scotland, 1943.
MacMaster, Richard K., and Donald R. Jacobs. *A Gentle Wind of God: The Influence of the East Africa Revival.* Harrisonburg, VA: Herald, 2006.
MacPherson, David. *The Incredible Cover-Up: The True Story of the Pre-Tribulation Rapture.* Medford, OR: Omega, 1975.
Maddox, Marion. *God under Howard: The Rise of the Religious Right in Australian Politics.* Sydney: Allen & Unwin, 2005.
Mahaffey, Jerome Dean. *The Accidental Revolutionary: George Whitefield and the Creation of America.* Waco, TX: Baylor University Press, 2011.
Makovsky, Michael. *Churchill's Promised Land: Zionism and Statecraft.* New Haven, CT: Yale University Press, 2007.
Makower, Katharine. *The Coming of the Rain: The Life of Dr. Joe Church—A Personal Account of Revival in Rwanda.* Carlisle, UK: Paternoster, 1999.
Mandeville, Bernard. *The Fable of the Bees: or Private Vices, Publick Benefits by Bernard Mandeville, with a Commentary, Critical, Historical and Explanatory*, edited by F. B. Kaye [pseud. for Frederick Benjamin Kugelman]. Oxford: Oxford University Press, 1924.
Manetsch, Scott M. *Theodore Beza and the Quest for Peace in France, 1572–1598.* Leiden: Brill, 2000.
Mangum, R. Todd. *The Dispensational-Covenantal Rift: The Fissuring of American Evangelical Theology from 1936–1944.* Eugene, OR: Wipf & Stock, 2007.
Mangum, R. Todd, and Mark Sweetman. *The Scofield Bible: Its History and Impact on the Evangelical Church.* Carlisle, UK: Paternoster, 2009.
Manning, Bernard Lord. *The Hymns of Wesley and Watts: Five Informal Papers.* London: Epworth, 1942.
―――. *The Protestant Dissenting Deputies.* Cambridge: Cambridge University Press, 1952.
Mansfield, Stephen. *Derek Prince: A Biography.* Lake Mary, FL: Charisma, 2005.
Manwaring, Randle. *From Controversy to Co-existence: Evangelicals in the Church of England, 1914–1980.* Cambridge: Cambridge University Press, 1985.
Marcel, Pierre Charles. *The Christian Philosophy of Herman Dooyeweerd.* I: *The Transcendental Critique of Theoretical Thought*, II: *The General Theory of Law Spheres.* 2 vols. Aalten, The Netherlands: Wordbridge, 2013.
Marks, John. *Reasons to Believe: One Man's Journey Among the Evangelicals and the Faith He Left Behind.* San Francisco: Harper Collins, 2008.
Marley, David John. *Pat Robertson: An American Life.* Lanham, MD: Rowman & Littlefield, 2007.
Marlow, Hilary. *Biblical Prophets and Contemporary Environmental Ethics.* New York: Oxford University Press, 2010.
Marquardt, Manfred. *John Wesley's Social Ethics: Praxis and Principles.* Nashville: Abingdon, 1992.
Marquart, Kurt E. *Anatomy of an Explosion: Missouri in Lutheran Perspective.* Fort Wayne, IN: Concordia Theological Seminary, 1977.
Marsden, George M. "Defining Fundamentalism." *Christian Scholar's Review* 1 (1971) 141–151.
―――. "Demythologizing Evangelicalism: A Review of Donald W. Dayton's *Discovering an Evangelical Heritage.*" *Christian Scholar's Review* 7 (1977) 203–7.

———. *The Evangelical Mind and the New School Presbyterian Experience: A Case Study of Thought and Theology in Nineteenth-Century America*. New Haven, CT: Yale University Press, 1970.

———. *Fundamentalism and American Culture: The Shaping of Twentieth-Century Evangelicalism, 1870-1925*. New York: Oxford University Press, 1980.

———. "Fundamentalism as an American Phenomenon, A Comparison with English Evangelicalism." *Church History* 46 (1977) 215-32.

———. *Jonathan Edwards: A Life*. New Haven, CT: Yale University Press, 2003.

———. *Reforming Fundamentalism: Fuller Seminary and the New Evangelicalism*. Grand Rapids: Eerdmans, 1987.

———. "Response to Don Dayton." *Christian Scholar's Review* 23 (1993) 34-40.

———. *The Twilight of the American Enlightenment: the 1950s and the Crisis of Liberal Belief*. New York: Basic, 2014.

———. *Understanding Fundamentalism and Evangelicalism*. Grand Rapids: Eerdmans, 1991.

Marsden, George M., ed. *Evangelicalism and Modern America*. Grand Rapids: Eerdmans, 1984.

Marsh, Charles. *Wayward Christian Soldiers: Freeing the Gospel from Political Captivity*. New York: Oxford University Press, 2007.

Marshall, I. Howard. *Biblical Inspiration*. Grand Rapids: Eerdmans, 1982.

Marshall, Paul. *Their Blood Cries Out: The Worldwide Tragedy of Modern Christians Who Are Dying for Their Faith*. Dallas, TX: Word, 1997.

———. *Thine is the Kingdom: A Biblical Perspective on the Nature of Government and Politics Today*. Basingstoke, UK: Marshall, Morgan & Scott, 1984.

Marshall, Paul, with Lela Gilbert. *Heaven is Not My Home: Living in the Now of God's Creation*. Nashville: Word, 1998.

Martin, David. *Pentecostalism: The World Their Parish*. Oxford: Blackwell, 2002.

Martin, Linette. *Hans Rookmaaker: A Biography*. Downers Grove, IL: InterVarsity, 1979.

Martin, William. *A Prophet with Honor: The Billy Graham Story*. New York: William Morrow, 1991.

———. *With God on Our Side: The Rise of the Religious Right in America*. New York: Broadway, 1996.

Martz, Larry. *Ministry of Greed: The Inside Story of the Televangelists and their Holy Wars*. London: Weidenfeld & Nicolson, 1988.

Mason, J. C. S. *The Moravian Church and the Missionary Awakening in England, 1760-1800*. Woodbridge, UK: Boydell & Brewer, 2001.

Massa, Mark S. *Charles Augustus Briggs and the Crisis of Historical Criticism*. Minneapolis: Fortress, 1990.

Masters, Peter. *The Healing Epidemic* [with additional section: "A Medical View of Miraculous Healing" by Verna Wright]. London: Wakeman, 1988.

Masters, Peter, and John C. Whitcomb. *The Charismatic Phenomenon*. London: Wakeman, 1982.

Mathias, Peter. *The First Industrial Nation: The Economic History of Britain, 1700-1914*. 2nd ed. London: Routledge, 1983.

Mathison, Keith A. [postmillennial]. *Dispensationalism: Rightly Dividing the People of God?* Phillipsburg, NJ: Presbyterian & Reformed, 1995.

———. *Postmillennialism: An Eschatology of Hope*. Phillipsburg, NJ: Presbyterian & Reformed, 1999.

Matthews, H. F. *Methodism and the Education of the People*. London: Epworth, 1949.
Maughan, Steven S. *Mighty England Do Good: Culture, Faith, Empire, and World in the Foreign Missions of the Church of England, 1850-1915*. Grand Rapids: Eerdmans, 2014.
Maze, Scott. *Theodorus Frelinghuysen's Evangelism: Catalyst to the First Great Awakening*. Grand Rapids: Reformation Heritage, 2011.
McAlpine, Robin. *Post Charismatic?: Where Are We Now? Where Have We Come From? Where Are We Going?* Colorado Springs, CO: Cook, 2008.
McCaslands, David. *Oswald Chambers: Abandoned to God: The Life Story of the Author of My Utmost for His Highest*. Grand Rapids: Discovery, 1998.
McClung, Grant, ed. *Azusa Street and Beyond: 100 Years of Commentary on the Global Pentecostal / Charismatic Movement*. Orlando, FL: Bridge-Logos, 2005.
McConnachie, John. "The Teaching of Karl Barth: A New Positive Movement in German Theology." *Hibbert Journal* 25 (1926-27) 385-400.
McCormack, Bruce L., and Clifford B. Anderson, eds. *Karl Barth and American Evangelicalism*. Grand Rapids: Eerdmans, 2011.
McDermott, Gerald R. *Jonathan Edwards Confronts the Gods: Christian theology, Enlightenment Religion, and Non-Christian Faiths*. New York: Oxford University Press, 2000.
McGirr, Lisa. *Suburban Warriors: The Origins of the New American Right*. Princeton, NJ: Princeton University Press, 2001.
McGowan, Andrew Thomson Blake. *The Divine Authenticity of Scripture: Retrieving an Evangelical Heritage*. Downers Grove, IL: InterVarsity, 2007.
McGowan, Chris. *In the Beginning: A Scientist Shows Why the Creationists Are Wrong*. Amherst, NY: Prometheus, 1984.
McGrath, Alister. *Evangelicalism and the Future of Christianity*. Downers Grove, IL: InterVarsity, 1995.
———. *In the Beginning: The Story of the King James Bible and How it Changed a Nation, a Language, and a Culture*. London: Hodder & Stoughton, 2001.
———. *To Know and Serve God: A Biography of James I. Packer*. London: Hodder & Stoughton, 1997.
McIlhenny, Ryan C., ed. *Kingdoms Apart: Engaging the Two Kingdoms Perspective*. Phillipsburg, NJ: Presbyterian & Reformed, 2012.
McKay, William Paul, and Ken Abraham. *Billy: The Untold Story of a Young Billy Graham and the Test of Faith that Almost Changed Everything*. Nashville: Thomas Nelson, 2008.
McKim, Donald K., ed. *The Authoritative Word: Essays on the Nature of Scripture*. Grand Rapids: Eerdmans, 1983.
McLaren, Brian. *A Generous Orthodoxy*. Grand Rapids: Zondervan, 2004.
McLeod, Hugh. *The Religious Crisis of the 1960s*. Oxford: Oxford University Press, 2007.
McNeile, Hugh. *England's Protest is England's Shield, For the Battle is the Lord's*. London: Hatchard, 1829.
———. *Lectures on the Church of England*. London: Hatchard, 1840.
———. *Letters to a Friend who has Felt it his Duty to Secede from the Church of England*. London: Hatchard, 1834.
———. *Popular Lectures on the Prophesies Relative to the Jewish Nation*. London: Hatchard, 1830.

M'Crie, Thomas. *The Life of Andrew Melville Containing Illustrations of the Ecclesiastical and Literary History of Scotland*. 2 vols. Edinburgh: William Blackwood, 1824.
McVicar, Michael J. *Christian Reconstruction: R.J. Rushdoony and American Religious Conservatism*. Chapel Hill: University of North Carolina Press, 2015.
Mekkes, Johan P. A. *Creation, Revelation, and Philosophy*. Sioux Center, IA: Dordt College, 2010.
Metzger, Bruce Manning. *Reminiscences of an Octogenarian*. Peabody, MA: Hendrickson, 2007.
———. *The Text of the New Testament: Its Transmission, Corruption and Restoration*. 2nd ed. New York: Oxford University Press, 1968.
Meyer, Stephen C. *Signature in the Cell: DNA and the Evidence for Intelligent Design*. San Francisco: Harper One, 2009.
Middleton, J. Richard. *The Liberating Image: The Imago Dei in Genesis 1*. Grand Rapids: Brazos, 2005.
———. *A New Heaven and a New Earth: Reclaiming Biblical Eschatology*. Grand Rapids: Baker, 2014.
Miller, Calvin. *The Vanishing Evangelical: Saving the Church from Its Own Success and Restoring What Really Matters*. Grand Rapids: Baker, 2013.
Miller, Donald E., et al., eds. *Spirit and Power: The Global Impact of Pentecostalism*. New York: Oxford University Press, 2013.
Miller, Keith B., ed. *Perspectives on an Evolving Creation*. Grand Rapids: Eerdmans, 2003.
Miller, Stephen P. *The Age of Evangelicalism: America's Born-Again Years*. New York: Oxford University Press, 2014.
———. *Billy Graham and the Rise of the Republican South*. Philadelphia: University of Pennsylvania Press, 2009.
Milton, John. *Complete Poetry and Selected Prose of John Milton*. New York: Random House, 1950.
Mitchel, Patrick. *Evangelicalism and National Identity in Ulster, 1921–1998*. New York: Oxford University Press, 2004.
Moberg, David O. *The Great Reversal: Evangelicalism versus Social Concern*. London: Scripture Union, 1973.
Moen, Matthew C. *The Christian Right and Congress*. Tuscaloosa: University of Alabama Press, 1989.
———. *The Transformation of the Christian Right*. Tuscaloosa: University of Alabama Press, 1992.
Mol, Hans. *The Faith of Australians*. Sydney: George Allen & Unwin, 1985.
Montague, Ashley, ed. *Science and Creationism*. New York: Oxford University Press, 1984.
Moore, James R. *The Post-Darwinian Controversies: A Study of the Protestant Struggle to Come to Terms with Darwin in Great Britain and America, 1870–1900*. Cambridge: Cambridge University Press, 1979.
Moore, Seth David. *The Shepherding Movement: Controversy and Charismatic Ecclesiology*. London: T. & T. Clark, 2003.
Moore, Terry Michael. *Consider the Lilies: A Plea for Creational Theology*. Phillipsburg, NJ: Presbyterian & Reformed, 2005.
Moorhead, James H. *World Without End: Mainstream American Protestant Visions of the Last Things, 1880–1925*. Bloomington: Indiana University Press, 1999.

More, Hannah. *Thoughts On The Importance Of The Manners Of The Great, To General Society: And An Estimate Of The Religion Of The Fashionable World*. London: Cadell, 1788.

Moreton, Bethany. *To Serve God and Wal-Mart: The Making of Christian Free Enterprise*. Cambridge, MA: Harvard University Press, 2009.

Morgan, Derec Llwyd. *The Great Awakening in Wales*. London: Epworth, 1988.

Morison, Frank [pseud. for Albert Henry Ross]. *Who Moved the Stone?* London: Faber & Faber, 1930.

Morris, Henry M. *The Bible and Modern Science*. Chicago: Moody, 1968.

———. *Biblical Catastrophism And Geology*. Philadelphia: Presbyterian & Reformed, 1963.

———. *Biblical Cosmology and Modern Science*. Nutley, NJ: Craig, 1970.

———. *Evolution and the Modern Christian*. Philadelphia: Presbyterian & Reformed, 1967.

———. *The Genesis Record: A Scientific and Devotional Commentary on the Book of Beginnings*. Grand Rapids: Baker, 1976.

———. *The God Who Is Real: A Creationist Approach to Evangelism and Missions*. Grand Rapids: Baker, 1988.

———. *History of Modern Creationism*. San Diego, CA: Master, 1984.

———. *The Long War Against God: The History and Impact of the Creation / Evolution Conflict*. Grand Rapids: Baker, 1989.

———. *The Remarkable Birth of Planet Earth*. Grand Rapids: Bethany, 1972.

———. *The Twilight of Evolution*. Grand Rapids: Baker, 1972.

Morris, Henry M., and Duane Gish, eds. *The Battle for Creation*. San Diego, CA: Creation-Life, 1976.

Morris, Henry M., and John C. Whitcomb. *The Genesis Flood: The Biblical Record and Its Scientific Implications*. Philadelphia: Presbyterian & Reformed, 1961.

Morris, John. *The Young Earth: The Real History of the Earth—Past, Present, and Future*. San Diego, CA: Master, 2007.

Morris, Tim, and Don Petcher. *Science and Grace: God's Reign in the Natural Sciences*. Wheaton: Crossway, 2006.

Moule, Handley C. G. *A Memoir of T.D. Harford-Battersby: Together with Some Account of the Keswick Convention*. London: Seeley, 1890.

Mouw, Richard J. *Abraham Kuyper: A Short and Personal Introduction*. Grand Rapids: Eerdmans, 2011.

———. *Called to the Life of the Mind: Some Advice for Evangelical Scholars*. Grand Rapids: Eerdmans, 2015.

———. *The Challenges of Cultural Discipleship: Essays in the Line of Abraham Kuyper*. Grand Rapids: Eerdmans, 2012.

———. *When the Kings Come Marching In: Isaiah and the New Jerusalem*. Grand Rapids: Eerdmans, 1983.

Mouw, Richard J., and Mark A. Noll. *Wonderful Words of Life: Hymns in American Protestant History and Theology*. Grand Rapids: Eerdmans, 2004.

Muether, John R. *Cornelius Van Til: Reformed Apologist and Churchman*. Philipsburg, NJ: Presbyterian & Reformed, 2008.

Mullin, Robert Bruce. *The Puritan As Yankee: A Life of Horace Bushnell*. Grand Rapids: Eerdmans, 2002.

Murphy, Nancey. *Beyond Liberalism and Fundamentalism: How Modern and Postmodern Philosophy Set the Theological Agenda*. London: T. & T. Clark, 1996.
Murray, Iain. *Australian Christian Life from 1788: An Introduction*. Edinburgh: Banner of Truth, 1988.
———. *D. Martyn Lloyd-Jones: The Fight of Faith, 1939-1981*. Edinburgh: Banner of Truth, 1990.
———. *D. Martyn Lloyd-Jones: The First Forty Years, 1899-1939*. Edinburgh: Banner of Truth, 1982.
———. *Evangelicalism Divided: A Record of Crucial Change in the Years 1950 to 2000*. Edinburgh: Banner of Truth, 2000.
———. *The Forgotten Spurgeon*. London: Banner of Truth, 1966.
———. *Jonathan Edwards: A New Biography*. Edinburgh: Banner of Truth, 1987.
———. *The Life of Arthur W. Pink*. Revised ed. Edinburgh: Banner of Truth, 2004.
———. *Revival and Revivalism: The Making and Marring of American Evangelicalism, 1750-1858*. Edinburgh: Banner of Truth, 1994.
———. *Wesley and the Men Who Followed*. Edinburgh: Banner of Truth, 2003.
Neal, Daniel. *History of the Puritans; or, The Rise, Principles, and Sufferings of the Protestant Dissenters, to the Glorious Era of the Revolution*, edited by Edward Parsons. 2 vols. London: Longman, Hurst, Rees, Orme and Brown, 1811.
Neatby, W. B. *A History of the Plymouth Brethren*. London: Hodder & Stoughton, 1901.
Nelson, Rudolph. *The Making and Unmaking of an Evangelical Mind: The Case of Edward John Carnell*. New York: Cambridge University Press, 1987.
Neuhaus, Richard John, ed. *American Apostasy: The Triumph of "Other" Gospels*. Grand Rapids: Eerdmans, 1989.
New, Alfred H. *The Coronet and the Cross: or Memorials of the Right Hon. Selina Countess of Huntingdon Compiled from Authentic Documents*. London: Partridge, 1857.
Newbigin, Lesslie. *Foolishness to the Greeks: The Gospel and Western Culture*. Grand Rapids: Eerdmans, 1988.
———. *The Gospel in a Pluralist Society*. Grand Rapids: Eerdmans, 1989.
———. *The Reunion of the Church: A Defence of the South India Scheme*. London: SCM, 1948.
Newsome, David. *The Parting of Friends: A Study of the Wilberforces and Henry Manning*. London: John Murray, 1966.
Nias, J. C. S. *Gorham and the Bishop of Exeter*. London: SPCK, 1951.
Nicholson, Ernest. *The Pentateuch in the Twentieth Century: The Legacy of Julius Wellhausen*. Oxford: Oxford University Press, 1998.
Nicole, Roger R. "The Inspiration and Authority of Scripture: J. D. G. Dunn versus B. B. Warfield." *Churchman* 97/3 (1984) 198-215, 98/1 (1984) 7-27, 98/3 (1984) 198-208.
Nicole, Roger R., and J. Ramsey Michaels, eds. *Inerrancy and Common Sense*. Grand Rapids: Baker, 1980.
Nicolson, Adam. *God's Secretaries: The Making of the King James Bible*. New York: Harper Collins, 2003.
Niebuhr, H. Richard. *The Kingdom of God in America*. New York: Harper & Row, 1937. Fiftieth anniversary ed.: Middletown, CT: Wesleyan University Press, 1988.
Nischan, Bodo. *Lutherans and Calvinists in the Age of Confessionalism*. Aldershot, UK: Ashgate, 1999.
Nolan, William A. *Healing: A Doctor in Search of a Miracle*. New York: Random, 1974.

Noll, Mark A. *American Evangelical Christianity: An Introduction*. Oxford: Blackwell, 2001.
———. *America's God: From Jonathan Edwards to Abraham Lincoln*. New York: Oxford University Press, 2002.
———. *Between Faith and Criticism: Evangelicals, Scholarship, and the Bible in America*. 2nd ed. Grand Rapids: Baker, 1991.
———. *Christians in the American Revolution*. Grand Rapids: Eerdmans, 1977.
———. *The Civil War as a Theological Crisis*. Chapel Hill: University of North Carolina Press, 2006.
———. "Common Sense Traditions and American Evangelical Thought." *American Quarterly* 37 (Summer 1985) 216–238.
———. *God and Mammon: Protestants, Money, and the Market, 1790–1860*. New York: Oxford University Press, 2001.
———. *Jesus Christ and the Life of the Mind*. Grand Rapids: Eerdmans, 2012.
———. *The Old Religion in a New World: The History of North American Christianity*. Grand Rapids: Eerdmans, 2002.
———. *One Nation Under God? Christian Faith and Political Action in America*. San Francisco: Harper & Row, 1988.
———. *Princeton and the Republic, 1768–1822: The Search for a Christian Enlightenment in the Era of Samuel Stanhope Smith*. Princeton, NJ: Princeton University Press, 1989.
———. *The Rise of Evangelicalism: The Age of Edwards, Whitefield and the Wesleys*. A History of Evangelicalism: People, Movements and Ideas in the English-Speaking World, Vol. I. Downers Grove, IL: InterVarsity, 2003.
———. *The Scandal of the Evangelical Mind*. Grand Rapids: Eerdmans, 1996.
———. *Where Shall my Wond'ring Soul Begin?: The Landscape of Evangelical Piety and Thought*. Grand Rapids: Eerdmans, 2000.
Noll, Mark A., ed. *The Princeton Theology, 1812–1921: Scripture, Science, and Theological Methodism from Archibald Alexander to Benjamin Breckinridge Warfield*. Grand Rapids: Baker, 1983.
Noll, Mark A., et al. *The Search for Christian America*. Westchester, IL: Crossway, 1983.
Noll, Mark A., and David N. Livingstone, eds. *Evolution, Science, and Scripture, Selected Writings, by B. B. Warfield*. Grand Rapids: Baker, 2000.
Noll, Mark A., and David W. Bebbington, eds. *Evangelicalism: Comparative Studies of Popular Protestantism in North America, the British Isles, and Beyond, 1700–1990*. New York: Oxford University Press, 1994.
Northcott, Michael. *An Angel Directs the Storm: Apocalyptic Religion and American Empire*. London: Tauris, 2004.
Norton, David. *The King James Bible: A Short History from Tyndale to Today*. Cambridge and New York: Cambridge University Press, 2011.
Numbers, Ronald L. *The Creationists: The Evolution of Scientific Creationism*. Berkeley, CA: University of California Press, 1992. Revised ed.: *The Creationists: From Scientific Creationism to Intelligent Design*. Cambridge, MA: Harvard University Press, 2006.
———. *Science and Christianity in Pulpit and Pew*. New York: Oxford University Press, 2007.
Oberman, Heiko Augustinus. *Luther: Man between God and the Devil*. New Haven, CT: Yale University Press, 1989.

———. *The Two Reformations: The Journey from the Last Days to the New World.* New Haven, CT: Yale University Press, 2003.
O'Brian, P. T., and D. G. Peterson, eds. *God Who is Rich in Mercy: Essays Presented to David Broughton Knox.* Sydney: Lancer, 1986.
Oden, Thomas C. *The Rebirth of Orthodoxy: Signs of New Life in Christianity.* San Francisco: Harper One, 2003.
Oldroyd, David R. *Thinking about the Earth: a History of Ideas in Geology.* Cambridge, MA: Harvard University Press, 1996.
Oliver, William H. *Prophets and Millennialists: The Uses of Biblical Prophecy in England from the 1790s to the 1840s.* Auckland, New Zealand: Auckland University Press, 1978.
Olson, Roger E. "The Reality of Evangelicalism: A Response to Michael S. Horton." *Christian Scholar's Review* 31 (2001) 157–62.
———. *Reformed and Always Reforming: the Postconservative Approach to Evangelical Theology.* Grand Rapids: Baker, 2007.
Olson, Steve. *Mapping Human History: Discovering the Past Through Our Genes.* Boston: Houghton, Mifflin, 2002.
Opie, John. *Jonathan Edwards and the Enlightenment.* New York: Heath, 1969.
Orr, James. *The Christian View of God and the World as Centering in the Incarnation.* Edinburgh: Andrew Elliot, 1897.
———. *The Problem of the Old Testament Considered with Reference to Recent Criticism.* London: Nisbet, 1907.
———. *Revelation and Inspiration.* London: Gerald Duckworth, 1910.
Orthodox Presbyterian Church. *The Standards of Government Discipline and Worship of The Orthodox Presbyterian Church.* Philadelphia: Committee on the Constitution of the Orthodox Presbyterian Church, 1941.
Osborn, H. H. *Pioneers in the East African Revival.* Winchester, UK: Apologia, 2000.
Osborne, Eric. *The Beginning of Christian Philosophy.* Cambridge: Cambridge University Press, 1981.
———. *The Emergence of Christian Theology.* Cambridge: Cambridge University Press, 1993.
———. *Tertullian: First Theologian of the West.* Cambridge: Cambridge University Press, 1997.
Overman, Dean L. *A Case Against Accident and Self-Organization.* Lanham, MD: Rowman & Littlefield, 2001.
Packer, James I. *Beyond the Battle for the Bible.* Westchester, IL: Cornerstone, 1980.
———. *The Evangelical Anglican Identity Problem: An Analysis.* Oxford: Latimer, 1978.
———. *Evangelism and the Sovereignty of God.* London: Inter-Varsity, 1961.
———. *Faithfulness and Holiness: The Witness of J. C. Ryle.* Wheaton: Crossway, 2002.
———.*'Fundamentalism and the Word of God' Some Evangelical Principles.* London: Inter-Varsity Fellowship, 1958.
———. *God Has Spoken: Revelation and the Bible.* London: Hodder & Stoughton, 1965.
———. "Hermeneutics and Biblical Authority." *Themelios* 1 (1975) 3–12.
———. *In Step with the Spirit.* Grand Rapids: Revell, 1984.
———. "'Keswick' and the Reformed Doctrine of Sanctification." *Evangelical Quarterly* 27/3 (1955) 153–167.
———. *Knowing God.* Downers Grove, IL: InterVarsity, 1973.

———. *A Quest for Godliness: The Puritan Vision of the Christian Life*. Wheaton: Crossway, 1994.

Packer, James I., ed. *All in Each Place: Towards Reunion in England*. Abingdon, UK: Marcham Manor, 1965.

Parker, Kenneth L., and Erick H. Moser. Eds. *The Rise of Historical Consciousness Among the Christian Churches*. Studies in Religion and Social Order. Lanham, MD: University Press of America, 2013.

Patterson, Paige. *Anatomy of a Reformation: The Southern Baptist Convention 1978–2004*. Fort Worth, TX: Southwestern Baptist Theological Seminary, 2005.

Paul, Robert S. *The Lord Protector: Religion and Politics in the Life of Oliver Cromwell*. London: Lutterworth, 1955.

Payne, Philip Barton. *Man and Woman, One in Christ: An Exegetical and Theological Study of Paul's Letters*. Grand Rapids: Zondervan, 2009.

Peck, Janice. *The Gods of Televangelism*. New York: Hampton, 1993.

Peck, John R., and Charles Strohmer. *Uncommon Sense: God's Wisdom for our Complex and Changing World*. London: SPCK, 1998.

Pelikan, Jaroslav. *Interpreting the Bible and the Constitution*. New Haven, CT: Yale University Press, 2004.

Pennock, Robert T., ed. *Intelligent Design Creationism and its Critics: Philosophical, Theological and Scientific Perspectives*. Cambridge, MA: Massachusetts Institute of Technology, 2001.

Pentecost, J. Dwight [pre-millennial dispensationalist]. *Things to Come: A Study in Biblical Eschatology*. Findlay, OH: Dunham, 1958.

Pestana, Carla Gardina. *Protestant Empire: Religion and the Making of the British Atlantic World*. Philadelphia: University of Pennsylvania Press, 2009.

Phillips, John Bertram. *Four Prophets: Amos—Hosea—First Isaiah—Micah: A Modern Translation from the Hebrew*. London: Geoffrey Bles, 1963.

———. *The New Testament in Modern English*. London: Geoffrey Bles, 1958.

———. *The Ring of Truth: A Translator's Testimony*. London: Hodder & Stoughton, 1967.

Phillips, Kevin. *American Theocracy: The Peril and Politics of Radical Religion, Oil, and Borrowed Money in the 21st Century*. New York: Viking, 2006.

Pickering, Ernest D. *The Tragedy of Compromise: The Origin and Impact of the New Evangelicalism*. Greenville, SC: Bob Jones University Press, 2000.

Piggin, Stuart. *Evangelical Christianity in Australia: Spirit, Word and World*. Melbourne: Oxford University Press, 1996.

Pinnock, Clark H. *The Scripture Principle*. San Francisco: Harper & Row, 1984.

Pinnock, Clark H., and Barry L. Callen. *The Scripture Principle: Reclaiming the Full Authority of the Bible*. Grand Rapids: Baker, 2006.

Podmore, Colin. *The Moravian Church in England, 1728–1760*. Oxford: Oxford University Press, 1998.

Poole-Connor, E. J. *The Apostasy of English Nonconformity*. London: Thyne, 1933.

———. *Evangelicalism in England*. Worthing, UK: Walter, 1951.

Popma, K. J. *A Battle for Righteousness: The Message of the Book of Job*. Belleville, Canada: Essence, 1998.

Porter, Andrew. *The Imperial Horizon of British Protestant Missions, 1880–1914*. Grand Rapids: Eerdmans, 2003.

Potter, G. R. *Zwingli*. Cambridge: Cambridge University Press, 1976.

Poythress, Vern S. *Understanding Dispensationalists*. 2nd ed. Phillipsburg, NJ: Presbyterian & Reformed, 1994.
Pressler, Paul. *A Hill on Which to Die: One Southern Baptist's Journey*. Revised ed. Nashville: Broadman & Holman, 2002.
Price, George McCready. *Evolutionary Geology and The New Catastrophism*. Mountain View, CA: Pacific, 1926.
———. *The Fundamentals of Geology and Their Bearings on the Doctrine of a Literal Creation*. Mountain View, CA: Pacific, 1913.
———. *Illogical Geology: The Weakest Point in the Evolution Theory*. Los Angeles: Modern Heretic, 1906.
———. *The New Geology*. Mountain View, CA: Pacific, 1923.
———. *The Phantom of Organic Evolution*. New York: Revell, 1924.
———. *The Predicament of Evolution*. Nashville: Southern, 1925.
Quebedeaux, Richard. *The Worldly Evangelicals*. New York: Harper Collins, 1980.
Rack, Henry D. *Reasonable Enthusiast: John Wesley and the Rise of Methodism*. London: Epworth, 1989.
Radosh, Allis and Ronald. *A Safe Haven: Harry S. Truman and the Founding of Israel*. New York: Harper Collins, 2009.
Radosh, Daniel. *Rapture Ready! Adventures in the Parallel Universe of Christian Pop Culture*. New York: Scribner, 2008.
Ramm, Bernard. *The Christian View of Science and Scripture*. Grand Rapids: Eerdmans, 1954.
Randal, Kelvin. *Evangelicals Etcetera: Conflict and Conviction in the Church of England's Parties*. Aldershot, UK: Ashgate, 2005.
Randall, Ian M. *Educating Evangelicalism: The Origins, Development and Impact of London Bible College*. Carlisle, UK: Paternoster, 2000.
———. *Evangelical Experiences: A Study in the Spirituality of English Evangelicalism, 1918–1939*. Carlisle, UK: Paternoster, 1999.
Rattenbury, J. Ernest. *The Conversion of the Wesleys: A Critical Study*. London: Epworth, 1938.
Rawlyk, George A., and Mark A. Noll, eds. *Amazing Grace: Evangelicalism in Australia, Britain, Canada and the United States*. Grand Rapids: Baker, 1993.
Redecop, Gloria Neufeld. *Bad Girls and Boys Go to Hell (or not): Engaging Fundamentalist Evangelicalism*. Eugene, OR: Wipf & Stock, 2012.
Reventlow, Henning Graf. *The Authority of the Bible and the Rise of the Modern World*. London: SCM, 1984.
Rian, Edwin H. *The Presbyterian Conflict*. Grand Rapids: Eerdmans, 1940.
Ribuffo, Leo P. *The Old Christian Right: The Protestant Far Right from the Great Depression to the Cold War*. Philadelphia: Temple University Press, 1983.
Richardson, Alan. *The Bible in an Age of Science*. London: SCM, 1961.
Richardson, Michael. *Amazing Faith: The Authorized Biography of Bill Bright, Founder of Campus Crusade for Christ*. Colorado Springs, CO: Water Brook, 2001.
Ridderbos, Herman N. *The Authority of the New Testament Scriptures*. Phillipsburg, NJ: Presbyterian & Reformed, 1963. Revised ed.: *Redemptive History and the New Testament Scriptures*. Phillipsburg, NJ: Presbyterian & Reformed, 1968.
———. *The Coming of the Kingdom*. Philadelphia: Presbyterian & Reformed, 1962.
———. *Paul and Jesus: Origins and Character of Paul's Preaching of Christ*. Philadelphia: Presbyterian & Reformed, 1958.

———. *Studies in Scripture and Its Authority*. St. Catherines, Canada: Paideia, 1978.
Riddlebarger, Kim [a-millennial]. *A Case for Amillennialism: Understanding the End Times*. Grand Rapids: Baker, 2003.
———. *The Man of Sin: Uncovering the Truth about the Antichrist*. Grand Rapids: Baker, 2006.
Ridley, Jasper. *John Knox*. London: Oxford University Press, 1968.
———. *Thomas Cranmer*. London: Oxford University Press, 1962.
Rios, Christopher M. *After the Monkey Trial: Evangelical Scientists and a New Creationism*. New York: Fordham University Press, 2014.
Rivers, Isobel, and David L. Wykes. *Dissenting Praise: Dissent and the Hymn in England and Wales*. New York: Oxford University Press, 2011.
Robbins, Keith, ed. *Protestant Evangelicalism: Britain, Ireland, Germany and America, c. 1750–c. 1950: Essays in Honour of W. R. Ward*. Oxford: Basil Blackwell, 1990.
Robeck, Cecil M. *The Azusa Street Mission and Revival: The Birth of the Global Pentecostal Movement*. Nashville: Thomas Nelson, 2006.
Robeck, Cecil M., and Amos Yong, eds. *The Cambridge Companion to Pentecostalism*. Cambridge: Cambridge University Press, 2015.
Robertson, O. Palmer. [a-millennial]. *The Christ of the Covenants*. Grand Rapids: Baker, 1980; Philadelphia: Presbyterian & Reformed, 1981.
———. *The Final Word: A Biblical Response to the Case for Tongues and Prophesy Today*. Edinburgh: Banner of Truth, 1993.
———. *The Israel of God: Yesterday, Today, and Tomorrow*. Phillipsburg, NJ: Presbyterian & Reformed, 2000.
Robinson, James M. *A New Quest for the Historical Jesus*. London: SCM, 1959.
Robinson, John Arthur Thomas. *The Priority of John*. London: SCM, 1985.
———. *Redating the New Testament*. London: SCM, 1976.
Rogers, Jack Bartlett. *Confessions of a Conservative Evangelical*. 2nd ed. Louisville, KY: Geneva, 2001.
———. *Scripture in the Westminster Confession: A Problem of Historical Interpretation for American Presbyterianism*. Kampen, The Netherlands: Kok, 1966.
Rogers, Jack Bartlett, and Donald K. McKim. *The Authority and Interpretation of the Bible: An Historical Approach*. San Francisco: Harper & Row, 1979.
Rookmaaker, Hans. *The Creative Gift: Essays on Art and the Christian Life*. Westchester, IL: Cornerstone, 1981.
———. *Modern Art and the Death of a Culture*. London: Inter-Varsity, 1970.
Rosell, Garth M. *The Surprising Work of God: Harold John Ockenga, Billy Graham, and the Rebirth of Evangelicalism*. Grand Rapids: Baker, 2008.
Rosell, Garth M., and Richard A. F. Dupuis, eds. *The Memoirs of Charles G. Finney: The Complete Restored Text*. Grand Rapids: Zondervan, 1989.
Rosman, Doreen M. *Evangelicals and Culture*. London: Croom Helm, 1984.
Roston, Murray. *Prophet and Poet: The Bible and the Growth of Romanticism*. London: Faber & Faber, 1965.
Rougeau, Vincent D. *Christians in the American Empire: Faith and Citizenship in the New World Order*. New York: Oxford University Press, 2008.
Rowley, H. H. *Darius and Mede and the Four World Empires in the Book of Daniel: A Historical Study of Contemporary Theories*. Cardiff: University of Wales Press, 1964.

Rudwick, Martin J. S. *Earth's Deep History: How It Was Discovered and Why It Matters.* Chicago: University of Chicago Press, 2014.

Ruegsegger, Ronald W. *Reflections on Francis Schaeffer.* Grand Rapids: Zondervan, 1986.

Runia, Klaas. *Karl Barth's Doctrine of Holy Scripture.* Grand Rapids: Eerdmans, 1962.

———. *Reformation Today.* London: Banner of Truth, 1968

Runner, H. Evan. *The Relation of the Bible to Learning.* Toronto, Canada: Wedge, 1970.

———. *Scriptural Religion and Political Task.* Toronto, Canada: Wedge, 1974.

Rupp, E. Gordon. *Religion in England 1688–1791.* London: Oxford University Press, 1986.

Rupp, E. Gordon, and Benjamin Drewery, eds. *Martin Luther.* London: Edward Arnold, 1970.

Rushdoony, Rousas John. *The Institutes of Biblical Law.* Philadelphia: Presbyterian & Reformed, 1973.

Ruthven, Jon Mark. *On the Cessation of Charismata: The Protestant Polemic on Post-Biblical Miracles.* Revised ed. Tulsa, OK: Word & Spirit, 2013.

Rutz, Michael. *British Zion: Congregationalism, Politics and Empire.* Waco, TX: Baylor University Press, 2011.

Ryle, John Charles. *The Christian Leaders of the Last Century; or, England a Hundred Years Ago.* London: Nelson, 1899.

———. *Knots Untied, being Plain Statements on Disputed Points in Religion, from the Standpoint of an Evangelical Churchman.* Tenth ed. London: Charles Thynne, 1885.

Ryrie, Charles Caldwell [pre-millennial dispensationalist]. *The Basis of the Premillennial Faith.* New York: Loizeaux, 1953.

———. *The Bible and Tomorrow's News.* Wheaton: Victor, 1969.

———. *Dispensationalism.* Chicago: Moody, 1995.

———. *Dispensationalism Today.* Chicago: Moody, 1965.

———. *Final Countdown.* Wheaton: Victor, 1982.

Samuelson, Kurt. *Religion and Economic Action: the Protestant Ethic, the Rise of Capitalism, and the Abuses of Scholarship*, edited by D. C. Coleman. Translated by E. Geoffrey French. New York: Basic, 1961.

Sandeen, Ernest R. "Defining Fundamentalism: A Reply to Professor Marsden." *Christian Scholar's Review* 1 (1972) 227–233.

———. *The Origins of Fundamentalism: Toward a Historical Interpretation.* Minneapolis: Fortress, 1968.

———. *The Roots of Fundamentalism: British and American Millenarianism, 1800–1930.* Chicago: University of Chicago Press, 1970.

Saunders, Teddy, and Hugh Sansom. *David Watson, A Biography.* Sevenoaks, UK: Hodder & Stoughton, 1992.

Sayers, Dorothy. *The Man Born To Be King: A Play-Cycle on the Life of our Lord and Saviour Jesus Christ.* London: Victor Gollancz, 1943.

Schaeffer, Francis. *A Christian Manifesto.* Wheaton: Good News, 1982.

———. *The Church at the End of the Twentieth Century.* London: Norfolk, 1970.

———. *Death in the City.* London: Inter-Varsity, 1969.

———. *Escape from Reason.* London: Inter-Varsity, 1968.

———. *The God Who is There.* London: Hodder & Stoughton, 1968.

———. *The Great Evangelical Disaster.* Westchester, IL: Crossway, 1984.

———. *He is There and He is Not Silent.* Wheaton: Tyndale House, 1972.

———. *How Should We Then Live? The Rise and Decline of Western Thought and Culture*. Grand Rapids: Revell, 1976.

———. *Whatever Happened to the Human Race? Exposing our Rapid yet Subtle Loss of Human Rights*. Old Tappan, NJ: Revell, 1979.

Schaeffer, Frank. *Crazy for God: How I Grew Up as One of the Elect, Helped Found the Religious Right, and Lived to Take All (or Almost All) of It Back*. New York: Carrol & Graf, 2007.

———. *Patience with God: Faith for People who don't Like Religion (or Atheism)*. Boston: Da Capo, 2009.

———. *Sham Pearls for Real Swine: Beyond the Cultural Dark Age—A Quest for Renaissance*. Brentwood, TN: Wolgemuth & Hyatt, 1990.

Schafer, Axel R. *American Evangelicals and the 1960s*. Madison: University of Wisconsin Press, 2013.

———. *Countercultural Conservatives: American Evangelicalism from the Postwar Revival to the New Christian Right*. Madison: University of Wisconsin Press, 2011.

Schenk, H. G. *The Mind of the European Romantics: An Essay in Cultural History*. London: Constable, 1966.

Schlossberg, Herbert. *Conflict and Crisis in the Religious Life of Late Victorian England*. Piscataway, NJ: Transaction, 2009.

———. *The Silent Revolution and The Making of Victorian England*. Columbus: Ohio State University Press, 2000.

Schlossberg, Herbert, et al., eds. *Christianity and Economics in the Post-Cold War Era: The Oxford Declaration and Beyond*. Grand Rapids: Eerdmans, 1994.

Schurden, Walter B. *The Struggle for the Soul of the SBC: Moderate Responses to the Fundamentalist Movement*. Macon, GA: Mercer University Press, 1994.

Schuurman, Egbert. *Perspectives on Technology and Culture*. Sioux Center, IA: Dordt College, 1995.

———. *Technology and the Future: A Philosophical Challenge*. Toronto, Canada: Wedge, 1980.

Schwarz, Hans. *Creation*. Grand Rapids: Eerdmans, 2002.

———. *Eschatology*. Grand Rapids: Eerdmans, 2000.

Schweitzer, Albert. *The Quest of the Historical Jesus: A Critical Study of its Progress from Reimarus to Wrede*. London: Adam & Charles Black, 1910.

Scofield, Cyrus I., ed. [pre-millennial dispensationalist]. *The Scofield Reference Bible: The Holy Bible containing the Old and New Testaments. Authorized Version*. New York: Oxford University Press, 1909.

Scorgie, Glen G. *A Call for Continuity: The Theological Contribution of James Orr*. Macon, GA: Mercer University Press, 1988.

Seel, John. *The Evangelical Forfeit*. Grand Rapids: Baker, 1993.

Seerveld, Calvin G. *Bearing Fresh Olive Leaves: Alternative Steps in Understanding Art*. Carlisle, UK: Piquant and Toronto, Canada: Tuppence, 2000.

———. *A Christian Critique of Art and Literature*. Sioux Center, IA: Dordt College, 1995.

———. *How to Read the Bible to Hear God Speak: A Study in Numbers 22–4*. Sioux Center, IA: Dordt College, 2003.

———. *In the Fields of the Lord: A Calvin Seerveld Reader*, edited by Craig Bartholomew. Carlisle, UK: Piquant, Toronto: Tuppence, 2000.

———. *Rainbows for the Fallen World: Aesthetic Life and Artistic Task*. Toronto, Canada: Tuppence, 1980.
Semmel, Bernard. *The Methodist Revolution*. New York: Basic, 1973.
Shantz, Douglas H. *Introduction to German Pietism: Protestant Renewal at the Dawn of Modern Europe*. Baltimore, MD: Johns Hopkins University Press, 2013.
Shapiro, Adam R. *Trying Biology: The Scopes Trial, Textbooks, and the Antievolution Movement in American Schools*. Chicago: University of Chicago Press, 2013.
Sheehan, Jonathan. *The Enlightenment Bible: Translation, Scholarship, Culture*. Princeton, NJ: Princeton University Press, 2005.
Shenton, Timothy. *The Life of Rowland Hill: The Second Whitefield*. Grand Rapids: Reformation Heritage, 2012.
Shibley, Mark A. *Resurgent Evangelicalism in the United States: Mapping Cultural Change since 1970*. Columbia: University of South Carolina Press, 1996.
Shor, Ira. *Culture Wars: School and Society in the Conservative Restoration, 1969–1984*. Boston: Routledge and Kegan Paul, 1986.
Shortland, Michael, ed. *Hugh Miller and the Controversies of Victorian Science*. London: Oxford University Press, 1996.
Shuff, Roger N. *Searching for the True Church: Brethren and Evangelicals in Mid-twentieth Century England*. Eugene, OR: Wipf & Stock, 2006.
Simeon, Charles. *The Entire Works of the Rev. Charles Simeon M.A. With Copious Indexes*, ed. Thomas H. Horne. 21 vols. London: Bohn, 1844–5.
Simon, John S. *John Wesley and the Advance of Methodism*. London: Epworth, 1925.
———. *John Wesley and the Methodist Societies*. London: Epworth, 1923.
———. *John Wesley and the Religious Societies*. London: Epworth, 1921.
———. *John Wesley: The Last Phase*. London: Epworth, 1934.
———. *John Wesley: The Master-Builder*. London: Epworth, 1927.
Sizer, Stephen. *Christian Zionism: Road-map to Armageddon?* Downers Grove, IL: InterVarsity, 2007.
———. *Zion's Christian Soldiers? The Bible, Israel and the Church*. Downers Grove, IL: InterVarsity, 2007.
Skeats, Herbert S., and Charles S. Miall. *History of the Free Churches of England, 1688–1891*. London: Alexander & Shepheard, 1891.
Skevington Wood, Arthur. *The Burning Heart: John Wesley, Evangelist*. Exeter, UK: Paternoster, 1967.
———. *The Inextinguishable Blaze: Spiritual Renewal and Advance in the Eighteenth Century*. London: Paternoster, 1960.
Skillen, James W. *The Good of Politics: A Biblical, Historical, and Contemporary Introduction*. Grand Rapids: Baker, 2014.
———. *In Pursuit of Justice: Christian-Democratic Explorations*. Lanham, MD: Rowman & Littlefield, 2004.
———. *Recharging the American Experiment: Principled Pluralism for Genuine Civic Community*. Grand Rapids: Baker, 1994.
———. *With or Against the World? America's Role Among the Nations*. Lanham, MD: Rowman & Littlefield, 2005.
Skilton, John H., ed. *Scripture and Confession: A Book about Confessions Old and New*. Nutley, NJ: Presbyterian & Reformed, 1973.
Smart, James D. *The Strange Silence of the Bible in the Church: A Study in Hermeneutics*. Louisville, KY: Westminster John Knox, 1970.

Smart, Robert Davis. *Jonathan Edwards's Apologetic for the Great Awakening*. Grand Rapids: Reformation Heritage, 2011.
Smidt, Corwin E. *American Evangelicals Today*. Lanham, MD: Rowman & Littlefield, 2013.
Smit, Meijer Cornelis. *Toward a Christian Conception of History*. Lanham, MD: University Press of America, 2002.
Smith, Christian. *The Bible Made Impossible: Why Biblicism Is Not a Truly Evangelical Way of Reading Scripture*. Grand Rapids: Brazos, 2011.
———. *Christian America? What Evangelicals Really Want*. Oakland: University of California Press, 2000.
Smith, David W. *Transforming the World: The Social Impact of British Evangelicalism*. Carlisle, UK: Paternoster, 1998.
Smith, Gary Scott. *The Seeds of Secularization: Calvinism, Culture, and Pluralism in America, 1870–1915*. Grand Rapids: Christian University Press, 1985.
Smith, Mark, ed. *British Evangelical Identities Past and present: Aspects of the History and Sociology of Evangelicalism in Britain and Ireland*. Eugene, OR: Wipf & Stock, 2009.
Smith, Wilbur M. *Therefore Stand: A Plea for a Vigorous Apologetic in the Present Crisis of Evangelical Christianity*. Boston: Wilde, 1945.
Smyth, Charles. *Simeon and Church Order: A Study in the Origins of the Cambridge Revival in the Eighteenth Century*. Cambridge: Cambridge University Press, 1940.
Snoke, David. *A Biblical Case for an Old Earth*. Grand Rapids: Baker, 2006.
Southgate, Christopher. *The Groaning of Creation: God, Evolution, and the Problem of Evil*. Louisville, KY: Westminster John Knox, 2008.
Spain, Rufus. *At Ease in Zion: Social History of Southern Baptists, 1877–1914*. Nashville: Vanderbilt University Press, 1967.
Spanner, Douglas. *Biblical Creation and the Theory of Evolution*. Exeter, UK: Paternoster, 1987.
Spargo, Tamsin. *The Writing of John Bunyan*. Aldershot, UK: Ashgate, 1997.
Sparks, Kenton L. *God's Word in Human Words: An Evangelical Appreciation of Critical Biblical Scholarship*. Grand Rapids: Baker, 2008.
Spector, Stephen. *Evangelicals and Israel: The Story of American Christian Zionism*. New York: Oxford University Press, 2008.
Spykman, Gordon J. *Reformational Theology*. Grand Rapids: Eerdmans, 1994.
Stackhouse, John G. *What Does it Mean to be Saved? Broadening Evangelical Horizons of Salvation*. Grand Rapids: Baker, 2002.
Standaert, Michael. *Skipping Towards Armageddon: The Politics and Propaganda of the Left Behind Novels and the LaHaye Empire*. New York: Soft Skull, 2006.
Stanford, Charles. *Joseph Alleine: His Companions & Times; A Memorial of "Black Bartholomew," 1662*. London: Jackson, Walford & Hodder, [1861].
Stanley, Brian. *The Global Diffusion of Evangelicalism: The Age of Billy Graham and John Stott*. A History of Evangelicalism: People, Movements and Ideas in the English-Speaking World, Vol. V. Downers Grove, IL: InterVarsity, 2014.
Stanley Smith, A.C. *Road to Revival: The Story of the Rwanda Mission*. London: CMS, 1946.
Staudinger, Hugo. *The Trustworthiness of the Gospels*. Edinburgh: Handsel, 1981.
Stead, Geoffrey and Margaret. *The Exotic Plant: The History of the Moravian Church in Britain, 1742–2000*. London: Epworth, 2004.

Steer, Roger. *Basic Christian: The Inside Story of John Stott.* Downers Grove, IL: InterVarsity, 2010.

———. *Church on Fire: The Story of Anglican Evangelicals.* London: Hodder & Stoughton, 1998. US ed.: *Guarding the Holy Fire: The Evangelicalism of John R. W. Stott, J. I. Packer, and Alister McGrath.* Grand Rapids: Baker, 1999.

Stein, Robert H. *Studying the Synoptic Problem: Origin and Interpretation.* Grand Rapids: Baker, 2001.

Stephens, Randall J. *The Fire Spreads: Holiness and Pentecostalism in the American South.* Cambridge, MA: Harvard University Press, 2007.

Stephens, Randall W., and Karl W. Giberson. *The Anointed: Evangelical Truth in a Secular Age.* Cambridge, MA: Harvard University Press, 2011.

St John, Patricia. *Breath of Life: The Story of the Rwanda Mission.* London: Norfolk, 1971.

Stock, Eugene. *The History of the Church Missionary Society: Its Environment, Its Men and Its Works.* 3 vols. London: Church Missionary Society, 1899.

Stoeffler, F. Ernest. *The Rise of Evangelical Pietism.* Leiden: Brill, 1965.

Stoldt, Hans-Herbert. *History and Criticism of the Marcan Hypothesis.* Edinburgh: T. & T. Clark and Macon, GA: Mercer University Press, 1980.

Stonehouse, Ned B. *J. Gresham Machen: A Biographical Memoir.* Grand Rapids: Eerdmans, 1954.

Stonehouse, Ned B., and Paul Wolley. *The Infallible Word: A Symposium by Members of the Faculty of Westminster Theological Seminary.* Philadelphia: Presbyterian & Reformed, 1946.

Storkey, Alan. *A Christian Social Perspective.* Leicester, UK: Inter-Varsity, 1979.

———. *Jesus and Politics: Confronting the Powers.* Grand Rapids: Baker, 2005.

Storkey, Elaine. *What's Right with Feminism.* Grand Rapids: Eerdmans, 1986.

Storms, Sam [a-millennial]. *Kingdom Come: The Amillennial Alternative.* Fearn, UK: Mentor, 2013.

Stott, John R. W. *The Baptism and Fullness of the Holy Spirit.* London: Inter-Varsity, 1964.

———. *Basic Christianity.* London: Inter-Varsity, 1958.

———. *Evangelical Truth: A Personal Plea for Unity, Integrity, and Faithfulness.* Downers Grove, IL: InterVarsity, 1999.

———. *Your Confirmation.* London: Hodder & Stoughton, 1958.

Stout, Harry S. *The Divine Dramatist: George Whitefield and the Rise of Modern Evangelicalism.* Grand Rapids: Eerdmans, 1991.

———. *Upon the Altar of the Nation: A Moral History of the Civil War.* New York: Viking, 2006.

Streeter, Burnett Hillman. *The Four Gospels, a Study of Origins treating of the Manuscript Tradition, Sources, Authorship, and Dates.* London: Macmillan, 1930.

Strom, Jonathan, et al, eds. *Pietism in Germany and North America, 1680–1820.* Aldershot, UK: Ashgate, 2009.

Stunt, Timothy C. F. *From Awakening to Secession: Radical Evangelicals in Switzerland and Britain, 1815–1835.* Edinburgh: T. & T. Clark, 2000.

Sutton, Jerry. *The Baptist Reformation: The Conservative Resurgence in the Southern Baptist Convention.* Nashville: Broadman & Holman, 2000.

Sutton, Matthew Avery. *Aimee Semple McPherson and the Resurrection of Christian America.* Cambridge, MA: Harvard University Press, 2009.

———. *American Apocalypse: A History of Modern Evangelicalism*. Cambridge, MA: Harvard University Press, 2014.

———. *Jerry Falwell and the Rise of the Religious Right: A Brief History with Documents*. New York: Bedford St. Martin's, 2012.

Swartz, David R. *Moral Minority: The Evangelical Left in an Age of Conservatism: Politics and Culture in Modern America*. Philadelphia: University of Pennsylvania Press, 2012.

Sweeney, Douglas A. *The American Evangelical Story: A History of the Movement*. Grand Rapids: Baker, 2005.

———. "The Essential Evangelicalism Dialect: The Historiography of the Early Neo-Evangelical Movement and the Observer-Participant Dilemma." *Church History* 60 (1991) 70–84.

———. "Fundamentalism and the Neo-Evangelicals." *Fides et Historia* 24 (1992) 81–96.

———. "Historiographical Dialects: On Marsden, Dayton, and the Inner logic of Evangelical History." *Christian Scholar's Review* 23 (1993) 48–52.

———. *Nathaniel Taylor, New Haven Theology, and the Legacy of Jonathan Edwards*. New York: Oxford University Press, 2003.

Sweeney, Douglas A., and Allen C. Guelzo. *The New England Theology: From Jonathan Edwards to Edwards Amasa Park*. Grand Rapids: Baker, 2006.

Swindoll, Charles R., et al. [pre-millennial dispensationalists]. *The Road to Armageddon: A Biblical Understanding of Prophecy and End Time Events*. Nashville: Thomas Nelson, 2004.

Synan, Vinson. *An Eye-Witness Remembers the Century of the Holy Spirit*. Grand Rapids: Chosen, 2010.

———. *The Holiness-Pentecostal Movement in the United States*. Grand Rapids: Eerdmans, 1971.

———. *The Holiness-Pentecostal Tradition: Charismatic Movements in the Twentieth Century*. 2nd ed. Grand Rapids: Eerdmans, 1997.

Synan, Vinson, ed. *Aspects of Pentecostal / Charismatic Origins*. Plainfield, NJ: Bridge Logos, 1975.

Tarico, Valerie. *The Dark Side: How Evangelical Teachings Corrupt Love and Truth*. Seattle, WA: Dea, 2006.

Tatlow, Tissington. *The Story of the Student Christian Movement of Great Britain and Ireland*. London: SCM, 1933.

Taylor, Ernest Richard. *Methodism and Politics, 1791–1851*. Cambridge: Cambridge University Press, 1935.

Taylor, Paul, *The Six Days of Genesis: A Scientific Appreciation of Genesis 1–11*. San Diego, CA: Master, 2007.

Telford, John. *The Life of John Wesley*. London: Epworth, 1947.

Temperley, Howard. *British Anti Slavery, 1833–1870*. London: Longman, 1972.

Templeton, Charles. *An Anecdotal Memoir*. Toronto: McClelland & Stewart, 1983.

———. *Farewell to God: My Reasons for Rejecting the Christian Faith*. Toronto: McClelland & Stewart, 1996.

Thaxton, Charles B., et al. *The Mystery of Life's Origin: Reassessing Current Theories*. New York: Philosophical Library, 1984.

Thiele, Edwin Richard. *The Mysterious Numbers of the Hebrew Kings: A Reconstruction of the Chronology of the Kingdoms of Israel and Judah*. Chicago: University of Chicago Press, 1951.

Thistelton, Anthony. *The Holy Spirit: In Biblical Teaching, through the Centuries, and Today*. Grand Rapids: Eerdmans, 2013.

———. *New Horizons in Hermeneutics: The Theory and Practice of Transforming Biblical Reading*. Grand Rapids: Zondervan, 1992.

———. *Thiselton on Hermeneutics: Collected works with New Essays*. Grand Rapids: Eerdmans, 2006.

———. *The Two Horizons: New Testament Hermeneutics and Philosophical Description with Special Reference to Heidegger, Bultmann, Gadamer, and Wittgenstein*. Grand Rapids: Eerdmans, 1980.

Thomas, Keith. *Religion and the Decline of Magic*. London: Weidenfeld & Nicolson, 1971.

Thuesen, Peter J. *In Discordance with the Scriptures: American Protestant Battles over Translating the Bible*. New York: Oxford University Press, 1999.

Tietjen, John. *Memoirs in Exile: Confessional Hope and Institutional Conflict*. Minneapolis: Augsburg Fortress, 1990.

Tillich, Paul. *Perspectives on Nineteenth and Twentieth Century Theology*, edited and introduced by Carl E. Braaten. London: SCM, 1967.

Tinker, Melvin, ed. *The Anglican Evangelical Crisis*. Fearn, UK: Christian Focus, 1995.

Todd, Mary. *Authority Vested: A Story of Identity and Change in the Lutheran Church-Missouri Synod*. Grand Rapids: Eerdmans, 2000.

Tomkins, Stephen. *The Clapham Sect: How Wilberforce's Circle Transformed Britain*. Grand Rapids: Kregel, 2010.

———. *William Wilberforce: A Biography*. Grand Rapids: Eerdmans, 2007.

Tomlinson, Dave. *The Post-Evangelical*. London: Triangle, 1995.

Toon, Peter. *Evangelical Theology, 1833–1856: a Response to Tractarianism*. London: Marshall, Morgan & Scott, 1979.

———. "The Parker Society." *Historical Magazine of the Protestant Episcopal Church* 46 (September 1977) 323–332.

Toon, Peter, and Michael Smout. *John Charles Ryle: Evangelical Bishop*. Cambridge: Clarke, 1976.

Torres, Hector, and C. Peter Wagner ["New Apostolic Reformation" advocates]. *The Restoration of the Apostles and Prophets and How it will Revolutionize Ministry in the 21st Century*. Nashville: Thomas Nelson, 2001.

Tripp, Dick. *The Biblical Mandate for Caring for Creation*. Eugene, OR: Wipf & Stock, 2013.

Troost, Andree. *What is Reformational Philosophy? An Introduction to the Cosmonomic Philosophy of Herman Dooyeweerd*. Grand Rapids: Paideia, 2012.

Tucker, Ruth A. *Walking Away from Faith: Unraveling the Mystery of Belief and Unbelief*. Downers Grove, IL: InterVarsity, 2002.

Turner, John G. *Bill Bright and Campus Crusade for Christ: The Renewal of Evangelicalism in Postwar America*. Chapel Hill: University of North Carolina Press, 2008.

Turner, John M. *John Wesley: The Evangelical Revival and the Rise of Methodism in England*. London: Epworth, 2003.

Turretin, Francis. *Institutes of Elenctic Theology*, edited by James T. Dennison. 3 vols. Translated by George M. Giger. Phillipsburg, NJ: Presbyterian & Reformed, 1997.

Tyerman, Luke. *The Life and Times of the Rev. John Wesley M.A., founder of the Methodists*. 3 vols. London: Hodder & Stoughton, 1872.

———. *The Life of the Rev. George Whitefield, B.A. of Pembroke College, Oxford*. 2 vols. London: Hodder & Stoughton, 1877.

———. *The Oxford Methodists: Memoirs of the Rev. Messrs. Clayton, Ingham, Gambold, Hervey, and Broughton, with Biographical Notices of Others*. London: Hodder & Stoughton, 1873.

———. *Wesley's Designated Successor: The Life, Letters and Literary Labours of the Rev. John William Fletcher, Vicar of Madeley*. London: Hodder & Stoughton, 1882.

Tyson, John R. *Assist Me to Proclaim: The Life and Hymns of Charles Wesley*. Grand Rapids: Eerdmans, 2008.

———. *The Ways of the Wesleys: A Short Introduction*. Grand Rapids: Eerdmans, 2014.

Tyson, John R., and Boyd S. Schlenther. *In the Midst of Early Methodism: Lady Huntingdon and Her Correspondence*. Lanham, MD: Scarecrow, 2006.

Urquhart, Colin. *When the Spirit Comes*. London: Hodder & Stoughton, 1974.

Usher, Roland G. *The Reconstruction of the English Church*. 2 vols. New York: Appleton, 1910.

Valeri, Mark. *Law and Providence in Joseph Bellamy's New England*. New York: Oxford University Press, 1994.

Vance, Laurence M. *King James, His Bible and Its Translators*. Pensacola, FL: Vance, 2006.

Van de Fliert, J. R. "Bible, Man and Science: A Reply." *International Reformed Bulletin* number 38 (July, 1969) 34–39.

———. "Fundamentalism and the Fundamentals of Geology." *International Reformed Bulletin* numbers 32–33 (January-April, 1968) 5–27.

VanderMey, Randall J. *God Talk: The Triteness and Truth in Christian Clichés*. Downers Grove, IL: InterVarsity, 1993.

Vander Stelt. John C. *Philosophy and Scripture: A Study in Old Princeton and Westminster Theology*. Marlton, PA: Mack, 1978.

Vanderwaal, Cornelis. *Hal Lindsey and Biblical Prophesy*. St. Catherines, Canada: Paideia, 1970.

Van Deursen, Arie Theodorus. *The Distinctive Character of the Free University in Amsterdam, 1880–2005: A Commemorative History*. Translated by Herbert Donald Morton. Grand Rapids: Eerdmans, 2008.

Van de Walle, Bernie A. *The Heart of the Gospel: A.B. Simpson, the Fourfold Gospel, and Late Nineteenth-Century Evangelical Theology*. Eugene, OR: Wipf & Stock, 2009.

VanDoodewaard, William. *The Marrow Controversy and Seceder Tradition: Atonement. Saving Faith, and the Gospel Offer in Scotland (1718–1799)*. Grand Rapids: Reformation Heritage, 2011.

Van Dyke, Fred. *Redeeming Creation: The Biblical Basis for Environmental Stewardship*. Downers Grove, IL: InterVarsity, 1996.

Vanhoozer, Kevin J. *The Drama of Doctrine: A Canonical Linguistic Approach to Christian Theology*. Nashville: Westminster John Knox, 2005.

Van Leeuwen, Mary Stewart, ed. *After Eden: Facing the Challenge of Gender Reconciliation*. Grand Rapids: Eerdmans, 1993.

Van Riessen, Hendrik. *The Society of the Future*. Philadelphia: Presbyterian & Reformed, 1957.

Van Til, Cornelius. *Christianity and Barthianism*. Grand Rapids: Baker, 1962.

---. *The Defense of the Faith*. Philadelphia: Presbyterian & Reformed, 1955.

---. *The New Modernism: An Appraisal of the Theology of Barth and Brunner*. Philadelphia: Presbyterian & Reformed, 1946.

Vassady, Bela. *Limping Along: Confessions of a Pilgrim Theologian*. Grand Rapids: Eerdmans, 1985.

Vaughan, Frank. *A History of the Free Church of England otherwise called the Reformed Episcopal Church*. London: Free Church of England, 1938.

Veitch, Thomas Stewart. *Chief Men Among the Brethren*. London: Pickering & Inglis, 1919.

---. *The Story of the Brethren Movement: A Simple and Straightforward Account of the Features and Failures of a Sincere Attempt to carry out the Principles of Scripture During the Last 100 years*. London: Pickering & Inglis, 1933.

Verburg, Marcel E. *Herman Dooyeweerd: The Life and Work of a Christian Philosopher*. Jordan Station, Canada: Paideia, 2015.

Vickers, Jason E., et al., eds. *Methodist and Pietist: Retrieving the Evangelical United Brethren Tradition*. Nashville: Kingswood, 2011.

Vollenhoven, D. H. T. "The Significance of Calvinism for the Reformation of Philosophy." *Evangelical Quarterly* 4/2 (April 1932) 128-60 and 4/4 (October 1932) 398-427.

Vos, Geerhardus. *Biblical Theology: Old and New Testaments*. Grand Rapids: Eerdmans, 1948.

---. *The Eschatology of the Old Testament*. Phillipsburg, NJ: Presbyterian & Reformed, 2001.

---. *Redemptive History and Biblical Interpretation*. Phillipsburg, NJ: Presbyterian & Reformed, 1980.

Vulliamy, C. E. *John Wesley* London: Epworth, 1954.

Wacker, Grant. *America's Pastor: Billy Graham and the Shaping of a Nation*. Cambridge, MA: Harvard University Press, 2014.

---. *Augustus H. Strong and the Dilemma of Historical Consciousness*. Macon, GA: Mercer University Press, 1985.

Wagner, C. Peter ["New Apostolic Reformation" advocate]. *Apostles and Prophets: The Foundation of the Church*. Ventura, CA: Regal, 2000.

---. *Apostles Today: Biblical Government for Biblical Power*. Ventura, CA: Regal, 2007.

---. *Churchquake: How the New Apostolic Reformation Is Shaking Up the Church As We Know It*. Ventura, CA: Regal, 1999.

---. *New Apostolic Churches*. Ventura, CA: Regal, 1998.

Walker, Andrew. *Restoring the Kingdom: The Radical Christianity of the House Church Movement*. London: Hodder & Stoughton, 1985.

Wallace, Ronald S. *On the Interpretation and Use of the Bible: With Reflections on Experience*. Edinburgh: Scottish Academic, 1999.

Waller, P. J. *Democracy and Sectarianism: A Political and Social History of Liverpool, 1868-1939*. Liverpool, UK: Liverpool University Press, 1981.

Walsh, Brian J., and J. Richard Middleton. *The Transforming Vision: Shaping a Christian World View*. Downers Grove, IL: InterVarsity, 1984.

---. *Truth is Stranger than it Used to Be: Biblical Faith in a Postmodern Age*. Downers Grove, IL: InterVarsity, 1995.

Walsh, John, et al, eds. *The Church of England, c. 1689-c.1833, from Tolerance to Tractarianism*. Cambridge: Cambridge University Press, 1993.

Walton, John H. *Ancient Near Eastern Thought and the Old Testament: Introducing the Conceptual World of the Hebrew Bible*. Grand Rapids: Baker, 2006.

———. *Genesis 1 as Ancient Cosmology*. Winona Lake, IN: Eisenbrauns, 2011.

———. *The Lost World of Adam and Eve: Genesis 2–3 and the Human Origins Debate*. Downers Grove, IL: InterVarsity, 2015.

———. *The Lost World of Genesis One: Ancient Cosmology and the Origins Debate*. Downers Grove, IL: InterVarsity, 2009.

Walvoord, John F. [pre-millennial dispensationalist]. *Armageddon, Oil and the Middle East Crisis: What the Bible says about the Future of the Middle East and the End of Western Civilization*. Grand Rapids: Zondervan, 1991.

———. *Blessed Hope and Tribulation*. Grand Rapids: Zondervan, 1976.

———. *Israel, the Nations, and the Church in Prophesy*. Grand Rapids: Zondervan, 1978.

———. *Major Bible Prophesies: 37 Crucial Promises that Affect you Today*. San Francisco: Harper Collins, 1994.

———. *The Millennial Kingdom*. Grand Rapids: Dunham, 1959.

———. *Prophecy: 14 Essential Keys to Understanding the Final Drama*. Nashville: Nelson, 1993.

———. *Prophecy in the New Millennium: A Fresh Look at Future Events*. Grand Rapids: Kregel, 2001.

———. *The Rapture Question*. Grand Rapids: Zondervan, 1957.

———. *The Return of the Lord*. Grand Rapids: Zondervan, 1983.

Walvoord, John F., and Mark Hitchcock. *Armageddon, Oil, and Terror: What the Bible says about the Future*. Carol Stream, IL: Tyndale, 2007.

Ward, William Reginald. *Christianity Under the Ancien Régime, 1648–1789*. Cambridge: Cambridge University Press, 1999.

———. *Early Evangelicalism: A Global Intellectual History, 1670–1789*. Cambridge: Cambridge University Press, 2006.

———. *The Protestant Evangelical Awakening*. Cambridge: Cambridge University Press, 1992.

———. *Religion and Society in England, 1790–1850*. London: Batsford, 1972.

Ward, W. Reginald, and Richard P. Heitzenrater, eds. *The Works of John Wesley*, Vol. 18: *Journals and Diaries I, 1735–1738*. Nashville: Abingdon, 1988.

Warfield, Benjamin Breckinridge. *Counterfeit Miracles*. New York: Charles Scribner's Sons, 1918. Republished as: *Miracles: Yesterday and Today, Real and Counterfeit*. Grand Rapids: Eerdmans, 1965.

Warner, Robert. *Reinventing English Evangelicalism, 1966–2001*. Milton Keynes, UK: Paternoster, 2007.

Warner, Wellman J. *The Wesleyan Movement in the Industrial Revolution*. London: Longmans, Green, 1930.

Watson, David Christopher Knight. *You Are My God: An Autobiography*. London: Hodder & Stoughton, 1983.

Watson, Justin. *The Christian Coalition: Dreams of Restoration, Demands for Recognition*. New York: Palgrave Macmillan, 1997.

Watt, David Harrington. *A Transforming Faith: Explorations of Twentieth Century American Evangelicalism*. Brunswick, NJ: Rutgers University Press, 1991.

Watts, Isaac. *The Poetical Works of Isaac Watts, Doctor of Divinity, With the Life of the Author*. 7 vols. Edinburgh: Apollo, 1782.

Weaver, C. Douglas. *The Healer-Prophet: William Marrion Branham: A Study of the Prophetic in American Pentecostalism*. Revised edition, edited by David Edwin Harrell. Macon, GA: Mercer University Press, 2000.
Webber, Robert E. *Ancient Future Faith: Rethinking Evangelicalism for a Postmodern World*. Grand Rapids: Baker, 1999.
———. *Evangelicals on the Canterbury Trail: Why Evangelicals are Attracted to the Liturgical Church*. Revised ed. New York: Morehouse, 2012.
Weber, Max. *The Protestant Ethic and the Spirit of Capitalism*. Translated by Talcott Parsons. London: George Allan & Unwin, 1930.
Weber, Timothy P. *Living in the Shadow of the Second Coming: American Premillennialism, 1875–1925*. New York: Oxford University Press, 1979.
———. *On the Road to Armageddon: How Evangelicals became Israel's Best Friend*. Grand Rapids: Baker, 2004.
Webster, Douglas D. *Selling Jesus: What's Wrong with Marketing the Church*. Downers Grove, IL: InterVarsity, 1992.
Weinlick, John R. *Count Zinzendorf: The Story of His Life and Leadership in the Renewed Moravian Church*. Nashville: Abingdon, 1956.
Welch, Edwin. *Spiritual Pilgrim: A Reassessment of the Life of the Countess of Huntingdon*. Cardiff: University of Wales Press, 1995.
Wells, David F. *The Courage to Be Protestant: Truth-lovers, Marketers, and Emergents in the Postmodern World*. Grand Rapids: Eerdmans, 2008.
———. *God in the Wasteland: The Reality of Truth in a World of Fading Dreams*. Grand Rapids: Eerdmans, 1994.
———. *No Place for Truth, Or Whatever Happened to Evangelical Theology?* Grand Rapids: Eerdmans, 1993.
Wells, Paul Ronald. *James Barr and the Bible: Critique of a New Liberalism*. Phillipsburg, NJ: Presbyterian & Reformed, 1980.
Wenham, John. *Easter Enigma: Are the Resurrection Accounts in Conflict?* Exeter, UK: Paternoster, 1984.
———. *Facing Hell: The Story of a Nobody. An Autobiography, 1913–1996*. Carlisle, UK: Paternoster, 1998.
———. *Redating Matthew, Mark and Luke: A Fresh Assault on the Synoptic Problem*. Leicester, UK: Inter-Varsity, 1992.
Weremchuk, Max S. *John Nelson Darby: A Biography*. Neptune, NJ: Loizeaux, 1993.
Werrell, Ralph S. *The Roots of Tyndale's Theology*. Cambridge: James Clarke, 2013.
———. *The Theology of William Tyndale*. Cambridge: James Clarke, 2006.
Wessels, Anton. *Europe: Was it Ever Really Christian? The Interaction between Gospel and Culture*. London: SCM, 1994.
Westerkamp, Marilyn. *Triumph of the Laity: Scots-Irish Piety and the Great Awakening, 1625–1760*. New York: Oxford University Press, 1998.
Whitefield, George. *The Letters of George Whitefield For the Period 1734–1742*. Edinburgh: Banner of Truth, 1976.
Whorton, Mark S. *Peril in Paradise: Theology, Science, and the Age of the Earth*. Waynesboro, GA: Authentic, 2005.
Whybray, Roger Norman. *Introduction to the Pentateuch*. Grand Rapids: Eerdmans, 1995.
———. *The Making of the Pentateuch: A Methodological Study*. Sheffield, UK: Sheffield Academic, 1987.

Wigger, John H. *American Saint: Francis Asbury and the Methodists.* New York: Oxford University Press, 2009.
———. *Taking Heaven by Storm: Methodism and the Rise of Popular Christianity in America.* Champaign: University of Illinois Press, 2001.
Wigger, John H., and Nathan O. Hatch, eds. *Methodism and the Shaping of American Culture.* Nashville: Abingdon, 2001.
Wilberforce, William. *A Practical View of the Prevailing Religious System of Professing Christians, in the Higher and Middle Classes, Contrasted With Real Christianity.* London: Cadell & Davies, 1797.
Wilcox, Clyde. *God's Warriors: The Christian Right in Twentieth-Century America.* Baltimore, MD: Johns Hopkins University Press, 1992.
———. *Onward Christian Soldiers? The Religious Right in American Politics.* Boulder, CO: Westview, 2006.
Wilkerson, David, with John and Elizabeth Sherrill. *The Cross and the Switchblade.* New York: Geis, 1963; London: Hodder & Stoughton, 1967.
Wilkinson, Paul Richard. *For Zion's Sake: Christian Zionism and the Role of John Nelson Darby.* Eugene, OR: Wipf & Stock, 2008.
Williams, Cyril G. *Tongues of the Spirit: A Study of Pentecostal Glossolalia and Related Phenomena.* Cardiff: University of Wales Press, 1981.
Williams, Michael D. *As Far as the Curse is Found: The Covenant Story of Redemption.* Phillipsburg, NJ: Presbyterian & Reformed, 2005.
Wimber, Carol. *John Wimber: The Way it Was.* London: Hodder & Stoughton, 1999.
Wirzba, Norman. *From Nature to Creation: A Christian Vision for Understanding and Loving Our World.* Grand Rapids: Baker, 2015.
———. *The Paradise of God: Religion in an Ecological Age.* New York: Oxford University Press, 2003.
Witherington, Ben, III. *The Problem with Evangelical Theology: Testing the Exegetical Foundations of Calvinism, Dispensationalism, and Wesleyanism.* Waco, TX: Baylor University Press, 2005.
Witte, John. *Law and Protestantism: The Legal Teachings of the Lutheran Reformation.* Cambridge: Cambridge University Press, 2002.
———. *The Reformation of Rights: Law, Religion, and Human Rights in Early Modern Calvinism.* Cambridge: Cambridge University Press, 2007.
Wolffe, John. *The Expansion of Evangelicalism: The Age of Wilberforce, More, Chalmers and Finney.* A History of Evangelicalism: People, Movements and Ideas in the English-Speaking World, Vol. II. Downers Grove, IL: InterVarsity, 2007.
———. *God and Greater Britain: Religion and National Life in Britain and Ireland, 1843-1945.* London: Routledge, 1994.
———. *The Protestant Crusade in Great Britain, 1829-1860.* London: Oxford University Press, 1991.
Wolffe, John, ed. *Evangelical Faith and Public Zeal: Evangelicals and Society in Britain, 1780-1980.* London: SPCK, 1995.
Wolters, Albert. *Creation Regained: Biblical Basis for a Reformational Worldview.* Grand Rapids: Eerdmans, 1985.
Woodbridge, Charles J. *The New Evangelicalism.* Greenville SC: Bob Jones University Press, 1970.
Woodbridge, John D. *Biblical Authority: A Critique of the Rogers / McKim Proposal.* Grand Rapids: Zondervan, 1982.

Worthen, Molly. *Apostles of Reason: The Crisis of Authority in American Evangelicalism.* New York: Oxford University Press, 2013.

Worthing, Mark W. *God, Creation, and Contemporary Physics.* Minneapolis: Fortress, 1996.

Wright, N. T. *The Challenge of Jesus: Rediscovering Who Jesus Was and Is.* Downers Grove, IL: Inter-Varsity, 1999.

———. *The Climax of the Covenant: Christ and the Law in Pauline Theology.* Minneapolis: Fortress, 1991.

———. *Jesus and the Victory of God.* Christian Origins and the Question of God. Vol. 2. London: SPCK, 1996.

———. *The New Testament and the People of God.* Christian Origins and the Question of God. London: SPCK, 1992.

———. *Paul and the Faithfulness of God.* Christian Origins and the Question of God. Vol. 4, Parts I–II and III–IV. 2 vols. London: SPCK, 2013.

———. *The Resurrection of the Son of God.* Christian Origins and the Question of God. Vol. 3. London: SPCK, 2003.

———. *Scripture and the Authority of God.* London: SPCK, 2005. US ed.: *The Last Word: Beyond the Bible toward a New Understanding of the Authority of Scripture.* San Francisco: Harper Collins, 2005.

———. *Surprised by Hope: Rethinking Heaven, the Resurrection, and the Mission of the Church.* San Francisco: Harper One, 2008.

———. *What Saint Paul Really Said: Was Paul of Tarsus the Real Founder of Christianity?* Grand Rapids: Eerdmans, 1997.

Würthwein, Ernst. *The Text of the Old Testament: An Introduction to the Biblia Hebraica.* Grand Rapids: Eerdmans, 1979.

Yarnell, Malcolm B., III, ed. *The Anabaptists and the Contemporary Baptists: Restoring New Testament Christianity; Essays in Honor of Paige Patterson.* Nashville: Broadmen & Holman, 2013.

Yates, Timothy. *The Conversion of the Maori: Years of Religious and Social Change.* Grand Rapids: Eerdmans, 2013.

Yeager, Jonathan. *Enlightened Evangelicalism: The Life and Thought of John Erskine.* New York: Oxford University Press, 2011.

Yeo, John J. *Plundering the Egyptians: The Old Testament and Historical Criticism at Westminster Theological Seminary (1929–1998).* Lanham, MD: University Press of America, 2010.

Young, Davis A. *The Biblical Flood: A Case Study of the Church's Response to Extrabiblical Evidence.* Grand Rapids: Eerdmans, 1995.

———. *Christianity and the Age of the Earth.* Grand Rapids: Zondervan, 1982.

———. *John Calvin and the Natural World.* Lanham, MD: University Press of America, 2007.

Young, Davis A., and Ralph F. Stearley. *The Bible, Rocks and Time: Geological Evidence for the Age of the Earth.* Downers Grove, IL: InterVarsity, 2008.

Young, Edward J. *Thy Word is Truth.* Grand Rapids: Eerdmans, 1957.

Young, Michael P. *Bearing Witness against Sin: The Birth of the American Social Movement.* Chicago: University of Chicago Press, 2007.

Zakai, Avihu. *Jonathan Edwards's Philosophy of History: The Reenchantment of the World in the Age of Enlightenment.* Princeton, NJ: Princeton University Press, 2003.

Zimmerman, Paul A. *A Seminary in Crisis: The Inside Story of the Preus Fact Finding Committee*. St. Louis, MO: Concordia, 2007.

Zinzendorf, Nicholas Ludwig von. *Nine Public Lectures on Important Subjects in Religion, Preached in Fetter Lane Chapel in London in the Year 1746*, edited by George W. Forell. Des Moines: University of Iowa Press, 1973.

Zylstra, Bernard, ed. and translator. *Statement of the Principles and General Political Program of the Anti-Revolutionary Party*. The Hague: Anti-Revolutionary Party, 1961.

INDEX OF PERSONS

A page number with a 'n' indicates that the reference is to a footnote.

Alexander, Archibald, 106, 127-28
Alleine, Joseph, 72
Allenby, Edmund, 175
Allis, Oswald T., 135
Ambrose of Milan, 21
Ames, William, 47
Amyraut, Moses, 50-51
Andrewes, Lancelot, 63
Ansberry, Christopher B., 206
Anselm of Canterbury, 44
Aquinas, Thomas, 23-24, 44, 128, 187
Arius, 17
Armerding, Carl E., 156
Arminius, Jacob, 47, 90
Arndt, Johann, 77
Asbury, Francis, 105
Ashley-Cooper, Anthony (Seventh Earl of Shaftesbury), 94
Astruc, Jean, 114
Atherton, Henry, 137
Augustine of Hippo, 19-24, 28-29, 44, 83

Bach, Johan Sebastian, 79
Bacon, Francis, 83, 108, 128, 161
Bacote, Vincent E., 159
Baker, Heidi, 169
Bakker, James, and Tammy Faye, 169
Ball, Hannah, 93
Balthus, Pietje, 189
Bancroft, Richard, 59

Bannerman, James, 104
Barclay, Oliver, 5, 195-96
Barr, James, 157-58
Barrow, Henry, 59
Barth, Karl, 133-34, 145-46, 188, 224
Bartholomew, Craig G., 195, 218
Baur, Ferdinand Christian, 115
Bavinck, Herman, 155, 159
Baxter, Richard, 67
Baxter, Robert, 99
Beale, Gregory K., 158
Bebbington, David W., 5-6, 72, 79, 112, 189, 192, 201, 203, 217
Behe, Michael, 164
Bellamy, Joseph, 106
Ben-Gurion, David, 175
Bennett, Dennis J., 167
Bentley, Todd, 169
Berkouwer, Gerrit Cornelis, 155, 159
Bernini, Giovanni, 185
Berridge, John, 92
Beecher, Lyman, 110
Beza, Theodore, 46-47, 51, 61-62, 153
Biéler, André, 211 n.6
Blaurock, George, 32
Bloesch, Donald G., 159
Blomberg, Craig, 150
Boardman, William Edwin, 119
Boer, Harry R., 156
Böhme, Jacob, 78
Bonar, Andrew A., 122

Bonar, Horatius, 121
Bonhoeffer, Dietrich, 134
Borg, Marcus, 206
Boston, Thomas, 72, 89
Bovell, Carlos R., 159
Brainerd, David, 106
Branham, William M., 168–69
Brickner, David, 177
Bridge, William, 67
Briggs, Charles A., 129–30
Bright, Bill, 170
Bromiley, Geoffrey, 146
Brookes, James Hall, 121, 126
Brooks, Thomas, 70
Browne, Robert, 59
Browne, Rodney Howard, 170
Bruce, F.F., 149–50
Bryan, William Jennings, 124, 132, 140
Buchanan, James, 104
Bullinger, Heinrich, 28, 30–31, 33, 37
Bunyan, John, 71
Burroughs, Jeremiah, 67
Bush, George W., 188
Buswell, J. Oliver, 135
Butterfield, Herbert, xii

Cain, Paul, 168
Calovius, Abraham, 77
Calvin, John, 21, 28, 31, 35–37, 44–48, 50, 52, 57, 60–62, 72, 83, 137, 191–92, 211
Campbell, Alexander, 109
Campbell Morgan, George, 125
Candlish, Robert Smith, 104
Cannistraci, David, 171
Cappel, Louis, 50–51
Carnell, Edward John, 145–47
Carson, Donald A., 154, 156
Carter, Jimmy, 187
Cartwright, Peter, 109
Cartwright, Thomas, 58–59, 61–62
Casaubon, Isaac, 51
Cassian, John, 20
Cassuto, Moshe David, 115
Catherine of Aragon, 56–57
Chafer, Lewis Sperry, 126
Chalmers, Thomas, 104
Chaplin, Jonathan, 195, 213

Charlemagne, 106
Charles I (King of England and Scotland), 64–66, 68
Charles II (King of England and Scotland), 67–69
Charles V (Holy Roman Emperor), 26
Chauncy, Charles, 106
Chemnitz, Martin, 77
Childs, Brevard S., 133
Chillingworth, William, 84
Chrysostom, John, 97
Churchill, Winston S., 138
Clark, Gordon Haddon, 145
Clement VII (pope), 56
Clouser, Roy A., 193
Coffin, Henry Sloane, 132
Coke, Thomas, 105
Colenso, John William, 118
Colson, Charles Wendell, 187
Comenius, Jan Amos, 78–79
Constantine the Great, 16–19, 22, 28, 32, 198, 200
Coornhert, Dirck Volkertszoon, 47
Copernicus, Nicolaus, 52
Cosin, John, 63
Cowper, William, 93
Cox, Richard, 57
Cranmer, Thomas, 56–57
Crick, Francis H.C., 163
Criswell, Wallie Amos, 157
Cromwell, Oliver, 65–68
Cromwell, Thomas, 56
Crossan, John Dominic, 206
Cudworth, Ralph, 84
Cunningham, William, 104

Darby, John Nelson, 98, 100–01, 103, 121, 152
Darwin, Charles, 113–14, 118, 161–64
Davenport, James, 106
Delitzsch, Franz, 117
Dembski, William, 164
Dengerink, Jan, 193
Denton, Michael J., 164
Diocletian, 16
Disraeli, Benjamin, 120
Doddridge, Philip, 72, 88

INDEX OF PERSONS

Dooyeweerd, Herman, 189, 191–93, 195–96, 203 n.4
Draper, John William, 162
Driver, Samuel Rolles, 115
Drummond, Henry, 99
du Plessis, David, 167
Dunn, James D. G., 150, 157
Dwight, Timothy, 106

Edward VI (King of England), 56–57
Edwards, Jonathan, 72, 82–84, 87, 90–91, 106–8, 110, 127
Eichhorn, Johan Gottfried, 116
Einstein, Albert, 166
Elias, John, 93
Eliot, George, 115
Elizabeth I (Queen of England), 57–59, 63, 96
Elliott, Charlotte, 121
Elliott, Ralph H., 156, 158
Episcopius, Simon, 47
Erasmus of Rotterdam, 25, 153
Erastus, Thomas, 62
Erdman, William J., 121
Erskine, Ebenezer, 72, 89
Erskine, Ralph, 89
Evans, Craig A., 150
Ewald, Heinrich, 116

Fairbairn, Patrick, 121
Falwell, Jerry L., 169, 176
Feti, Domenico, 78
Field, John, 58
Finney, Charles Grandison, 109–110, 121, 130
Fisher, Edward, 89
Flavel, John, 70
Fletcher, John (of Madeley), 92, 119, 124
Fosdick, Harry Emerson, 132
France, Richard Thomas, 150, 157 n.2
Francke, August Hermann, 78
Franklin, Benjamin, 84
Franklin, Rosalind E., 163
Frei, Hans Wilhelm, 133
Fuller, Daniel, 146
Fuller, Andrew, 107, 145
Fuller, Charles Edward, 140–41

Funk, Robert W., 206

Geertsema, Henk, 193
Gerhard, Johann, 77
Gesenius, Wilhelm, 116
Gillespie, George, 66
Gillies, John, 89
Gladstone, William Ewart, 120
Godbey, William Baxter, 125
Gödel, Kurt, 166
Goheen, Michael, 218
Gomarus, Franciscus, 47
Goode, William, 103
Goodwin, Thomas, 67, 70
Gore, Charles, 126
Gorham, George C., 113
Goudzwaard, Bob, 184, 193
Gould, Stephen Jay, 161, 166
Graaf, S.G. de, 216
Graf, Karl Heinrich, 114
Graham, William (Billy) Franklin, 141–44, 147, 149, 168
Grebel, Conrad, 32
Green, Ashbel, 106
Greenwood, John, 59
Gregory of Rimini, 24
Greydanus, Sidney, 218
Griesbach, Johann Jakob, 115, 153
Griffin, Edward, 106
Griffioen, Sander, 193
Griffiths, Brian, 184
Grimshaw, William, 92
Grindal, Edmund, 58
Groen van Prinsterer, Guillaume, 189–190, 196
Grubb, Norman Percy, 123
Grudem, Wayne, 170
Guinness, Os, 187
Gunkel, Hermann, 116
Gurnall, William, 84
Guthrie, Donald, 149

Hagee, John C., 169, 176
Hales, John, 84
Ham, Kenneth Alfred, 164
Ham, Mordecai, 142
Hamon, William (Bill), 171
Harford-Battersby, Thomas D., 119

INDEX OF PERSONS

Harnack, Adolf von, 116
Harper, Michael, 167
Harris, Harriet A., 158
Harris, Howell, 93
Hatch, Nathan, 188
Hauerwas, Stanley, 133, 188
Hays, Christopher M., 206
Hearst, William Randolph, 143
Hegel, Georg Wilhelm Friedrich, 115
Heidegger, Johan Heinrich, 51
Hendriksen, William B., 135
Hengstenberg, Ernst Wilhelm, 117
Henry VIII (King of England), 56, 58
Henry, Carl Ferdinand Howard, 145
Henry, Matthew, 71
Herbert, A.G., 147
Herrmann, Johann Wilhelm, 116
Hill, David Octavius, 104
Hill, Rowland, 93
Hinn, T.B. (Benny), 169
Hodge, Archibald Alexander, 127–29
Hodge, Charles, 127–29
Hoeven, Johan van der, 193
Hoffman, Melchior, 34, 174
Hofstadter, Richard, 147
Hooker, Richard, 59–60, 62–64, 84, 86
Hooper, John, 56–57
Hooykaas, Reyer, 195
Hopkins, Samuel, 106
Hort, F.J.A., 153
Hubbard, David Allan, 145–47
Hughes, Hugh Price, 120
Humbard, A. Rex Emmanuel, 169
Hume, David, 108
Humphrey, Lawrence, 58
Hus, John, 29, 55, 78
Hutter, Jacob, 34
Huxley, Thomas H., 113

Ireton, Henry, 67
Ironside, Henry Allen, 125
Irving, Edward, 98–100, 103
Irwin, Benjamin Hardin, 124

James I (King of England), and VI (King of Scotland), 63–64
James II (King of England), and VII (King of Scotland), 69

Jan of Leiden, 43
Jeffreys, George, 125
Jewell, John, 58
Johnson, Douglas, 195
Johnson, Michael R., 166
Johnson, Philip E., 164
Johnson, Torrey Maynard, 141
Jones, Bob, 140, 145
Jones, Griffith, 72
Julian the Apostate, 18
Justin Martyr, 21
Juxon, William, 70

Kantzer, Kenneth S., 156
Karlstadt, Andreas von, 30
Käsemann, Ernst, 117
Keble, John, 96
Keener, Craig S., 150
Keil, Carl Friedrich, 117
Kendall, Robert T., 168
Kennedy, D. James, 169
Kennedy, John (of Dingwall), 122
Kierkegaard, Søren, 187
Klapwijk, Jacob, 193
Kline, Meredith G., 159
Knox, John, 28, 57, 60–62, 64
Koyzis, David T., 213
Krummacher, Friedrich Wilhelm, 117
Kuhn, Thomas S., 195
Kuiper, Roelof, 193
Kuyper, Abraham, 155, 189–192, 196, 204, 224

Lacunza, Manuel de, 99
Ladd, George Eldon, 145, 147
Larsen, Timothy, 5, 6 n.4
Latimer, Hugh, 56–57
Laud, William, 63, 65
Law, William, 85
Lewis, Clive Staples, 138
Lewis, Sinclair, 140
Lincoln, Abraham, 110
Lindsell, Harold, 145–47, 154
Lindsey, Harold Lee (Hal), 176
Livingstone, David N., 161
Lloyd-Jones, David Martyn, 148–49, 168, 196
Locke, John, 83, 191

INDEX OF PERSONS

Louis XIII (King of France), 48
Loyola, Ignatius, 46
Lucinius, 17
Luther, Martin, 9–10, 21, 24–27,
    29–32, 35, 37, 44, 52, 55, 78–79,
    83, 85, 186, 191

Macartney, Clarence Edward, 132,
    134, 141
Machen, John Gresham, 127, 132–35,
    145–46
Machiavelli, Niccolò, 25
MacKay, Donald MacCrimmon, 195
MacRae, Alan A., 135
Malebranch, Nicole, 83
Mandeville, Bernard de, 81
Manning, Bernard Lord, 137
Manning, Henry Edward, 96, 113
Manton, Thomas, 70
Marsden, George M., 146 n.2, 156, 188
Marshall, Ian H., 150
Marx, Karl, 211
Mather, Moses, 106
Mathias, Jan, (of Haarlem), 34, 174
Maurits, Prince of Orange, 47
McCartney, Bill, 171
McGowan, A.T.B., 159
McGrath, Alister, 5–6
McIntire, Carl T., 135, 140–41, 145
McKim, Donald, 155–56
McLaren, Brian, 183
McNeile, Hugh, 94, 99
McPherson, Amy Semple, 140
Meinecke, Friedrich, 114
Mekkes, Johan Peter Albertus, 189
Melanchthon, Philip, 29–30, 47, 77
Melville, Andrew, 61, 63
Mencken, H.L., 140
Mendel, Gregor Johann, 163
Meyer, Frederick B., 119
Meyer, Stephen C., 164
Middleton, J. Richard, 195, 218
Miescher, Johannes Friedrich, 163
Miller, Hugh, 104, 161
Miller, William, 121
Milner, Joseph, 92
Milton, John, 67
Mohler, R. Albert, 157

Moody, Dwight L., 121–22, 130, 136,
    143
Moore, Hannah, 93
Moore, James R., 161
More, Henry, 84
Morison, Frank, 138
Morris, Henry M., 163–64
Moule, Handley, 119
Moulin, Pierre du, 47, 51
Müntzer, Thomas, 33
Murray, Iain H., 148–49 n.4, 196
Murray, John, 137

Nee, Watchman, 171
Needham, George C., 121
Nettleton, Asahel, 106, 110
Nevin, John Williamson, 106
Newbigin, Lesslie, 218
Newman, John Henry, 96, 113
Newton, Benjamin Wills, 100
Newton, John, 93
Niebuhr, Helmut Richard, 133
Niebuhr, K.P. Reinhold, 133
Nietzsche, Friedrich, 181
Noll, Mark A., 156, 188
Norris, John Frank, 139–40
Nye, Philip, 67

Oastler, Richard, 94
Ockenga, Harold John, 141, 145, 147
Oden, Thomas C., 199
Oldenbarnevelt, Johan van, 47–48
Olford, Stephen F., 147
Orr, James, 159
Orr, J. Edwin, 147
Osiander, Andreas, 52
Osteen, Joel Scott, 169
Otto I (Holy Roman Emperor), 22
Owen, John, 70

Packer, James I., 147–149, 155, 157
Paley, William, 164
Palmer, Phoebe, 199
Parham, Charles Fox, 124
Parker, Matthew, 97
Patterson, Paige, 157
Patton, Francis Landey, 127
Payson, Edward, 106

Peake, Arthur Samuel, 115
Pen-Lewis, Jessie, 124
Percival, Spencer, 94
Perkins, William, 47, 71
Phillips, John B., 7, 138
Philo of Alexandria, 14
Pink, Arthur, 137
Piper, John, 170
Placeus, Josua, 50
Plato, 21, 44–45, 181
Plotinus, 21
Polycarp, 211
Poole Connor, Edward Joshua, 137
Popma, Klaas Jan, 193
Pressler, H. Paul, 157
Preus, Robert D., 156
Price, George McCready, 164
Prince, Derek, 176
Prynne, William, 67
Ptolemy, Claudius, 52
Pulkingham, Graham, 167
Pusey, Edward, 96
Pym, John, 65

Raikes, Robert, 93
Rainy, Robert, 104
Ramm, Bernard, 162
Ramus, Petrus, 46
Rauschenbusch, Walter, 120
Reagan, Ronald, 184, 187–88
Redpath, Alan, 147
Rees, Thomas B., 147
Reid, Thomas, 108, 127
Reimarus, Herman Samuel, 117
Reuss, Édouard G.E., 114
Rheticus, Georg Joachim, 52
Rice, John R., 139, 145
Ridderbos, Herman, 159
Ridley, Nicolas, 56–57
Riessen, Hendrik van, 193
Rivet, André, 51
Roberts, Evan, 124
Roberts, Granville (Oral), 168
Robertson, M.G. (Pat), 169, 176–77
Robertson Smith, William, 122, 129
Rogers, Jack B., 155
Romaine, William, 92

Rookmaaker, Hans H., 187, 189, 192–93
Rosell, Marvin, 141
Ross, Albert Henry, 138
Rousseau, Jean-Jacques, 187
Rowlands, Daniel, 93
Runner, H. Evan, 193–94
Rushdoony, Rousas John, 170
Ryder, Henry, 94
Ryle, Herbert Edward, 122
Ryle, John Charles, 119, 121–22, 136
Ryrie, Charles Caldwell, 126

Sampson, Thomas, 58
Sankey, Ira D., 121, 136
Sayers, Dorothy Leigh, 138
Schaeffer, Francis A., 135, 186–89, 191
Schaeffer, Frankie, 187
Schleiermacher, Friedrich D.E., 116
Schrödinger, Erwin, 166
Schrotenboer, Paul G., 194
Schuller, Robert H., 169
Schuurman, Egbert, 193
Schweitzer, Albert, 117
Scofield, Cyrus I., 126, 152
Scopes, John T., 132, 139–40
Seerveld, Calvin G., 193–94
Selina, Countess of Huntingdon, 89
Seymour, William Joseph, 124
Shea, George Beverley, 143
Shields, Thomas Todhunter, 137
Sibbes, Richard, 59
Simeon, Charles, 92
Simon, Richard, 114
Simons, Menno, 34
Simpson, George G., 166
Simpson, Sidrach, 67
Skillen, James W., 193, 213
Smit, Meyer Cornelis, 193
Smith, George Adam, 143
Smith, Hannah Whitall, 119
Smith, Henry Preserved, 129–30
Smith, Wilbur Moorehead, 145, 147
Spanner, Douglas, 166
Sparks, Kenton L., 206
Spencer, Herbert, 113
Spener, Philipp Jacob, 77–78
Spinoza, Benedict, 114, 206

Sprague, William, 106
Spring, Gardiner, 106
Spurgeon, Charles Haddon, 119, 121–22
Spykman, Gordon J., 6, 194
Stafleu, Marinus Dirk, 193
Stewart, Dugald, 108
Stewart, Lyman, 131
Stewart, Milton, 131
Stillingfleet, Edward, 84
Stone, Perry, 169
Stonehouse, Ned Bernard, 135
Stott, John R.W., 148–150, 158, 167
Strauss, David Friedrich, 115
Studd, Charles Thomas, 123
Styles, Ezra, 106
Sunday, Billy, 130
Swaggart, Jimmy Lee, 169
Synan, H. Vinson, 171

Taylor, Charles Hudson, 123
Taylor, Jeremy, 63
Taylor, Nathaniel, 106–8, 110
Templeton, Charles Bradley, 142–43, 147
Tennent, Gilbert, 106
Tertullian, 12–13
Tetzel, John, 186
Thatcher, Margaret, 184
Theodosius I, 16, 18–19, 22, 28, 32,
Thornton, Henry, 93
Toplady, Augustus Montague, 91
Torres, Hector, 171
Torrey, Rubin A., 122, 125
Trapp, John, 84
Travers, Walter, 58, 61
Troeltsch, Ernst, 116
Troost, Andree, 193
Turretin, François, 51, 128
Tyler, Bennet, 106, 110
Tyndale, William, 25, 55

Urquhart, Colin, 167
Ursinus, Zacharias, 46
Ussher, James, 160, 163
Uytenbogaert, John, 47

Van de Fliert, J.R., 163

Van Impe, Jack, 169
Van Til, Cornelius, 146, 188
Vassady, Béla, 145
Venn, Henry, 93
Vermigli, Peter Martyr, 46
Vincentius of Lérins, 199
Voetius, Gisbertus, 47
Vollenhoven, Dirk H.T., 191–93, 193
Vos, Geerhardus Johannes, 143, 159

Wagner, C. Peter, 170–71
Walker, Samuel, 92
Wallace, Alfred R., 113, 161
Walsh, Brian, 195
Walton, John H., 160
Walvoord, John F., 126
Warfield, Benjamin Breckenridge, 127, 129, 161, 168
Warren, Rick, 171
Washington, George, 105
Watson, David, 167
Watson, James D., 163
Watts, Isaac, 72, 88
Weber, Max, 71, 204
Weiss, Johannes, 116
Wellhausen, Julius, 114–15
Wells, Ronald, 189
Wenham, John, 149
Wentworth, Thomas, 65
Wesley, Charles, 84–85, 89, 91, 103, 124, 127
Wesley, John, 9–10, 13, 21, 25, 51, 53, 55, 80–82, 85–92, 94, 103, 107, 127
Wesley, Samuel, 51, 84, 86
Wesley, Susannah, 85
Westcott, B.F., 153
Whichcote, Benjamin, 84
Whitcomb, John C., 163
White, Andrew Dickson, 162
Whitefield, George, 82–91, 127
Whitgift, William, 59
Whittingham, William, 57, 64
Whybray, Roger N., 115
Wigglesworth, Smith, 167
Wilberforce, William, 93–94
Wilcox, Thomas, 58
Wilkerson, David, 167

Wilkinson, Bruce, 171
William of Ockham, 24
Williams, William (Pantycelyn), 93
Wilson, Robert Dick, 127
Wimber, John, 170
Witherington III, Ben, 150
Withers, George, 62, 104
Witherspoon, Thomas, 108, 138
Woodbridge, Charles, 145–46
Woodbridge, John D., 155–56
Wrede, Georg Friedrich Eduard William, 117
Wright, J. Elwin, 141
Wright, Nicolas Thomas, 150, 206, 218

Wycliffe, William, 29, 55, 205
Wyrtzen, Jack, 141

Yeo, Jonathan J., 159
Yoder, Howard, 188
Young, Davis A., 166
Young, Edward J., 135

Zanchius, Jerome, 46
Zinzendorf, Nikolaus Ludwig von, 78–80, 100
Zuidema, Sytse Ulbe, 193
Zwingli, Huldrych, 28, 30–33, 37
Zylstra, Bernard, 194

www.ingramcontent.com/pod-product-compliance
Lightning Source LLC
Chambersburg PA
CBHW071234230426
43668CB00011B/1433